Law and the Human Sciences

Semiotics and the Human Sciences

Roberta Kevelson
General Editor

Vol. 3

PETER LANG
New York • San Francisco • Bern
Frankfurt am Main • Berlin • Wien • Paris

Law and the Human Sciences

Fifth Round Table
on Law and Semiotics

Edited by
Roberta Kevelson

PETER LANG
New York • San Francisco • Bern
Frankfurt am Main • Berlin • Wien • Paris

Library of Congress Cataloging-in-Publication Data

Round Table on Law and Semiotics (5th : 1991 :
Pennsylvania State University)
Law and the human sciences / Fifth Round Table on
Law and Semiotics; edited by Roberta Kevelson.
p. cm. — (Semiotics and the human sciences ;
vol. 3)
Includes bibliographical references.
1. Semiotics (Law). 2. Law and anthroposophy.
3. Law—Philosophy. I. Kevelson, Roberta. II. Title
III. Series.
K213.R68 1992 340'.1—dc20 91-37475
ISBN 0-8204-1815-3 CIP
ISSN 1054-8386

Die Deutsche Bibliothek-CIP-Einheitsaufnahme

Law and the human sciences ; ed. by Roberta
Kevelson.—New York; Berlin; Bern; Frankfurt/M.;
Paris; Wien: Lang, 1992
(Semiotics and the human sciences ; Vol. 3)
ISBN 0-8204-1815-3
NE: Kevelson, Roberta [Hrsg.]; GT

The paper in this book meets the guidelines for permanence and
durability of the Committee on Production Guidelines for
Book Longevity of the Council on Library Resources.

Printed in the United States of America.

Table of Contents

Chapter 1

Introduction: Discovery, 'Reason's Conscience', the Human Sciences

Roberta Kevelson

I

When the call for papers went out for this year's Round Table on Law and Semiotics, with the main theme of the conference given as LAW AND THE HUMAN SCIENCES, it was noted as a janus-faced, pivotal stage in the development of this idea called Legal Semiotics. We regard the evolution of complex sign-systems such as the idea of law as part of our indebtedness to Peirce. He pioneered and opened up the field of semiotics as an area for ongoing inquiry. More accurately it might be said that he came upon it at one edge, at the boundary shared with American pragmatism in philosophy and with Legal Realism in Law. Certainly there are other edges, e.g. Continental hermeneutics, Prague linguistics, Greimasian structural linguistics approach to semiotics/semiology.

This fifth-year Round Table may be regarded as a mediational device. All of Legal Semiotics regarded as an investigatory tool may be understood as a discovery of legal meaning, and as a means of discovery, i.e., a way of producing such evidence that may be further evaluated in judgments of Law's acts and transactions with other sign-systems in the whole sphere of social organization.

Such other sign systems are institutions such as the political, the economic, the artistic, the familial, the educational, the religious, and so forth.

Law is such a complex character on our human stage. As character, it is also a composite, complicated, continually evolving idea. Law is a system of signs, (Kevelson, 1988). It is a standard-bearer of social value.

From a Peircean point of view law is a member of the Sciences of Discovery; Law is partly a Questor of new Properties and partly a Restorer of old States. Law is dependent, in Peirce's schemes, upon abstract Ethical principles of Normative Sciences. Ethics in turn, is governed by Aesthetics (Esthetics), and is referent, in *its* turn, for all of Peirce's Expanded Logic which, in tripartite division, includes Grammar, Critic, and Rhetoric or the Methodology of Semiotics.

II

Briefly and anecdotally, the following may be of interest: In July of 1902 Peirce applied for a grant from the Carnegie Foundation to enable him to finally complete his lifelong work on the Sciences of Discovery. In Ms L-75 Peirce outlines this work; it is the cap he foresaw for his theory of signs. In this application Law occupies a special place in one of the two major branches of the Sciences of Discovery, at the Level of Firstness, or what constitutes the Iconic level of sign function.

Law falls within the category of the 'idioscopic division' which Peirce calls 'Psychognosy,' and which, as the counterpart in the sciences of discovery of 'Physiognosy,' includes all of what we understand today as the physical sciences. One branch of 'psychognosy' includes, in Peirce's schema, all of the social sciences, i.e., psychology, sociology, linguistics, history, criticisms of all the fine arts, etc., and also includes the subdivisions of 'ethnology' which, along with the theory and practice of the law, refers to folklore, religion, ethnology of technology, cosmogony, etc. In brief, without taking more time here than may be appropriate for an introduction, Peirce sets out as the base of the sciences of discovery, the *reportorial* aspects of legal theory. The *speculative* aspects of law are carried forward into the mediate level, which is the philosophical level of the sciences of discovery. The middle category of philosophy is that division he called Normative Sciences, which is headed by Esthetics or the Science of Value.

Here in the Normative Sciences Law's referents are discovered, processed and carried forward into the third and highest level of Discovery within his 'Idioscopy.' Idioscopy, a term adapted from Bentham by Peirce, concerns investigation and creation of that which is novel, particular and unique, and which becomes a major factor in the creating of new general laws of human value.

This is a simplistic description of a complex and multidimensional scheme of Peirce's theory of signs. Elaborated, we would see that Law is that motif which runs through the whole of Peirce's semiotics as a connective and recurrent thread. Thus Law is, inferentially speaking, a representation with respect to that complex system of human rationality we call society. Law is to society what Peirce's 'Reason's Conscience' is to individual relationships of questioner and answerer in all semiotic processes of message transactions.

In Ms 693, assumed to have been written around the same period that the Carnegie application was submitted, we find an important essay, 'Reason's Conscience: A Practical Treatise on the Theory of Discovery Wherein Logic is Conceived as Semiotic.' In this essay Peirce places the Normative Sciences as pivotal of his semiotic reason. It is via the Esthetic normative code that that which is hypothetical, or is hypothetically observed, becomes codified and carried forward into the outer world of human affairs, into the various subdivisions of the human sciences, into overlapping spheres of human meaning.

For a rich and full discussion on Peirce's development of the idea of observation and evidence I recommend Max Fisch's important paper which traces the evolution of Peirce's notion of semiotic into this last stage in which the whole of his expanded logic (representing the practical logical structure of legal reasoning as an Interpretant sign) is presented, (Fisch, 1978, *Peirce's General Theory of Signs* reprinted in Fisch, 1986: 321-355; see also Kevelson, 1988, 1990).

Peirce's 'architectonic' theory of semiotics shows the physical sciences and the social or human sciences branching from the same node, where each is characterized predominantly by its ability to take note of and incorporate that which is peculiar and novel rather than that which is general and already a part of the symbolic code of each division of discovery/inquiry. It is the Coenoscopic instrument of discovery -- also a Benthamite term of neologism which looks at general ideas and signs. Thus the Coenscopic sciences and the Idioscopic divisions of the Sciences of discovery are not in a relationship of subordination and superordination; rather they serve different functions. In the same sense of parallel functions, neither are the human sciences mere spin-offs of the physical sciences, but they each attend to different aspects of the phenomenal world.

Yet we find quite a different emphasis developed by Foucault who is probably the person most responsible for placing the term, 'human sciences' in our public domain. Indeed, his understanding of 'human sciences' is visible and ambiguously so; what he meant by the function of the human sciences is far from clear. Visibility, as I use the term, is that which permits a possibility to become an observable; but it is no guarantee that a possibility will become realized as a consequential idea.

Foucault's notion of the human sciences is manipulative, or is as Habermas insists, determined and deterministic. Indeed, problems of modernity and postmodernity can be said to turn on facets of this problem of the *meaning* of the human sciences.

David Hoy, one of the early contributors to Round Table discussions, astutely points to the fact that it is Foucault's own rhetoric which backfires on him and which structurally contradicts the semantic import of his own writing (Hoy, 1986; 11-18). Hoy notes that Foucault's very notion of 'system' undoes him, since in Foucault's context a system is assumed to be static and the genuine process of systemic change is not realizable. Hoy's major criticism of Foucault's concept of the human sciences centers on Foucault's failure to provide a resource for production, transformation and distribution of values. What is wanted is a pervasive force to unify the various sciences even as it would respect differences among them. Indeed, it is such differences that permit units of human meaning to be relational units rather than atomistic ones (see Kevelson, 1990). The problem, as I have examined elsewhere, has much to do with problems of observables and relations in space, or with facts and community interwoven with legal ideas of place, property and reciprocal, connective human rights.

This is so full a volume that it does not permit one to do more than merely point here and there. But in addition to Peircean and continental hermeneutist influences on law and the human sciences, I want also to say a few words about the Prague Linguistic Circle's contribution, and about Thomas G. Winner, who speaks of this Prague influence. Therefore, the following brief remarks will conclude the Peircean and Foucaultian strains for now and lead to a few remarks that will introduce Winner on Prague School Semiotics.

The human sciences, says Foucault, are those inquiries about 'man' as the two-faced one. The 'object and knower of knowledge,' refers to 'man' whose heads look in and out rather than left and right or simultaneously at past and future. These few sciences which came into existence in the nineteenth century are, unlike anything called science before them, not mappings of ideas of an earlier age. They are not interpretants in Peirce's sense of an initial idea which 'acts' like a model of a system of thought. Nor are Foucault's 'human sciences' like images or iconic functions of new thought-signs, spontaneously as Peircean 'Firsts' and as novel, invented thoughts become in our time self-referring discourses as are poems, paintings or any artworks that are self-referring and yet are *not* autonomous.

But the idea of the human sciences, newly born, is not in my opinion intended as an honorific term: indeed, this idea comes into the world, according to Ian Hacking and others, with connotations of 'greenness' clinging to its name: Hacking speaks of Foucault's human sciences as the 'immature sciences.' But it is this discourse, or knowledge of knowledge as a kind of power, i.e., a constituting medium, which permits us to make ourselves, as artifacts, into such selves as we would want to be. Hacking is insistent that ideas are partners in search of authenticity of relationship between I and Thou; yet he shows Foucault's idea of the human sciences not as monologic as a whole, but rather as a shifting of power, from one authorial discourse to another. One might say that this view of Foucault's 'human sciences' represents or mirrors powershifts in the world of nation-states prior to now.

What seems at first to be genuinely anarchistic in Foucault's notion of the human sciences turns out to be nihilistic. Those outer-directed narratives, says Hacking, leave out the indispensable link and basic structure of human relationships in free community; such free relations are based upon the idea of inner dialogue, a construction which lies at the heart of Peircean thought. Such outer-directed narrative of Foucault, in Hacking's sense, "Omits the permanent heartland of subjectivity . . . it is less knowledge produced in the human sciences that we use as our guide in life than self-knowledge. To say this is not to return to subjectivity. There is nothing private about this use of acquired words and practical techniques. The cunning of conscience and self-knowledge is to make it *feel* private,'' (Hacking, 1986:236, cited in D. Hoy, *Foucault: A Critical Reader*).

The fact is that Foucault is primarily concerned with relations of abstract power rather than human interpersonal relations; he is caught up with struggles between the terms 'legal' and 'legitimate' rather than with the conflicts between actual and experiential legal systems that represent opposing human values. This makes it hard for me to grasp why legal semioticians of any stripe would expect to find in Foucault's thought basic paradigms and theoretical grounds for a semiotics of law.

Yet the idea of the human sciences -- the 'immature sciences' -- do provide us with an intellectual position, often lifted from its original context and recast as a target to hit against. As Habermas points out, no repressive system, including a repressive legal system, can bring about freedom, (Habermas, as suggested in 'Questions and Counterquestions' in R. Bernstein, 1985:196). A legal system which interprets and represents the value of freedom can do so only if it grows out of the free reciprocity of communicative exchange between free people. This highest value, freedom, is the referent value of Peirce's semiotics; here law functions as link and as a pivot between possible and ideal, between physical and metaphysical. Freedom is possible as a value because the vague and the nondetermined are sustained all along the complicated way of pushing and stretching the boundaries of the Real.

As Tom Winner's student, I began to appreciate how the Prague Theorists conceived of the creating of meaning as free exchange of value, in dialogue, e.g. as that which Jan Mukarovsky called 'semantic reversals.'

Professor Thomas G. Winner is at present Director of the Semiotic Program at Boston University. He was a student of the late Roman Jakobson, and he was my advisor in my own doctoral work on semiotics at Brown University in the 1970's. Tom Winner was born in Prague. He took his doctoral degree at Columbia University, and he taught at several of the most prestigious universities in this country and abroad. It was his introductory course in Poetics and Semiotics which led me into Peirce, into semiotics, and hence into legal semiotics.

I have here a manuscript by Tom Winner which is especially detailed with respect to his own meticulous scholarship in Slavic poetics and linguistics, but which contains as well important insight on the origins and contributions of the Prague Linguistic Circle with respect to modern semiotics. It is, in part, a complex and technical study. But Tom Winner suggested that I may excerpt from this very long and full study whatever material I find of particular importance for our purposes in legal semiotics and which may have especially significant bearing for our present topic here on Law and the Human Sciences. I take such liberties with his permission.

In addition to what I learned from Tom Winner about the Prague Linguistic Circle and its enormous influence in the areas of discourse analysis, poetics, cross-reference, relations between all coordinate functions of semiosis, the role of marked language against unmarked and normative language, and interrelationships between aesthetic functions in artworks as *in other social subsystems* as well, what I also learned is Tom's inimitable respect for the purposes and freedoms of other people. He gave me a wide berth to study what mattered most to me, and he was there as teacher, facilitator, resource person, and as critic and friend in my own discovery procedure into law and the human sciences via semiotics. An abridged version of the manuscript he sent me follows; I have deleted passages which focused on more technical aspects of Slavic language and literature than this readership may be concerned with here.

III
Papers and Authors in this Forum

The Fifth Round Table on Law and Semiotics was programmatically subdivided into special topics of a general nature which were intended to provide more of a binding force to the colloquium than to address particular problems and issues. These subcategories are: The Idea of the Human Sciences and Paradigms of Legal Semiotics; Toward a Legal Aesthetics; Law Language, Styles, Genres and Related Topics; International Law and Legal Cultures; Interactions With Respect to Law, Politics and Economics; Strategies of Legal Rhetoric. To say this in no way minimizes the importances of these subtopics *as such.*

It is only when a field has been tightly defined and monitored that given paradigms may be regarded as the only paradigms which are acceptable for investigation and analysis; other concerns, as Kuhn well noted, come to be regarded as anomalous. We have tried to avoid imposing paradigmatic grids on early stages of legal semiotics inquiry for, as noted earlier, to do so would prematurely set forth a reduced model in the name of a general and abstract model.

To digress, it is also for this reason that Peirce had objected to the notion of 'abstraction' in referring to the Quality or first sign of an image of a most general understanding of something comes to be selected from its usual and customary ground in the photosemiotics of his Phenomenology. Rather, Peirce calls his method a 'prescinding' of a quality from its customary environment rather than an abstraction, because we choose it in order to examine an idea in ways that have thus far been overlooked. We isolate a Quality rather than reduce the ground. I discuss this distinction in some detail in Kevelson, 1987, in particular in the chapter on phenomenology. For example, ideas like works of art may be possessed and in that sense 'owned' by individual members of any given society, but artworks, as is the case of all cultural properties, belong to the public with respect to the special Quality they represent *as* value. This distinction between possession and property is part of a problem to be taken up at future Round Tables; it is at this time part of work in progress.

The point here is that regardless of how an idea comes to be born, how it is brought from possibility into the light of public inquiry, it is *as* existent, *not* the owned possession of any single person or institution but rather, as a cultural value it is part of the public domain. Eventually, as is the way even of trade names such as Vaseline and Xerox and Frigidaire, such terms become assimilated into public speech where they take on meaning not intended nor predicted by their coiners.

So with Legal Semiotics, and all the suggested subtopics for sessions at Round Table meetings: Those who respond, who choose to engage in this dialogic exchange, do claim the right to interpret the 'given' as data and to transform it, i.e., to *make meaning* in response to perceived meaningful *signs as ideas*.

Thus the resultant Round Table of this fifth anniversary composed itself into somewhat different categories than those programmatically suggested. Actually we find the following groups emerging 'naturally' and spontaneously:

I, *Law and Economics*, organized and chaired by Robin Malloy, Professor of Law and Economics at Syracuse University, was the most cohesive group. This session introduced concepts such as 'simulation', 'complexity', and 'nonlinearity' to semiotics's views on law and economics. The members of this group were in addition to Robin Paul Malloy, Denis J. Brion of the Law Faculty of Washington and Lee University, Gordon Whitney, who brings his expertise as former staff member of AT&T Bell Laboratories to the making of 'A Semiotic Model of Economic Theory', Richard Janikowski who teaches Criminology and Criminal Justice at Memphis State University, and Pertti Ahonen of the Law and Economics Faculty of the University of Tampere in Finland.

II, which focused on 'Legal Cultures' was probably the most comprehensive of this year's topics, is broadly anthropological but clearly divisible into a) theoretic approaches to the problems of law and semiotics from anthropological theory and b) semiotic perspectives on cross-cultural conflicts. In the first category is Professor Irene Portis-Winner who provides a background to the study of legal semiotics through anthropologists such as Hoebel whose direct influence on Llewellyn and legal Realism is now proverbial. Irene Portis Winner teaches at the Massachusetts College of Art and is well known for her work on the semiotics of culture.

This approach similarly underlies Michael Green's paper, 'Legal Language and Metaphysical Metaphors.' Here it is clear that categories are somewhat less than useful compartments in the bringing forth of new and experimental ideas. Professor Green's work lays out in great detail comparative mythologies which are resourceful for several kinds of legal systems and legal orders. Green is a member of the Philosophy Department of SUNY at Oneonta.

In a germane mode Ralph Lindgren, Professor of Philosophy at Lehigh University, looks at evolution of rituals as a model of semiosis, i.e., of semiotic processes conventionalized and made culture-specific. Lindgren's work contribures to an emergent semiotic interest in customary law, and for semiosis itself as a metaphor-producing function of relations in law.

Within this anthropological approach to semiotics and the human sciences we also find attention focused on current problems, such as terrorism and violations of human rights in international law. The latter is the topic of Professor P.C. Bedwa's paper. Professor Bedwa teaches in the Department of Law at the Guru Nanak Dev University in the Amritsar region of India. The former, namely the issue of terrorism, is taken up by Professor Michael Saltman of the Departments of Sociology and Anthropology at the University of Haifa in Israel. Peter Winn, grounded in both philosophy and anthropology, and now Special Assistant District Attorney in Austin, Texas, brings together both these threads in his paper which examines legal instruments in connection with ideas of legal rituals.

Several papers which I am here mentioning as being a good fit in other categories could be just as appropriately included here. In fact at the closing plenary session of the Fifth Round Table it was generally conceded that the anthropological approach was the most dimensional at this year's meeting.

Closely following was III, *Law and Language*, which includes papers that deal with verbal strategies in legal rhetoric. Among contributors working in this broad sphere are the following: Tom Winner, whose paper, discussed briefly, is primarily of a linguistic nature, but is also speculative and theoretical.

Dr. Eve Wilson of the Computing Laboratories of University of Kent in Canterbury England brings forward the linguistic 'functional' approach, which through Halliday as well as through the Prague Linguistic School, has made enormous contributions to our own inquiry of aspects of legal semiotics. Wilson deals with linguistic structures of indeterminacy and uncertainty in law language. She suggests how this linguistic overlapping of boundaries is carried forward into more global aspects of legal procedure.

Bill Scott's paper on Codification approaches the phenomena of legal codes also from the perspective of linguistic analyses; his work moves between linguistics and problems of metaphysics and includes as well problems in sociopolitical and aesthetic theory. Professor Scott heads the Communications Department at Glasgow Technical Institute in Scotland.

An historical view is presented here by William Pencak, Professor of History at Penn State. Bill's paper brings a semiotic point of view to some open-ended questions on an unsolved event of suspected revolution in colonial Massachusetts. Pencak is well known for his work in legal semiotics.

Robert Ginsberg, Professor of Philosophy at Penn State, examines the role of law in the history of higher education in the United States. He sees law as a multidisciplinary hub among the liberal arts studies which radiate from it. His paper opened discussion on how legal semiotics may be shaped for the classroom, at graduate, undergraduate, and professional and postdoctoral levels.

In a broad stroke we show Legal Aesthetics as a rubric or arc covering many perspectives. In common use, the term Aesthetics currently and most usually connotes art history and art criticism; presumably a Legal Aesthetics would link topics of this kind to those characteristic which commonly fall in the traditional category of The Law. But several papers of a very different kind of Legal Aesthetics were presented at the Fifth Round Table, e.g., papers by Peter Goodrich, Yifat Hachamovitch, Costa Douzinas, Thomas Beebee and others. By request some of these papers are included in a forthcoming volume on Law and Aesthetics which should appear early in 1992 in the Series, on topics in Aesthetics, edited by Robert Ginsberg and published by Peter Lang.

But in this present volume we are including several major contributions to this new idea of a legal aesthetics and a new approach to the topic:

David Caudill's paper, 'Jacques Lacan and our State of Affairs: Preliminary Remarks on Law as Other' relates value (aesthetics) to law via law and psychoanalysis. He examines the notion of linguistic determinants which become translated or transmuted into legal values. Professor Caudill is a member of the Law Faculty of the Washington and Lee University.

Andrew McThenia is also a Professor of Law at Washington and Lee University. His contribution to the idea of a legal aesthetics centers on the interaction of law and morality. McThenia has recourse to works of fiction in his paper, 'Inadequate Stories.' This paper also has important bearing on current work in the area of Narratology in Legal Semiotics, e.g., B. Jackson (1988; W. Twining, 1988, 1991). The connection between law language and various styles of literature was first taken up by Kevelson in 1977 in *Inlaws/Outlaws*, on the catalytic function of the Robin Hood Ballads in conflicting legal systems.

Martha Kemper, who teaches Theater Arts at the Penn State University, discusses several kinds of law in conflict in her '*Antigone*.' She reminds us with an actor's insight that law as a system of internal contradictions is part of the heritage of western civilizations in particular, but may also characterize conflicting notions of legality and legitimacy on a global scale.

Roberta Kevelson is Distinguished Professor of Philosophy at Penn State and directs the Center for Semiotic Research. While not anthropological in its main thrust, but broadly theoretical and focused on a Peircean aesthetics in legal semiotics, Kevelson's paper, 'Pragmatics, Utopic Construction, Legal Myths,' points to neglected correspondences between Durkheim and Peirce which center on the 'method of pragmatism.' In particular, she points to other aspects of competing ideologies in the mythological structures of legal cultures. Such internal oppositions become highlighted in problems of conflicts of law in international law which currently confront us.

Jay Knaack's paper, 'Metaphysics of Punishing,' explores relationships between values and ethics also, but from the viewpoints of major jurisprudential thought and current theoretical oppositional views on legal punishment. Professor

Knaack raises questions on the relative effectual results of cooperation versus coercion as motives in legal punishing. Jay Knaack heads the Department of Philosophy and Religious Studies at the University of West Florida.

Alison Young's paper, 'The Body of Criminality: The Politics of Ordinariness,' argues that the very notion of criminality as a discourse in the law is a construction of rhetorical strategies in which argument is used to create a 'body' of linguistic data that is taken to represent a presumed object-body of fact. Here in Young's papers, we are also confronted with value shifts and permutations in the instruments of the law, i.e., in law as medium for much craft if not for artwork *as such*. Alison Young is a Lecturer in Law at Lancaster University in England.

Paul Ryan's paper, 'A Sign of Itself,' takes its title from Peirce's writings. Ryan takes his main argument from Peirce as well. In fact, he shows that Peirce's theory of iconicity may act as a model of regulatory and self-creative processes such that, ideally, would characterize free and open legal systems. Paul Ryan's paper is carried over from the Fourth Round Table on Law and Semiotics (1990) where it was originally presented and was received with much enthusiasm and interest. Ryan is a video artist, an ecologist, and a free-lance writer whose base is in New York.

Although the main thrust of Michel Rosenfeld's paper, 'The Semiotics of Justice: Reading Across the Boundaries Between Law, Ethics and Politics,' is not intended to develop an axiological/aesthetic thesis, he points up this topic significantly. Rosenfeld's concern is with major distinctions between Luhman's 'theory of legal autopoeisis' and Weinrib's 'new legal formalism.' Rosenfeld's own position is supportive of the Luhmanian view, but with important qualifications; Professor Rosenfeld is at the Cardozo Law School.

Michael Pendleton, Professor of Law at Murdoch University is Australia, shows how outmoded linguistic instruments, still in use by legal systems, may constrain and distort the ways in which various kinds of property is described and, therefore, is regarded as meaningful signs.

Finally, these papers in respective, unique, transdisciplinary and crosscultural style, need to be met according to the special ways they each present themselves. They must be seen, as well, as members of this company or community which forms a kind of bond by means of our common language of Legal Semiotics. We have then a common tongue (after a fashion) and more than two dozen remarkable idiolects presented here. If a single theme can be said to connect us, I think it is our mutual concern to bring crosscurrents and conflicts into the open and to evolve out of such conflicting themes that raise some more general and more unifying linkages.

IV

In acknowledgement, we want to thank the wide circle of supporters of the Center for Semiotic Research in Law, Government and Economics of Penn State, since it is through the Center that these Round Tables exist and that these volumes are produced. Thus, we extend our appreciation to the Penn State Commonwealth Educational System, The College of the Liberal Arts, The Offices of Research and Graduate Studies, The Berks Campus, The University Libraries and to all individual persons who have helped our project. We thank, also, The Xerox Foundation for its supportive grants which assist in the publications of the Center and in related Center activities. And, not least, we thank Cindy Palecek and her staff for bringing these manuscripts into publishable form.

The Center encourages inquiries for the sponsoring of special colloquia and possible publishing of works on special topics in semiotics of law, government and economics, singly and/or jointly.

Chapter 2

Pragmatic Aspects of the Political Economy of Law: With Applications to Environmental Policies

Pertti Ahonen[1]

I

Abstract

The basic level of the pragmatics of the political economy of law can be spelled out in terms that culminate with an elementary binary structure of pairwise comparisons between alternatives available to individuals. An intermediate level of the pragmatics culminates with propositions supposed to be testable, often empirically. The pragmatics is crowned with arguments that apply rules of formal logic to prove certain propositions. However, it is not rare that the arguments 'feed back' to the empirical testing and the pragmatic basis, which may lead to new, interesting perspectives. Cases drawn from environmental policies illustrate the general points made and their limits.

II

Elements of the Pragmatics of Political Economy

A mere enumeration of the *objects* studied in political economy does not suffice for the delineation of its proper scope, as the range of the objects nowadays covers not only the economic aspects as narrowly conceived and their extensions to politics, but stretches to culture, everyday life, and beyond.[2] What better indicates what is typical of modern political economy is the prevalence of special mathematical and logical languages and the special *signs* of these languages as well as special graphical sign systems with their signs.[3] A pragmatic account of modern political economy that discusses objects and signs must also fix its attention to the *signification* that arises in the minds of expert and lay interpreters as intended and unintended effects of the special languages, sign systems and their signs conventionally used for spelling out the objects in question.[4]

It is convenient to focus on the different aspects of the signification that takes place in modern political economy. Here, a hierarchy of the aspects is useful for arranging the discussion. *First*, we can distinguish *basic concepts* and *models*, preferably few or even only one to facilitate the analysis. The concepts and models also include the fundamental assumptions concerning certain '*possible objects*', such as objects which it is useful for research to posit for its purposes but which cannot be considered either true or false as such. Political economy is famous for its construction of certain generic objects, '*types*', such as those of 'rational choice' and the '*homo economicus*', and for its assumptions that these objects somehow transcend concrete objects such as real-world acts or real-world individuals, which remain as if mere '*tokens*'. In its substituting the *nomothetic* study of generic 'types' and related general scientific laws for the *idiographic* study of individual cases and their specificity, political economy largely abandons the study of qualitative and intuitive aspects typical of the pursuit and the criticism of the arts. *Second*, there are *propositions* that convey information on that which is considered to exist. Such propositions may be either true (in stating that something exists when it 'really' does) or false (in the opposite case), or the propositions may possess different degrees of truth or falsehood. *Third*, there are *arguments* whose criterion is validity or invalidity according to logic. While propositions concern the *existence* of something, arguments deal with the *truth* of that something.[5]

Our focus is on the basic concepts and models, the propositions, and the arguments of the political economy of law, with a special reference to environmental policy. *Our object of study cannot be any of the objects studied by political economy*, including the objects studied by the political economy of environment, but the *object is political economy* itself, with a special reference to its latter subset, or fractions of the both sets. Our task bears some analogy to the contemporary study of the rhetoric of economics by economists themselves (Klamer, 1984, McCloskey, 1985, 1990), but our perspective still is fundamentally different (cf., however, certain articles in Samuels, 1990).

III
The Model of Rational Choice: Pairwise Choices Between 'Given' Alternatives

A. The Coase Theorem and Beyond

First there was law, then there was legal theory, and much later a political economy of law materialized. Despite that the *Coase theorem* (first spelled out in Coase, 1960) has been subject to fundamental criticisms by pro-government liberals and Marxists as well, it remains the true bedrock of the contemporary political economy of law, often called '*law and economics*'.[6]

The Coase theorem builds on several assumptions. *First*, the *transaction costs* some of which necessarily arise as a second-order consequence of the transactions (the mutual economic dealings) of market actors are relatively low.

Second, there is a mechanism (such as a *legal order*) for enforcing contracts upon actors reluctant to fulfill their obligations and for mediating the actors' disputes, and this mechanism is exogenous *vis-à-vis* the actors. *Third*, a freely transferable '*numeraire* good' such as money is available. *Fourth*, there are *property rights* that the actors hold towards the objects being transacted.

The assumptions given, the Coase theorem deals with any situation where the actions of at least one of the actors hurt at least one other actor. Here, in the terms of technical terminology, socially significant *externalities*, also called *external effects*, are present. The externalities may be 'negative' ones: a producer's production or a consumer's consumption hurts non-producers or non-consumers, therefore imposing them costs that are also costs from the entire society's point of view but not from that of the original producer or consumer. If you have a factory upstream, you may have no incentive to prevent your effluent from polluting the water of the downstream users. The externalities may be 'positive' ones: others draw out benefits from a producer's production or a consumer's consumption without the producer or the consumer being able to impose much of the cost upon the 'external users', which may lead to undersupply from society's (all users') point of view. Even without technical limitations preventing your elimination of the effluent of your upstream factory, your necessity to compete might prevent your role as environmentally conscious entrepreneur.

The Coase theorem argues that in situations of externalities *everyone* involved can reach mutually advantageous bargains voluntarily. As far as there is a unique outcome that maximizes social wealth, the actors involved will reach that outcome *no matter what the prior assignment of property rights and liabilities*. A further implication of the Coase theorem is the claim that the externalities are no justification for government intervention *à la* American tradition (*regulation* of certain industries) nor *à la* the tradition of Western Continental Europe (*direct government provision* guaranteed through public sector growth and occasional nationalization), but governments should only assure alienable property rights that can be defended in institutions of law to ensure that transaction costs stay low and that the markets function.[7] Importantly, *environmental policies are a subset of the entire set of questions that lie within the domain where the Coase theorem is supposedly valid.*

B. *Homo Economicus* Unveiled

While there is no doubt that Coase, an economist, was well versed in the formalisms of economics, he chose to argue in terms that made his theorem accessible to relatively wide audiences. This fact may have disguised that his fundamental concepts and models are basically the same as those of orthodox economics: the model underlying the Coase theorem is nothing but the *model made up of the axioms of rational choice*.[8] The model includes a *generic model* of *homo economicus* as the key acting subject dealt with in economic discourse, and the model implies the use of the methods of 'comparative statics' borrowed early from such sources as physics (e.g., Mirowski, 1989), i.e., comparing different equilibria expressed in the terms of maxima and minima by the means of differential calculus.

The axioms of rational choice apply to actors ('i'), who make choices among *given alternatives*. For the axioms it is of no special consequence with what values the i valuate the alternatives, nor what is the source of the alternatives available, such as pre-existent property rights and a corresponding pre-existent distribution of income, wealth, and welfare.

According to the axioms, *first*, each individual, i, evaluates each of its alternatives solely on the basis of the *outcome*, x_i, that arises from the alternative.

Second, each i has a *transitive* and complete *preference ordering* between all x_i.[9] Third, there is a mathematical function that gives the numerical representation of the preference ordering by each i, namely the *utility function*, $u(x_i)$, or $u = u(x_i)$, which gives i's valuation of its alternatives according to the transitive preference ordering based on the outcomes, x_i. *Fourth*, the actors are '*rational egoists*', who are indifferent towards each others' preference orderings: each i prefers what s/he does irrespective of what any -i does. *Fifth*, each i acts in such a way that it *optimizes* (typically, maximizes) the value of its utility function $u(x_i)$ within the important constraint of the scarce *resources* available to i. *Sixth*, the *marginal utility* available to i decreases by each additional increment of whatever it is that i desires.

The model made up of the axioms of rational choice, including the model of *homo economicus*, boils down to an *elementary binary structure* of pairwise comparisons between alternatives posed to an individual. Here, comparison between j alternatives a, b, c, ..., j can be condensed into pairwise comparisons between a and b, b and c, and so on, until j-1 and j are compared.[10]

Different interpretations of the model of rational choice have been proposed, from the view that the model is an '*ideal type*' that phenomenologically 'brackets' the inessential features and thereby focuses attention to the essential ones (Weber, 1985); to the '*predictivist*' view that the model's only true test is its predictive ability with respect to a 'reality'; to the '*instrumentalist*' view that the model is a mere tool (about these interpretations, Caldwell, 1984). A *pragmatist* view does agree with the other views to the extent that they see that a model may not be either true or false as such, but the pragmatist view abandons the other views where they make methodological prescriptions, such as predictivist or instrumentalist ones. The model of rational choice and the aligned model of *homo economicus* can therefore be seen as models of *possible objects* whether these objects (here, simply, the object called 'rational choice' and the related object called '*homo economicus*') ever exist in any 'real reality'. Here, it is *enough* for the pragmatist view to fix its attention on this and other similar models and, through the models, on the possible objects being modeled.

At this point it is enough to remind only of a further circumstance: the choice of models of possible objects may be conditioned by certain relationships between the [possible] objects and the signs available for spelling out features of these [possible] objects. For instance, there is little doubt of the conditioning exerted by mathematical language on what have been considered legitimate objects of study in political economy.

IV
Testable 'Coasean' Propositions

The pragmatist idea that propositions should be seen as statements that convey information on what is considered to exist should not be taken too literally or narrowly in a context such as that of political economy. Here, it is unusual that the objects being studied were 'essences' of any kind, but it is typical that the objects are quantities, including quantities typical of certain relationships whose strength is being expressed. In political economy, it is conventional that the question of the truth vs. falsehood of propositions, in turn, tends to boil down to the empirical verification or falsification of the quantities, including the strength of relationships, exceeding certain threshold values, such as values that are from some point of view absolute, values that are comparatively high or low, or values important according to some statistical test.[11]

The 'law and economics' building upon the Coase theorem is often categorized into a more encompassing group of approaches labeled with such names as the '*public choice -- property rights school*'. Within this 'school' with broad boundaries, it is commonplace to test theoretical propositions concerning the desirability of market allocation as opposed to government allocation with such empirical measures as comparisons of productivity in 'private' businesses and in operations run by government, or in voluntary arrangements and in arrangements established and maintained by government.[12]

Proponents of 'law and economics' would definitely hold that, for instance, an arrangement where government carries a tax or a fee on certain emissions or, what really amounts to the same, prohibits the emissions,[13] is less efficient than an arrangement where the actors can engage among themselves in transactions buying and selling rights to pollute and freedoms from the emissions. In the latter case no less than a market has been created for selling and buying the rights and freedoms. However, the empirical tests trying to demonstrate if governments or markets are more efficient have not been fully conclusive,[14] following the common fate of empirical research -- by the way well-known to methodology claimed 'positivist' as well -- that no amount of verification or falsification is really ever finally enough given all the conceivable circumstances and the incessantly changing times.

V

Arguments in Political Economy: Strengths and Weaknesses of the Force of Logic

From a pragmatist point of view, arguments can be seen as closely linked to propositions. While the pragmatist interest concerning the latter focuses on the *existence* of something, including the existence of relationships, the similar interest concerning the arguments focuses on the *truth* of certain propositions, including the truth of propositions that concern the existence of certain relationships.

In political economy in particular, the best renowned arguments are typically cast as *indirect proofs* through the demonstration of logical *paradoxes*. Here, the valid[15] argument which the proof includes typically starts from a set of premises at least one of which is *untrue*[16] but which are all first assumed to hold true for the purpose of the proof. Towards the end of the argument and through it, it will be then shown that at least one of the premises does not hold. In the terms of technical terminology, the relationships in question are typically functions in the mathematical sense that are, through the 'rules' that the functions include, supposed to provide a 'mapping' of the preferences of a set of individuals onto the result of their collective choice.[17]

Three arguments with an indirect proof, each famous in political economy, include the *Arrow (impossibility) theorem* also called the *Arrow paradox*, the *Sen paradox*, and the *Gibbard-Satterthwaite impossibility theorem*. It is possible to sketch the general form of the basic proposition made in each of these and several other cases in the purpose of obtaining a certain valid argument concerning the circumstance that at least one of the premises turns out to be false:

> It is not true that a certain set of true premises holding simultaneously define a function that provides a logically solid path from the preferences of a set of individuals to the results of their common choice or decision.

The Arrow theorem involves the proof of the impossibility of a *social welfare function* (SWF), which would map individual preferences onto a collectively preferred combination of *collective goods* (e.g., world peace; a thick ozone layer for all nations; national security; freedom from transborder toxic emissions for a nation; local police protection) and *individual goods* (perfectly divisible goods from whose consumption it is easy to close off any outsider, such as many daily consumables). Arrow's proof builds on five premises, axioms that are supposed to hold simultaneously.

First, there is the *Pareto principle* that not a single individual's well-being must be increased if the price is any decrease in the well-being of at least one other individual. *Second*, there is the principle of *non-dictatorship* that the preferences of no single individual should dictate the result of the collective choice. *Third*, the resulting social preference ordering should be *transitive*.[18] *Fourth*, there must be an *unrestricted domain* of all the alternatives being considered by all the relevant individuals. *Fifth*, there must be an *independence from irrelevant alternatives*: the collective choice must be dependent only on the very alternatives being considered. Arrow's indirect proof starts from the assumption that the axioms may hold simultaneously, and he ends up proving that if the other axioms hold, the non-dictatorship axiom is violated.[19]

According to the *Sen paradox* (1970, 1976), even if the Arrowian non-dictatorship axiom were relieved in the sense of allowing each single individual involved in the social choice to be decisive for the social choice over one pair of alternatives, and the conditions of unrestricted domain and the Pareto principle would hold, the transitivity condition would be violated, thus leading to a cycle and therefore indecisiveness and instability.[20] The Sen paradox is also known as the proof that '*Paretian liberals*' do not exist in the sense that the force of logic alone does not suffice for guaranteeing individuals simultaneously a domain of the exertion of their liberal rights at least in small matters and freedom from such redistribution that takes from some individuals and gives that which is taken away to other individuals.[21] In the general context of political economy, including the political economy of environment, the Sen paradox can be taken as a representative of such proofs of the inexistence of social choice functions that focus on the problems of cycles, instability and indecisiveness.[22]

The *Gibbard-Satterthwaite paradox* applies to functions that are less ambitious than the true social choice functions (SCF), namely social decision functions (SDF).[23] While an SCF consists of collective choice rules that transform individual preference profiles into social preference relations, an SDF only transforms preference profiles into single winners. In the latter case, the Arrowian axioms of transitivity and universal domain are dropped, but certain of the implicit Arrowian requirements not casted as axioms by him may receive this status. The Gibbard-Satterthwaite theorem also drops the Arrowian requirement of the Pareto principle, and builds on altogether four axioms.

First, there is *universality*, which is an Arrowian requirement here elevated into the status of an axiom: the SDF should not apply only to easy cases but also hard ones such as those with no unanimity whatsoever. *Second*, there is the Arrowian *non-dictatorship*. *Third*, there is *nondegeneracy* (nontriviality): not a single one of the alternatives at hand must be trivial in the sense of its being the loser in every one of the relevant choices. *Fourth*, there is *nonmanipulability* (cheatproofness), according to which not a single one of the individuals in question should be able to secure his or her preferred outcome by strategically misrepresenting his or her own preferences to at least one other individual. The Gibbard-Satterthwaite proof starts from the assumption that all the four axioms hold simultaneously, but the proof ends up with the result that if the other axioms hold, non-dictatorship is violated. In political economy, including the political economy of environment, the Gibbard-Satterthwaite theorem can be taken to imply the difficulties in avoiding situations of some individuals' '*free-riding*' on others, who must then bear the cost of carrying out what all the individuals, including the free-riders, 'really' prefer and would express to prefer in the absence of the benefits of concealing their preferences.[24]

In environmental policy, a 'classical' case of the risks of 'free-riding' involves 'common property resources' available freely to all but dependent on due care as to their renewability. Without any constraints whatsoever, every individual has an incentive to maximize his or her exploitation of the resources and ignore their regeneration, because the other individuals would 'automatically' share the benefits of the regenerative efforts. The final result is that the resources may be lost for good. Certain forest areas of the world (early, many Mediterranean forests; later, some fractions of the agricultural land of such countries as the United States; nowadays the Amazonia, and the Sahel of Africa) or fisheries with given species of fish or sea mammals suffice for examples. One suggested institutional solution is a Coasean one: the introduction of property rights if possible, hopefully giving each owner enjoying the fruits of the regeneration sufficient incentives to be concerned with assuring the regeneration. Other suggested ways out of the dilemma include altruism, conventions, repetitious 'playing' of the 'game' in question with the result that the players develop a good 'reputation' that they do not wish to spoil, and such models as TAT ('tit for tat', never start cheating, forgive ex-cheaters, but revenge chronic cheating) (for many of these models, Kreps, 1989).

A certain drawback of the arguments proper of modern political economy is their limited number especially as concerns truly different arguments. This has, after some time, tended to lead to a certain exhaustion of new topics to study. The fact that this is also a drawback of a certain research strategy heavily relying on formal logic has been an incentive for broadening the scope of research to cover 'feedbacks' from the arguments back to the propositions supposed to be proven empirically, and maybe even further, to the pragmatic basis of the political economy based on the axioms of rational choice.

VI

From Arguments Back to Testable Propositions in Political Economy

Because the valid proof of arguments, including the proof proper of the truth or the lack of truth of their premises, is a matter of logic only, it might hold true also in political economy that not too many prospects for continuing research might remain once the proofs have been construed. However, increasingly many researchers have taken a further '*pragmatist turn*', studying the *relevance* of arguments, including arguments that involve paradoxes, in varying contexts. Beside modelling that introduces different contexts, importantly institutional contexts, by the means of the methods of comparative statics (see especially the now-paradigmatic cases of McKelvey, 1976 and Shepsle, 1979), an important methodological device is *simulation*.

Here, simulation sheds new light on the objects created by research -- in this case, the arguments, including the paradoxes -- by developing or introducing new languages and, sometimes, other new sign systems, for spelling out crucial characteristics of the objects in various contexts where the objects are supposedly applicable. Simulation also creates new, artificial objects -- models of simulation and different elements of such models -- that reproduce features of certain existing or possible more 'real' or more 'real world' objects in order to enable the study of the relevance of the scientific objects *vis-à-vis* the 'real' or 'real world' ones. In this respect simulation is a variant of *experimentation*, and in this sense there is hardly any other except experimental simulation.

As any simulation, simulation in political economy, including simulation concerning questions relevant for environmental policy, may involve *iconic* models or *symbolic* models of the aspects being modeled.[25] Accounting for the direction where current simulations proceed in political economy (Kahneman, et al. 1990) it is useful to introduce a term for a third type of models situated between the two former types, namely *indexical* models,[26] which already have many applications. *Iconic models* display close *similarities*, perhaps physical ones or ones of form, with the objects being modeled. *Indexical models* may not display any similarities with the objects being modeled, but these models refer directly to the objects through physical causality or contiguity (*à la* smoke *vis-à-vis* fire) or through a certain *conventional* use of a symbol (*à la* pronouns, which refer only in spatio-temporal contexts of certain kinds). *Symbolic models* lack both the similarity and the direct determination *vis-à-vis* their objects; they are purely conventional; as signs, they can be seen as such complicated 'icons' which beside their literal meaning (such as a mathematical formula or a computer model made up of certain equations, certain data inputs and certain types of expected outputs) have a further, 'ideal' significance (such as that of being a model of something of interest in political economy). We should by no means rule out the possibility that the same simulation may involve both iconic, indexical and symbolic aspects.

The simulations of the Coase theorem, which is one of the important foci of the political economy of law in questions of environmental policy, are not yet too many, which defends the choice of taking only one example of a simulation (Kahneman, et al., 1990).[27] A prediction of the Coase theorem is that, certain assumptions given, market actors may 'internalize' economic externalities through mutually advantageous trades and multilateral bargaining without government intervention and, which is the most important point for the present simulation, that the actors will reach that outcome, maximizing social wealth, no matter what the prior assignment of property rights and liabilities.

The model of Kahneman et al. in their experimental simulation is, *first* of all, iconic, namely one involving students playing roles of market actors. *Second*, the model is also an indexical one: the hypothesis being tested was one of an '*endowment effect*', where the possession of an object (a kind of 'here-ness' providing a reference point), might decrease inviduals' *willingness to accept* a price as low for the object as the price that corresponds with the *willingness to pay* for the very same object by the very same individuals when they do not possess the object (indicating a 'there-ness' of the object as a reference point). *Third* and finally, the model is a symbolic one: what 'literally' were different groups of students at the Simon Fraser University of Canada were seen as capable of symbolizing many important situations that may prevail in economic markets. The simulation indeed suggested that relatively strong endowment effects exist, and Kahneman et al. (1990: 1345) therefore project their model as follows:

> 'Endowment effects can also be observed for firms and other organizations. Endowment effects are predicted for property rights acquired by historic accident or fortuitous circumstances, such as government licenses, landing rights, or transferable pollution permits.'

VII

From Arguments and Testable Propositions Back to the Model of Rational Choice

Simulations such as that of Kahneman et al. imply the need for sensitivity when applying the models of rational choice and the *homo economicus* in various contexts. This renders further support to the view that beside the delineation of objects and the definition of scientific languages and other scientific sign systems, also signification matters in political economy, as the features of the objects being studied with the help of the sign systems may have various effects among the different interpreters.

There is one point where many directions of research on political economy have been developing a constantly growing strong consensus: *institutions and the study of institutions matter*. The Coase theorem already opens path for attention to institutions, and simulations suggesting problems in the applications of the theorem can also be seen as building bricks for further institutions, this time institutions that might correct some of the problems in question (Frey and Eichenberger, 1991, Alt and Shepsle, 1990).

Institutional solutions have also been searched for problems of cycles, instability, indecisiveness and, in the extreme, chaos in decision-making. The solutions range from constitutional or conventional, including cultural, restrictions to the allowable scope of decision-making in given decision-making bodies to multi-staged decision procedures to assumptions of foresight instead of 'myopia' among the decision-making individuals (Shepsle, 1979, Kreps, 1984, Ferejohn and Krehbiel, 1987, Ordeshook and Schwartz, 1987, Alt and Shepsle, 1990).

The simulation of Kahneman et al. actually builds on a foundation of research first started in the 1940's with criticisms towards the model of rational choice and the related model of the *homo economicus*, and this research included a sensitivity towards questions of institutions at the outset. It was the Nobel laureate *Herbert A. Simon*, who already in his *Administrative Behavior* (1947) emphasized the cognitive limits of human beings and the possibilities to compensate some of these limits through such institutions as administrations. As continued by Simon, by *James G. March* (e.g. 1988) and others (e.g., Brunsson, 1985, March and Olsen, 1989), this idea that rationality is '*bounded*' in any concrete context in many including cognitive ways, has been expanding towards a more encompassing notion of the 'anomalies' in political economy; the consequences of the anomalies including the manipulability of individuals through strategic action; the possibilities to correct or compensate some of the anomalies through institutions flexible enough to adapt to the requirements of the different contexts of decision-making, choice, and the idiosyncrasies of decision-makers. A certain 'pragmatics of political economy' has emerged, including a 'pragmatics of social choice', and also developing features of a 'pragmatics of the political economy of law', bearing some resemblance with and having certain links to existing elements of such a general pragmatics as that of human communication (Watzlawick, et al., 1967).

VIII

Conclusions in the Light of 'Real-World' Examples of the Political Economy of Environment

The Coase theorem, even after having been qualified by such an experimental simulation as that of Kahneman et al., bears a certain credibility as a blueprint for internalizing economic externalities without government intervention irrespective of the initial endowment of individuals with the rights and liabilities which, according to the theorem, could be made objects of market exchange. However, there are 'real world' settings where 'effective demand' in the economic sense, that is, willingness to pay conditioned by the endowment of each actor, is not considered a completely adequate basis for distributing power and influence.

Klevorick and Kramer (1973) analyze the example of German water partnerships, *Genossenschaften*, for the management of water quality of certain rivers. The partnerships have two kinds of members, those whose action has the second-order consequence of producing most of the effluents, namely business firms, on the one hand, and municipal governments representing households who also are responsible for part of the effluent, on the other. The firms' representation depends basically on the volume of their effluent which the partnerships should work to clean, and the municipal representation is a direct function of the amount population. While Klevorick and Kramer are able to prove that in the system of a stylized partnership also such equilibria exist where no tax is carried from the firms nor the households in order to finance installations for the cleaning, also such equilibria exist where the tax rate is > 0. Moreover, many of the partnerships have *de facto* adopted *institutional* rules that place a high floor on the relative voting strength of those of their members who or which prefer a high elimination rate of the effluent, such as the households represented by the municipalities as opposed to firms with a high volume of effluent, or downstream communities and firms as opposed to their counterparts upstream.

There are also cases that render direct support to solutions *à la* Coase theorem. It may be no coincidence *that some of such cases of an evident applicability of the Coase theorem involve property rights based on national boundaries that cannot be transcended,* in which case there is no analogous (transnational) government equally capable of redistribution as might be the case within a single nation. A first case involves the transboundary air pollution between the USSR to Finland (Kaitala, et al., 1990). Here, the most visible problem includes the damage to Finnish forests in the furthest northeast of this country, caused by acidification resulting from sulphur and nitrogen compounds, predominantly emitted by Soviet nickel industries applying technologies that have a low elimination rate of these chemicals. The results of an analysis seeing the situation as 'a dynamic acid rain game', a cooperative or a noncooperative one, suggest that in order to obtain a cooperative solution Finland -- joined by Norway and Sweden which also suffer from the Soviet emissions -- should to an extent compensate, in other words 'bribe', the polluting country to decrease its emissions. And indeed in 1991 a Finnish-Swedish-Norwegian project is under way to help the USSR renew its facilities for nickel smelting. The aid includes such elements as loans with liberal terms and exports of (Finnish) smelting technology that eliminates practically all of the emissions.[28]

While transborder acid rain may be a serious problem for the nation that falls victim to it, violent international conflict launched by questions of natural resources are no less than matters of world peace and the functionality of the 'world system'. One of the proclaimed reasons for the war in the Persian Gulf in early 1991 was Iraqi dissatisfaction with the management of the oil deposits on the border of this country and its neighboring Kuwait, including Iraqi accusations of Kuwaiti pumping of oil from under the surface of Iraqi lands. Ending with a lengthy quotation from Stephen (1988: 19-20; see also Libecap and Wiggins, 1985) one can ask, *mutatis mutandis*, to what extent the loss to life, health and property that ensued in the Gulf might have been avoided with a proper management following more or less Coasean lines:[29]

> 'The . . . reservoir . . . under the surface will be determined by geological factors unrelated to the pattern of surface landownership. [W]hen . . . extracted from one part of the field, oil from other parts

. . . flows towards the areas from which . . . extracted. [T]he reservoir . . . is . . . a common property resource for everyone who has the right to drill on the surface . . . . These people have an incentive to extract the oil quickly before someone else does. [To avoid the problems that may ensue] . . . [t]he technical solution is to handle the reservoir as a unit combining extraction and pumping . . . to maintain pressure [a procedure called 'unitization']. . . .

The evidence . . . supports the argument . . . that an absence of exclusive property rights leads to . . . inefficient utilisation. . . However, it cannot be taken as necessarily supporting exclusive *private* {read here also as '*national*'} property rights. . . . Similar benefits are obtained . . . where . . . rights are vested in the state {read here also as 'transnational government'} rather than the surface landowner and the licence to extract . . . is auctioned . . .'[30]

ENDNOTES

1. Pertti Ahonen is University Professor of Public Administration at the University of Tampere, Finland.

2. Beside the political economy of markets and the economics of politics, McKenzie and Tullock, 1989, provide ample examples of the political economy of such topics as child production, sexual behavior, affection, crime, and lying and cheating.

3. In mathematics, the development of the special languages and their signs is covered in any comprehensive treatment of the history of mathematics. See, e.g., Kramer, 1982. An example of the consequences of the use of special languages and their signs in the economic sciences is the need for elementary books dedicated exactly to giving elementary interpretations of the common conventions, e.g., Eastman, 1984.

   Political economy also widely utilizes the graphical sign languages of mathematics. An interesting passage in this respect is Ordeshook 1986: 16-28, where the author introduces such common notions of modern political economy as 'city block preferences' and

'Euclidean preference contours' (ellipsoids or circles that depict preferences concerning given points in a plane or a space through the distance of these points from a best preferred point, a 'saturation point' or a 'bliss point'). Euclidean preferences have become an extremely common tool of political science, as any of the post-1975 volumes of such journals as *American Political Science Review* proves. We may also ponder to what extent the simultaneous introduction of formal languages and proofs and the new graphics have rendered parts of the political science community functionally illiterate.

For graphical sign languages, see also Bertin, 1983. Weingast, 1991, is on the way of writing a book on the Euclidean preferences used for analyzing the 'bliss points', and the accompanying graphics.

4. This brings in a specific approach to questions of *meaning*, namely a *pragmatist* approach that stresses the important role of use, users and usage for signs to have meaning with reference to objects. Here, the reference goes to Peirce, 8.179, 8.184, 5.474.

5. *Id.*, 3: 254-263.

6. From a pragmatist point of view it is also interesting how the Coase theorem has, for reasons outside its proper argument, breeded deep cleavages of opinion. The mere importance that the concepts of 'property' and 'property rights' have according to the theorem have activated accusations by social critics for 'conservatism'. Certain accusations may have been justified, but this has been so for reasons outside the discourse of the theorem, which happens to have been adopted, since the 1960's, by many by defenders of the status quo and the prevailing property rights. As a counterexample, we can point out to the fact that also such an approach exists as 'analytic Marxism', applying rational choice to engine Marxist social criticism, e.g., Elster, 1985, Roemer, 1986.

7. The argument follows the clear presentation of Ordeshook 1986: 353. In more technical terminology, the situation and the arrangement seen as desirable according to the Coase theorem make up one type of *core*, which can, among others, be defined as one type of equilibrium in a *noncooperative game*: a set of the players' those payoff vectors that are not dominated by any other similar set, *Id.*: 340-345.

   About different theories of regulation, see, e.g., Gujarati, 1984: 21-51. Here, 'traditional' theory is the one supporting government regulation, and its challenger is the one proceeding in the lines of 'self-regulation', Coasean or other.

8. For a contemporary statement of the model or models, Kreps, 1990: 18-37.

9. Transitivity is a property which can be expressed as follows: it must be so that $x_1 > x_2 > x_3 < x_1$. The sign '$>$' reads here not as 'more than' but as 'better than' or 'preferred [ordinally] more than', and the sign '$<$' is its opposite.

It has been known at least since the work of *Marquis de Condorcet* in the 18th century and Reverend Charles L. Dodgson (better known as the author *Lewis Carroll*) (see Black, 1958, where passages of Condorcet and Dodgson are included) that lack of transitivity involves cycles in choices. Thus if we have three individuals i, i = A, B and C, choosing between three alternatives j, j = x, y and z, and A's preferences are x > y > z, B's, z > x > y, and C's, y > z > x, a cycle results. This includes that any conceivable collective choice (x, y or z) involves the very worst j of one of the i (and also the best j of one other of the i). We can also conclude that even where two of the i would agree on the choice of one of the j, thus giving one of them its best j and the other one its second best i, then the third i could easily tempt the i with its second best j to abandon the first deal in order to obtain its best j, which would give the third i its second best j, and so on. So cycles also involve *instability*.

10. The benefits and the problems of binary structures, which are evidently the simplest of structures, as opposed to other structures such as ternary ones as the basis of concept formation should be elaborated separately. For a discussion of some of the similarities between the 'comparative statics' of marginalist economics (such as that of *Léon Walras*) and the binary structural linguistics of *Ferdinand de Saussure,* 1972/1916, as stressed by Saussure himself, see Ahonen, 1989. For a discussion on similarities between 19th century physics and 19th century economics, Mirowski, 1989.

11. The stress is here on 'tends'; this is no evaluation of the desirability or the undesirability of this state of affairs.

12. Mueller, 1989: 247-347 for a rich variety of examples.

13. Here, the prohibitions also impose a price on the emissions to the polluter, such as a fine payable in the case of non-compliance. This, by the way, also implies that crime is also a matter of economic rationality, and that there are markets for crime, too.

14. From a pragmatist point of view it is also striking that many scholars who have wished to prove the vices of government have indeed been able to do so, whereas many scholars who have wanted to prove the opposite have not been less successful. It is true that there are also scholars who are 'honest' in the sense that they have not attained only results as if prescribed by their own convictions, although even here we should not completely rule out strategic action which occasionally displays evidence that is not completely in line with what the scholar wishes to prove.

15. Here, 'validity' signifies the logical validity of the argument.

16. Notice that valid arguments may involve either true or untrue premises, or a combination true and untrue premises.

17. Let us take an example. Let R_i denote all the preference relations of a single individual i (i = 1, 2, ..., n) between all the alternatives available to i, X the set of all the

alternatives among which the i choose(s), 2^X the set of all the subsets of X, and B the result of the aggregation of the individuals' preferences into a result of collective choice. Then a *social choice function* (SCF), i.e., a set of rules according to which it is (or would be) possible to proceed from the individuals' preferences to B can be written as:

$$F: X \times R_1 \times R_2 \times \ldots \times R_n \rightarrow B$$

Political elections between two or more candidates or choice between two or more alternatives in decision-making bodies of two or more members are concrete examples of SCF:s in action. (For more, Nurmi, 1987.)

18. About transitivity, see endnote 9.

19. Arrow, 1963. I omit the lengthy proof despite that it is a most essential part of any argument of the kind dealt with here. Vickrey's, 1960, version of the proof, often cited in intermediate to advanced texts on economics, is one of the most easily accessible. Versions where the proof of the impossibility of an SWF focuses on the violation of some other of the axioms while the others hold also exist; therefore the Arrow theorem is not really only a theorem on the necessary dictatorship involved in SWF:s (and such of their applications as societal central planning). See also my discussion below on the Sen paradox.

20. About cycles, see endnote 9. I omit the proof.

21. Sen himself takes refuge to the 'extra-logical' idea that the Pareto principle should, to a certain extent, defer to liberal rights at least in certain situations. Here, individuals might be able to exert permissiveness and decide that some of their own preferences, such as some of their preferences concerning others' doings in moral issues, might not, after all, be of such a central concern.

22. About cycles, see endnote 9. For the seminal expansion of this focus in a 'chaos theorem' of social choice, see McKelvey, 1976. For a less abstract and easily accessible application of the Sen thinking, see Hammond and Miller, 1985.

23. The two first articles where the paradox was presented were Gibbard, 1973 and Satterthwaite, 1975.

24. I omit the proof. It is also conceivable to prove that provided that all the other axioms hold, the nonmanipulability axiom is violated.

    'Free-riding' also involves individuals' concealment of their true preferences. Despite that an individual might really prefer that a collective good preventing the destruction of common property resources be produced, s/he might, when asked, strategically misrepresent his or her preferences, hoping that the others would bear the burden and the individual could (continue to) 'ride free'.

25. These terms, making part of the established terminology of simulation as it is well known to researchers of various disciplines, stem, which is less widely acknowledged, directly from Peirce, e.g., Peirce 2.275.

26. Loc. cit.

27. For further simulations, see entries in the bibliography of Kahneman et al. (1990). See also Nurmi, 1990, who conducts a series of simulation studies in order to investigate the frequency or the probability of several types of logical paradoxes of voting in different 'cultures' of preferences, each made up of voters with preferences that resemble each other to a certain degree, from a higher to a lesser homogeneity.

    I am grateful for *Dr. Floyd Rudmin* for pointing out to me that there is an important class of relevant models beyond the ones discussed by me, namely strictly non-Bayesian models.

28. An air pollution example can, even without recourse to game theory, here be used to illustrate the Coase theorem (adapted from Mueller, 1989: 28-31). Let us assume that F's (Finland's) net income *per annum* (p.a.) from forestry in her northernmost part is $ 100 M (million) with S's (Soviet Union's) emissions, S's net income from her activities that have second-order consequences is $ 25 M *p.a.*, and F's net income without the emissions would be $ 130 M.

    Could Finland prohibit S's production altogether the 'society' (F, S) would be better off than with the emissions, as $ 130 M - $ 100 M > $ 25 M. But F cannot prohibit S's emissions due to the latter's property rights in the absence of effective international law at F's disposal, and therefore it pays F to offer S, on the condition that S cease production altogether, a bribe *b* up to $ 25 M *p.a.* Alternatively, F might buy S's factories with a price $ 25 M/i, where i is the cost of capital, which with an exemplary i of 15 per cent gives $ 25 M/.15 = 167 M. In certain cases bribes that only provide for the limitation of S's production and the partial elimination of the emissions might be conceivable.

    To see that the results of this kind are independent of the assignment of property rights, let us assume that S's net income is $ 40 M *p.a.*, F's as before, i.e., $ 100 M *p.a.*, and there is efficient international law that enables F to have S's production prohibited altogether. Then, the collectively efficient solution would involve S's bribe *b* to F up to $ 10 M, $0 \leq b \leq$ $ 10 M, as $ 40 M - ($ 130 - $ 100 M) = $ 10 M.

29. This is not to say that, even from a rational choice point of view, the dissatisfactory management of the oil deposits was the *only* reason by far to the armed conflict. De Mesquita, 1991, points out that there is a class of games where a relatively weak player which is unwilling to negotiate in its belief that the stronger player or players will not launch an attack is the most dangerous one from the point of view of crisis escalation. In the Gulf conflict Iraq was an evident example of such a player.

30. Beside the above examples, we must also mention here the approach of *Oliver Williamson* (e.g., 1985), asking why institutions emerge, which has invited his approach the name of '*neo-institutionalism*'. For brief, Williamson argues that institutions are there in order for their users to evade transactions costs by the means of 'internalization' through intra-organizational - and extra-organizational - hierarchies. For a discussion on Williamson in a context of law and economics, see Stephen, 1988: 184-193.

Another but a very different approach to the rise of institutions is that of Calvert, 1991, who uses game theory in order to investigate if and how rational actors might learn to cooperate by learning to coordinate their actions under constantly varying conditions. More exactly, Calvert studies how 'multilateral games' such as 'society' might be reducible to dyadic games between two actors at a time; how people learn to cooperate; how conventions arise and are maintained.

REFERENCES

Ahonen, Pertti, 1989, "The Meaning of Money: Comparing a Peircean and Saussurean Perspective," in *Law and Semiotics III*, Roberta Kevelson, ed., 13-29, New York: Plenum Press.

Alt, James E. and Kenneth Shepsle, eds., 1990, *Perspectives on Positive Political Economy*, Cambridge: Cambridge University Press.

Arrow, Kenneth J., 1963/1950, *Social Choice and Individual Values*, rev. ed., New York: John Wiley and Sons.

Bertin, Jacques, 1983, *Semiology of Graphics: Diagrams, Networks, Maps*, William J. Berg, trans., Madison: University of Wisconsin Press.

Brunsson, Nils, 1985, *The Irrational Organization: Irrationality as a Basis for Organizational Action and Change*, Chichester: Wiley.

Bueno de Mesquita, Bruce, 1991, "Norms of Cooperation," presentation given at the School of Engineering, Stanford University, April 11, 1991. The author's address at the time of the presentation: Hoover Institution, Stanford CA 94305, USA.

Caldwell, Bruce, ed., 1985, *Appraisal and Criticism in Economics: A Book of Readings*, Boston: Allen & Unwin.

Calvert, Randall, 1991, "Elements of a Theory of Society Among Rational Actors," paper presented at the *Public Choice Society Annual Meeting*, New Orleans, March 15- 17, 1991.

Coase, Ronald, 1960, "The Problem of Social Cost," *Journal of Law and Economics* 3, 1-44.

Eastman, Byron D., 1984, *Interpreting Mathematical Economics and Econometrics*, New York: St. Martin's Press.

Elster, Jon, 1985, *Making Sense of Marx*, Cambridge: Cambridge University Press.

Ferejohn, John A. and Keith Krehbiel, 1987, "The Budget Process and the Size of the Budget," *American Journal of Political Science* 31, 296-320.

Frey, Bruno S. and Reiner Eichenberger, 1991 "Anomalies in Political Economy," *Public Choice* 68, 71-89.

Gibbard, Allen, 1973, "Manipulation of Voting Schemes: A General Result," *Econometrica* 41, 587-602.

Gujarati, Damodar, 1984, *Government and Business*, New York: McGraw-Hill.

Hammond, Thomas H. and Gary J. Miller, 1985, "A Social Choice Perspective on Expertise and Authority in a Bureaucracy," *American Journal of Political Science* 29, 1-28.

Kahneman, Daniel, Jack L. Knetsch and Richard H. Thaler, 1990, "Experimental Tests of the Endowment Effect and the Coase Theorem," *Journal of Political Economy* 98 (1990), 1325-1348.

Kaitala, Veijo, Matti Pohjola, and Olli Tahvonen, 1990, Transboundary Air Pollution Between Finland and the USSR - A Dynamic Acid Rain Game, *Labour Institute of Economic Research*, Working Papers 99, Helsinki.

Klamer, Arjo, 1974, *Conversations with Economists: New Classical Economists and Opponents Speak Out on the Current Controversy in Macroeconomics*, Lanham MD: Rowman and Allanheld.

Klevorick, Alvin K. and Gerald H. Kramer, 1973, "Social Choice on Pollution Management: The Genossenschaften," *Journal of Public Economics* 2, 101-146.

Kramer, Edna E., 1982/1971, *The Nature and Growth of Modern Mathematics*, Princeton NJ: Princeton University Press.

Kreps, David M., 1984, "Corporate Culture and Economic Theory," paper presented to the *Second Mitsubishi Bank Conference on Technology and Business Strategy*, Stanford University, Stanford CA, mimeo. Also in Alt and Shepsle, 1990: 90-143.

_____, 1990, *Intermediate Microeconomics*, Princeton University Press, Princeton NJ.

Libecap, G.D. and Wiggins, S.N., 1985, "The Influence of Private Contractual Failure on Regulation: The Case of Oil Field Unitization," *Journal of Political Economy* 93: 690-714.

March, James G., 1988, *Decisions and Organizations*, Oxford: Basil Blackwell.

March, James G. and Johan P. Olsen, 1989, *Rediscovering Institutions: The Organizational Basis of Politics*, New York: Free Press.

McCloskey, Donald, 1985, *The Rhetoric of Economics*, Madison: University of Wisconsin Press.

_____, 1990, *If You Are So Smart: The Narrative of Economic Expertise*, Chicago: University of Chicago Press.

McKelvey, Richard D., 1976, "Intransitivities in Multidimensional Voting Models and Some Implications for Agenda Control," *Journal of Economic Theory* 12, 472- 482.

McKenzie, Richard B. and Gordon Tullock, 1989, *The Best of the New World of Economics*, 5. ed. Homewood IL: Irwin.

Mirowski, Philip, 1989, *More Heat Than Light*, Cambridge: Cambridge University Press.

Mueller, Dennis C., 1989, *Public Choice II*, Cambridge: Cambridge University Press.

Nurmi, Hannu, 1987, *Comparing Voting Systems*, Dordrecht: Reidel.

Nurmi, Hannu, 1990, "Impartial Culture Simulation of Voting Systems: An Assessment," paper presented at the *European Consortium for Political Research (ECPR) Joint Session of Workshops, Bochum, April 2-7, 1990*, The author's address: Department of Political Science, University of Turku, 20500 Turku, Finland. Mimeo, forthcoming.

Ordeshook, Peter C., 1986, *Game Theory and Political Theory*, Cambridge: Cambridge University Press.

Ordeshook, Peter C. and Thomas Schwartz, 1987, "Agendas and the Control of Political Outcomes," *American Political Science Review* 81, 179-199.

Peirce, C(harles) S(anders), 1931-1958, *Collected Papers*, Charles Hartshorne and Paul Weiss, eds., Vols. 1-2 [1931], 5-6 [1935] and Arthur W. Burks, ed., Vols. 7-8 [1958], Cambridge Mass: Harvard University Press.

Roemer, John, ed., 1985, *Analytical Marxism*, Cambridge: Cambridge University Press.

Samuels, Warren J., ed., 1990, *Economics as Discourse.: An Analysis of the Language of Economists*, Dordrecht: Kluwer.

Satterthwaite, Mark A., 1975, "Strategy-Proofness and Arrow's Conditions: Existence and Correspondence Theorems for Voting Procedures and Social Welfare Functions," *Journal of Economic Theory* 10, 187-217.

Saussure, Ferdinand de, 1972/1916, *Cours de linguistique générale*, Tullio de Mauro, ed., Paris: Payot.

Sen, Amartya, 1970, *Collective Choice and Social Welfare*, San Francisco: Holden-Day.

_____, 1976, "Liberty, Unanimity, and Rights," *Economica* 43, 217-245.

Shepsle, Kenneth A., 1979, "Institutional Arrangements and Equilibrium in Multidimensional Voting Models," *American Journal of Political Science* 23, 27-60.

Simon, Herbert A., 1947, *Administrative Behavior*, New York: Macmillan.

Stephen, Frank H., 1988, *The Economics of the Law*, Brighton: Wheatsheaf.

Vickrey, William, 1960, "Utility, Strategy, and Social Decision Rules," *Quarterly Journal of Economics* 74, 507- 535.

Watzlawick, Paul, Janet H. Beavin, and Don D. Jackson, 1967, *Pragmatics of Human Communication*, New York: Norton.

Weber, Max, 1978/1921, *Economy and Society: An Outline of Interpretive Sociology*, Guenther Roth and Klaus Wittich, trans., Berkeley: University of California Press.

Weingast, Barry, 1991, Ongoing work, referred to by him to the author, Stanford University, Stanford, CA, April 12, 1991.

Chapter 3

International Law and Legal Cultures in the Present Day Context

P.C. Bedwa[1]

I

The rapid development of means of transport and communication, and the increasing contact between the citizens and commercial organizations of different countries, developments in legal, political and economic systems whether in the positive or negative side in any part of the world have deep impact on the legal, political and economic systems of almost all countries today. These developments, systematic or spontaneous have impact upon all nations and give birth to new legal cultures[2]. This is the natural consequence of the interaction between the law and society in a wider perspective. The interaction between the law and society can be seen at several levels: the judicial process and its socio-cultural linkage; law as an indicator of the nature of societical complexity, and its attendant problems of interaction; and finally law as an agent of modernization and social change. A sociology of law would have to deal with all these levels of interaction, and this interaction evolves new legal cultures. In this paper an effort is being made to evaluate as to whether the legal changes brought out in India with the promulgation of the Constitution of India and the enactment of certain municipal laws for the amelioration of the lot of women in certain specific areas, to keep pace with the global communion, have the realistic impact on the society and served the desired objectives or these laws simply satisfy the political ego and in their actual application their impact becomes a farce.

Throughout the recorded history of mankind, woman has been considered unequal with man; she has been oppressed, exploited and ill-treated in all ancient and medieval male-dominated societies. They have been treated just like ordinary Chattels incapable of enjoying any rights as human beings and in family and society their status was no better than those of slaves. They were condemned to perpetual subjugation to their fathers, husbands and guardians. 'Such' says Gibbon, 'was the stern and haughty spirit of ancient law that women were condemned to perpetual tutelage of priests, husbands or guardians; a sex created to please and to obey was never supposed to have obtained the age of reason and experience.'[3] As such women were never treated at par with men in matters relating to marriage, divorce, right to property and inheritance under the ancient laws.[4]

In Roman law a woman was under the tutelage of her father during his life and after his death of her agnates by blood or adoption. When married she and her whole property passed into power and possession of her husband. In fact, she herself was treated as a property by her husband and had no more right than a purchased slave. At certain stages of the Roman law a husband was given a right to kill his wife if she was found to have poisoned somebody or treated somebody with wine or adopted else's child. The Romans did not allow a woman to exercise any civil or public office.[5] In Sparta, female infants and such women who could not be expected to give birth to healthy sons were often destroyed and the result of it was that the proportion of women in the population was reduced and one woman had several husbands.[6] By old Athenians, woman was treated only as a property that was marketable and could be transferred one to the other.[7] Professor Westermark says that in Greece man recognized in her no other end than to minister to his pleasure or to become the mother of his children. Plato classes women together with children and other servants, and states generally that in all the pursuits of mankind the female sex inferior to the male. Euripides says, 'Women are impotent for good, but clever contrivers of all evils'.[8]

In Persia, a country so near to that from which woman got her Magna Carta of liberty and secured of protection of honor and respect, men were notoriously voluptuous; and to them woman was nothing more than an object to gratify their base passions. Every wealthy man kept crowds of females in his house.[9]

Woman under Christianity has been really a pitiable creature inspite of all her education and culture. Buddhism treats her badly, Judaism worse, but Christianity worst of all. Christianity considers her a criminal of the gravest type and so much unholy that she cannot even touch alter or raise her voice in church. The great Christian Saint Chrysostom remarked that woman is a necessary evil, a natural temptation, a desirable calamity, a domestic peril, a deadly fascination and a painted ill. Lord Jesus Christ is reported to have ordained to woman that 'Thy desire shall be to thy husband and he shall rule over thee.'[10]

Christianity has feathered upon woman the cold-blooded murder of not only of an ordinary human being but the very son of God. As regards rights and privileges of woman Christianity has said or done nothing of any consequence.[11]

In ancient India, the position of woman was not as deplorable as elsewhere. In Vedic age, the Indian woman enjoyed a high status in society. During those days the woman played an important role in religious and social functions and the girls had an effective say in the selection of their husbands.[12] They could fight wars, join in festivals and take part in philosophical discussions. She could remain unmarried if she so desired. Rig Veda extols the virtues of women even greater than that of men. The concept of Ardhnarishwar speaks of the equality of women. The philosophy of the Shakti cult is concerned around the superiority and destructive strength of women. But in the Smriti period the whole position was changed when 'Manu', a great law giver of India, clamped down the freedom of the women. According to him a woman must be subject to her father in childhood, to her husband in youth and when her lord is dead to her sons. A woman must never be independent.[13] Marriage was considered essential for her and widowhood was a curse. The custom of Sati was prevalent under which she had to burn herself alive with the dead body of her husband. She was sometimes made wife of several brothers at the same time.[14]

In Japan, in olden times women were not allowed to pray or to take part in religious exercises. In China, they were not supposed to go in the temples. The wise men of China have offered free advice for the benefit of husbands in these words, 'Listen to the counsel of the wife, but act against it.' As far as the Arabs themselves are concerned, they treated women badly before the advent of great world reformer Prophet Mohammed. Their country produced worse than anybody did. They buried alive their daughters. Women suffered degradation and had no legal right whatsoever.[15] There was no limit to polygamy.

II

The above state of affairs establishes the fact that almost all personal laws throughout the world were against the interests of women, and it is only a matter of satisfaction that under the Islamic law, as propagated by the Prophet Mohammed in the seventh century, women got a legal position superior than that of her counter parts under other religions.[16] As soon as a woman comes of age, the law of Islam vests in her all the rights of an independent human being.[17] Prophet's laws of inheritance, of marriage, of divorce of guardianship all are indicative of his deep insight into human nature. His laws held as good fourteen centuries ago as they do today. He provided the right to property to women, while the civilized England provided this right to christian women only a few years back; and also on such matters as custody of children which still remain unlegislated in these Islands.[18]

The above study reveals that the traditional system in almost all societies denied equality to women in every respect, and this humiliating treatment of women for centuries created a sense of social awareness by drawing the attention of a supine society to the need for change. It has now been recognized by the United Nations General Assembly under Article 1 which declares thus[19] -

> 'Discrimination against women, denying or limiting as it does their equality of rights with men, is fundamentally unjust and constitutes an offense against human dignity.'

Under the U.S.S.R. Constitution women and men have been provided equal rights.[20] The American constitution via its twenty-seventh Amendment says:

> 'Equality of rights under the law shall not be denied or abridged by the United States on account of sex.'[21]

Such like provisions to ameliorate the status of women have been enshrined in the constitution of many countries and in this context it will be most appropriate to refer to some of the important provisions of the Constitution of India which in fact is a breathing, pulsating reality of social change in the status of women in India.[22] Parts III and IV of the constitution provide for the socio-economic emancipation of women. Article 14 runs as follows:

> 'The State shall not deny to any person equality before the law or the equal protection of the laws within the territory in India.'[23]

Further Article 15(1) lays down that

> 'State shall not discriminate against any citizen on grounds only of religion, race, caste, sex, place of birth or any of them.'

Furthermore Article 15(3) specifically mentions that

> 'Nothing in this article shall prevent the State from framing any special provision for *women* and children.'[24]

So while discrimination against women has been prohibited, no bar has been imposed to discriminate in favor of women. Thus Article 15(1) has been of paramount importance in appropriating to women to establish the socio-economic equality through the instrumentality of law.[25]

Article 16(1) which declares that, 'There shall be equality of opportunity for all citizens in matters relating to employment or appointment to any office under the State,' foists the banner of equality which is the hallmark of the Indian Constitution. Further emphasis is stressed on Article 16(1) by Article 16(2) which provides 'No citizen shall on ground only of religion, race, caste, sex, descent, place of birth, residence or any of them be ineligible for or discriminated against in respect of any employment or office under the State.'

Articles 14, 15 and 16 are so interlinked that one article can be invoked to construe the scope of the other. Article 14 guarantees the general right of equality and Articles 15 and 16 are instances of the same right in favor of citizens in some special circumstances. Article 15(1) and 16(2) prohibit that discrimination should not be made only and only on the ground of sex. In *Yusuf Abdul Aziz v. State of Bombay*[26] the Hon'ble Court observed -

> 'Sex is a sound classification and although there can be no discrimination in general on that ground, the Constitution provides for special provisions in the case of women . . . .[27]

Further in *Air India v. Nargesh Mirza*[28] where the Supreme Court forbade discrimination only on the ground of sex. The most important aspect of the decision was that of declaring the pregnancy bar to Air-hostesses unconstitutional. The court observed that after having utilized her services for four years, to terminate her service, if she becomes pregnant amounts to interference with and divert the ordinary course of human nature. The termination of service under such circumstances is not only *callous and crude act but is an open insult to the Indian Womanhood and abhorrent to the notions of civilized society.*[29] Sex like race and national origin is a characteristic determined solely by accident of birth. Hence *imposition of special disability upon the members of a particular sex appears to violate the basic concept of equality, which is the cornerstone of our constitution and Indian Legal System.*[30]

At the same time, it would be more appropriate to mention the *Constitution (Forty second) Amendent Act,* 1976 which introduces the innovative concept of Fundamental Duties of the Indian citizens. For this purpose, a new Part IV consisting of Article 51 A has been added to the Indian Constitution laying down 10 fundamental duties. Article 51 A (e), restricts the observance of *'Practices derogatory to the dignity of women.'* This provision found its manifestation through the enactment of the *Indecent Representation of Woman (Prohibition) Act,* 1986. This is an act to prohibit indecent representation of women through advertisements or in publications, writings, paintings, figures or in any other manner and for matters connected therewith or incidental thereto.[31] This is indicative that Parliament is fully alive in ameliorating the alround status of women in India. In addition Part IV of the Constitution *'Directive principles of State policy'* directly protects and enhances the status of women in all aspects of life -- social, cultural, political and economic.

III

The above study indicates that the constitution prohibits the State from discriminating against women on the ground of sex and directs the State to promote women's welfare. But at the same time we cannot ignore the fact that even before the independence of India, British government keeping in view certain changes at the international level took notice of certain burning social needs of the Indian society for ameliorating the lot of females, and provided certain *provisions* in the Indian Penal Code, 1860, Criminal Procedure Code, 1898, Indian Evidence Act, 1872 etc. etc. in the interest of women. Though several other Acts affecting the women were also passed during the British period but these reforms were half hearted.[33]

The earnest efforts for the amelioration of the social status of the women especially the Hindu women began with the independence of India and most appropriately after the adoption of the Constitution of India. A number of enactments like *Hindu Marriage Act,* 1955, *Hindu Succession Act,* 1965, *Hindu Adoption and Maintenance Act*, 1956 and *Hindu Minority and Guardianship Act*, 1956, *Dowry Prohibition Act*, 1961 and *Commission of Sati (Prevention) Act,* 1987 were enacted by the Parliament to bring dynamic social changes in the Hindu law especially in the status of Hindu women. Thus through the instrumentality of law, ardent effort has been made by the Parliament to bring social changes in the Hindu society in order to ameliorate the social status of Hindu woman.

Consequently, the problem for deep evaluation under the fast-changing social values of modern age is

> whether ostentatious celebrations of International Women's year on international academic seminars, figurative speeches of politicians, judges, lawyers, guarantees enshrined in Chapters III and IV of the

Constitution of India and the enactment of various laws for the amelioration of the status of women, have been successful in bringing the social change in the traditional outlook of the society towards the women to the extent as anticipated by the legislature and the society, and whether all these efforts for social change in the status of women would solve the problem relating to the alround welfare of women without changing the socio-economic and political outlook of the society as a whole and the system of working of the judiciary in particular.[34]

IV

The author is of the view that such efforts would never be successful and nothing substantial would be achieved unless the judiciary extricates itself from the age old rotten technicalities of the procedural law established by the British, and dedicates itself in imparting speedy social justice keeping in view the pressing need of ameliorating the lot of the women who had suffered for centuries for their only fault of being females, in the hands of the male-dominated society.[35]

It is a matter of great satisfaction that the woman has gradually come to acquire considerable emancipation from the complexes and ills with which she had been suffering for long. Today's woman has come to have better acceptability and respectability, better status of equality with man, better rights and privileges, better opportunities and avenues, in all spheres of national life -- social, economic and political. Hence in the emancipation and liberation of woman, in the recognition of her legitimate place in the family and the society, in the recognition and protection of her interests, rights and privileges, and in the gradual enhancement of status, the law has played a great role as an instrument of change keeping pace with the international communion. Despite all these constitutional and legislative efforts our experience on the working of law whether constitutional, family or criminal is not at all satisfactory and conducive to solve the burning and pressing needs of the women who have suffered for centuries in the male-dominated society.[36] The law if we say does not work at all will not be wrong. Law is only helpful to those who have richness, resourcefulness or have the support of the people having muscle strength. Under the present social, economic and political set up it is awfully difficult to get justice from any quarter whether administrative or judicial. The reason is obvious and not far off to seek. We admit that moral, social, cultural and political values of pre-independence have become irrelevant in almost all spheres of human life in India. Except a few industrialists, bureaucrats, politicians and their supporters, people have lost their faith not only in the administrative and judicial system of the country but the constitution itself.

Some of the underlying reasons for the non working of the laws are (1) working of the courts and the attitude of the judicial officers and the doubtful honesty, integrity and sincerity of the lawyers and the police and civil administration (exceptions are microscopic). (2) Civil and criminal procedural law in India is highly complicated and defective and it helps in bringing more injustice and inconvenience than justice to the people who come to the courts to seek justice. (3) Delay in adjudication is procured by the lawyers by applying delaying devices (may be legal under the technicalities of the Civil and Criminal procedure code) on the initiative of the clients to harass the opposite party as well as for their own financial interests. (4) The courts mostly are not at all interested in deciding the cases speedily even if where the statutory period is fixed under certain enactments. (5) The courts (trial as well as appellate) do not even adhere to any set statutory procedure in most of the cases while allowing adjournments and giving the dates for months and months for next hearings. (6) The litigants are treated by the lawyers and the courts mostly depending upon their financial and social status. The attitude of the lawyers and the working of the courts is so cumbersome and degrading that people (especially women) mostly avoid to seek legal remedies and prefer to suffer silently.

To achieve the desired objectives of the legislations active public participation and social awareness are the needs of the present time to see that law actually works as desired by the legislature.

ENDNOTES

1. P.C. Bedwa is Professor and Reader in the Department of Laws, Guru Nanak Dev University, Amritsar, India and Senior Lecturer at the University of Maiduguri, Nigeria in 1989.

2. International developments do effect the municipal laws too.

3. Kidwai, M.H., 1976, *Woman under different social and religious laws*, 1.

4. Jahwari, S., 'Reformation of discriminatory laws against men,' *Lawyer*, Vol. 13, No. 2, Feb. 81, 1.

5. *Supra.*

6. Kapoor, Viney, 1986, *Position of women in Islam -- An Appraisal*, unpublished, 3.

7. *Id.*

8. *Supra*, 3.

9. *Supra,* 6, p 3.

10. *Supra.*

11. *Supra.*

12. Hemlatha, Devi, V., 'Constitution -- Women and Socio-economic justice,' *Lawyer* Vol. 14-4, Apr. 82, 60.

13. Colebrook, H.T., *A Digest of Hindu Law*, 1807: 109.

14. Even up to the present day polygamy is still prevalent in the Hindu society despite its abolition, in one form or the other.

15. Gaya, Iqbal, 1980, *Lectures on Muslim Law in India*, 2. See also Schacht, 1965, *An Introduction to Islamic Law*, 7.

16. Mohamood, Tahir, 1972, *Islamic Law in Modern India*, 188.

17. *Id.*

18. The views of certain jurists that Mohammedan law is a conglomeration of chaotic rules based on the arbitrary dictates of a revengeful semiotic deity and on the decisions -- sometimes apocryphal, often without reason -- of the Prophet of Islam, coupled with the fatwas and deductions of fanatic mullas and Muftis and Kazis throughout the middle ages, does not in fact reflect the correct position of Islamic law. See Fyzee, A.A.A., 1963, *A Modern Approach to Islam.*

19. November 7, 1967, *Declaration of Elimination of Discrimination Against Women.*

20. Article 35 of *Constitutional (Fundamental Law) of the Union of Soviet Specialist Republics*, adopted on October 7, 1977.

21. Section 1.

22. Articles 14;15 (1), (2), (3); 16 (1), (2).

23. Corresponds to the *14th Amendment of the United States' Constitution.*

24. Emphasis supplied.

25. Bhatia, Arvind, 1989, *Women, Law and Social Change -- An Appraisal*, unpublished, 7.

26. AIR 1954 S.C. 321.

27. This view was re-affirmed in *Miss C.B. Mathamma v. Union of India*, AIR 1979 S.C. 1868.

28. AIR 1981 S.C. 1829.

29. Emphasis supplied.

30. Emphasis supplied.

31. Bhatia, Arvind, *Supra* 10, 16.

32. Emphasis added.

33. Christian Marriage Act, 1872; Dissolution of Muslim Marriages Act, 1939; Guardians & Wards Act, 1890; Hindu Widows Marriage Act, 1856; Indian Divorce Act, 1869; Indian Succession Act, 1925; Parsee Marriage and Divorce Act, 1936; and Hindu Women's Right to Property Act, 1937, etc.

34. Bhatia, Arvind, *Supra* 18, 19.

35. *Id.*

36. This is not only the State of affairs in India, but almost all countries who got independence from British are facing the same problems even in more acuteness.

Chapter 4

Rhetoric and the Law of Enterprise

Denis J. Brion[1]

I

The focus of this essay is the troubled intersection in legal doctrine between productive enterprise and rights in land. The starting point is the propensity for American productive enterprise, with the implicit approval of the judicial system, to extract natural resources as inputs to manufacturing processes in a way that amounts to their partial or complete expropriation from their former owners. The economic effects of this expropriation, moreover, coupled with the physical externalities that also tend to characterize the resource exploitation process, cause a considerable redistribution of wealth in favor of entrepreneurs, and often enough the gratuitous destruction of values significant to the former owners of these resources and to society at large.

The extreme example is the case of Appalachia, where, beginning in the late nineteenth century, urban-centered enterprise acquired and severed first Appalachian timber and then Appalachian coal in a way that has turned the region into what amounts to a third world economy. The Appalachian experience is an extreme case because of the broad scope of the resource exploitation that occurred and the equally broad scope of the economic, social, and cultural effects that ensued. This tendency toward exploitation and suppression, however less extreme in extent that it typically occurs, is a general phenomenon in the American experience.

There is, of course, a considerable gap between this pattern of exploitation and suppression and the thrust of the principles that underlie our notion of the Rule of Law, those principles that find expression in our 'founding documents,' the Declaration of Independence, the federal Constitution, and the Bill of Rights, and those implicit principles that lie behind the common law tradition and the particular cultural myth that has evolved in American culture. These deep principles include such concepts as the substantial autonomy of the individual from interference either from government or from fellow citizens, an equality of political and economic opportunity, and an equality of civic and social worth that is intolerant to large disparities in material wealth across society. This essay seeks to explore how it has come to be that the law, despite the sharp inconsistency with its deep principles, has generally ratified and facilitated this pattern of exploitation and suppression.

My thesis is threefold. First, a sufficient explanation for this gap does not require a conspiracy theory, a theory, that is, that understands the law as operating to facilitate the purposes of the power elite in society through the conscious design of the officials -- judges and legislators -- of the legal system. Rather, this gap arises from the fact that there prevails in American culture a world view that is entirely consistent with the way of resolving the clash of enterprise and entitlements to land that gives rise to this gap. For the purposes of the ensuing discussion, I use the term 'capitalist ethic' to denominate this world view. This world view is ubiquitous, permeating not only legal discourse but also all other loci of public discourse, coexisting, however paradoxically, with the deep principles of the Rule of Law that find expression in that same discourse.

Second, this world view is powerful, certainly powerful enough to generate and maintain circumstances strongly at odds with deeply held political principles. We cannot escape having a world view. It is not inevitable, however, that the capitalist ethic prevails as our world view. Rather, the capitalist ethic arose in particular historical circumstances. Other world views are entirely possible and we have the power to choose among them. Third, then, understanding how a world view comes to prevail is worthwhile because this understanding is a necessary condition for undermining the hegemony of a world view that, because of the undesirable consequences that it generates, is no longer, on balance, satisfactory.

If my thesis holds up, it is valuable because it makes it possible to conceive the law as having a measure of autonomy from the political and economic elite in society. It avoids a conception of the law as a sterile formality whose doctrines provide only predictive indeterminacy for the judicial process because doctrine serves as only a mask for a judicial function of ratifying and justifying the depredations of the economic elite.

This essay, for reasons of length, will be suggestive rather than exhaustive. It will first briefly identify the gap between legal principle and judicial practice through an analysis of cases representative of competing claims over entitlements to land. It will then describe the historical process by which the capitalist world view developed in American culture generally and in the law particularly. Finally, it will explore the mechanism by which this world view dominates discourse, allowing a pattern of human interaction to occur that is strongly at odds with basic political principles. Exposing this mechanism to scrutiny, I submit, is useful as a first step in becoming better able to control, rather than be controlled by, the power of world views.

II

Enterprise and the Law

A dictionary definition of 'entrepreneur' is 'one who organizes, manages, and assumes the risk of a business or enterprise.'[2] When courts adjudicate disputes over conflicting claims to natural resources, their decisions demonstrate a striking, consistent, and strongly favorable attitude toward the enterprising risk taker. This attitude is evident across a wide spectrum of cases involving disputes over natural resource extraction, private nuisance, urban redevelopment, and the land regulation process.

As I recounted at the third in this series of Round Tables on Law and Semiotics, the extreme example is the substantial disruption of the culture and physical landscape of Appalachia that accompanied the severance of the region's timber and coal resources that began in the late nineteenth century.[3] This disruption has been especially severe in the Cumberland Plateau of Eastern Kentucky. The Kentucky Supreme Court facilitated this destructive process by their interpretation of deeds of conveyance of mineral rights, which on their face granted a limited right to entrepreneurs to remove coal in a nondisruptive fashion. The Court reinterpreted these deeds as contracts whose overwhelming purpose was to subordinate entirely the rights and uses of the native landowner to the needs of the entrepreneurs, holding them free of liability for any consequential harm to the land and to the landowner's uses consequential on the exploitation of the coal.[4]

This hospitable judicial attitude is not confined to the exploitation of Appalachia's resources. The city of Virginia Beach in Virginia, having overdrawn its local sources of water supply and having declared a 'water crisis', has proposed to draw on a reservoir located along the Roanoke River some one hundred miles to the west, a proposal that the Virginia and North Carolina communities lying along the Roanoke River have vigorously opposed.[5] The economic reality is that the City is simply selling its currently available water for too low a price; all it need do is raise the price to a market-clearing level. The legal reality is long-standing common law doctrine that accords the right to use the water only to landowners riparian to the river and that seeks to maintain the physical integrity of the watershed by confining water use to land within that watershed.[6]

Regardless, the courts have defined the issue in the dispute between Virginia Beach and the Roanoke River Basin communities in terms of impact; the courts will block the withdrawal only if the protesting communities can show environmental harm resulting from the withdrawal that will outweigh the benefit to Virginia Beach and its residents accruing from the withdrawal. In other words, the riparian owners, who, at common law, at present own the right to use the water, will lose that right unless there is a showing of one particular consequential harm that outweighs a benefit that the courts have already defined as 'vital to human wealth and welfare.'[7] By casting the principal legal issue in this way, the courts have all but ensured an outcome favorable to the proposed withdrawal. In so doing, they have implicitly accepted theories of the economic process that define the productive economy as centered around the urban complex, which has a right to expropriate and exploit the resources of its hinterland, whoever might own them.[8] The judicial decisions that gave a particular interpretation to the Kentucky mineral deeds similarly treated the Cumberland Plateau as the hinterlands of the urban based economies which consumed its coal.

This judicial preference, then, favors the more intensive resource user over the more entrepreneurially passive resource owner, a preference that is replicated in a wide variety of disputes involving potentially productive resources. In the law of nuisance, which traditionally has forbidden one individual to use his land in a way that harms the land of another, the courts tend to shield the harm-causing landowner if his use is more economically intensive.[9] Courts show the same strong preference in disputes over public urban redevelopment and private land development projects[10] and in disputes that arise within the public land regulation process.[11]

A consistent bias, then, underlies the way in which courts resolve the clash between enterprise and more passive holders of interests in land. This bias manifests itself as a reallocation of land to economically more productive uses by redistributing the entitlements to that land to the entrepreneur, who will then exploit it for private gain. When the courts offer a rationale for this redistribution, it consists of no more than simply equating the public interest with the facilitation of private productive activity.

This rather straightforward policy, however, does not square well with rather basic political principles. Even in terms of the efficient allocation of society's resources to productive activities, a principle that is quite relevant to these apparent judicial attempts to facilitate enterprise, there is a considerable shortfall. As Ronald Coase tells us, a judicial attempt at reallocation will serve efficiency only if there is an antecedent misallocation of resources that persists because of transactional barriers to reallocation. If this is not the case, then these reallocations do no more than provide a subsidy to the productive enterprise, a subsidy which, under the circumstances, disserves efficiency.

Indeed, the most direct effect of these decisions is to redistribute wealth from the landowner to the entrepreneur through the partial or complete expropriation of rights in land. If the redistribution does not serve efficiency, its direction will tend to exacerbate societal inequalities in the distribution of wealth. If the redistribution does serve efficiency, it nevertheless concentrates on a few, random members of society the cost of serving the general public interest.

Moreover, the functional effect of this underlying bias is to reverse the conventional conception of rights in land. This conception, which flows from William Blackstone's notion of ownership as 'an absolute despotism',[12] cannot of course prevail in its pure form in a constitutional order that gives equal claim to the exercise of governmental power to serve the common good. Property, that is, is partially socialized by the very nature of the constitutional order. The judicial bias in favor of entrepreneurs, however, tends to establish a regime in which the productive activities of individuals generate the structure of property rights. As a result, the conceptual nature of property shifts from the one extreme of inviolate antecedent entitlements based on Blackstonian dominion to the opposite extreme of complete contingency.

A final effect of this bias is to change the nature of political society itself. Even a conception of ownership[13] that is fully consonant with Blackstonian 'despotism' nevertheless recognizes a limitation on this despotism, a prohibition on use that harms others. This limitation flows from the pragmatic recognition that, in order for any one land owner to enjoy that dominion, she must be free from harmful intrusions occasioned by the enjoyment of ownership by other landowners.[14] This captures John Rawls's notions that we can put into practice a strong commitment to the abstract concept of individual liberty only through a system of liberties, and that a system of liberties has no practical significance if the beneficiaries of that system lack the means to enjoy it. This bias, then, tends to generate a societal structure in which there not only is an enduring economic hierarchy but also a hierarchy of effective liberty.

III

The Evolution of a World View

Having exposed a bias in the judicial approach to particular kinds of disputes over rights in land, a bias that tends to disserve resource allocational efficiency, to exacerbate disparities in wealth distribution across society, and to undermine the practical value of the American system of political liberties, we will turn in this section to consider with more particularity a way of looking at the world that I am calling the capitalist ethic. The purpose of this section is to recount what likely is an already familiar tale, how this world view has evolved over time both in general political discourse and in the law. Because of this familiarity, this recounting will be brief and suggestive rather than exhaustive.

A. The historical development of the capitalist ethic

At the beginning of the nineteenth century, the United States was roughly divided into two distinct cultures, a division that was replicated politically, economically, and socially.[15] The bulk of the population was rural and engaged in agriculture, with the rest located in the commercial cities of the East Coast. Because the Industrial Revolution was as yet in its initial phases, most of what America produced was agricultural products and raw materials severed from the land. The market in goods and services tended toward the atomistic and competitive and was largely local and regional in scope.[16] The political spectrum generally split between the urban-based, commercial minded Federalists and the rural-based agriculturalist Democrats.[17]

The rapid process of industrialization in the pre Civil War period drew young people from rural areas and absorbed a substantial part of the influx of immigrants. Because of the greater growth in the part of the population involved in commerce and manufacturing, and because of the relative economic dynamism and affluence that they enjoyed, the political influence of the non-agricultural sector grew as well. Because industrialization went forward much more rapidly in the Northeast and Midwest, a cultural split between the agriculturalist, hereditarily hierarchical South and the increasingly manufactural, meritrocraticialy hierarchical North became exacerbated.[18]

The destructiveness of the Civil War that followed was a consequence in part of the industrial development that preceded it -- the traditional series of pitched battles carried out with technologically sophisticated weaponry.[19] The particular scope and technological sophistication of the Northern economy made possible the development of the strategic doctrine that led to victory.[20] The North engaged in massive mobilization to achieve massive firepower, applying it to pin down and overwhelm a foe whose strength was in maneuver and whose weakness was in numbers.[21]

As the victors, the politically dominant North put into practice the lessons learned during the War, particularly with the massive mobilization of resources deployed to achieve large ends.[22] The latter part of the nineteenth century saw the development of mass industrial enterprise and the emergence of mass, national markets.[23] Because the scale of government lagged behind the developing scale of productive enterprise, the consequent laissez faire circumstances led to abusive industrial practices -- monopoly, physical spillover effects, economic instability, harsh conditions for productive workers, and defective quality in consumer products -- and extreme disparities in the distribution of wealth across society.[24]

The Progressive Movement, the reaction to the excesses of the time, achieved a measure of success -- the establishment of governmental entities to enforce quality standards on food and drug products,[25] to impose standards on working conditions[26], to regulate shipping rates,[27] and to proceed against the most egregious monopolies.[28] While the Progressives did not achieve a substantial amelioration in the distribution of wealth, they did establish the acceptance of the concept of more activist and larger-scale government.[29] This in turn achieved an in-kind redistribution to the economically less advantaged in the form of better working conditions, higher and more uniform quality in consumer products, a greatly improved system of public education, and a substantial improvement in the infrastructure of utility services and public parks, in turn improving the general health, providing broadly available recreational opportunities, and improving the aesthetics of the built environment. The Progressive Movement thereby achieved a significant measure of public order.[30]

There was, as well, an achievement of order in a different sense. The Progressive Era saw the emergence of an expanded professional and managerial middle class, and the advanced educational institutions required for their training, whose function was implementing the new terms of the public order. However they may have perceived the nature of this function, they performed it as minions of the new economic elite, but at the same time implementing the expanding role of large enterprise in the economic system and, most importantly, justifying the emerging economic and social structure.[31] Society had become much more highly structural, with paternalism and hierarchy as salient attributes.

The twentieth century has largely seen the working out of the consequences of the late nineteenth century emergence of large enterprise and the Progressive Era reaction to it. The early part of this century saw the development of techniques of mass production which in turn made possible mass markets in consumer goods.[32] There was a new round of entrepreneurial excesses, this time in the unregulated financial markets, in the era of prosperity that followed the First World War.[33] During the Depression years that followed, government turned more fully to the entrepreneurial model of large scale organization in order to address the symptoms and the perceived causes of the Depression.[34]

Our own era has seen the almost complete breakdown of the distinction between the private sphere and the public.[35] This breakdown is the result of interest group capture of the regulatory process, intensive interest group lobbying of Congress and the state legislatures, and the continuous movement of the members of the professional and management class from position to position at the policy-making levels of government and productive enterprise.[36] The result is a continually reinforced identity of world view in the routine functions of government and productive -- it would be anachronistic to say 'private' -- enterprise. The American economic order is best characterized as democratic capitalism.[37]

Present day American capitalism is, of course, highly derivative from its classical conception. The essence of capitalism, according to the classic definition, is private control over the means of production.[38] From the unregulated free market competition of the nineteenth century has emerged a largely oligopolistic, bureaucratized, mass scale productive system serving a mass market for consumer goods.

On the nominally public side of society is another largely bureaucratized regulatory system whose formal purpose is to foster competition,[39] regulate natural monopoly,[40] control the negative spillovers of productive activities,[41] insure fair trade practices,[42] and enforce minimum standards of working conditions[43] and consumer product quality.[44] Because producers have successfully captured these regulatory processes, in practice these processes only partially ameliorate the negative aspects of the productive system, in effect legitimating the negative aspects that remain.[45] Moreover, because producers have captured the legislative process as well,[46] they successfully use the system of public finance for the subsidy of the costs of capital, infrastructure, and research and development.

The result is a societal structure with strong hierarchies of wealth and of political power.[47] Enterprise liability is limited both at the level of investment -- the core function of the corporate form -- and at the level of production. And enterprise enjoys substantial subsidies from the system of public finance. Because the productive system remains capitalistic -- the means of production remain in private ownership -- the present day state capitalist system achieves, according to the pejorative aphorism, 'the privatization of profit and the socialization of loss.'

B. The Parallel Development of the Law

Morton Horwitz has provided an incisive description of the evolution of American law during the first half of the nineteenth century.[48] At the beginning of this period, the common law generally reflected the static sensibilities of the rural population rather than the dynamic sensibilities of the considerably smaller urban population. The underlying thrust of doctrine was precommercial and antidevelopment, tended to ratify the moral sense of the community, and was paternalistic and regulative, oriented to notions of fair exchange. Its character tended to capture the Jeffersonian suspicion of cities in favor of replicating the cosmos of the sturdy yeoman.[49]

As industrialization proceeded, the common law began to reflect the needs of the emerging market oriented society by becoming facilitative rather than regulative. Common law judicial decisions tended to subsidize enterprise and deregulate bargain, tending as well to establish an implicit structure of legal rules that carried a high degree of certainty and predictability, characteristics of crucial importance to the efficient trade of entitlements on increasingly active markets. Doctrines of public law, by contrast, tended toward the antiutilitarian and the formalistic, thereby, as Horwitz argues, limiting the legislative power to redistribute the newly acquired wealth of the emerging entrepreneurs.[50]

The balance of the nineteenth century saw the shift of common law as well to the formalism of public law.[51] The establishment of the Harvard Law School around the concept of 'scientific formalism' marked the beginnings of the university-based law school as the exemplar of legal education, a model that has come to achieve almost complete dominance.[52] Scientific formalism, Horwitz argues, served the post-Civil War economic elite because of its positive project of searching out the implicit structure of rules in the mass of judicial decisions and its normative acceptance of this implicit structure as the expression of what the law ought to be. By this time, of course, this implicit structure would largely capture the pro-entrepreneur thrust that judicial decisions had been following for several decades. A move to legal formalism, then, would serve to protect what the economic elite had gained.[53]

Scientific formalism reached its zenith with the launching of the Restatement project in the 1920s. The project was the undertaking of the American Law Institute, made up of distinguished members of bench, bar, and legal academia. The legal establishment, that is, comprised the Institute.[54]

The Legal Realist movement that began in legal academia at about this time, however, sought to undercut the pretensions of scientific formalism, in the process leading to the unmasking of the implicit bias in the supposedly neutral structure of common law principles.[55] Perhaps because the legal realist movement had a liberating effect, courts turned more openly to incorporating considerations of social policy into the rationale that they offered for their decisions.[56] Over the last several decades, this more open analytical style has led to a considerable shift away from a judicial appeal to formalistic principles. Tort doctrine, for instance, increasingly serves a loss spreading function in determining liability for harms from consumer products.[57] In contract disputes, courts tend to step away openly from rigid doctrinal rules.[58] In constitutional law, the enforcement of equal protection principles by the Warren Court was an exercise in social policy analysis on a grand scale.[59]

If, however, our earlier exploration of the enterprise-entitlements disputes accurately captures the thrust of what the judiciary is doing, then, in a functional sense, little has changed since the early part of the nineteenth century when the common law began to transform itself into an instrument that functioned to facilitate the enterprise of America's emerging capitalists. Once the law had largely reworked itself along these facilitative lines, it turned to formalism. This had the effect of freezing these newly evolved doctrines into place just at the time when the Gilded Age capitalists sought to make permanent their newly won economic and political dominance.

When the Legal Realists had the bad manners to point out that formalist doctrine worked for all the world as a facade behind which the courts exercised substantial latitude in the way that they resolved disputes, the law turned again, embracing social policy analysis. And it did so just at the time when the emerging administrative state began to take on broad powers fully capable of controlling the costs that the capitalist system always tends to thrust onto the rest of society. And, as we have seen, the substantive content of the social policy to which the courts appeal has the effect of facilitating the enterprise of the capitalist system; that is, the courts seem to apply the social policy of a very narrow part of society.

The law, then, seems to have undergone a series of substantial transformations in the style of its doctrinal veneer, while the courts applied doctrine to dispute in a way that consistently and continually tracked the needs of the capitalist system and facilitated the workings of that system. It is true, of course, that a substantial part of the most recent transformation has consisted of the adoption of strong protection for an expanding array of individual rights and strong requirements for equal protection and due process for these rights-holders. Our dispute analysis, however, tends to show that the courts, in adopting these strong protections for the individual, are doing little more than establishing the formal status of the individual while the real status, in terms of economic and political power, continues to be a function of a far different, and more hidden, substantive approach to dispute resolution.

We are left, then, with a substantial and enduring gap between the formal and real status of the individual, a gap that is explainable as a functional capitalist hegemony over the law. A basic thesis of this essay, however, is that this gap does not require a conspiracy theory to explain its existence, a theory, that is, that there is a tacit but conscious identity of interest between the economic elite and the judiciary. An explanation, however, is necessary. The parallel development of the productive system and of the law toward an increasingly effective synergy is so uncanny that it would be unconvincingly facile to reject the conspiracy theory as a mere 'post hoc' argument. We must turn, then, to the task of explaining how this enduring hegemony of the capitalist ethic over the law has come about.

IV

Mechanisms

If the foregoing account of the workings of the law is accurate, then the judiciary is ratifying a systematic practice of entrepreneurs to expropriate interests in land in order to incorporate these interests into their productive activities. The entrepreneurs, that is, are engaging in acts of violence. And when their victims appeal to the judicial process for relief, the courts ratify the entrepreneurs' acts. In response, then, the courts exercise power over the victims, who, as Cicero would put it, 'submit to justice without violence.'[60]

The question of interest is how does it happen that the victims of this violence then become subject to a disadvantageous exercise of judicial power? To cast our inquiry in terms of power has, as the ensuing discussion will attempt to demonstrate, the advantage of allowing us to pursue a particular theory of power. This theory, I will argue, makes possible a crucial step on the path toward explaining these instances of judicial ratification of violence without having to posit a consciously coopted judiciary.

A. Power

Steven Lukes offers this definition of power: '*A* exercises power over *B* when *A* affects *B* in a manner contrary to *B*'s interests.'[61] The theory that Lukes uses to derive this definition offers a complex description of power as operating in three dimensions. When an individual, *A*, exercises power in the first dimension, she makes decisions on issues over which there is an observable conflict of subjective interests.[62] When she exercises power in the second dimension, she is 'creating' or reinforcing social and political values and institutional practices that limit the scope of the political process to public consideration of only those issues which are comparatively innocuous to her. Power exercised in the second dimension, then, amounts to setting the agenda of contestable issues, the mobilization of bias.[63] Power exercised in both of these dimensions involve contexts of overt conflict.

This two-dimensional description captures familiar and readily observable ways in which the powerful exercise power. It does not, however, provide an explanation of how it can be, in a formally open political system, populated with a citizenry that is relatively observant and relatively well educated, that an enduring stratification of power exists. Surely people recognize this situation and are able to react to it by using the political process to induce change. Surely also, if courts are indeed not coopted by the power elite, they will protect the powerless from the powerful.

Lukes' answer is that a further, deeper dimension of power also operates.[64] Those who have power have the opportunity to dominate discourse. And this dominance makes possible the supreme and most insidious exercise of power to prevent people, to whatever degree, from having grievances by shaping their perceptions, cognitions and preferences in such a way that they accept their role in the existing order of things, either because they can see or imagine no alternative to it, or because they see it as natural and unchangeable, or because they value it as divinely ordained and beneficial.[65]

The exercise of power in this third dimension -- 'shaping . . . perceptions, cognitions and preferences' -- is an exercise in rhetoric. As such, it allows *A* to affect *B* in a manner contrary to *B*'s interests by blinding *B* to the understanding of his real interests.[66]

The workings of this rhetorical dimension of power is nicely illustrated by the career of the legendary small town newspaper editor, William Allen White.[67] In 1895, the twenty-seven year old White purchased the struggling Emporia, Kansas *Gazette*. Already strongly a Republican in his political sentiments, he achieved rapid success in reviving the *Gazette* by simultaneously engaging in the commercial boosterism of the moribund farming community of Emporia.[68]

White's Progressive Republicanism -- 'booster Progressivism' as he termed it -- evolved substantially over the years, precisely in parallel with the concurrent development of the American economy as the capitalist system matured.[69] White's boosterism was necessarily accepting of the economic disparities that a vibrant local commerce sustained by the local political system inevitably entailed. White's Progressivism was nevertheless strongly imbued with the values of cohesion and mutual concern that characterize the American small community at its best.

As the American economy evolved, however, it set into motion forces that undermined the community values of which White was such a strong proponent. Emporia, a rural backwater when White began his newspaper career, evolved, with his considerable assistance, to become for a short time a thriving, relatively independent commercial center for a considerable surrounding agricultural area.[70] As mass markets for consumer goods developed in the early twentieth century, however, both the nature of the *Gazette* and the nature of Emporia itself changed. The town lost its economic independence and much of its economic and social vitality as it became little more than a destination point for consumer goods manufactured elsewhere. The *Gazette* as well became less a chronicle of the local community than a consumer of news and opinion syndicated on a national scale. The effect was a loss of whatever intimacy and communal spirit that Emporia enjoyed for all too brief a time in the late nineteenth century.[71]

What is significant is the role of White and his *Gazette* in this process of evolution. He helped develop his own role of national political influence through the podium that the newspaper provided him. He maintained that position through the newspaper while, at the same time, and with the help of his position in the business elite, eventually driving off all serious competition from other local newspapers. With a dominating position in the public discourse of Emporia, and a powerful position in national public discourse as well, White was a conscious and highly effective instrument in the implementation of the Progressive order -- establishing the primacy of commerce and industry in the hierarchy of political values at all levels of government and implementing the hierarchical, paternalistic character of the economic order, with upper middle class professionals such as White the willing accomplices of the dominant productive elite, and with that elite capturing to its own ends the processes of a growing, bureaucratic government.[72]

The example of William Allen White illustrates the power of rhetoric. He presented turn of the century Emporia in such compelling terms as to create an image in the minds of his national audience of a town as the idyllic embodiment of American cultural virtues.[73] He did so as one of the leading participants in a particular national discourse. The subject of the discourse was the set of values that was to dominate American culture. As the cultural historian Alan Trachtenberg has incisively shown, the set of values that White and others of these leading participants advocated was congruent with, and thereby effectuated, the emerging capitalist ethic.[74]

When White was at the peak of his rhetorical powers, however, it is not likely that he expressed a view of enterprise that would have commanded the assent of the majority of his contemporary citizens.[75] Certainly a considerable body of Emporians, those of more modest means, held views of the local elite that resonated more closely with the acerbic views of another contemporary, Thorstein Veblen: 'The country town of the great American farming region is the perfect flower of self-help and cupidity standardized on the American plan.'[76]

Nevertheless, Veblen's views are, if remembered at all, remembered as a quaint curiosity. White's views are woven into the fabric of today's public discourse. At all levels of government, we carry out the debate over political issues with a concern over the 'business climate.' The law of tort is imbued with doctrinal devices whose purpose is to limit liability for harms arising out of productive activities.[77] The Sales Article of the Uniform Commercial Code enjoins the ratification of what business people do as the self-reflexive norm for the standards of performance to which the courts are to hold them.[78] It is only against this background of assumptions that we debate over such pressing problems as environmental degradation, discrimination, the role of public education, and the limits of public expenditure. When we act through our organs of government, we do so almost uniformly by compromising the values at stake in these problems with the needs of the business climate.

We have a habitual way of looking at the world. Various theorists have described it variously. Thomas Kuhn has explored the idea of 'paradigms' in scientific thought.[79] Stanley Fish has explored the idea of 'interpretive communities' in the reading of texts.[80] Suzanne Langer has advanced the notion of 'philosophic epochs' in Western thought.[81]

Each of them describes what appears to be an enduring necessity in the process of human interaction within any particular culture, that there be some overarching set of assumptions about how we order our relations among ourselves and between ourselves and our physical environment. This set of assumptions makes up a world view. There is no single set of assumptions that is exhaustive of the possibilities; any set, however, that generates a world view necessarily captures a subset of the totality of the mutually conflicting values that humans find compelling. We could just as easily follow the agrarian assumptions of the Jeffersonian-Jacksonian Democrats of the early nineteenth century, or, indeed, the thoroughly enchanted[82] assumptions of Native Americans. And, I argue, the capitalist ethic is another such set of assumptions.

What seems to be necessary is that these assumptions, whatever their particular configuration, must be relatively enduring in the crucial area of public discourse; we seem not to be able to engage in the radical and continual renegotiation of these assumptions as we carry out our interactions. At the same time, however, the world view that these assumptions generate is as much a product of human interactions as it is a framework for it. This mutually synergistic process of creating a world view and shaping human interaction lies at the core of the concept that reality is a social construct; world views, though held by individuals, are a social, not an individual, phenomenon.

It is the argument of this essay that this set of assumptions, this necessary, durable, non-determined world view, is as well a function of rhetoric. Arguments work -- they have force[83] -- to the extent that they provide the listener with a world view, or they appeal to, or change, the listener's world view. Rhetoric has this potential for force because reality is a social construction. We necessarily, as individuals, form a tentative world view. Necessarily also, we have a need to seek its confirmation in social discourse. This is why Plato and other classic philosophers so feared rhetoric[84] -- it is powerful, and power is corruptible.

The exercise of rhetorical power is an exercise of power in the third dimension. As such, it is an exercise in providing, resonating with, or changing the listener's world view in a way that makes the listener powerless. The listener, that is, becomes blinded to his own interests and to the fact that the powerful are acting detrimentally to those interests.

The world view, then, is strongly determined by the exercise of power in the third dimension. As an historical matter, beginning in the late nineteenth century, a set of assumptions congenial to the needs and purpose of the emerging entrepreneurial elite emerged to dominate public discourse. From this discourse emerged the world view that I have denominated the capitalist ethic.

We can readily see something of the same process occurring in the early to mid nineteenth century transformation of the common law that Horwitz has described.[85] Make the entirely plausible assumption that, because of the expense of litigation, litigants in those pre-Legal Aid days tended to be affluent -- people of means, typically commercial means, disputing over matters of moment, again typically commercial matters. Although the typical dispute was over the entitlements to, and the spoils from, these commercial matters, the basic values and beliefs of these disputants were not in dispute -- both sides reflected the values of the emerging capitalists. The judges, then, were in a very real sense the audience of a rhetorical process that flowed from a single world view. It should not be the least bit surprising that the law -- what the judges did about these disputes -- began strongly to reflect the values of the mutually disputing litigants that were not in mutual dispute. The arguments of the litigants flowed from these values operating as implicit premises; the judges would not have to be consciously serving these values in order to adopt them as the implicit premises for the way that they resolved these disputes.

Thus, we can understand how the judiciary came to ratify the expropriative actions of entrepreneurs. Once having subconsciously adopted the unstated premises that underlay the rhetoric of argument in disputes between entrepreneurs, the judiciary carried these premises as a world view over into disputes between entrepreneur and passive landowner. This increasingly was the natural thing to do as the larger discourse in which the judiciary, as members of the emerging professional class, participated increasingly went forward on the basis of this world view. And the resulting judicial opinions that rationalized the outcome of disputes between entrepreneur and passive landowner, increasingly couched as they were in terms of this world view, simply became the next step in the larger rhetorical process.

In terms of the overall thesis of this essay, however, this argument is not complete in itself. We have, perhaps as much as any culture, institutionalized a pluralism of values in our political discourse and in our legal discourse. The 'rights revolution' of recent decades includes an expanding range of concerns. In legal discourse, the judicial process includes at the minimum a dualistic pluralism through the adversarial system. More than ever before, academic legal discourse now amounts to a multifaceted pluralism. We have seen how a particular world view came to dominate public discourse, particularly legal discourse. The question remains, how this world view has endured in the face of all this pluralism.

B. The semiotic process

My answer to this question lies in the nature of language, the tool which we use in order to carry out our public discourse. More particularly, it lies in the process of meaning by which the act of using language comes to have a substantive content. The concept of the linguistic sign provides a way of understanding this process of meaning. Charles Sanders Peirce posited a triadic conception of the linguistic sign:

> A *Sign*, or *Represantamen*, is a First which stands in such a genuine triadic relation to a Second, called its *Object*, as to be capable of determining a Third, called its *Interpretant*, to assume the same triadic relation to its Object in which it stands itself to the same Object. The triadic relation is *genuine*, that is its three members are bound together by it in a way that does not consist in any complexus of dyadic relations.[86]

However cryptic this conception might appear, it is especially powerful for our purposes because it moves beyond the familiar concept[87] of the arbitrary linguistic sign made up of the dyadic elements of signifier and signified. The richness of Peirce's concept emerges in his definition of the triadic sign:

> A sign or *representamen*, is something which stands to somebody for something in some respect or capacity. It addresses somebody, that is creates in the mind of that person an equivalent sign, or perhaps a more developed sign. That sign which it creates I call the *interpretant* of the first sign. The sign stands for something, its *object*. It stands for that object, not in all respects, but in reference to a sort of idea, which I have sometimes called the *ground* of the representamen.[88]

Peirce's concept moves beyond the structuralism of the dyadic sign by focussing instead on meaning as a process. Moreover, through the Interpretant, it incorporates the human mind into the sign. Meaning, then, is not a fixed content lodged in some reified objective reality. Rather, it is a process that goes on in interacting minds.

Perhaps the most important element of Peirce's conception is the ground, that 'sort of idea.' The concept of the ground allows us to understand that language is not a transparent window on the world of physical phenomena. Rather, it is a filter of these phenomena. Moreover, the phenomena that we experience are themselves a selection of what is 'out there', a selection determined by the nature of the limitations of our senses and by the psychological limits of our capacity for processing sensations.[89]

Peirce's conception of the linguistic sign allows us to make consistent propositions that provide a way of understanding the process of meaning in legal discourse. The ground is the implicit set of rules that determine which phenomena are selected and how they interrelate in the system of signs. The arbitrary sign,[90] then, is arbitrary only at the level of the relationship between sign and object. The sign is not arbitrary at the level of the ground because it is the ground that carries out the filtering function. Because filtering is a process of selection, the ground, then, is a deep ideology that determines the content of language. And, because we can conceptualize only through language, language creates the world that we experience.

Substantively, the ground must be a matter of belief. It cannot be a matter of fact because it functions as a filter for fact. It cannot be a matter of truth because the filtering function is the process that determines truth.

If meaning is the connection between fact and truth, then the ground consists of the deep assumptions that underlie the world view. It operates at the level of the subconscious as the world view operates at the level of the conscious. Like the world view, then, the ground arises out of a social process, the feedback process between individual and group, carried out as discourse, that determines our reality.

In discourse, we argue in terms of world views. If an argument carries the day, it is because there is agreement on the substance of the world view, at least by the end of the discourse. If an argument is not convincing, it is because there is no agreement on world view.[91] If an exercise of rhetoric is discourse that proceeds within a paradigm, then an argument is successful to the extent that it presents a paradigm that derives from the listener's ground better than any competing paradigm that might be present in that discourse.

Assume further that the particular substantive content of the ground of our language consists of the assumptions that made up the Cartesian Revolution -- the radical dichotomy between subject and object, the mechanistic world that Newton's Laws describe, and the general scientific paradigm that grew out of these postulates, that we can know the world as an objective reality.[92]

The capitalist ethic is entirely consistent with these assumptions, a world view that enjoins humankind to seize the day and conquer unruly nature, positing the radically free and autonomous individual whose basic function is domination and not husbandry.[93]

These various propositions that flow consistently from Peirce's conception of language provide, then, an explanation for the judicial outcomes that ensue when enterprise and entitlements to land come into conflict. These outcomes, despite their radical conflict with the deep principles of our constitutional order, nevertheless come far more easily to the judicial mind because they are so fully consistent with the Cartesian postulates that make up the particular substantive content of the ground of our language. The American judiciary is largely drawn from those who are politically active, those, that is, who partake most fully in the Enlightenment-grounded language of our public discourse. An opinion that is inconsistent with this ground 'just won't write' precisely because the language in which the judge must write it is not compatible to the task. It is not compatible because, despite the cacophony of competing world views that now characterizes judicial and legal academic discourse, the Enlightenment-based ground as yet remains largely intact. And because it remains largely intact, it creates our language and thus our world. Thus, when judges ratify entrepreneurial violence, they are only acting consistently with the ground of our world -- they are 'getting real.'

V
Conclusion

We now have an explanation for the radical gap between outcome and principle that requires no conspiracy theory. In legal discourse, legal doctrine and capitalist ethic meet the Cartesian postulates embedded in the ground of our language. Judges do what they do because it is the most compatible thing to do.

As the recent revolution in science also teaches us, the entire Cartesian ground is a biased reading of reality.[94] It is nothing more or less than an ideology. It is 'mere rhetoric.'

We cannot escape having an ideology. We can, however, escape a particular ideology when it no longer serves us well, and replace it with one that will immediately be more useful for the problems at hand.[95] The foregoing discussion is an attempt to show the mechanism by which a world view gains hegemony. A Florida philosopher put it well when he said, 'We have met the enemy and he is us.'[96] By implication also, this discussion shows how a different world view can replace it. Doing so is hard work. But it amounts only to 'mere rhetoric.'

ENDNOTES

1. Denis J. Brion is Professor of Law at Washington and Lee Law School. An extended verison of this essay appears in volume 42 of the Syracuse Law Review. The author gratefully acknowledges the helpful comments of Judith McMorrow on the drafts of this essay.

2. *Webster's Third International Dictionary*, 1971, 759.

3. Brion, 1989, "Making the Appalachian World: The Judicial Conception of the Land," in R. Kevelson, ed., *Law & Semiotics*, Vol. 3, 73, New York: Plenum.

4. The cases are collected and analyzed in *id.*

5. The particulars of the dispute are recounted in *City of Virginia Beach v. Roanoke River Basin Ass'n*, 776 F.2d 484 (4th Cir. 1985); *State of North Carolina v. Hudson*, 731 F.Supp. 1261 (E.D. N.C. 1990); United States Army Corps of Engineers, *Water Supply Study, Hampton Roads, Va. -- Feasibility Report and Final Environmental Impact Study*, Dec. 1984.

6. E.g., *Young v. City of Asheville*, 241 N.C. 618, 86 S.E.2d 408 (1955); *Pernell v. City of Henderson*, 220 N.C. 79, 16 S.E.2d 449 (1941); *Dunlap v. North Carolina Power & Light Co.*, 212 N.C. 814, 195 S.E. 43 (1938); *Greer v. Durham Water Co.*, 127 N.C. 349, 37 S.E. 474 (1900: *Town of Purceville v. Potts*, 179 Va. 514, 19 S.E.2d 700 (1942); *Virginia Hot Springs Co. v. Hoover*, 143 Va. 460, 130 S.E. 408 (1925); *Commonwealth v. City of Newport News*, 158 Va. 521, 164 S.E. 689 (1923); *Davis v. Town of Harrisonburg*, 116 Va. 864, 83 S.E. 401 (1914); *Mumpower v. City of Bristol*, 90 Va. 151, 17 S.E. 853 (1893); *Carpenter v. Gold*, 88 Va. 551, 14 S.E. 329 (1892).

7. *State of North Carolina v. Hudson*, 731 F.Supp. 1261, 1272 (E.D.N.C. 1990).

8. J. Jacobs, 1984, *Cities and the Wealth of Nations: Principles of Economic Life*,; M. Storper and R. Walker, 1989, *The Capitalist Imperative: Territory, Technology, and Industrial Growth*, hereinafter *Stroper & Walker*.

9. E.g., *Boomer v. Atlantic Cement Co.*, 26 N.Y.2d 219, 257 N.E.2d 870 (1970); *Prah v. Maretti*, 108 Wis.2d 223, 321 N.W.2d 182 (1982); *Bove v. Donner-Hanna Coke Co.*,

236 A.D. 37, 258 N.Y.S. 229 (Sup. Ct. 1932). See generally, *Restatement (Second) of Torts* § 826 (1977).

10. E.g., *Berman v. Parker*, 348 U.S. 26 (1954); *J. Weingarten, Inc. v. Northgate Mall, Inc.*, 404 So.2d 896 (La. 1981); *Poletown Neighborhood Council v. City of Detroit*, 410 Mich. 616, 304 N.W.2d 455 (1981).

11. E.g., *Geotech Reclamation Indus., Inc. v. Hamrick*, 886 F.2d 662 (4th Cir. 1989); *Udell v. Haas*, 21 N.Y.2d 463, 235 N.E.2d 897 (1968); *Matthews v. Board of Zoning Appeals*, 218 Va. 270, 237 S.E.2d 128 (1977).

12. W. Blackstone, 2 *Commentaries* *2.

13. Such a conception is set out in Honorè, 1961, "Ownership", in *Oxford Essays in Jurisprudence*, A. Guest, ed., 107.

14. *Id.* 123.

15. J. Burns, 1982, *The Vineyard of Liberty* 42-63, 315-350; F. McDonald, 1985, *Novus Ordo Seclorum: The Intellectual Origins of the Constitution* 185-224; D. Rodgers, 1987, *Contested Truths: Keywords in American Politics since Independence* 63-79, 84-101, 112-130, 147-156, hereinafter *Rodgers*; R. Wiebe, 1984, *The Opening of American Society: From the Adoption of the Constitution to the Eve of Disunion* 209-252, hereinafter *Opening*.

16. *Opening*, *supra*, 146-152.

17. *Id.* 257-264.

18. D. Potter, 1976, *The Impending Crisis*, 1848-1861, 30-44.

19. G. McWhiney & P. Jamieson, 1982, *Attack and Die: Civil War Tactics and the Southern Heritage* 3-98.

20. M. Adams, 1978, *Our Masters the Rebels: A Speculations on Union Military Failure in the East, 1861-1865*, 152-174, hereinafter *Adams*; J. McPherson, 1988, *The Battle Cry of Freedom: The Civil War Era*, 816-818, hereinafter *McPherson*.

21. *Adams*, *supra*, 152-174; S. Foote, 1974, *The Civil War: A Narrative*, Vol. 3, 13-16; *McPherson*, *supra*, 722.

22. G. Frederickson, 1965, *The Inner Civil War: Northern Intellectuals and the Crisis of the Union*, 98-112, 199-225, hereinafter *Frederickson*.

23. R. Wiebe, 1967, *The Search for Order*, 1877-1920, 44-75, hereinafter *Order*; M. Josephson, 1962, *The Robber Barons: The Great American Capitalists*, 1861-1901, 253-289, 375-403, hereinafter *Josephson*.

24. *Josephson*, *supra*, 315-346; *Order*, *supra*, 76-110.

25. The Pure Food Act, 1906, Pub. L. 59-384, 34 Stat. 768.

26. The Child Labor Act, 1969, Pub. L. 64-249, 39 Stat. 675.

27. The Interstate Commerce Act, 1877, Pub. L. 49-104, 24 Stat. 379.

28. The Sherman Act, 1890, Pub. L. 51-647, 26 Stat. 209.

29. *Order*, note 23 *supra*, 164-195.

30. *Id*. 196-223.

31. *Frederickson*, note 22 *supra*, 199-216; J. Gaventa, 1980, *Power and Powerlessness: Quiescence and Rebellion in an Appalachian Valley*, 66-72, hereinafter *Gaventa*; *Order*, note 23 *supra*, 111-132, 196-223.

32. *Storper & Walker*, note 8 *supra*, at 88, 206-207.

33. The tale is recounted in M. Josephson, 1972, *The Money Lords: The Great Financial Capitalists, 1925-1950.*

34. J. Galbraith, 1956, rev. ed., *American Capitalism: The Concept of Countervailing Power*, 108-153; see generally, A. Schlesinger, Jr., 1958, *The Coming of the New Deal.*

35. R. Bartlett, 1973, *Economic Foundations of Political Power*, hereinafter *Bartlett*; C. Lindblom, 1977, *Politics and Markets: The World's Political-Economic Systems*, 170-188, hereinafter *Lindblom*.

36. Taylor, "Can Big Owners Make a Difference?", *Harvard Bus. Rev.*, Sept.-Oct. 1990; Turque, "The Ethics Rules Don't Fix Congress's Problems," *Newsweek*, Dec. 31, 1990, at 46; *Federal Contract Policy: "Revolving Door" Issue Tops Legislative Agenda*, Bureau of Nat'l Aff. Daily Report for Executives, Special Report DER No. 13, Jan. 18, 1991.

37. S. Bowles & H. Ginter, 1986, *Democracy & Capitalism* 3; *Lindblom*, note 35 *supra*, at 132-133, 189-200 offers 'polyarchy' as the descriptive term.

38. Or, more particularly, a process based on the private ownership of the means of production and on the use of wealth to generate and accumulate more wealth. See R. Heilbroner, 1985, *The Nature and Logic of Capitalism*, 13-16, 343-35.

39. The Department of Justice, 1988, 15 *U.S.C.* §§ 1-31.

40. The Federal Communications Commission, 1988, 47 *U.S.C.* §§ 151-613.

41. The Environmental Protection Agency, 1988, 42 *U.S.C.* §§ 7401-7642 clean air; 1988, 33 *U.S.C.* §§ 1251-1387, clean water.

42. The Federal Trade Commission, 15 *U.S.C.* §§ 41-77.

43. The Occupational Safety and Health Administration, 1988, 29 *U.S.C.* §§ 651-678.

44. The Food and Drug Administration, 1988, 21 *U.S.C.* §§ 301-392.

45. A pollution discharge permit, for example, by definition does not eliminate pollution entirely; in essence, then, it legitimates the amount of pollution that it does not eliminate. Producer influence -- the phenomenon of regulatory capture --works to maximize the amount of pollution thereby legitimated.

46. *Bartlett*, note 35 *supra*, at 65-69, 103-112.

47. See generally, R. Kuttner, 1984, *The Economic Illusion: False Choices Between Prosperity and Social Justice;* K. Phillips, 1990, *The Politics of Rich and Poor: Wealth and the American Electorate in the Reagan Aftermath*.

48. M. Horwitz, 1977, *The Transformation of American Law*, 1780-1860, hereinafter '*Horwitz*'.

49. *Id.*, 253.

50. *Id.*, 255-256.

51. *Id.*, 256-266.

52. Woodard, 1986, "Progress and Poverty in American Law and Legal Education," 37 *Syracuse L. Rev.* 795, 807-811, hereinafter *Progress and Poverty*; Woodard, 1968, "The Limits of Legal Realism: An Historical Perspective," 54 *Va. L. Rev.* 689, 705-718, hereinafter *Legal Realism*.

53. *Horwitz*, note 48 *supra*, 266.

54. *Legal Realism*, note 52 *supra*, 702.

55. *Rodgers*, note 15 *supra*, 203-211; *Progress and Poverty*, note 51 *supra*, 820.

56. *Progress and Poverty*, note 51 *supra*, 834, 846-849.

57. G. Calabresi, 1970, *The Costs of Accidents: A Legal and Economic Analysis*, 39-67.

58. E.g., *Columbia Nitrogen Corv. Royster Co.*, 451 F.2d 3 (4th Cir. 1971); *Roto-Lith, Ltd. v. F.P. Bartlett & Co.*, 297 F.2d 497 1st Cir. 1962; *Southern Concrete Servs. v. Mableton Contractors, Inc.*, 407 F.Supp. 581 (N.D. Ga. 1975).

59. E.g., *Reynolds v. Sims*, 377 U.S. 533 (1964); *Brown v. Board of Educ.*, 347 U.S. 483 (1954).

60. Cicero, *De Inventione*, in 2 *Cicero* 2, H. Hubbell ed. & trans., 1968, quoted in S. Fish, 1989, *Doing What Comes Naturally: Change, Rhetoric, and the Practice of Theory in Literary and Legal Studies*, 482, hereinafter *Fish*.

61. S. Lukes, 1974, *Power: A Radical View*, 27, hereinafter *Lukes*.

62. *Id.*, 11-15.

63. *Id.*, 16-20. Lukes defines the mobilization of bias as 'a set of predominant values, beliefs, rituals, and institutional procedures 'rules of the game' that operate systematically and consistently to the benefit of certain persons and groups at the expense of others.' *Id.*, 17.

64. *Id.*, 21-25.

65. *Id.*, 24.

66. *Gaventa*, note 31 *supra*, is a compelling presentation of an empirical confirmation of the workings of Lukes's three dimensional conceptualization of the operation of power.

67. S. Griffith, 1989, *Home Town News: William Allen White and the Emporia Gazette*, hereinafter *Griffith*.

68. *Id.*, 13-63.

69. *Id.*, 92-138, 187-241.

70. *Id.*, 67-91.

71. *Id.*, 159-184.

72. *Order*, note 23 *supra*, is an extended description of the emergence of the professional and bureaucratic middle class in the decades immediately around the turn of the century as the implementers of and apologists for the capitalist order.

73. *Griffith*, note 67 *supra*, 151-55, 234-39.

74. A. Trachtenberg, 1982, *The Incorporation of America: Culture & Society in the Gilded Age*.

75. There was no lack of cracks in the smooth facade of order and communal harmony that White tried to portray. *Griffith*, note 67 *supra*, 99-106.

76. T. Veblen, 1967, *Absentee Ownership: The Case of America*, 142.

77. As long ago as the early 1880s, Oliver Wendell Holmes, Jr., captured the rationale for these devices:

> A man need not, it is true, do this or that act,--the term *act* implies a choice,--but he must act somehow. Furthermore, the public generally profits by individual activity. As action cannot be avoided, and tends to the public good, there is obviously no policy in throwing the hazard of what is at once desirable and inevitable on the actor.

O. Holmes, Jr., 1963, *The Common Law*, M. Howe ed., 77; Calabresi, 1961, "Some Thoughts on Risk Distribution and the Law of Torts," 70 *Yale L.J.*, 499, 507-516.

78. E.g., *U.C.C.* § 1-105, comment 3; *Id.*, § 1-205, comment 5; *Id.*, § 2-314a.

79. T. Kuhn, 1970, *The Structure of Scientific Revolutions*, 2d ed., hereinafter *Kuhn*.

80. *Fish*, note 60 *supra*; S. Fish, 1980, *Is There a Text in This Class? The Authority of Interpretive Communities*.

81. S. Langer, 1957, 3d ed., *Philosophy in a New Key: A Study in the Symbolism of Reason, Rite, and Art*, 9, hereinafter *Langer*.

82. M. Berman, 1981, *The Reenchantment of the World*, 135-189, hereinafter *Berman*.

83. *Fish*, note 60 *supra*, 471-524.

84. *Id.*, 476-478; Lanham, 1988, "The "Q" Question, 87 *So. Atl. Q.*, 653, 653-681.

85. See notes 48-59 *supra* and accompanying text.

86. 2 C. Peirce, 1931-1935, *The Collected Papers of Charles Sanders Peirce*, 274, hereinafter *Peirce*, quoted in J. Sheriff, 1989, *The Fate of Meaning*, 58-59, hereinafter *Sheriff*.

87. F. De Saussure, 1966, ppb. ed., *Course in General Linguistics*, 65-78, hereinafter *de Saussure*.

88. *Peirce*, note 86 *supra*, 228, quoted in *Sheriff*, note 86 *supra*, 56.

89. J. Jaynes, 1976, *The Origin of Consciousness in the Breakdown of the Bicameral Mind*, 56-66; L. Mumford, 1966, *Technics and Human Development*, 48-63.

90. Onomatopoeia aside, there is no necessary relationship between the signifier and the signified in the Sausserian linguistic sign -- 'dog' in English, 'chien' in French, and 'hund' in German are all signifiers for the same signified. *F. de Saussure*, note 87 *supra*, 65-78.

91. For a thorough discussion, see A. MacIntyre, 1981, *After Virtue: A Study in Moral Theory*, 6-21.

92. *Berman*, note 82 *supra*, 69-132.

93. The contrast here is between two competing conceptions of the relation between humans and the natural world -- subordination and stewardship. For a discussion, D. Ehrenfeld, 1978, *The Arrogance of Humanism*; F. Elder, 1970, *Crisis in Eden: A Religious Study of Man and Environment*.

94. E.g., J. Gleick, 1987, *Chaos: The Making of a New Science*; I. Prigogine & I. Stengers, 1984, *Order Out of Chaos: Man's New Dialogue With Nature*.

95. *Kuhn,* note 79 *supra*, 52-76; *Langer*, note 81 *supra*, 3-25.

96. Walt Kelly, *Pogo*, in J. Bartlett, 1980, 15th ed., *Familiar Quotations*, 455.

Chapter 5

Jacques Lacan and Our State of Affairs: Preliminary Remarks on Law as Other

David S. Caudill[1]

(moi)a:	'Lacan must be read as a rejection of the legacy of Descartes.'
autre:	'But did he reject Peirce?'
(moi)a:	'I'm not sure; in certain senses, he *did* reject Paris....'

--actual verbal interchange at a semiotics conference.*

I

What is the meaning, or at least one meaning, of Jacques Lacan's work in psychoanalysis for our common project: to understand how law operates in and reflects linguistic and social practices and processes? I choose to approach the question, appropriately I trust, by briefly considering several uses of Freud in the critical legal tradition, a tradition in which I will include certain legal realists and law-and-society scholars, as well as those associated with critical legal studies. This approach has the advantage of tying my inquiry to *legal* theory and *Freudian* theory -- two popularly-understood anchors -- to avoid the splintering into confusion that often accompanies discussions of Lacan. I concede, nevertheless, that my pretentiously 'royal road' to Lacan is but one of a hundred ways to read him. As evidenced by the ever-expanding literature concerning Lacan, he alternatively inspires praise and criticism from feminists, literary theorists, aestheticians, semioticians, historians, philosophers, and, of course, psychiatrists, psychologists, psycho-therapists, and psycho-analysts. I will be content to speak from the place of one seeking to understand the critique of legal ideology, by which I mean the triadic inquiry: (1) What is ideology? (i.e., is it a set of communal beliefs, or if not, is it the commonality of language?); (2) How does ideology function in legal processes and institutions?; and (3) How does the critic of ideology remain self-critical?

Recall that we credit Freud with many concepts that have become 'common sense,'[2] four of which are relevant to my approach:

First, the recognition of sexuality or sexual desire as a force; when we pay attention to that which is seemingly an individual and private matter, we realize that sexuality reflects social repression, that 'normal' sexuality is not biological (except in the narrowest sense),[3] and that society organizes even our instincts.[4] This is much more than a reduction of life to the erotic, of which Freud was accused;[5]

Second, the recognition of an unconscious, into which painful desires and ideas are driven or repressed, such that reality is distorted or denied;[6]

Third, the promise of access to the dynamics of mental life through an analytic method;[7] and

Fourth, the understanding that the first three concepts are significant for our understanding of society. The reason that some social theorists employ psychoanalysis is that a picture emerges as to how the social world constructs the human subject and reproduces ideological patterns -- society does not merely affect our otherwise individual and mental experiences, it actually forms them.[8]

I proceed below through a series of didactic schemata, with the understanding that they are inadequate representations of anything other than the outline of my remarks.

II

Traditional

ego-------------------seeks *law* as a father-substitute

---

id: desire

Designating my first scheme as a 'traditional' use of Freud, I have in mind Jerome Frank in the 1930's and Professor Schoenfeld nowadays. Frank identified the basic social *myth* that law is precise and coherent, and then analogized (i) a child's search for security and authority in his or her father, with (ii) society's craving for finality and rules.[9] We are unwilling, Frank observes, to concede that law is biased, thus we delude ourselves into thinking that we are governed by reason.[10] Frank acknowledged that his explanation was only partial,[11] and the radical implications of his analysis were thereafter, it seems, ignored. Psychoanalysis was soon welcomed into socio-legal theory as *just another* helpful insight, and even then, it was often regarded as superficial.[12] Much 'law and social psychoanalysis' literature betrays an obsessional fear that psychoanalysis will misused.[13] After all, Freud has been discredited by mainstream psychology and psychiatry.[14] The message is usually: use Freud sparingly.[15]

By the time we reach Schoenfeld, psychoanalytic explanations of socio-legal phenomena are tentative and simplistic.[16] For example, the growing acceptance of judicial review (of Congressional law) in the decades immediately following the Civil War *might* be explained by the citizenry's 'unconscious wish for parental direction' after a traumatic event.[17] To underscore how speculative this is, Schoenfeld concedes that he has failed in his explanation to consider the insights of sociology, political science, history and economics.[18] Schoenfeld apologizes for Freud, but is hardly an apologist.

III
Law-and-Society

conscious racism----------------------eliminated by *law*

———————————

unconscious racism

For want of a better term to describe a much more sophisticated use of psychoanalytic socio-legal categories, I borrow the term law-and-society from that so-named interdisciplinary movement with roots in legal realism. I have in mind Charles Lawrence's recent critique of equal protection laws, which takes Freud seriously.[19] I could also mention Bienenfeld in the 1950's[20] and Ehrenzweig in the 1960's,[21] both enthusiastic proponents of psychoanalytic jurisprudence, but a contemporary example will suffice.

Lawrence sees the ideology of equal opportunity as a symptom, a defense mechanism for emotional disturbances.[22] That is, we feel the tensions between (i) a social order in which racism persists, and (ii) our ideals of equality, and we resolve those tensions by a selective perception of social and legal realities.[23] When equal protection laws, for example, require a finding of discriminatory intent to establish unlawful discrimination, only conscious racism will be eliminated.[24] Unconscious racism, due to this intentionalist scheme, maintains unequal treatment throughout society.

Lawrence shows how we repress, that is, how we think and act contrary to, personal and cultural morality. There is a remnant of Marcuse here -- 'repression from without is maintained by repression from within.'[25] Nevertheless, Lawrence feels compelled to qualify his argument by clarifying that he is not defending psychoanalysis as definitive -- he is only using, he says, its conceptual vocabulary.[26]

IV
Critical Legal Studies

social self--------------------------established by *Law*

____

unconscious desire

It is not until we consider the eclectic Critical Legal Studies movement that Freudian categories are fearlessly employed. The Neo-Marxian and Structuralist traditions that inform much that we call critical legal scholarship were less concerned with how psychoanalysis fared within the psychiatric establishment.

I have in mind Peter Gabel's work when I diagram the split between the social self and desire, which is the split between the knowledge the subject has of himself and the subject.[27] (The similarity of this aspect of Gabel's approach with R.D. Laing's 'divided self' is worth noting, because Lacan's theory of subjectivity is an indirect critique of the idea of 'true' and 'false' selves.[28]) The unconscious desire identified by Gabel is the desire for confirmation and connectedness.[29] Families unwittingly throw children into a series of roles that in each case alienate the child from his or her desire, a desire that is repressed to maintain such roles.[30] Politicians feed this desire with fantasies.[31] Most important for the present inquiry, legal culture mediates between individual and national needs to create a collective, social denial.[32] Law is seen by nearly everyone as authoritative, which for Gabel evidences a projection by underconfirmed subjects.[33]

Other critical legal scholars have characterized legal thought as a form of denial,[34] or emphasized the *unconscious* self-construction of legal reality,[35] but Gabel is much more systematic in setting forth the contours of a socio-legal psychoanalysis. Significantly, Gabel's work is based in large part on the theories of Jacques Lacan.

V
Lacan

> By way of 'fixing our ideas' and the souls suffering here, I will apply the [subject's relation to the Other] to schema L....[36]

A. *Schema L* (*see* Appendix)

Lacan's quadripartite *Schema L*,[37] while useful to illustrate certain features of (i) his theory of the structure of human intersubjectivity, as well as (ii) his famous concept of the 'mirror stage' of infant development,[38] in no way *captures* Lacanian psychoanalysis. The Scheme was never intended to be a reductionistic theory in itself.[39] Moreover, dozens of such schemata appear in the writings of

Lacan and his commentators, each one trying to illustrate a few isolated relationships in a field that is ultimately indecipherable. I offer below a translation of the *Schema L*, one of many possible translations, that emphasizes the place of legal processes and institutions in Lacanian theory, even though my emphasis was rarely Lacan's, and even though he did not use his *Schema L* in those rare instances.

B. Law as Other

Several features of a scheme I call 'Law as Other' (*see* Appendix) are significant for socio-legal theory:

(1) On the left-hand side, there is no simple conscious/unconscious distinction, and no ego in control of an id. Recall that Lacan firmly rejected the later Freud's emphasis on a socially-adaptive ego that masters its environment.[40] For Lacan, the ego misconstrues, neglects, and ignores -- the legendary short session of analysis with Lacan ended, sometimes after a few minutes, when the ego would begin to lie.[41] The arrowed lines in the scheme point *to* the ego or self, which only *assumes* an image of control.

(2) Moreover, there is not really an ego or self at all in the Freudian sense, because such words 'imply a wholeness or totality' that is itself illusory.[42] Thus the ego is often termed 'zero' by Lacanian theorists, and by the time an identity ('one') is received, the ego has become dependent upon culture, or in socio-legal terms, has been captured by the system of laws.[43] The subject that appears on the surface to be unified is split in the diagram between the subject of speech and the identificatory function, both of which function at conscious and unconscious 'levels,' and both of which would more accurately be splintered into hundreds of variations.[44] The subject is a network of relations of need and demand with many *others* -- family members, friends, colleagues, boss, analyst.

Again, the arrowed lines depict significations *received from* language, from other people, and from the Big 'O' *Other* -- we are bound to the social structure, the right-hand side of the scheme, the 'outside-within-us' that gives us identity and purpose through signs and social practices. We even get an idealized image, a mis-recognition, of autonomy and freedom.

(3) As to the *Other*, the term has multiple meanings for Lacan and his disciples, but it is typically exterior as well as determinative.[45] It is initially the place of the parents, especially the father as the initial representative of law,[46] and it is therefore the place from which language is received -- the outside from which we are named. As parents lose their hold on discourse, the Other is the community, the place of social order or rules of discourse that we internalize.[47] Primarily, for Lacan, the Other is unconscious discourse, the place of Desire, and is therefore analogous to the discourse of our dreams and slips of the tongue[48] -- in Freudian terms, the place of clarity and truth.[49]

(4) The *moi* (or what I have called the Ego) in the lower left-hand corner includes for Lacan the ego and the id in the Freudian topology.[50] Freud's super-ego, associated with internalized social morality and other ideals, is now the mechanism that represses the *moi* and forms the split-off social speaking subject.[51] This mechanism is the equivalent of a system of language and law,[52] and might be represented by the arrowed lines from the Other to the (split) subject. Again, however, the social network is early in life internalized[53] and is not just an *outsider* to which the subject submits.

(5) The Speaking Subject functions to *represent* itself, but in fact masks itself. It is a mechanism of defense and denial, pretending to be independent of the Other, while in actuality its language is imprinted with cultural myths.[54]

(6) Finally, note the arrowed line from others to the identificatery ego, representing the gaze or desire to which the ego responds in constructing its self image.

At the obvious risk of rushing to find 'practical' -- and perhaps simplistic -- applications of Lacanian theory for socio-legal analysis, or, worse yet, of appearing to move 'beyond' Lacan before we have come to terms with the richness of his systematic description of our sociality, I begin to consider below -- and it is only a beginning -- the potential of Lacanian theory for analysis of the institutions of legal education and of the practice of real estate law. My tentativeness is not, however, a critique of Lacan, but is rather a self-critical move.

VI

Law School

The diagram I call 'Law School' (*see* Appendix) is based (roughly) upon Peter Goodrich's analysis of legal education in Great Britain.[55] Goodrich uses Lacan (as well as Kristeva and others) to demonstrate that law schools make exemplary patients for social psychoanalysis. The analysand resists such an analysis, of course,[56] but listen and you hear the fabrications of the speaking subject -- as it attempts to stabilize the ego, as the rules of law are internalized.[57] (Again, the diagram reflects a particular emphasis -- mine -- on the law professor as an *other*[58]; the relationships would change slightly if the other is a fellow law student, a parent, or an interviewer from a law firm.)

VII

Law Practice

In the diagram called 'Law Practice' (*see* Appendix), I have in mind, first, the problem of the incoherency of the law prohibiting regulatory takings without compensation, an incoherency reproduced in the dozens of law review articles that try to clarify Supreme Court jurisprudence,[59] and reproduced as well in city council chambers wherein litigators fabricate the takings doctrine. The outcome of regulatory takings cases rests primarily on unconscious beliefs or stories about greedy developers and helpless municipalities, or vice versa.[60] A second example is the myth of equal bargaining power in real estate financing, that is, the rule or presumption of contract law that, with respect to agreements signed by sophisticated parties, certifies that the parties had equal bargaining power.[61] Courts generally believe that a borrower freely negotiates its loan agreement.[62] This myth actually limits the conceivable outcomes of lender liability cases until juries -- not educated to believe in the myth -- are introduced.[63]

VIII

Conclusion

My primary focus here is not on the details of the last three schemata (Law as Other, Law School, Law Practice), but on the observation that each represents a pathological problem, not a solution or cure. Each represents an assessment of what we are up against. Each explains, in a preliminary fashion, why change for Lacan is a slow and complex process. Rational or autonomous control is out of the question -- we *need* legal and social processes because they are us, they are the field in which we exist. Unconscious belief is curable, but belief is not. Lacan,

I think, allows for the possibility of beginning to select what we take from others, from society, and from law.[64] Peter Goodrich identifies psychoanalysis itself as offensive to social systems, and he follows Lacan in recommending self-subversive styles of writing and of life.[65] Less optimistic Lacanians see only a tragic choice between 'alienation into language' and inability to function socially.[66] Lacan, indeed, emphasized the potentially bankrupting price to be paid for knowledge -- our consistency, our illusionary substance or enjoyment, might dissolve.[67]

Does Lacan help those who try to rise above inadequate and simplistic critiques of legal ideology, or does he ruin the project by demonstrating how little self is left in the social-to-the-core subject? It's too early to tell, but there is in Lacan an attractive willingness to acknowledge our state of affairs.

APPENDIX

SCHEMA L:

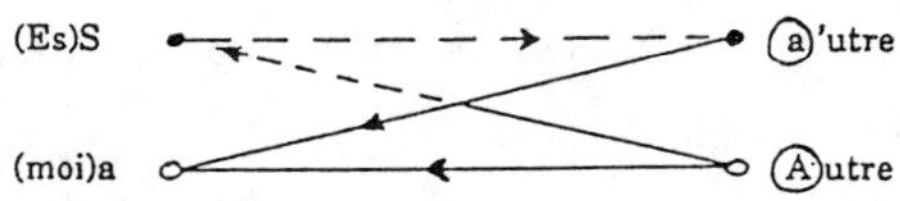

[Refer to note 36, supra]

LAW AS OTHER:

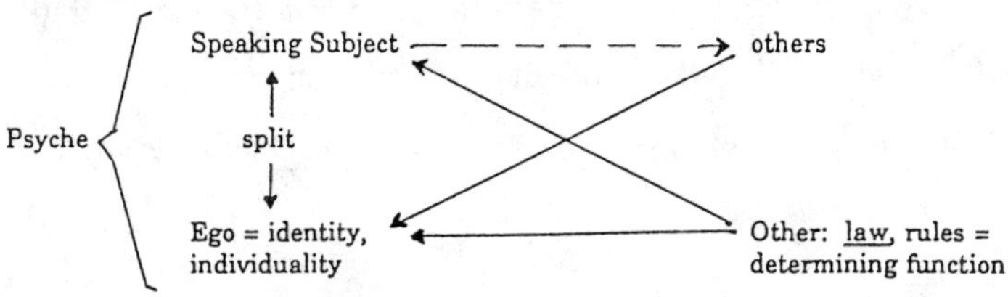

LAW SCHOOL:

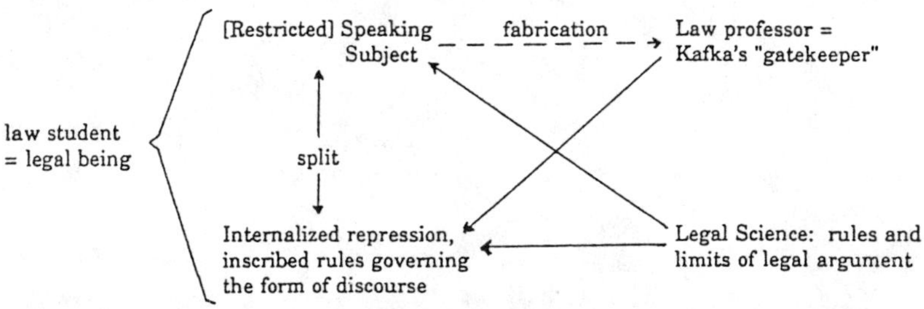

LAW PRACTICE:

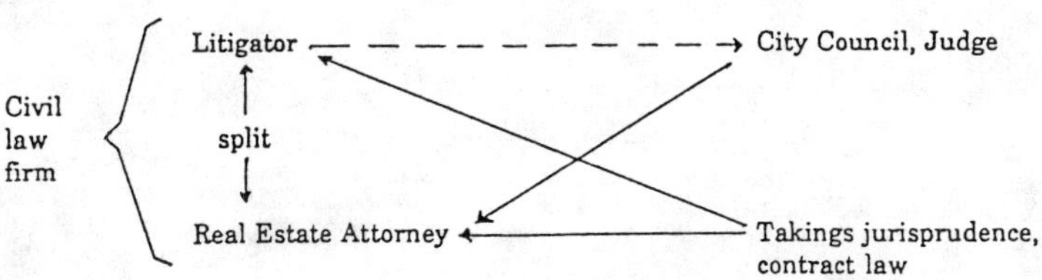

ENDNOTES

1. David S. Caudill is Assistant Professor of Law, Washington and Lee University.

2. S. S. Frosh, 1987, *The Politics of Psychoanalysis: An Introduction to Freudian and Post-Freudian Theory 1.* Freudian 'concepts of repression, sexual desire and the unconscious [are] often implicit in [our] 'common sense' understandings of ourselves and each other.'

3. S. Freud, 1957, *Five Lectures on Psycho-Analysis*, 42, J. Strachey, ed. & trans.:

> A child has its sexual instincts and activities from the first; it comes into the world with them; and, after an important course of development passing through many stages, they lead to what is known as the normal sexuality of the adult.

4. *Frosh*, *supra* note 2, 46. Freud describes 'the way society enters into the essence of the human individual, organizing the instincts where usually we consider that we are most privately ourselves.'

5. Freud, Five Lectures, *supra* note 3, 40-41:

> [T]his assertion of [the predominance of erotic life] will not be willingly believed. Even workers who are ready to follow my psychological studies are inclined to think that I over-estimate the part played by sexual factors.

6. *Id.*, 21-28, Freud identified, in his early studies of patients suffering from hysteria,

> a wishful impulse which was in sharp contrast to the subject's other wishes and which proved incompatible with the ethical and aesthetic standards of his personality.... [The] idea which had appeared before consciousness as the vehicle of this irreconcilable wish fell a victim to repression, was pushed out of consciousness with all its attached memories, and was forgotten.... [Repression] was thus revealed as one of the devices serving to protect the mental personality.

7. S. Freud, 1952, *An Autobiographical Study 77*, J. Strachey trans.:

> The analyst, who listens composedly but without any constrained effort to the stream of associations and who, from his experience, has a general notion of what to expect, can make use of the material brought to light by the patient . . . to infer the unconscious material itself; or if the resistance is stronger he will be able to recognize its character from the associations, as they seem to become more remote from the subject, and will explain it to the patient.

8. Frosh, *supra* note 2, 11:

> [Psychoanalysis] contains the possibilities for an approach that analyzes the mechanisms by which the social world enters into the experience of each individual, constructing the human 'subject' and reproducing itself through the perpetuation of particular patterns of ideology.

That is, our social relations are

> themselves only available because of the particular ideological structures that dominate within a society....
>
> [Social] structures are incorporated into individual consciousness and have a formative role on the ordering of the psyche.

Id., 47, 48.

9. J. Frank, 1930, *Law and the Modern Mind,* 8-9, 13-31.

10. *Id.*, 31-32.

11. *Id.*, 13-31.

12. See, e.g., Goldstein, 1968, "Psychoanalysis and Jurisprudence," 77 *Yale L.J.* 1053, 1054. Integration of psychoanalysis and law 'is not close at hand, and the scant beginning has occurred only at a relatively superficial descriptive level.'

13. See e.g., *id.* 1060-64, 1071.

14. Gilman, 1987, "The Struggle of Psychiatry with Psychoanalysis: Who Won?," 13 *Critical Inquiry*, 293.

15. Goldstein, *supra* note 12, 1076-77.

16. C. G. Schoenfeld, 1973, *Psychoanalysis and the Law.* Psychoanalytic explanations are acknowledged to be 'at best *partial.*' *Id.*, 7 emphasis in original.

17. *Id.*, 114.

18. *Id.* Schoenfeld remarks that his 'admittedly speculative' account 'fails to treat of matters that a sociologist, a political scientist, an historian, an economist, or others, might well deem highly relevant.'

19. Lawrence, 1983," *'Justice' or 'Just Us': Racism and the Role of Ideology,"* book review, 35 *Stan. L. Rev.*, 831, hereinafter *Justice*; "The Id, the Ego, and Equal Protection: Reckoning with Unconscious Racism," 1987, 39, *Stan L. Rev.*, 317, hereinafter *Equal Protection.*

20. An unfinished manuscript on psychoanalysis and law by Franz Rudolf Bienenfeld 1886-1961 was published in two parts entitled "Prolegomena to a Psychoanalysis of Law and Justice," 1965, 53, *Calif. L. Rev.*, 957 [Part I], 1254 [Part II].

21. A. Ehrenzweig, 1971, *Psychoanalytic Jurisprudence: On Ethics, Aesthetics, and 'Law' -- On Crime, Tort, and Procedure.*

22. Lawrence, *Justice, supra* note 19, 841-42.

23. *Id.*, 842, 848.

24. Lawrence, *Equal Protection, supra* note 19, 322-23, 329.

25. H. Marcuse, 1955, *Eros and Civilization, A Philosophical Inquiry Into Freud,* 16.

26. Lawrence, *Equal Protection, supra* note 19, 331 n.55.

27. Gabel, 1989, "Dukakis's Defeat and the Transformative Possibilities of Legal Culture," *Tikkun*, Mar./Apr., 16; *id.*, 15 acknowledging that Lacanian 'psychoanalysis is based on a fundamental split between the subject and the knowledge he has of himself'.

28. R. D. Laing, 1971, *The Politics of the Family and Other Essays 3-19*; E. Ragland-Sullivan, 1987, *Jacques Lacan and the Philosophy of Psychoanalysis 62*:

    > Laing following Winnicott makes a Rousseauesque division between true and false images of self 'true' belonging to the natural and good inner self and "false" to the distorting, repressive effects of the social realm . . . . Lacan's subject, on the other hand, is a paradox of true and false . . . . No final separation exists, therefore, between the inside and outside realms.

29. Gabel, *supra* note 27, 16.

30. *Id.*

31. *Id.*, 15.

32. *Id.*, 107-08.

33. *Id.*, 108-09.

34. Trubek, 1984, "Where the Action Is: Critical Legal Studies and Empiricism," 36, *Stan. L. Rev.*, 575, 607.

35. Kelman, 1984, "Trashing," 36, *Stan. L. Rev.*, 293, 304.

36. J. Lacan, 1977, *Écrits: A Selection 193,* A. Sheridan, trans.

37. Schema L appears in "Le séminaire sur 'La lettre volée,'" in *Écrits,* 1966, 53; a simplified version appears in *Écrits: A Selection, supra* note 36, 193, in the essay entitled 'On a question preliminary to any possible treatment of psychosis', to signify 'that the condition of the subject S, neurosis or psychosis, is dependent on what is being unfolded in the Other O.'

38. "Le séminaire..," *supra* note 37, 9 as translated by A. Wilden in his notes following Lacan's "The Function of Language in Psychoanalysis," in J. Lacan, *Speech and Language in Psychoanalysis*, Wilden trans. & commentary 1968, 107 n. 48:

> Thus it is if man comes to thinking the Symbolic order, it is because he is caught in it from the first in his being. The illusion that he has formed it by his consciousness results from the fact that it was by way of a *béance* specific to his Imaginary relation to his counterpart, that he was able to enter into this order as a subject. But he was only able to make this entrance by the radical defile of [*parole*] ... which ... is reproduced each time that the subject addresses himself to the Other ... who can nullify the subject himself ... by making himself an object in order to deceive him. This dialectic of intersubjectivity, whose use I have shown to be necessary -- from the theory of transference to the structure of paranoia, itself -- ... is readily backed up by the [*Schema L*] which has long been familiar to my students.... The two middle terms represent the coupled reciprocal Imaginary objectification which I have emphasized in the *stade du miroir.*

For Lacan's description of the mirror stage, *Écrits: A Selection, supra* note 36, 1-7.

39. *Cf. Écrits: A Selection, supra* note 35, 214, discussing *Schema I,* the structure of the subject at the termination of the psychotic process:

> [It] would be better to confine this schema to the waste-bin, if, like so many others, it was to lead anyone to forget in an intuitive image the analysis on which it is based.

40. *Écrits: A Selection, supra* note 36, 22.

41. S. Schneiderman, 1983, *Jacques Lacan: The Death of an Intellectual Hero,* 151. 'Almost by definition, the ego can never be the master of the short session.' *Id.*, 134.

42. Ragland-Sullivan, *supra* note 28, 2.

43. Goodrich, 1990, *Languages of Law: From Logics of Memory to Nomadic Masks*, 281-82:

> Ego . . . is in law a lack, an absence that is filled by entry into the symbolic. . . .

> The entry of the individual into the symbolic, the transition from zero to one, from lack to identity, is the condition of institutional existence, the capture of the subject by law.

44. Ragland-Sullivan, *supra* note 28, 42-43.

45. *Id.*, xii, ' . . . this *Autre* . . . intervenes in Lacan's theory on several levels, but all of which distinguish themselves by a dimension of exteriority and a determining function in relation to the human subject.'

46. *Écrits: A Selection, supra* note 36, 68. 'It is in the *name of the father* that we must recognize the support of the symbolic function which, from the dawn of history, has identified his person with the figure of the law.'

47. Ragland-Sullivan, *supra* note 28, 17, *citing* Schneiderman, 1975, "Psychoanalysis and *Hamlet*," DAI 72, 23503A.

48. *Écrits: A Selection, supra* note 36, 193:

> What is being unfolded [in the Other for the subject] is articulated like a discourse (the unconscious is the discourse of the Other), whose syntax Freud first sought to define for those bits that come to us in certain privileged moments, in dreams, in slips of the tongue....

49. Ragland-Sullivan, *supra* note 28, 39 clarity and 'truth' reside in the unconscious Other(A) . . . .

50. Ragland-Sullivan, *supra* note 28, 54, Lacan 'collapsed the Freudian id and ego into the *moi* . . . .'.

51. *Id.*, '. . . the identificatory *moi* is repressed as an ideal ego and the social *je* is formed, and thus [the superego is] a part of both subjects.'

52. *Id.*, 57.

53. *Id.*, 56, when an infant submits 'to the laws that structure its particular social network and [internalizes] them, it has acquired a superego.'

54. *Id.*, 63-64, 'Language . . . imprints the cultural myths which adults later assume they have consciously deduced or learned.'

55. Goodrich, 1987, "Psychoanalysis in Legal Education: Notes on the Violence of the Sign," R. Kevelson, ed., *Law and Semiotics*, Vol. 1, 193.

56. *Id.*, 197, the subject's defenses as 'the first obstacle of any analytic or therapeutic relation'.

57. *Id.*, 196, '. . . analysis is led eventually to question an order of repression . . . in which the laws governing the forms of discourse are inscribed in the very constitution of subjectivity.'; 200 "the student of law internalizes the limits of legal argument"; 201 ". . . the essence of any grammar [is] to standardize and control meaning . . . ."; 205:

> It is the subject that fabricates the law through an act of denial, through a non-recognition or repression of subjectivity and desire in favour of entry into the symbolic as the fiction of law.

58. *Id.*, 198:

> In analytic terms . . . it is the teaching relationship, the form of language of the substantive disciplines, the methodologies of argument and the structures of evaluation and examination that are all at some point to be questioned, in terms of their internal and external disciplinary functions.

59. Bray, Caudill & Owen, "Once Again, the Trilogy in Retrospect: An Essay on the Virtues of Development Agreements in Texas," *32 S. Tex. L. Rev. 1*, 14-26, for a discussion of numerous such articles.

60. *Id.*, 26-28, citing Williams, 1988, "Legal Discourse, Social Vision and the Supreme Court's Land Use Planning Law: The Genealogy of the Lochnerian Recurrence in First English Lutheran Church and Nollan, *59 U. Colo. L. Rev. 427*, 428-29, 446-73. Judicial adoption of a particular "social vision" as determinative; two competing discourses -- property as a fundamental right *versus* judicial deference in socioeconomic matters -- reflect such visions; Alexander, 1988, "Takings, Narratives, and Power," 88 *Colum. L. Rev.*, 1752, 1752-68, 'narratives of power' lie below abstract, doctrinal analyses.

61. Mortgage loan borrowers, particularly commercial borrowers, invariably can read, and after consulting with their attorney, can understand standard loan documents and give what is known as an informed and voluntary consent. Such a borrower presumably has bargaining power, equal to the lender, so as to eliminate unacceptable provisions in loan documents through negotiation. *J. Calamari & J. Perillo*, 1987, Contracts 418-24 3rd ed. Those who have represented borrowers know, however, the difficulties in negotiating against a bank's 'standard documentation'; often, nowadays, the initial loan commitment signed by a borrower *is* an agreement which limits the terms of the loan to the bank's "standard documentation." In real estate law practice, loan documents are seldom "negotiated" in the manner of sale agreements, leases, or easements.

62. *Lovell v. Western Life Insurance Co.*, 754 S.W.2d 298 Tex.Ap-- Amarillo, 1988, a case involving a claim of breach of good faith and fair dealing brought by a borrower mortgagor against a lender:

> The duty of good faith and fair dealing does not exist in Texas unless intentionally created by express language or unless a special

relationship of trust or confidence exists between the parties to the contract. *Arnold* . . . 725 S.W.2d 165, 167 Tex. 1987 . . . .

> In the insurance context, a special relationship arises out of the parties' unequal bargaining power . . . .

725 S.W.2d at 167.

> . . . In analyzing the transaction in the instant case, we find [no] imbalance of bargaining power.

754 S.W.2d at 301-302.

63. Interview, "Juror Comments on $46 Million Judgment," *Lender Liability Law Report*, Jan. 1988, 4:

> '...well, what was it that convinced the remainder of the jury that Bank of America [in *Kruse v. Bank of America*, 248 Cal. Rptr. 217 Cal Ap1988] was liable?'
>
> [Jury Foreman:] 'The fact that the bank's witnesses lied so much . . . . Every bank witness testified he had not instituted the loan request, even though three . . . had signed the loan request. One of [those who signed the request and approved it] testified . . . that in 'bank jargon,' an approval doesn't mean the bank actually approved the request, it means something else.'

64. S. Zizek, 1989, *The Sublime Object of Ideology,* 46:

> Lacan's last word would be a radical alienation of the subject [if the subject's] content [was] determined by an exterior signifying network . . . . But Lacan's basic thesis, at least in his last works, is that there is a possibility for the subject to obtain some contents, some kind of positive consistency, also outside the big Other, the alienating symbolic network.

65. Goodrich, *supra* note 55, 195, 210.

66. Ragland-Sullivan, *supra* note 28, 273.

67. Zizek, *supra* note 64, 68.

**The phonological play between 'Peirce' and 'Paris' reminds us of the power of the idiolect to create new, general cross-reference. Ed. note.*

Chapter 6

The Law as a Liberal Art

Robert Ginsberg[1]

I

Nay, law is a liberal profession, a trained practice with valuable social functions, that nets the practitioner a good income. Such is the view of the matter by the general public, and this view is decisive when undergraduate students think of law school and a career in law. In this view of law what counts is getting ahead. Getting ahead financially is a persuasive attraction. Success in law, with its financial rewards, means learning to get ahead in the practice. How to win your case, how to calculate the outcome, and how to make the best of the mess are the central concerns for legal practice. Law is a How To Do It art. Therefore, the only sensible reason for studying it is to learn how to do well in practicing it. What a mistake to approach law, which is an art of doing, as if one of the liberal arts, those fields of human perfection by study.

This mistake I shall develop in this essay in the form of a case for law within the general education requirements for the liberally educated person, in other words law as a liberal art for college students. Sometimes by pursuing a mistaken viewpoint to its fullest articulation, giving it the fairest hearing, we can discover that it is sound, after all. May law once recognized as a liberal art liberate us from other mistaken notions about the profession of law.

Two approaches in liberal arts are available for studying law: looking at law from the traditional disciplines, and looking at those disciplines from the perspective of law. Consider the example of history. We can do a history of law, and we can explore law's contribution to history. We discover the two are closely related. Law's own history is inextricably yet explicably enmeshed in the history of society.

Any major form of human activity can have its history and can be traced as contributing to the history of society. We know this is the case about the arts, for instance. But we have given scant attention to law in these terms. The reason is that law's history is unglamorous. For the most part, law changes its practice and principles by gradual adaptation. Though new laws may be made, the law is slow to change. That is one of its reliable virtues. Even so, the kind of change that subtly makes its presence in the law may mirror changes in awareness or of conduct in that larger world in which the law takes up its nest. Thus, history of labor law in the United States reveals developing notions in American thought about rights, ownership, dignity, organization, force, health, and protection. You could not write the history of such law without dealing at every moment with the general history of the country. Nor should we attempt to write the history of law in this field. The law and the social process go hand in hand. The cultural historian will be tempted to overlook the law as merely a consequence of the prevailing thought and power of the times; in other words, the law as another product of society. Yet the law is often a creatively shaping power in society. Law originates, judges, and enforces. Even it its small steps that spread as a fine netting, the law can restrain the movement of society and guide it in fresh directions. The law has consequences. Why, it governs.

In times of crisis the law faces history directly. The society turns to the law for the resolution of its controversies which it is not above to settle by other means. The law is the battleground, nonviolent and discursive, where the great conflicts of the times are fought. Abortion, capital punishment, euthanasia, the right to die, the right to life are life and death issues bristing with polemics that elude consensus and that are thrown into the lap of the law. Turning to the law may well be the first step taken in movements about these issues so that the cutting edge of social controversy takes a legal point.

What an admirable sight is a society arming itself for its internal conflicts with the law. At one moment the law is an instrument in the hands of partisan groups. At the next moment the law disarms some party by its bright disclosure of principle or its stern decisive ruling. The law itself falls under attack in these controversies as partisan, ignorant, or inept. The effort to change the law then occurs alongside the effective change in social existence by the law. Here the historian reaches a moving insight about the creative nature of law in the affairs of human beings: we do not get along well with one another. Law is our mutual appeal to resolve disputes by means of principle, process, and institution. We couldn't live together without law. It is a medium of our common existence, the mortar of our social edifice. Even with law we have a hard time living together. But we do better with it than without it.

II

The law rarely offers a simple solution to disputed values. The vary divergence of values initially at stake is related to the diversity of ways of getting the law to respond. The conflict thereby continues, though in a more orderly fashion. The law is equipped to handle dispute. What passes for law also becomes a matter of dispute. The solutions offered add to the problem. Consider the complexity of the American legal system's attempt to deal justly with racial discrimination and its consequences. The history of the law's involvement with this, America's quintessential problem, is a poignant tale of compromise, insight, innovation, delay and backsliding. The Constitution, as fundamental law of the land, recognized slavery yet put a future cap on the slave trade. Slavery was a right that states might recognize. The Dred Scott decision of the Supreme Court too nicely came down on the side of the owner of a slave, though the slave had made it to a free state. But law and political compromise could not prevent the final facing off between slave states and free states. The victory of the Union in the Civil War was followed by amendment to the Constitution, outlawing slavery.

The American struggle over slavery was transformed into a struggle over segregation. The Supreme Court's 1954 decision in *Brown v. Broad of Education* struck down legalized segregation of blacks and whites, but its aftermath was continued struggle over discrimination. The most recent controversy in society and in law on the racial issue centers around reverse discrimination, tokenism, quotas, affirmative action programs, and other forms of remediation for disadvantagement.

At each epoch of these twisting struggles the law is pushed forward to do the job of settling our problems; at each point the law is pushed back as constituting an obstacle to our advance. Law is the continuing dialogue that we are moved to amid the frequent shouting and the occasional shooting. The historian may teach students how our social problems in turn become clarified, intensified, and overcome by the workings of law. Law will be seen then as close to the core of the interactive process of social advance. While the law is a formalizing helper and an instrument for action, rarely does the law by itself solve our burning controversies. We resort to other resources of being human together.

Love may have to be called in where law is not enough. The lawyer, Mohandas K. Gandhi, discovered this in South Africa.

Yet our problems still may go unresolved. Abortion, for instance, appeared to have been settled as a national issue by a decision of the Supreme Court. But the Court's position will likely be modified as it considers new cases, responds to a new climate of dissatisfaction in the land, and undergoes a change of its membership. Appointment of new members, screened on abortion by the President and Congress, may shift the law. More directly, Congress may pass new laws that bypass the judicial restrictions. Stalemated at the federal level, the whole matter may be thrown back to the states. Abortion meanwhile can be a decisive election issue for state and federal legislators. Law enforcement officials go easy on supposed crimes of abortion, or they may stage public crackdowns. Civil disobedience has been employed on both sides of the conflict: against legalized abortion and against illegalization of abortion. Medical practitioners also may refuse to adhere strictly to the law. People may take the law into their own hands, letting conscience be their guide. Meanwhile religion insists on getting into the act, and a constitutional amendment is just around the corner. In sum, don't look in the law for all this to be resolved, because the law itself is being reshaped by the disagreements. Law is entangled in the problematics of our social existence. It makes itself available to the liberal arts for study as a powerful manifestation of our problem-driven life together.

While law contributes to historical understanding and to history, it has its own history. The history of law is neglected in law schools. More is at stake in the historical approach to law than the tracking of precedents. That kind of intellectual effort gathers what is pertinent to the case at hand from the past; it is part of the current practice. We may also look at law's past independently of applying it to our cases. In that case we may come to appreciate the development of legal notions, structures, and vocabulary.

The social context of law needs to be grasped as we appreciate law's identity at any epoch. History of law like history of science may entertain us with its richness of imagination and creativity. We may see how law reflects a cultural worldview, as, say, that of the Romans. We learn the valuable lesson that law, even when pronounced to be eternal and universal, has changed and continues to vary from place to place. These are the broad possibilities of human organization and interaction. The law's past is filled with mistakes and dead-ends, notable in its neglect of the humanity of women. We learn from these as well as its highpoints.

III

History has brought us to the cultural role of law. Different systems of law operate in different societies and cultures. The American law school concentrates on turning out practitioners for the American system. The rest of the world they lump together in the single course on Comparative Law. The emphasis may be on how to translate from one system to another so that the Americans can get ahead when crossing over into other systems. Our liberal arts curriculum in law will put aside the practical emphasis and the enthnocentric focus for a broader appreciation of cultures as illustrated by the role they reserve for law. Islamic law, for instance, draws no line between the secular and the religious. While strengthening that line has been a worthy success of systems of law in the West, for Islam the highest achievement is to make all of daily life holy. The Koran is the guide to law in society as well guiding the community of believers under God.

Soviet Law, oddly enough, approximates Islam in its insistence on communal governance over matters of daily life. While the Soviet system is its heyday was avowedly atheistic and had no place for religion, legal practice was meant to correct those who strayed from the path of communist faith. Law in such a cultural context has therapeutic value. Show trials make sense as public acknowledgement of guilt. The society is to be healed by such drama as is the contrite perpetrator of social injustice.

In Islam the lawbreaker is not just breaking the law; also violated is the pious life that binds us all. In the Soviet Union the lawbreaker was not just breaking the law; also violated was the solidarity with those engaged in the inevitable triumph of the world revolution. Both Islam and Marxism call for sacrifice and absolute obedience at the present time in the light of what is yet to come: a Day of Judgment when the world withers away, or a world of unity when states wither away. Marxism and Islam as social-political systems needs much critical understanding from insiders as well as outsiders in the last years of this century. The critique of communism is beginning to take on full steam by the insiders; Islam's self-critique lies ahead. Study of how such cultures treat law will help understand and critique.

Comparative Law, taught in the liberal arts as Law and Culture, would explore other systems, including the Napoleonic Code of Continental Europe (and of Quebec and Louisiana), and those traditional systems which operate in cultures once called primitive. Adding our lessons from the history of law, we will be treated to a global range of cultural visions of the place of law within human life. The two directions of understanding operate: we better grasp the diverse cultures of the world by studying their treatment of law, and we better understand the value of law by grasping its diverse functions in many cultures. Historian and cultural anthropologist join hands as liberal artists in expanding such understanding.

This argument for law among the liberal arts is a philosophic one, guided by notions of education, culture, values, human action, and organization. Philosophy is often characterized as a speculative pursuit removed from the cares of the world, whose successes are castles built on nothing more substantial than the air. Law, in contrast, is a profession engaged in day-to-day practice grounded firmly in the harsh facts of reality. Little exists in common between the arduous footwork of the legal practitioner and the armchair theorizing of the detached philosopher.

IV

Law attracts philosophers because it sits at the intersection of political theory and moral theory. If you start with a theory of polity sooner or later you will have to face the question of the operation of law within it. The foundation of a polity may itself be a kind of law: a constitution or social contract. A noble goal in political thinking is that government be of laws rather than of men and women. Government in that case is also governed by law. And if you begin with a theory of the moral life you will have to get on to law, as classic questions arise: Ought we to follow an immoral law? Does the moral law supersede the law of the land? The philosopher also finds many problems in law worth theorizing about that underlie issues in social philosophy: punishment, rights, obligations, coercion.

Regrettably, such philosophical concern with law has little place in law school, relegated, say, to, a non-required course in Jurisprudence. The practitioner of law doesn't want to be troubled by the deep questions philosophers ask about legal foundations and the relationship of law to politics, ethics, and society. Those grander vistas are for leisurely speculation and prolonged discussion, whereas would-be lawyers have to get on with the job. All the more reason for inclusion of such consideration in general education. Law is too important to our lives to leave it entirely to the practice of lawyers. Underlying their practice as well should be an informed sense of the larger realm in which law exists; state, society, and individuals are what at bottom count.

Philosophers enjoy the liberty of asking the probing questions that get to the unquestioned presuppositions. While the lawyer aims at resolution, successfully closing the case, the philosophical spirit moves in the other direction, opening further consideration of broader foundations, implications and alternatives. A philosopher-associate in a law office may not help the partnership win cases, but such a professional should increase everyone's appreciation of what they are doing -- of the value their work has to the world. I am waiting for my appointment as just such an associate.

The case we need to make to philosophers is for their learning from law for the better practice of philosophy. I recall the passionate arguments of Chaim Perelman at world congresses for philosophers to study such things as the traffic code. A body of law is instructive as a form of practical reasoning. It usually stands for a triumph of human beings in being reasonable in areas where they get into conflict. The law is won out of our difficulties, disagreements, and dangers. We may learn from this kind of reasoning as reasoning while we learn about ourselves as human beings.

We learn philosophically that law is *emergent*; it arises out of human interaction over a passage of time. Law thereby is anchored much more concretely than philosophy, for a philosophic theory may begin anywhere without empirical ties and push on anywhere for the sake of argument alone, without utility to human affairs. If law cannot enjoy that enormous freedom of philosophy, it captures the pungent presence of our embodiment as persons -- something with which philosophy needs more contact. Law is the extended record of answering human problems in practice by means of principles and procedures for the decent regulation of various forms of conduct with one another.

Philosophy envelopes all possibilities concerning reality and hypothetical values; law belongs to the lived reality and manifest values that people shape and share. The philosopher will find in close attention to the workings of the law features dear to the intellect, for law is not arbitrary or dogmatic, but it is corrigible and open to progress. Law is flexible enough to change where it is inadequate to the human situation or oppressive to human values. Recognizable advances in the practice and content of law, such as the outlawing of slavery, helped by philosophic understanding, show that law gets somewhere; it makes permanent contributions to humanity.

Not only does law regulate people, but it contributes to a person's due recognition of others as people. A law-abiding person is a responsible person. This means something other than blindly following the law whatever its justness. The responsible person is committed to the value of living by the law, under the rule of law, though that person my counteract particular laws that are unjust. Law must abide by a just treatment of persons, insists a law-abiding person. In the interplay between law and person, law is both a creation of people and an instrument for humanizing and civilizing, that is, for gently leading people to the responsible life appropriate to a social culture.

Another value in our study of law is that it brings the philosopher directly into contact with the unresolved problems of human interaction. Law is not simply the story of slow success; is also the recurring adventure of pressing crises. Law is in trouble because human beings are troubled. We make trouble for ourselves. Many kinds of solutions suggest themselves, but by their very presence they counteract one another. And problems solved make way for unresolved ones. Progress is not guaranteed. Regress always threatens. Look how the legal progress against capital punishments totters. The long sought and hard won achievements of law can be overthrown by extralegal action as well as from within law. What is at stake is everything, namely civilized life as the fabric of co-existence under the rule of law.

The sources of legal crises include the residual gap between existing laws and social justice, and the rapid outdistancing of law by new social situations and technological developments: the law is always behind. The excess of regulation may stifle creative initiative and only sustain bureaucracy, yet we may suffer from great neglect of legislative choice in making laws where they are needed: we have either too much or too little. Crisis arises from frontal attack on law and order as protective of the oppressors and enemy of the deprived, as well as from the backlash against law by those who have enjoyed privilege and prosperity and resent the demands of the unsuccessful: law is then unjust instrument of the others. More problems arise from the rivalry between law and the values in other important human activities, such as economics, politics, and education, and the exploitation of law by movements in every field in order to realize their values: all our problems are legal ones or else none of them are.

According to the popular view, the law is fixed while the particular case sets the problems for the lawyer. That case gets by or else is smashed on the rocks of the law. What really happens may be quite different, for the case may stand on some vast and immutable bedrock of human right which shatters the particular law when brought down upon it. The law gets changed in being applied. The lawyer is engaged in two kinds of activity: working within a framework of laws taken as given, and working to reconstitute or at least revise that framework. The law is both system and process. In this give and take, this openness and commitment, we have room for preservation of the valuable and for its innovation.

The philosopher sees that law continues to be a living reality of problems, not just a record of solutions. In the language of philosophy, law belongs not to being but to becoming. We too are more human becoming then human being. We may take a hand in what we are to become. We have to make law into what it ought to be to help us become who we must be. Insofar as philosophers see law as value process they witness the dynamism of humanity at work upon itself. And since help is needed in resolving crises, the philosopher only with great difficulty could resist getting into the act by speaking out on what should be done about matters of principle that make crises for law.

Law works out in practice issues that trouble the conduct of people by means of regulative principles: laws an legal procedures. Whenever philosophers turn their attention to a field of knowledge or practice, whether it be physics or politics, they look for the principles that order the subject matter and the rules of procedures that direct the activity. How is it put together? On what is it based? How does it proceed? In answering these questions we expose the logic and grounding of the field under investigation.

Law is admirably suited for such analysis: it invites logical cross-examination and intellectual judgment. Laws can be codified and arranged in deductive hierarchy. Fundamental principles of law, such as a bill of rights or a national constitution, can be identified as axioms and postulates of the legal system. Second-order or 'metalegal' laws may exist as laws about laws, a kind of logical complexity philosophers are fond of exploring. Laws themselves are not propositions or knowledge claims; they are directives of one kind or another of actions. Such directives or regulatives are purposeful, though ultimate goals and initial values may be tacit. In sum, a legal system is an applied (and applicable) ethics that still bears the traces of a theoretical framework.

The code of law is not itself equivalent to an ethical theory; instead, it fills in a range of particulars that work consistently for one or more ethical theories. But a legal system differs from an ethical theory in others ways than merely extent of application and particularization. The law is silent on certain moral admonitions traditional to ethics, such as Do Good to Others, and even Do Good to Yourself. Law is more concerned with the effective prevention of harm done to others. This is its number one value commitment. Punishment of those who do harm may be derived as corollary of this protective value if punishment deters. While law comes into play where sources of conflict in human interaction abound, unlegislated and unregulated fields of activity exist where law has not yet been needed. Ethics has a more positive manifest concern with the best values for leading your life. Law aims at protection; ethics aims at fulfillment.

Another side to law is often overlooked by those who draw the sharp line between law and ethics: the facilitative regulation, such as mandatory primary education, which makes opportunities available for human fulfillment. We might argue this is corollary to the protective value of law, for none should suffer from not having decent opportunity for their full human development. Yet we are sometimes told that law should not be used to solve social problems. But law is so used and sometimes should be. It is time for us to publicly recognize that primarily by law rather than by voluntary activity will people find available the means to develop their fuller humanity. Granted, we have to proceed carefully with the facilitative power of law. While we are told, 'You can't legislate morality,' we might legislate morally so that people will have a better chance at valuable lives. The facilitative and protective values of law need to be discussed together. Consider the debate on legality of public-funded abortions. Is striking down the law a protective mearue on behalf of the embryo, while supporting the law is a facilitative measure on behalf of the woman's dignity?

The philosopher moves two ways with law and theory, seeing how a kind of ethical theory can be applied protectively and facilitatively in law, and how law can be traced back through its internal system to theoretic and value commitments. While travelling back and forth in these directions, the philosopher is in a position to help out by pointing to inconsistencies or gaps in the system, by asking for clarifications of axioms or values, and by going into areas in which applications are yet to be made. We can have two-way traffic between philosophy and law.

A legal system is similar though not equivalent to an ethical theory. Other similarities abound between the kinds of reasoning that go in philosophy and in law. A thorough exercise in the forms of legal reasoning ought to strengthen the intellectual repertory of any thinking person. Legal training does involve the practice of inference and the evaluation of evidence. Similarly, philosophers have been concerned in their field with the criteria for inference and with problems of empirical judgment, including the status of causal connectives. The case method in law in which a particular case is broken down into its constituent general characteristics which can then be referred to previous procedures and subsumed under pertinent rulings, should remind philosophers of some valuable Scholastic techniques of reasoning.

The training law students will undergo in adversary procedures is similar to the philosopher's preparation in the skills of dialectic. In each field the student must recognize that the argument proffered can be joined by opposed arguments, and our responsibility extends to effective treatment of those arguments. Effective treatment means speaking to the issues in dispute, not performing courtroom tricks or sophistry. Philosophers and law students each can become more skillful practitioners in their field by becoming more appreciative of the nuance of practice encountered in the other field. Philosophy and law share a value placed on the responsible conduct of intellectual method which aims at resolution of problems but remains fair to others who have a say in the matter and join in reasoning.

The philosopher learns not only from the substance and method of law but also from its limits and connections with other fields. Law, I am obliged to announce, is not everything. Neither is philosophy. Some might jest that philosophy is not anything. But among the many things that philosophy can be is the comprehensive integration of the various fields of knowledge, value, and activity. It may join together, place side by side, or point out the differences between law and, say, political science, sociology, and economics. These fields interact, often they assume one another, sometimes they struggle among themselves for predominance.

Law as a living practice is not confined to statute books and the processing of legal papers. It deals with people and is shaped by them; this is its sociological dimension. Law also operates within a framework of political institutions, yet law helps to construct or adjust that framework. What makes law especially attractive as a profession nowadays is its opening out toward the people-dimension. Note how hopefully law is being enlisted in America in the movement for the rights of ethnic minorities and the majority sex.

Law, finally, revolves around justice. Philosophy has a notable concern with justice, evident in Plato's masterpiece *The Republic*. And citizens of a society governed by law have a stake in justice. By bringing law and philosophy together in the general education of our citizenry we may not only better understand justice but aid its implementation.

Law and literary study have much to offer each other. Exciting work by literary scholars has been focussed on the law as a kind of literature, structured about narrative, character, and speech acts.[2] The literature course now has room for legal materials as a genre of writing subject to recognizable canons of form and style. Heretofore the mystery of law was wrapped in obscurity of language and strangeness of formulae. Theories of communication, language, and interpretation can make such materials more accessible and more interesting to the general reader. Moreover, some legal materials, such as the dissents and opinions of Justice Holmes, are so elegantly composed they make good reading as intellectual literature. In the basic English reading course scientific and political texts are often introduced for study as modes of writing students will encounter as generally educated persons. Legal texts should be introduced at this level for the same reason. General students as well as future lawyers should be sensitized to the law as text-centered. Everything under law comes out a text sooner or later.

V

Far more enjoyable reading is the portrayal of law in imaginative and dramatic literature. Literature as a fine art has the power of making felt the reality which theory only couches in abstract terms. Literature draws us in such that our reality becomes engaged. Literature makes especially moving the broken edges of the law, the paradoxes, ironies, and tragedies: not just the great conflicts but the great unresolvable conflicts, the poignant, pressing dilemmas of being human.

The *Antigone* of Sophocles is an astonishing achievement of world literature in which people are crushed by the entanglements of law whichever way they turn. Antigone would rather die in respecting filial ties and religious rites than adhere to the letter of the state's law. Creon, the new ruler, would rather put Antigone -- his niece and future daughter-in-law -- to death in conformity with his decrees than give in to family members. His son, Haemon, having infuriated his father, would rather die with his betrothed than be an obedient son and citizen. Eurydice would rather kill herself over the loss of her son than live with a cruel husband, Creon. And the brothers Eteocles and Polynices, who started the crises of this play, preferred killing one another to working out their differences in alternate rulership of the state. They are all damned.

The powerful arguments by Antigone for obedience to a law higher than the state are all the more gripping because of her political helplessness, a mere young woman. Yet she is as fearless, resolute, and vigorous as any fighter for justice. Antigone is an awesome character -- and not just in the eyes of Creon. She is terrifying in her honesty. Her civil disobedience at the risk of death astonishes us all. We are frightened by her because of an excess that runs in the family. It is as if she embraces death above all and fits her disobedience to it as a sure instrument. Champion of upholding one vision of law, Antigone talks herself into becoming the fatal victim of law in another sense. Creon too gives in to excess, sticking stubbornly to his image as political authority, while not heeding the humane calls of family. He is to lose family and lose face as ruler.

Antigone has been an inspirer in other times and places. Thus, Jean Anouilh's version could find a place on the French stage during the German Occupation as ostensibly a classical piece, though it skillfully reminded its French audience of the bitter conflict between individual conscience and the power of the state. Some twenty years later, under other conditions of unrest in France, I saw a performance of Anouilh's play in modern-dress: trenchcoats. What a chilling evocation of oppression that was. I can still hear the echo of the gruff guard,

"Non, chef, . . . Oui chef," in response to the sinister orders by the boss of the state.

The Medea plays by Euripides and Seneca are another pair of terrific dramas that turn on matters of law and portray an equally unforgettable embodiment of womanhood. I have asked my students to perform readers' versions of the great argumentative scenes involving Antigone or Medea with the proviso that they may suspend the action and engage in further argument. The rest of the class is empowered as audience, chorus, or counselor to the characters, urging further reasoning on all sides. While leaving the original works of drama momentarily, the students give full life to the drama of the human conflicts. Medea was a monster, violating the most sacred law of nature by killing her two children, some protest, while others denounce Jason -- that opportunist who would fleece anyone in sight -- for his summary divorce of Medea.

Melville's *Billy Budd* is terrifying in its calm observation and smooth perfection as story. the mastery of form stands in painful contrast to the story it tells. Foretopman Billy is condemned to death for striking a fatal blow to the Master at Arms. It is as simple as that considered under the law. Yet our hero Billy suffers from a speech impediment; when unfairly accused by the bad-intentioned Claggart he struck out at the accuse! 'I did not mean to kill him. Could I have used my tongue I would not have struck him. But he foully lied to my face, and in the presence of my Captain, and I had to say something, and I could only say it with a blow. God help me!' Too bad. What has the goodness of the one man or the badness of the other to do with the exercise of justice? Captain Vere sees to it that justice is done blindly. Even Billy, with the rope around his neck, finds his voice to bless the just captain.

We are troubled no end by this work. It gives us no satisfaction concerning the lingering problem. Something has gone wrong with law if Billy has been hung, yet something is argued to be going right with law if it brings about this result though it means the death of so fine a person. Melville gets out of the story as its documenter. Billy is hoisted right out of it. Even the articulate, kind, and just Captain Vere passes on. The damn story sticks with us. We are left hanging.

Dostoyevski's *Crime and Punishment* is a superb work for undergraduates because it features a poor student who justifies murder to get ahead. Dostoyevski has probed the murderousness that lurks in all our hearts. The intricate untwisting of Raskolnikov's soul by the skilled inspector is a wonderful self-examination for us. Scarcely a day has passed in which I have not contemplated some serious crime; Dostoyevski knew that about me -- and perhaps about you. The novel is a valuable experience in the psychology of guilt and crime.

Malamud's *Fixer* is another remarkable case study of the soul caught in the machinations of the law, but this time it is the victim of laws miscarriage that we follow in his resolute unbending dignity. A genre exists of prison literature, fictional as well as factual, whose contributors, including Plato, Boethius, Cellini, Defoe, Dostoyevski, Dickens, Gorki and Wilde, provide the student of comparative literature with abundant riches for thematic comparison.

Cinema may be even more powerful than the novel in giving us the full experienced sense of other people's suffering. The great art form of our time, cinema offers a wealth of enjoyment to study of law. *Twelve Angry Men* is a classic of the juryroom, that sacrosanct chamber where we are judged by our peers. Henry Fonda does his level-headed best to keep the accused from being convicted while subject to a reasonable doubt. The drama has been displaced from street and courtroom to jury chamber.

Jimmy Stewart in *Anatomy of a Murder* shows that good old-fashioned, small-town, hard-working American spirit that wins the case, although we are obliged to wonder if -- gee whiz -- he has just allowed a murderer to get off the hook.

Paul Newman in *The Verdict* cleans up his act in time to fight the big institutions of hospitals and law firms on behalf of the victimized. He wins his case almost singlehandedly against the powerful legal maneuvering of James Mason. Justice is so sweet that Paul throws aside the whisky bottle and hangs up on the woman -- also a lawyer -- who twisted the rules of love and law.

I have spoken of the stars of law films as the heros, for that is the way we experience film. We do not lose sight that Paul Newman or Jimmy Stewart are present, embodied in their performance. They loom up larger than their roles. We forget the names of their characters. The films are designed that way and played for that effect. Consequently, we retain strong images of law's heroic personifications. Paul Muni as fugitive from a southern chain gang, Jimmy Stewart as Mr. Smith going to Washington to be senator, Sidney Poitier as urbane law enforcement officer displaced in the South fix our cultural vision of heroism in law. We also need new images and interpretations; especially desirable are women as heroes who shape law.

The prison film, the crime film, the detective film, the courtroom film are overlapping genres. They illustrate enriching artistic values, changing social values, and perduring legal problems.

While serious study of cinema has made its place into the liberal arts, television remains on the outside, a popular entertainment rather than a serious art form. But we live in a video culture, and we ought to examine it carefully. From Perry Mason and Rumpole of the Bailey to *Paper Chase* and *L.A. Law* television has an ongoing attachment to legal drama that gets into the behind-the-scenes excitement of the criminal justice process. Such popular entertainment may have considerable artistry. Often our subject of conversation upon greeting is last's night's show. Video experience is with us -- especially with our students -- in an unquestioned way. Much of their experience, including real events, comes through video. Our liberal arts course should get students to self-consciously question the myths and images of law shaped for them by video experience.

VI

The visual and architectural dimensions of law may be studied along with their literary manifestations. I take my students on field trips to see law in action in the buildings specifically designed for it. My campus is near the county seat in Media, Pennsylvania, which is graced by an old-fashioned, all-purpose court house. It is one thing to read about legal procedures, and quite another to approach this building, crowning the square at the center of town, lined with impressive lawns. We are awed by the law before we get inside.

Inside we experience the architectural planning for access, safety, and dignity. The courtroom impresses everyone. It is meant to do that. We observe the placement of the bench, the wood paneling, the symbols -- flags, justice blindfolded, county seal, murals -- all the reserved entrances. To the architecture and iconography of law we must add its costuming and planned movement. The judge enters in robes through a private door, the public stands, the judge takes a seated place above the heads of the others in the room. The attorneys also have their distinctive dress, their characteristic gestures, and their significant movement in space. Later we will meet with the judge in chambers, and then with the attorneys in the cafeteria. The visit is a reminder that law is no mere shuffling of papers but involves live people engaged in activity. The symbolic manifestation of much of the activity is not superficial; in a deeper sense law is semiotic ritual.

As we leave the court house a parking ticket is invariably found on the windshield of one of the student cars.

Another building we visit is the county prison. Before we go, most of the class, like most Americans, I suppose, favors capital punishment. Indeed, their sentiment is for throwing the key away for most criminals. Once we get to prison and are locked in ourselves we find the criminals are much like us. They could well be other students. The difference is that they made a big mistake and got themselves into trouble. They are eager to meet the students and talk with them about life and jobs and hopes. The prisoners envy the students who until this day may have felt no special value in their life as students.

We have read theories about punishment and experienced films and novels that portray the criminal mind, but here we are in jail with real people. We study the arrangements, for a prison is much more than cells. Facilities must be designed for health, nutrition, education, recreation, counseling, family visits, and other supportive services. In the arrangements of any prison we detect many of a society's values.

When the bars are opened, the door unlocked, and we are allowed to pass beyond the gates, we breathe the air of freedom. The popularity of capital punishment goes down fifty percent for the remainder of the term.

The range of these approaches to law is meant to bring it within our experience in its multi-dimensional presence in human culture. The liberal arts are the skills to be practiced throughout a lifetime by persons who would develop their humanity to the fullest. Law is part and parcel of our humanity. Every educated person ought to have a well-rounded critical familiarity with the law, for each of us is a person living under law and a co-creator of it. Understanding the imaginative power of law, the historical significance of law, the nature of legal reasoning, and the myths and images of law should be integral to general education. The law is a cultural achievement, human-shaped, in service to people, and immersed in our values. It should not remain a technical field reserved for the specialists or understood as apart from human life.

ENDNOTES

1. Robert Ginsberg is Professor of Philosophy at Penn State.

2. See my case for "The Law as Literature," forthcoming in a volume edited by Yeager Hudson and Creighton Peden for the series sponsored by the North American Society for Social Philosophy, "Social Philosophy Today", Edwin Mellen Press.

Chapter 7

Law, Forms of Life, and Metaphysical Metaphors

Michael Green[1]

I

The last one hundred years have seen an explosion of knowledge in anthropology and linguistics. One of the most important discoveries was that cultural objects exhibit specific, identifiable styles. As in music one can identify themes and variations, so in cultures one can do the same. A second important discovery was the unity of all the Indo-European languages. In this paper, I wish to speculate on the importance of these discoveries for an understanding of philosophy and philosophical approaches to law.

Dumezil found that the parthenons of Indo-European gods and goddesses from diverse Indo-European cultures had similar structures. These were divided into three groups. (Table I) The first group consisted of a pair of gods. These all developed different variations on the notion of sovereignty. One of the gods was a giver of laws and of the legitimate powers to uphold these laws. These were gods of judicial sovereignty. The other exhibited a development of the concept of magical sovereignty. He worked in conjunction with the previous god to bind those who would violate the established laws. For example, in India these two are represented by Mitra and Varuna. The word 'Mitra' is formed from a root that means 'to exchange regularly, peacefully, amicably.'[2] It is a deified social relation and not a natural phenomenon. Mitra is the sovereign of law and is responsible, through his laws, for the whole order of the universe. Varuna on the other hand is armed with knots and strings with which he seizes those who transgress the order of the universe.

These two gods of sovereignty, who were the primary concern of priests, were distinguished from two other groups of deities. The second function was occupied by a warrior god. This god had great agility and strength. He represented the offensive triumph over resistance and was essentially active in war. He granted victory to some and defeat to others. He possessed an ultimate weapon that allowed him to petrify his adversary so as to gain immediate victory from a distance. His realm was that of physical force, and he operated by means of lightning. From his perspective, the world was full of conflict and strife -- force and resistance. In India, this function was filled by Indra who, armed with his *vajra* (thunderbolt), fought the monsters that threatened his culture. He was, though, an unruly god and not firmly and always under control by the sovereign function. Thus at times he could turn against his own people. The sovereign function and the warrior function were also distinguished from a third function, usually consisting of goddesses, who presided over fertility and prosperity. These presided over the growth and development of plants and animals and had as their special providence the activities of farmers and herders. This, coupled with the linguistic work of Benveniste, has shown that Western culture sprang from a patrilineal social structure that recognized three basic functions: the production of economic assets by cultivators or herdsmen, the protection and/or expansion of the group by warriors, and the maintenance of sacred rites and rituals by priests. These various forms of life within the Proto-Indo-European culture provided themes that were developed in different directions by different Indo-European societies at different times.[3] Each mode of social action represented by each of the above three functions has its own distinctive patterns of conceptualization and basic metaphors in terms of which it organizes its conception of the world. Each provides the basis for a distinctive philosophical tradition.

Anyone who did not fit into one of these three functions was not a member of Indo-European civilization. Slaves, serfs and usually women were excluded from membership. However, from the fact that a group was excluded from the official social order, it didn't follow that it was prevented from formulating its own mode of social organization independently of the established order. Lewis, in his conception of ecstatic religions, and Wallace, in his conception of revitalization movements, have argued that individuals who have the least ability to modify their own lives within a given social context tend to resort to ecstatic states.[4] Within socially marginal individuals such states constitute a means of protest by politically impotent individuals. In some societies they constitute ritualized rebellions that arise at times of tension and conflict between superiors and inferiors and serve as a vehicle for manipulating and moderating the activities of those with power. In what Lewis calls main morality possession religions, there is constant use of such ecstatic states by individuals in order to strengthen and legitimize their authority. Such religions tend to arise within cultures subject to constantly recurring social and environmental pressures that militate against the formation of large, secure groups. In simple societies, for example the Eskimo, the shaman uses ecstatic states to act as an arbiter of social conflicts under conditions in which there are no other political control mechanisms. In the same vein, messianic religions arise with acute social disruption as religions of the oppressed.

If a philosophical system is grounded in a specific form of social practice and if each of the above four functions has its own distinctive social practice, then it should be possible to discover within Western civilization four main traditions of thought. I call these four traditions; scepters, swords, seeds, and spirits. The first develops variations upon the sovereignty theme. It conceives of the world and of society in terms of laws and hierarchical organization with metaphors draw from social relations of inferiors and superiors in which each has his or her allotted place. The second conceives of the world and society in terms of strife and struggle, as force and resistance with metaphors drawn from war. The third, the seed, conceives of the world and of society in terms of growth and development with metaphors drawn from agriculture. Finally, the fourth thinks in terms of transcending the given social order to directly participate in a source of truth and a type of reality that will legitimize its challenges to the existing order. Metaphors of possession and intoxication (conceived of as enrapture and possession) are central. Our task now is to articulate the social relations underlying these metaphors more clearly and then to trace their development into philosophical modes of thought about law.

II

Swords and Sovereigns: Law as Force

What is the form of life of a society in which the warrior gains ascendency? This happens when this function is able to break loose from its traditional role as subordinate to the priest and before it has become solidified into a feudal hierarchy. Usually a culture existing under these conditions is in a great state of flux and instability as war is continuous and total. In epics, such as the *Illiad* or *The Song of Roland,* one can acquire a glimpse of the warrior's form of life. The basic social unit in times of war was the band of young warriors serving a well-known leader.[5] The root of kingship within this form of life arose from the leader's distribution of the spoils of war after a raid. His power and influence was also dependent upon the number and power of his kin.[6] In Anglo Saxon, the lord was a food giver, i.e., one who shares the loaf. The leader had to engage in constant war in order to bring in enough booty to be able to feed his followers and provide them with gifts appropriate to their standing.[7] Gain and glory were the main motives of war for these individuals. Universalized into a metaphysics, the world was a battle camp full of never-ending struggle and strife as strength and counter-strength met to prove which was the better. The *Illiad* portrays the world as one of violence, conflict and struggle -- an endless oscillation in which the forces with the greatest power of the moment gain ascendency but are soon replaced by even greater ones. The basic juridical relationship was the trial by ordeal. Battles were essentially trials of strength, ordeals, in which an individual must prove himself better than his opponent. Thus, when Paris and Menelaos meet to fight, it is agreed that 'whichever proves the better man shall take both wealth and women home with him'.[8] By winning, one thereby proved himself to be the better man. Since strength is the usual prerequisite for victory, the best man was the strongest. Indeed, the 'best man' was equivalent to the 'best fighting man' so that the first and foremost in battle was the best. Each man had a certain virtue measured by his strength. Thus, to prove that he was more virtuous than another, he had to show that he was stronger than that other individual. Trials of strength were designed as such proofs. Whoever emerged victorious had shown himself to be more virtuous. Right was on his side. Victorious might was a proof of right. One finds a development of this view in Hobbes and, implicitly, in many legal positivists. Thus, I think it is true that behind the positivistic account of law is 'the visible shadow of a deeper reality: the determinate causal order.'[9]

Hobbes was well-versed in the classics.[10] He translated the *Illiad,* the *Odyssey* and Thucydides' *The Peloponnesian Wars*. According to him, forces and counterforces acted and reacted to give rise to the world as we know it. The world is a battle between opposing forces for supremacy and control. He attempts to give an account of law in terms of force. Individuals are locked in struggles for gain and glory. One can triumph only by having more power than another. However, because individuals are equal (an assumption probably made more plausible by the invention of firearms) none is ever able to fully gain ascendency. Instead, there arises a war of all against all in which life is 'nasty, brutish and short.' The only way to end this war is to establish a power that is stronger than any other individual or combinations of individuals and hence can keep the war within certain acceptable bounds. Thus, the individuals negotiate a truce and establish laws and an sovereign with a monopoly on force to maintain it. Each agrees to leave the other alone if that other in turn will leave him alone. Laws originate in the will of a sovereign and are imposed on a resistant medium, his subjects. They are threats, commands or decisions backed by force. As Hobbes asks:

> 'What man that has his natural senses . . . beleeves the Law can hurt him; that is, Words, and Paper, without the Hands, and Swords of men?'[11]
>
> Covenants without the Sword are but Words.[12]

and

> 'The sword of war is in the same hand, in which is the sword of justice.'[13]

In a world of mere force, laws -- indeed any values -- must themselves be forces if they are to have any effectiveness and hence reality. What is of utmost importance is that there be a civil authority strong enough to enforce its laws. The civil law affects our conduct by inducing in us the proper appetites and aversions. The most important such aversion is the fear that arises from the threat of punishment. This engenders an aversion to the prohibited modes of conduct and leads to conformity to the law. Legal obligation arises from the sovereign's threat to use his monopoly of force. The authority of law rests entirely on the sovereign's ability and will to harm those who disobey.[14] In a trial by ordeal between a subject and a sovereign, the sovereign is destined to win and thus there is no point in challenging his might. It is only under such conditions that individuals can coexist with a modicum of order.

III
The Scepter and the Sacred: Law as Kosmos

The Indo-Europeans for long periods of time were warriors and nomadic herdsmen -- children of the mist born of fire and ice who swept across the land subduing all in sight. When they set themselves up as rulers over conquored individuals, they established a hierarchically organized society with warriors and priests set over farmers and laborers. These invaders extended the shepherd-sheep metaphor to human relations. The rulers were the shepherds, who, through their loyal and obedient dogs (warriors), kept the flock from straying and protected it from wolves. Within this framework, each had a different station -- shepherds weren't sheep, nor were sheep shepherds. Each station had its own appropriate duties. The sheep were to provide clothing and food for the shepherd. The dogs were to be obedient to their superiors, refrain from preying on the sheep, and chase away wolves. The shepherd was to look out after the welfare of the flock so that it would prosper. Authority was exercised from the top down, and all were expected to be obedient to this authority. The scepter was the symbol of the shepherd's authority to exercise power over his sheep. Among the Greeks, the kings were called, scepter bearers. The word for scepter (*skeptron*) was derived from the word meaning 'to lean with all one's weight on something which gives support,'[15] as the shepherd does his staff. Thus, it is something that gives support to what one does and lends authority to one's actions. The scepter brought from Zeus to earth by a messenger and handed down from ruler to ruler was a symbol of that individual's authority to rule.[16] It symbolized order, control, law, authority and the demand for obedience. Among the early Romans, law arose from the rituals in accordance with which a specialized body of priests working with fixed texts and formulas pronounced authoritative decisions upon whether something did or did not conform to a given rule and thus could or could not be approved for performance.[17] Made into a metaphysics, each being in the universe had its own proper domain and privileges in a hierarchy of functions, ranks, honours, prerogratives and powers. Ultimately God commanded and forbade in a fixed and static order in which stability, continuity and regularity were the predominant characteristics. The universe was a Kosmos--a natural normative order. God delineated the hierarchy that had to be respected so that each individual could be kept forever within the limits of his own domain. Under his rule, the universe achieved stability and permanence. He established a just distribution of functions and privileges. The natural law tradition arose from this way of looking at the world. This view finds a clear development with Aquinas. The metaphors he uses to explicate the relation of God to his creatures involves hierarchical subordination. As Chief Governor, God is like a king commanding his administrators,[18] a chief craftsman disposing of the work of under-craftsmen,[19] and a commander arranging his troops.[20]

According to Aquinas, a law is an ordinance of reason, directed to the common good, made by one who is entrusted with the care of the community, and promulgated to his subjects.[21] The subjects owe their superior respect, honor, and obedience, or fidelity, reverence and service,[22] while the superior owes his inferiors influence and care.[23] The inferior should be well-subordinated to that by which it is regulated so that it can be led to the good.[24] The supreme measure of law is given by Eternal law, which in an ordinance of God's reason, directed toward the good of the whole universe and written into the very nature of each thing. It is from this that each thing derives the inclinations it has to its proper acts and ends. Natural law is that part of Eternal law which is implanted within rational creatures. It is innate, known by all, and constitutes the immanent ruling reason within each individual. Each individual has a natural inclination toward that which Eternal law decrees. These principles can never be completely erased from a person's heart.[25] From this is derived *synderesis*, the habitual knowledge of the first principles of conduct. The first principle is, obey God. He makes each thing in such a manner that it desires the good by natural tendency. One should not oppose this tendency, and, thus, should do good and avoid evil. Now, it follows from this that one should not oppose the specific tendencies toward continuing his existence, reproducing, caring for offspring, living in society, and knowing God that He has implanted in all rational beings as part of their nature.[26] The particular positive law of a community is derived from Natural Law in one of two ways. In one way, such as with criminal law, positive law can be related to Natural Law as a conclusion to premises. In another, such as with punishment, it arises as a determination or specification of it. A just law is in conformity with nature and reason and is binding on conscience. An unjust law is no law and doesn't bind. However, this is not a radical as it seems, since it is the responsibility of the ruler who has care for the community and not so much the subjects to determine whether a law is nor is not just.

The moral virtues derived from Natural Law are subordinate to the theological virtues of faith, hope, and charity, which are known by the Divine Law revealed in the Old and New Testaments. These are infused as God's free gift into the soul by the Holy Ghost. As such, they transcend reason and are superadded to an individual so as to incline him toward the good. They heal the soul from the illness of original sin, move free choice toward the good, bind and guard against temptations, preserve the good, and lead to glory (the beatific vision). Through belief in Christ and the Sacraments, an individual is led to grace. God punished us with original sin, so the passions (inferiors) are not necessarily obedient to reason (the superior). Then, He provided us with grace so that this 'illness' could be overcome. He also provided us with the state as a corrective to original sin. Since all were corrupted by original sin, the state and its laws were set up to maintain by force and coercion sufficient order to minimize the harms that sinful individuals would otherwise inflict on one another. Laws are part of God's design for maintaining order and punishing the wicked.

IV

Seeds and Self-Organization: Law as Process

The farmers and herders could develop their mode of life only when they have freed themselves to some extent from the other two functions. A glimpse of this type of social organization can be obtained from the work done on village communities such as that done by Bacon on the Hazara Mongols.[27] The basic unit is the extended patrilineal family group. The head of the household typically obtains the approval of the family members before disposing of any property or borrowing any money. All members of the family are interdependent. Individuals in need, such as orphans, the disabled, the elderly, or the sick, are provided with food and shelter.[28] A village can have a formal or an informal organization. Some villages do not seem to recognize the position of chief or headman.

Whereas others have a chief who is assisted by the heads of the respected families in the village. In some villages, these positions can be hereditary.[29] Whenever there is a problem, the leaders discuss it among themselves and with the other villagers. As Bacon states, 'any decision made followed the consensus of the village.'[30] Barth speaks of a similar arrangement among another group of nomadic individuals. The chief lacks the means to enforce a unilateral decision. Thus, he must attain unanimity every day as to whether the group should stay or go. Thus, large amounts of time are spent in discussion.[31] Individuals have a sense of mutual responsibility and dependency. Such relationships are typical of organic organizations. These are complex and dynamic systems in which there is reciprocal interaction and mutual adjustment among the parts based on high information processing. Centralization, standardization, stratification, differentiation and hierarchy are low.[32]

In agriculture, the growth of the wild plants into domesticated cereals depended upon human activity, while humans in turn came to depend upon the fruition of these seeds for the sustenance they needed in order to engage in the very activities of nurturing and caring for these crops. By a process of development and transformation, mutual interdependence was developed, sustained, and affirmed among originally distinct entities. On this view, individuals become what they were only through their reciprocal interrelationships. There is a strong emphasis upon development from potentiality to actuality along possible pathways that had been opened up by previous development. Law is this process of self-organization undertaken by a community working toward discovering and implementing a social consensus. Historically, this approach was strongly developed by Machiavelli and Rousseau. Communities are like self-organizing organisms. They arise in certain contexts, continue in existence under certain conditions, and then perish when these conditions pass away. The common interests and values developed through continual interaction provide for continuity by maintaining the integrity and unity of the community during these changes. These values will tend to be embedded in appropriate social structures, which will tend to persevere and to reinforce this specific way of life. Education is very important for maintaining continuity. Citizenship arises among those who are considered equal in some significant respect and thus are able to participate in the important social, religious, and political activities of that community. Because communities have different origins, they have diverse laws and institutions. To properly understand any community, then one must start with its origin, for this sets the parameters of possibilities within which it can develop. Those that begin in servitude have very reduced possibilities for development. Those with a good beginning have a better chance of getting on the straight road. As circumstances change, so the principles, rules, and institutions should change. Since they were adapted to other circumstances, they will not work in the new ones. As an organism has a state of health, so does a community. For the later, health consists in the rule of law, while disease consists of the rule of either the few or the many without law. Law is the nerve and life blood of freedom.[33] The government is the minister of the collective by upholding the laws enacted by the common will. Mismatches between the laws and the minister who is to uphold them, 'produce revolutions which bring things back within the order of nature.'[34] Also the same laws are not appropriate to all stages of development of a group, just as not all forms of government are.[35] Laws are an expression of the general will, which is just the process of making, amending, and executing decisions based upon the reciprocal interactions among the members of the community. Sovereignty only lives as the citizens of a community meet in a free deliberation among equals. The legal process is the '*agon* within the *agora*.'[36] It is grounded in a strong participatory democracy that requires constant individual participation. Such arrangements give to each individual a permanent control of the political process and serves to develop responsible and autonomous individuals.[37] Such law comes from all, applies to all, equally affects all and serves the good of all.[38] Law as the democratic process is the 'perfectibility of society in progress.'[39] When the general will is active, all rush to the assembly, and, when a new law is to be passed, the one proposing it is only saying what all others have felt.[40] Rousseau's *Social Contract* relies implicitly upon the history of the Roman Republic to sketch the history of the rise and fall of the general will of a community. It arises from under the yoke of a foreign tyrant, constitutes itself in a vigorously democratic form of life, and then is overcome by the very instrument it established to enforce its decisions, the government.

V

Spirits and Slavery: Law as Oppression

During times of rapid social change or among marginal individuals, i.e., individuals excluded from the social structure, societies can undergo revitalization processes. Such processes are:

> deliberate, organized attempts by some members of a society to construct a more satisfying culture by rapid acceptance of a pattern of multiple innovations.[41]

For example, the Seneca Indians of New York suffered severe cultural dislocation under the impact of the Europeans. The terms in which the individuals defined themselves could no longer be maintained. The widespread use of alcohol arose, the accusations of witchcraft increased, and fighting among factions was unending. Anomie, alienation and disillusionment were widespread. However, Handsome

Lake, inspired by a revelation from God, led a revitalization movement that redirected the social organization, and within a few years moral chaos was replaced by communities of devout, sober and partly literate farmers.[42] As a social structure breaks down and individuals can no longer maintain a sense of worth and dignity within that social system, an individual or group can formulate a new, utopian image of society. Often, these codes are formulated as a result of a prophetic or mystical experience. The individual undergoes what Wallace calls a mazeway resynthesis in which after a period of extreme stress the person's whole complex of values and beliefs are swept aside and replaced by new ones. The existing culture is thought of as corrupt and hence of needing to be destroyed and replaced by another. The new code is presented as offering salvation for the individual and society. It offers a way for individuals to recapture their self-respect and sense of self-worth. By means of hysterical conversion large masses of people can be converted to the movement. The heightened sense of mutual concern present in such movements provides a foretaste of the liberation to be achieved after the dismantling of the existing social relations. After the extermination of all evil, there would be a return to the lost anarcho-communistic order that existed at the beginning of time. There would be no human authorities, taxes, rents or dues. Such movements tend to conceive of the community as a homogeneous, unstructured unity that transcends the differentiations and contradictions of the established social order.[43] They emphasize universal human values such as peace, harmony, fertility of the mind and body, universal justice and the equality and brotherhood of all.[44] Law is oppression, and since the goal is to transcend all oppressing limitations, law must be transcended.

In the Thirteenth century Joachim of Fiore formulated a prophetic view of history that fed this tradition throughout the Middle Ages (and into the Modern). According to him, history had three ages. In the first, fear and servitude were central. In the second, faith and filial submission gained the ascendency. Finally, in the third age, which is to come, love, joy and freedom would prevail. In this new age, there would be no work. Individuals will have spiritual bodies so that they would not need any food. There would be no institutional authorities of any kind.[45] His view strongly influenced the Brethern of the Free Spirit. These people championed a quasi-mystical anarchism,

> an affirmation of freedom so reckless and unqualified that it amounted to a total denial of every kind of restraint and limitation.[46]

An individual was supposed to strive for direct communion with God, and was to recognize no authority at all save his own experiences.[47] They thought that every rational creature was blessed.[48] An individual could become wholly liquified in God so that one could not distinguish between the two.[49] They preached antinomianism and complete sexual freedom.[50] An individual who had become one with God was no longer bound to observe any law or command of another.[51] They denied the validity of private property and claimed that all things should be held in common.[52] As the Amaurians, they believed that the miracle of the Incarnation was repeated in each of them.[53] From them, it would spread to the whole world so that every person would be divine and would know himself as such.[54] Such Joachimite views survive even to modern times. He influenced Hegel who in turn influenced Marx. This latter undertook to secularize this tradition. For Marx, history moves from servititude (the Ancient mode of production) through filial submission (the Medieval mode of production) to freedom (the coming Communist mode of production). Those that are marginal in the current order, the proletariats, are going to rise up and destroy the whole capitalistic order. All its laws and legal institutions are based upon private property and, since this is the source of the oppression of the proletariat, must be destroyed. Instead of the Holy Ghost, Marx has the revolutionary spirit which will take possession of the masses and lead them to the New Jerusalem.[55] In this communistic society, scarcity, competition, exchange and the enslaving division of labor will all be overcome by creating an era of abundance.[56] In the religious version, God provided this abundance, while in the secular, technology. Finally, a true community based on the unconditional and all-round development of the individual will be formed,[57] the state will wither away and complete freedom, equality and brotherhood will reign.[58] Laws, since they are general, cannot take account of the concrete differences and circumstances of individuals and thus will always be a source of oppression.[59] With no laws, there would be no oppression.

Table I

*INDO-EUROPEAN PARTHENONS

Culture	First Function	Second Function	Third Function
Indic	Varuna-Mitra	Indra	Asvins-Nasatyas
Germanic	Odin-Tyr	Thor	Freyr-Freyja
Roman	Jupiter-Dius Fidius	Mars	Quirinus
Celtic	Lug-Nuadu	Ogma	(unclear)
Greek	Zeus-Hephaestus	Ares	Demeter-Kore
Iranian	Vohu Manah-Asa	Xsathra	Ameretat-Haurvatat and Armaiti

*based on Dumezil

ENDNOTES

1. Michael Green is Associate Professor of Philosophy at SUNY-Oneonta.

2. Dumezil, Georges, 1973, *Gods of the Ancient Northmen*, Einar Haugen, ed., Berkeley and Los Angeles: University of California Press, 39.

3. Dumezil, Georges, 1970, *The Destiny of the Warrior,* Alf Hiltebeitel, trans., Chicago: University of Chicago Press, 1970, and *Gods of the Ancient Northmen,* edited by Einar Haugen. Also, see Larson, Gerald James, 1974, C. Scott Littleton, Jaan Puhvel, eds., *Myth in Indo-European Antinquity,* Berkeley and Los Angeles: University of California Press, 1974, Littleton, C. Scott, 1982, *The New Comparative Mythology An Anthropological Assessment of the Theories of Georges Dumezil,* Third Edition, Berkeley and Los Angeles: University of California Press; and Benveniste, Emile, 1973, *Indo-European Language And Society,* Coral Gables, Florida: University of Miami Press.

4. Lewis, I. M., 1975, *Ecstatic Religion An Anthropological Study of Spirit Possession and Shamanism,* Baltimore: Penquin Books, Ltd.; Wallace, Anthony F. C., 1961, *Culture and Personality,* New York: Random House, and Wallace, Anthony F. C., 1966 *Religion An Anthropological View,* New York: Random House. Also, see Bourguignon, Erika, ed., 1973, *Religion, Altered States of Consciousness, and Social Change,* Columbus: Ohio State University Press, 1973 and Perry, John Weir, 1987, *The Heart of History Individuality in Evolution,* Albany: State University of New York Press: 1987.

5. Tacitus, *Germania,* XIII.

6. Jones, George Fenwick, 1963, *The Ethos of the Song of Roland,* Baltimore: Johns Hopkins Press, 20.

7. Jones, George Fenwick, *The Ethos of the Song of Roland,* 14.

8. Homer, 1983, *The Illiad,* W. H. D. Rouse, trans., New York: The New American Library, Inc., 41.

9. Weinreb, Lloyd, 1987, *Natural Law and Justice,* Cambridge, Massachusetts: Harvard University Press, 125.

10. Wolin, Sheldon S., 1970, *Hobbes and the Epic Tradition of Political Theory,* Los Angeles, California: William Andrews Clark Memorial Library.

11. Hobbes, Thomas, 1968, *Leviathan,* C. B. Macpherson, ed., Harmondsworth: Penquin, 699.

12. Hobbes, Thomas, *Leviathan,* 223.

13. Hobbes, Thomas, 1969, *The Elements of Law: Natural and Politic,* F. Tonnies, ed., introduction by M. M. Goldsmith, London: Frank Cass & Co., 107.

14. Dworkin, Ronald, 1977, *Taking Rights Seriously,* Cambridge, Massachusetts: Harvard University Press, 19.

15. Benveniste, Emile, *Indo-European Language And Society*, 325.

16. *Id.*, 326.

17. *Id.*, 391.

18. Aquinas, St. Thomas, *Summa Theologicae,* Ia-IIae, q. 93, a. 3.

19. *Id.*, q. 93, a. 3.

20. *Id.*, q. 44, a. 6.

21. *Id.*, q. 90, a. 1-4.

22. *Id.*, q. 100, a. 5.

23. *Id.*, q. 26, a. 9.

24. *Id.*, q. 92, a. 1.

25. *Id.*, q. 94, a. 4.

26. *Id.*, q. 106, a. 1; q. 94, a. 3; and q. 109, a. 3.

27. Bacon, Elizabeth, 1966, *Obok: a study of social structure in Eurasia,* New York: Johnson Reprint Corporation.

28. *Id.*, 12.

29. *Id.*, 21.

30. *Id.*, 21.

31. Barth, Fredrik, 1964, *Nomads of South Persia, New York: Humanities Press* 44.

32. Bennis, W. G., 1966, *Changing Organizations: Essays on the Development and Evolution of Human Organizations,* New York: McGraw-Hill. For the importance of the developmental framework in Rousseau, see Merle L. Perkins, 1974, *Jean-Jacques Rousseau On the Individual and Society,* Lexington, Kentucky: The University Press of Kentucky.

33. Machiavelli, Niccolo, 1975, *The Discourses of Niccolo Machiavelli,* Leslie J. Walker, trans., S. J., London: Routledge & Kegan Paul, 287.

34. Rousseau, J. J., 1968, *On Social Contract,* Gerard Hopkins, trans., in *Social Contract Essays by Locke, Hume, and Rousseau,* Sir Ernest Barker, ed., Oxford: Oxford University Press, 134.

35. *Id.,* 120.

36. Merquior, J. G., 1980, *Rousseau and Weber,* London: Routledge & Kegan Paul, 61.

37. *Id.,* 58.

38. Cell, Howard R. and James I. MacAdam, 1988, *Rousseau's Response to Hobbes,* New York: Peter Lang, 240.

39. Merquior, J. G., *Rousseau and Weber,* 71.

40. Rousseau, J. J., *On Social Contract,* 149.

41. Wallace, A. C., *Culture and Personality,* 144.

42. *Id.,* 146.

43. Turner, Victor W., 1969, *The Ritual Process Structure and Anti-Structure,* Chicago: Aldine Publishing Company, 92.

44. *Id.,* 134.

45. Knox, Ronald A., 1961, *Enthusiasm A Chapter in the History of Religion,* Oxford: Oxford University Press, 100.

46. *Id.,* 150.

47. *Id.,* 152.

48. *Id.,* 181.

49. *Id.,* 183.

50. *Id.,* 154.

51. *Id.,* 188.

52. *Id.,* 193.

53. *Id.,* 159.

54. *Id.,* 160.

55. On the importance of revolutionary spirit to Marxist movements, see Merquior, J. G., *Rousseau and Weber*, 125ff.

56. Marx, Karl, 1972, *Critique of the Gotha Program,* in *The Marx-Engels Reader,* 2nd ed., Robert C. Tucker, ed., New York: W. W. Norton and Company, 530-531.

57. See Marx's, 1973, definition of wealth in *Grundrisse,* Martin Nicolaus, trans., London: Allen Lane, 611.

58. For an explication of communistic justice, see Michael K. Green, 1983, "Marx, Utility, and Right," in *Political Theory,* Vol. 11, No. 3, August, 433-446.

59. Marx, Karl, Critique of the Gotha Program, in *The Marx-Engels Reader,* 530.

Chapter 8

Cost-Benefit Analysis in Criminal Procedure: Social Science Data, the Supreme Court, and the Exclusionary Rule[1]

W. Richard Janikowski[2]

I

Introduction

Polemics have beset the exclusionary rule since its inception. While Justice Douglas believed that the United States Supreme Court's decision in *Mapp v. Ohio*, 367 U.S. 643 (1961) had ended 'the storm of constitutional controversy' (p. 670) engendered by *Wolf v. Colorado*, 338 U.S. 25 (1949), the ensuing years have demonstrated that the storm 'had not only intensified -- but engulfed the fourth amendment exclusionary rule itself.' (Kamisar, 1983: 566). Critics have called for abandonment of the rule (Burger, 1964; Wright, 1972; Schlesinger, 1977; Wilkey, 1978) while defenders consider it a constitutional or political necessity (Sunderland, 1978; Kamisar, 1982; Canon, 1982). Others suggest a need to limit application of the exclusionary rule to those situations where police have acted willfully, maliciously, in bad faith or without reasonable cause (Coe, 1975; Ball, 1978; Jensen and Hart, 1982; Uviller, 1982). Moreover, various members of the Supreme Court at different times have called for re-examination of the scope of the rule: *Stone v. Powell*, 428 U.S. 465 (1976) (Burger, C.J., concurring, 496; White,

J., dissenting, p. 536); *Brown v. Illinois*, 422 U.S. 590 (1975) (Powell, J., concurring in part, 609-612); *Schneckloth v. Bustamonte*, 412 U.S. 218 (1973) (Powell, J. concurring, pp 261-271); *California v. Minjares*, 443 U.S. 916 (1979) (Rehnquist, J., dissenting from denial of stay).

Responding to these criticisms, the Court, since its decision in *Mapp,* has developed numerous exceptions to the exclusionary rule. While *Mapp had suggested a number of justifications for the exclusionary rule*, these subsequent decisions have emphasized that the primary, if not the sole, rationale for the exclusionary rule is the deterrence of unlawful police conduct. This process, culminating in the Court's decision in *Leon v. United States*, 486 U.S. 847 (1984), has relied substantially on social science data to justify redirecting the Court's analysis of the foundations of the exclusionary rule. As a result, the Court has significantly diminished the scope of the exclusionary rule to 'those areas where its remedial objectives are thought most efficaciously served' by application of a balancing of interests approach, essentially cost-benefit analysis, to determine the appropriateness of the exclusionary remedy in a particular area. This paper examines the development of this cost-benefit analysis and the manner in which the Court has used social science data as a rhetorical technique for explaining a new jurisprudential foundation for the exclusionary rule.

II

Formulating the Rule: A Constitutional Requirement

The United States Supreme Court first addressed the constitutional problem of excluding evidence obtained in violation of the Constitution in *Boyd v. United States*, 116 U.S. 616 (1886). The Court in *Boyd*, finding the Fourth and Fifth

Amendments as running 'almost into one each other' (630) concluded that the Amendments:

> . . . apply to all invasions on the part of the government and its employees of the sanctity of a man's home and the privacies of life. It is not the breaking of his doors, and the rummaging of his drawers, that constitutes the essence of the offense; but it is the invasion of his indefeasible right of personal security, personal liberty and private property . . . . Breaking into a house and opening boxes and drawers are circumstance of aggravation; but any forcible and compulsory extortion of a man's own testimony or of his private papers to be used as evidence to convict of crime or to forfeit his goods, is within the condemnation . . . .(*Boyd* at 635.)

Within thirty years, in *Weeks v. United States*, 232 U.S. 383 (1914), the Court would again be faced with the issue in a case involving the warrantless seizure of letters and articles by U.S. marshals. Finding that the marshals had acted without the 'sanction of law' (393) and in a manner that 'not even an order of court would have justified' (394), the Court elucidated a philosophical foundation for excluding the evidence that had been used to convict the defendant:

> The effect of the Fourth Amendment is to put the courts of the United States and Federal officials, in the exercise of their power and authority, under limitations and restraints as to the exercise of such power and authority, and to forever secure the people, their persons, houses, papers and effects against all unreasonable searches and seizures under the guise of law. This protection reaches all alike, whether accused of crime or not, and the duty of giving it force and effect is obligatory upon all entrusted under Federal system with the enforcement of the laws. The tendency of those who execute the

> criminal laws of the county to obtain conviction by means of unlawful seizures and enforced confessions, the latter often obtained after subjecting accused persons to unwarranted practices destructive of rights secured by the Federal Constitution, should find no sanction in the judgments of the courts which are charged at all times with the support of the Constitution . . . (*Weeks* at 392.)

The Court observed that allowing such evidence to be used in a criminal prosecution would be tantamount to declaring that the Fourth Amendment had no value and that 'so far as those thus place and concerned, might as well be stricken from the Constitution.' (393). Concluding that punishment of the guilty did not justify sacrificing 'those great principles established by years of endeavor and suffering' and embodied in 'the fundamental law of the land' (393), the Court stated that '{T}o sanction such proceedings would be to affirm by judicial decision a manifest neglect if not an open defiance of the prohibitions of the Constitution.' (394). Clearly the Supreme Court was unwilling to engage in a cost-benefit analysis regarding what it perceived as a fundamental right. As Yale Kamisar (1983) has noted

> Nowhere in *Weeks* is the exclusionary called a 'remedy' and nowhere in the opinion is there any discussion, or even mention, of the effectiveness of the exclusionary rule versus the effectiveness of tort remedies, internal self-discipline or other alternatives. Although few suspect this from the argument of the rule's opponents or from recent majority opinions of the Supreme Court, the *Weeks* opinion contains no language that expressly justifies the rule by reference to a supposed deterrent effect on police officials.
>
> Indeed, no less formidable a critic of the exclusionary rule than Chief Justice Burger recognized, before ascending to his present post,

that the *Weeks* case 'rest{s} on the Court's unwillingness to give even tacit approval to official defiance of constitutional provisions by admitting evidence secured in violation of the Constitution. The idea of deterrence may be lurking between the lines of the opinion but is not expressed.' (598)

This approach would be reiterated in *Silverthorne Lumber Co. v. United States*, 251 U.S. 385 (1920). In *Silverthorne* the government made copies of various documents, obtained during the course of a warrantless search, prior to their return to the defendants. The copies became the basis for a subpoena issued to the defendants for the original documents. In reversing a contempt order entered against the defendants for failure to comply with the subpoena, Justice Holmes, writing for the Court, noted that to allow the government to avoid the holding of *Weeks* by use of this type of two step process reduced the Fourth Amendment to a 'form of words.' (392). Announcing what would later become known as the 'fruit of the poisonous tree' doctrine, Holmes suggested that the essence of the Fourth Amendment was not merely that the original evidence was not to be used in court, 'but that it shall not be used at all.' (392). Essentially for thirty-five years following *Weeks* the Supreme Court rarely addressed the rationale of the exclusionary rule and never compared the relative merits of the exclusionary rule to alternative methods of enforcing the fourth amendment, (Kamisar, 1983), unless one considers that such a discussion was 'lurking' somewhere in the opinions.

Then in 1949 the Court in *Wolf v. Colorado*, 338 U.S. 25, appeared to retreat from its prior position. Using a fundamental rights approach, the *Wolf* Court, while finding 'no hesitation in saying that were a State affirmatively to sanction such police incursion into privacy it would run counter to the guaranty of the Fourth Amendment' (28), declined to impose the *Weeks* rule upon the states. The majority found that the *Weeks* doctrine 'was not derived from the explicit requirements of the Fourth Amendment' but was 'a matter of judicial implication.' (28). As such the Court believed it could not 'brush aside the experience of States which deem the incidence of such conduct by the police too slight' to require imposition of an exclusionary remedy. The Court concluded that the states had not left the right of privacy unprotected but had, and would in the future, develop alternative remedies. While not explicitly addressing the efficacy of the exclusionary rule as a remedy, the majority's focus on alternative remedies suggests the beginning of a cost-benefit analysis. This interpretation is reinforced by the Court approvingly quoting from Justice (then Judge) Cardozo's opinion in *People v. Defore*, 242 N.Y. 13 (1926):

> The question is whether protection for the individual would not be gained at a disproportionate loss of protection for society. On the one side is the social need that crime shall be repressed. On the other, the social need that law shall not be flouted by the insolence of office. There are dangers in any choice. The rule of the *Adams* case {176 N.Y. 351, 68 N.E. 636} strikes a balance between opposing interests. (Wolf at 32, fn. 2.)

Within twelve years, in *Mapp v. Ohio*, 367 U.S. 643 (1961) the Court would reverse itself. Holding that evidence obtained in violation of the Fourth Amendment was inadmissible in state criminal proceedings, the Court stated:

> Since the Fourth Amendment's right of privacy has been declared enforceable against the States through the Due Process Clause of the Fourteenth, it is enforceable against the Federal Government. Were it otherwise, then just as without the *Weeks* rule the assurances against unreasonable federal searches and seizures would be a 'form of

> words", valueless and undeserving of mention in a perpetual charter of inestimable human liberties, so too, without that rule the freedom from state invasions of privacy would be ephemeral and so neatly severed from its conceptual nexus with the freedom from all brutish means of coercing evidence as not to merit this Court's high regard as a freedom 'implicit in the 'concept of ordered liberty''. (*Mapp* at 655).

The Court appeared to base its decision in part on a finding that the experience of the states with alternative remedies had been 'worthless and futile'. (652). Additionally though, the Court recognized another imperative, judicial integrity, for its decision. Justice Clark observed that while some critics had suggested that '{t}he criminal is to go free because the constable has blundered", it is 'the law that sets him free.' (659). He reminded critics that '{N}othing can destroy a government more quickly than its failure to observe its own laws, or worse, its disregard of the character of its own existence' (p. 659), and directed their attention to Justice Brandeis' dissent in *Olmstead v. United States*, 277 U.S. 438 (1928):

> Our government is the potent, the omnipresent teacher. For good or for ill, it teaches the whole people by its example . . . . If the government becomes a lawbreaker, it breeds contempt for law; it invites every man to become a law unto himself; it invites anarchy. (*Olmstead* at 485).

While some critics (Schrock and Welsh, 1974) have suggested that it is not clear from the opinion whether the exclusionary rule is constitutionally required because of its deterrent intention, or because it actually works as a deterrent, Kamisar (1983) has cogently pointed out that when taken in its totality the opinion is fairly clear. It can be understood to say:

> We reaffirm the 'original understanding' of the exclusionary rule, as explained in *Weeks* and its progeny, that (anything to the contrary in *Wolf* notwithstanding) it is a constitutionally required rule, although not explicitly provided for in the text of the fourth amendment -- and moreover (again, anything to the contrary in *Wolf* notwithstanding), it is the most effective (or the only presently available effective) means of deterring police conduct. (623)

It therefore appeared that the basis for the exclusionary rule was an understanding that it was constitutionally required by the Fourth Amendment. In Professor Allen's (1961) words, 'the exclusionary rule is part of the Fourth Amendment; the Fourth Amendment is part of the Fourteenth; therefore, the exclusionary rule is part of the Fourteenth.' (26).

III
Reformulating the Rule: Deterrence

By 1974 this formulation of the rationale for the exclusionary rule began to be undermined. Beginning with *United States v. Calandra,* 414 U.S. 338 (1974), the Court in a series of decisions reconsidered the basis upon which the exclusionary rule rested. Now the Court would balance the deterrent effect of the rule against the cost to the government and society of excluding evidence (Whitebread and Slogin, 1986).

In *Calandra,* the Court found the exclusionary rule's primary purpose was 'to deter future unlawful police conduct and thereby effectuate the guarantee of the Fourth Amendment against unreasonable searches and seizures.' (Calandra, 348). Therefore the Court concluded that the rule was a judicially created remedy 'designed to safeguard Fourth Amendment rights generally through its deterrent effect, rather than a personal constitutional right of the party aggrieved.' (Calandra, 348). Accepting this formulation of the rationale for the exclusionary rule the court determined that extension of the rule to grand jury proceedings would depend on the costs of such action, suppressing evidence of guilt and potentially releasing factually guilty defendants, as compared to any accrued benefits. Applying the test, the court found that any incremental benefit was uncertain at best since any 'incentive to disregard the requirement of the Fourth Amendment solely to obtain an indictment from a grand jury is substantially negated by the inadmissibility of the illegally seized evidence in a subsequent criminal prosecution' (350), and therefore refused to extend the scope of the exclusionary to grand jury proceedings. The effect of *Calandra* was to uproot the exclusionary rule from a normative foundation and instead to rest it on an empirical evaluation of its effect. As Davies (1983) observed

> Under *Calandra's* reformulation of the rule's rationale, the Supreme Court has purportedly 'balanced' the costs of suppressing evidence of guilt and potentially releasing defendants who are factually guilty of crimes against the potential deterrent benefits of applying the rule in a variety of specific procedural settings . . . . Of course there is no empirical content to this 'balancing' approach to considering the costs and benefits of the rule in specific settings; no empirical measures exist of either the costs or the benefits purportedly involved. (626)

Curiously enough the Court recognized the problematic nature of its new formulation in a prior footnote (348, fn. 5)

> There is some disagreement as to the practical efficacy of the exclusionary rule, and as the Court noted in Elkins *v. United States {citation omitted} relevant '{e}mpirical statistics are not available.'*

Cf. Oaks, Studying the Exclusionary Rule in Search and Seizure, 37 U.Chi.L.Rev. 665 (1970).

However the Court would ignore the question by finding 'no occasion in the present case to consider the extent of the rule's efficacy in criminal trials". (348)

Utilizing the Calandra balancing approach, the Court developed the 'dissipation of taint' concept in *Brown v. Illinois*, 422 U.S. 590 (1975) reasoning that at some point 'the detrimental consequences of illegal police action become so attenuated that the deterrent effect of the exclusionary rule no longer justifies its costs.' (609) This analysis allowed the Court in *Stone v. Powell*, 428 U.S. 465 (1976) held that a state prisoner who has been afforded a full and fair opportunity to litigate a Fourth Amendment claim may not obtain federal habeas relief on the ground that unlawfully obtained evidence had been introduced at trial. In reaching this conclusion the Court emphasized the social costs of the exclusionary rule, which according to the majority are 'well known' (459) citing as evidence the study by Oaks (1970) and having previously determined in *United States v. Janis*, 428 U.S. 433 (1976) that '{j}urists and scholars uniformly have recognized that the exclusionary rule imposes a substantial cost on the societal interest in law enforcement by its proscription of what concededly is relevant evidence.' (448). Moreover, Justice Blackmun in *Janis*, following an extensive review of social science data on the deterrent effect of the rule, concluded that insufficient evidence existed to conclusively determine that a deterrent effect existed. As a result the *Powell* Court concluded that limiting the circumstances under which Fourth Amendment claims could be raised in federal habeas corpus proceedings would not reduce the rule's deterrent effect.

Thus in *Rakas v. Illinois*, 439 U.S. 128 (1978) the Court limited standing to challenge admission of the fruits of an illegal search and seizure to the actual victim of the police misconduct, having previously found in *Harris v. New York*, 401 U.S. 222 (1971) that even a defendant with standing could not prevent admission of such evidence for purposes of impeachment. In both cases the Court found that any incremental furthering of the exclusionary rule was outweighed by resulting costs.

Similarly, in *Michigan v. DeFillippo*, 443 U.S. 31 (1979), the Court refused to suppress evidence obtained by police officers relying in good faith on a criminal statute subsequently declared unconstitutional. Finally, in *United States v. Leon*, 468 U.S. 897 (1984) the Court announced a 'good faith' exception to the exclusionary rule judging that 'the marginal or non-existent benefits produced by suppressing evidence obtained in objectively reasonable reliance on a subsequently invalidated search warrant cannot justify the substantial costs of exclusion.' (922). This conclusion was reached by the Court after 'reviewing the findings of social science research concerning the effects of the exclusionary rule on the disposition of felony arrests. (Walker and Monahan, 1987: 562).

> Researchers have only recently begun to study extensively the effects of the exclusionary rule on the disposition of felony arrests. One study suggests that the rule results in the nonprosecution or nonconviction of between 0.6% and 2.35% of individuals arrested for felonies. {citation omitted} The estimates are higher for particular crimes the prosecution of which depends heavily on physical evidence. Davies' analysis of California data suggests that screening by police and prosecutors results in the release because of illegal searches or seizures of as many as 1.4% of all felony arrestees, id., at 650, and 0.9% of felony arrestees are released because of illegal searches and seizures at the preliminary hearing or after trial, id., at 654. {citations omitted}.

> Many of these researchers have concluded that the impact of the exclusionary rule is insubstantial, but the small percentages with which they deal mask a large absolute number of felons who are released because the cases against them were based in part on illegal searches or seizures . . . . Because we find that the rule can have no substantial deterrent effect in the sorts of situations under consideration in this case . . . , we conclude that it cannot pay its way in those situations. (*Leon*, 907)

In essence the Court determined that the exclusionary rule could not, and should not, be used to deter objectively reasonable police activity. The Court's analysis appears to indicate that a balancing approach has always been the focus of any test determining application of the exclusionary rule. Thus the *Leon* Court found that 'the balancing approach that has evolved during the years of experience with the rule provides strong support for the modification currently urged upon us' (*Leon*, 913). Further the Court concluded that 'the question whether the use of illegally obtained evidence in judicial proceedings represents judicial participation in a Fourth Amendment violation and offends the integrity of the courts is essentially the same as the inquiry into whether exclusion would serve a deterrent purpose' (*Leon*, 920, fn. 22). *Leon* therefore stands for the proposition that the fundamental purpose of the exclusionary rule is deterrence of unreasonable police conduct. However, *Leon* fails to adequately resolve in a principled manner the appropriateness of the Court's formulation of cost-benefit analysis as the foundation for the exclusionary rule.

IV

A Judicial Rhetoric of Social Science and the Exclusionary Rule

At first glance the Supreme Court's approach to the exclusionary rule since *Calandra* appears seductively appealing. The Court appears to move from abstract legal and constitutional theory to a practical consideration of the consequences of a specific social/political policy. Closer examination of the Court's reasoning reveals a rampant misuse (but *not* misunderstanding) of the social science research on the issues of deterrence and cost regarding the exclusionary rule.

The *Calandra* Court's attack on the exclusionary was primarily based on an analysis of social science research which suggested that the rule had little deterrent effect. However, at the time *Calandra* was decided little research was actually available regarding the effectiveness of the rule. The primary study available, done by Dallin Oaks in 1970 studying police conduct in certain cities, suggested no substantial effect. However, this conclusion, not supported by the data, was a personal opinion about the efficacy of the rule's deterrent effect. As observed by Davies, 'the Oaks study has been probably established something of a record for being widely cited as empirical support for a finding it did not really claim to make' (628). Davies analysis also concluded that the limits of social science methodology would prevent any conclusive determination from being made regarding the efficacy of the rule as a deterrent to police misconduct. However, while Justice Blackmun in *Janis* recognized '{t}he final conclusion is clear: No empirical researcher, proponent or opponent of the rule, has yet been able to establish with any assurance whether the rule has a deterrent effect', the Supreme Court continues to base its exclusionary rule decisions on the presumption that the research indicates no deterrent effect. This is especially problematic in light of anecdotal research (Canon, 1977) indicating that the *Mapp* decision beneficially affected police attitudes and training in the search and seizure area.

Moreover, the Court's emphasis on studies indicating the high societal costs of the use of the exclusionary sanction is questionable. The main study (NIJ 1982) relied upon by the Court has been severely criticized as methodologically flawed and misleading (Davies, 1983). Further, the Court's interpretation of the data itself is misleading. Justice White in *Gates v. Illinois* suggested that 30 percent of cases are lost due to exclusion of evidence. Zalman and Seigel though point out

> the 30 percent figure is grossly misleading. First, the NIJ study showed that 4.8 percent of all rejected felony cases are lost because of search and seizure problems. But this in no way indicates the cost of the exclusionary rule -- it does not show what proportion of cases are lost due to the rule; it instead shows that among those cases that prosecutors rejected, 4.8 percent were lost due to the rule. This is meaningless because the percentage calculated in this way can change dramatically depending on changes in the other reasons for dismissals. When the NIJ data of lost cases are calculated a base figure of total arrests, those lost due to the exclusionary rule drop to about 0.8 percent, more in line with the other studies. As for the 30 percent figure, it was drawn from a sample of 150 drug cases from two local prosecutor's offices in Los Angeles, which was not representative. (246)

Further, as noted various recent studies demonstrate that less than 1% of arrests are lost by virtue of the rule, and in half of these cases convictions are still obtained with other evidence. When confronted with this research and analysis the Court redirects its attention from the data to a more normative analysis. Thus the Court uses the data to conclude that any lost arrests constitute a significant social cost: 'the small percentages with which {the studies} deal mask a large absolute number of felons who are released.' (Leon, 688).

Many commentators examining this history of the exclusionary rule conclude that the 'misuse' of social science research by the Court was due to an ignorance of the available empirical studies (Zalman & Seigel, 1991). However, another explanation is not only possible, but plausible. The Court's use of the data can be viewed as a search for authority which can justify deviation from the prior decisions in *Weeks* and *Mapp* while masking, especially for those Justices dedicated to a theory of judicial restraint, the normative nature of the subsequent rulings. As has been observed by one commentator, social science data can be used by the Court much like precedent -- something to be 'located, not evaluated.' Thus the data can be used as a rhetorical technique to persuade readers that the Court's decision is based on a sound policy footing and not a preference for a particular normative approach. Review of the use of social science research in the exclusionary rule cases reveals precisely this approach. The Court was not ignorant of the relevant empirical studies or the criticisms of these studies, as demonstrated by the Court's citation of both in it's opinions, but chose to interpret the research at various times in manners that supported its policy objective.

V

Conclusion

In recent decades the United States Supreme Court has been increasingly willing to recognize social science research as a basis of authority for reaching decisions. Often however, the use of this research by the Court appears to be flawed, leading many commentators to conclude that the Court is ignorant of social science methodology and unable to properly interpret social science research results.

However such a conclusion may do injustice to the sophistication of the Court's persuasive techniques. It is suggested that careful attention needs to be paid to the precise manner in which the Justices use data and the its relationship to the policy objectives of the Court. In the exclusionary rule debate the Court since *Calandra* has made sophisticated use of social science data as means of attacking the exclusionary rule. As such social science research as used by the Court can best be understood as a rhetorical technique which enables the Court to justify changes in constitutional policy.

ENDNOTES

1. The author would like to acknowledge the assistance of Mr. Paul Posey, third year law student at the Cecils C. Humphrey School of Law, Memphis State University, in researching the material for this paper.

2. W. Richard Janikowski is Assistant Professor, Department of Criminology and Criminal Justice, Memphis State University.

REFERENCES

Allen, Francis, 1981, 'Federalism and the Fourth Amendment: A Requiem for Wolf,' *Supreme Court Review*, 1961:1-48.

Ball, Edna F., 1978, 'Good Faith and the Fourth Amendment: The 'Reasonable' Exception to the Exclusionary Rule,' *Journal of Criminal Law and Criminology*, 69:635-657.

Burger, Warren E., 1964, 'Who Will Watch the Watchman?' *American University Law Review*, 14:1-23.

Canon, Bradley C., 1982, 'Ideology and Reality in the Debate Over the Exclusionary Rule: A Conservative Argument for Its Retention,' *South Texas Law Journal*, 23:559-582.

Coe, Phillip S., 1975, 'The ALI Substantiality Test: A Flexible Approach to the Exclusionary Sanction,' *Georgia Law Review*, 10:1-51.

Davies, Thomas Y., 1983, 'A Hard Look at What We Know (and Still Need to Learn) About the 'Costs' of the Exclusionary Rule: The NIJ Study and Other Studies of 'Lost' Arrests,' *American Bar Foundation Research Journal*, 1983:611-690.

Jensen, D. Lowell and Rosemary Hart, 1987, 'The Good Faith Restatement of the Exclusionary Rule," *Journal of Criminal Law and Criminology*, 73:916-938.

Kamisar, Yale, 1982, 'How We Got the Fourth Amendment Exclusionary Rule and Why We Need It,' *Criminal Justice Ethics,* 1:3-

_____, 1983, 'Does (Did) (Should) the Exclusionary Rule Rest on a 'Principled Basis' Rather than an 'Empirical Proposition,'' *Creighton Law Review*, 16:565-667.

Oaks, Dallin, 1970, 'Studying the Exclusionary Rule in Search and Seizure,' *University of Chicago Law Review*, 37:665.

Schlesinger, Steven R., 1977, *Exclusionary Injustice,* New York: M. Dekker.

Schrock, Thomas S. and Robert C. Welsh, 1974, 'Up from Calandra: The Exclusionary Rule as a Constitutional Requirement,' *Minnesota Law Review*, 59:251-383.

Sunderland, Lane V, 1978, 'The Exclusionary Rule: A Requirement of Constitutional Principle,' *Journal of Criminal Law and Criminology*, 69:141-159.

Uviller, H. Richard, 1978, 'The Acquisition of Evidence for Criminal Prosecutions: Some Constitutional Premises and Practices in Transition,' *Vanderbilt Law Review*, 35:501-526.

'The U.S. Supreme Court 1988-89 Term.' 1989, August 16, *The Criminal Law Reporter, 45,* p. 4109-4110.

Whitebread, Charles and Christopher Slobogin, 1986, *Criminal Procedure: An Analysis of Cases and Concepts, 2nd ed.* Mineola, New York: Foundation Press, Inc.

Wilkey, Malcolm R., 1978, 'The Exclusionary Rule: Why Suppress Valid Evidence?' *Judicature* 62:215-232.

Wright, Charles A., 1972, 'Must the Criminal Go Free If the Constable Blunders,' *Texas Law Review* 50:736-745.

Zalman, Marvin and Larry Seigel, 1991, *Criminal Procedure: Constitution and Society*, St. Paul, Mn: West Publishing.

Cases Cited

Boyd v. United States, 116 U.S. 616 (1886)
Brown v. Illinois, 422 U.S. 590 (1975)
California v. Minjares, 443 U.S. 916 (1979)
Harris v. New York, 401 U.S. 222 (1971)
Leon v. United States, 486 U.S. 847 (1984)
Mapp v. Ohio, 367 U.S. 643 (1961)
Michigan v. DeFillippo, 443 U.S. 31 (1979)
Olmstead v. United States, 277 U.S. 438 (1928)
People v. DeFore, 242 N.Y. 13 (1926)
Rakas v. Illinois, 439 U.S. 128 (1978)
Schneckloth v. Bustamonte, 412 U.S. 218 (1973)
Silverthorne Lumber Co. v. United States, 251 U.S. 385 (1920)
Stone v. Powell, 428 U.S. 465 (1976)
United States v. Calandra, 414 U.S. 338 (1974)
Weeks v. United States, 232 U.S. 383 (1914)
Wolf v. Colorado, 338 U.S. 25 (1949)

Chapter 9

Antigone and the Law

Martha Kemper[1]

I

In order to understand the characters of Sophoclean tragedy we can view them as representatives or signs of a world view or moral code. According to Thomas Woodward, in his introduction to *Sophocles: A Collection of Critical Essays*, 'In themselves the heroes usually seem perverse, neurotic, or fanatical. But, just as we see them as symbols of a whole mentality, a world view, a moral code, so in their struggles we see the necessity for their behavior and temperament.' (Woodward, 1966: 7) In *Antigone*, three characters represent three codes of law. Creon represents the tyrant's law; the chorus, the communal law; and Antigone, the higher moral law of the gods.

In *Antigone,* Creon articulates the basic premise of the tyrant's law in dialogue with Haimon when he states, 'My voice is the one voice giving orders in the city.' (Fitzgerald, 1947: 482) His sense of entitlement as ruler leads him to create the edict which prohibits the burial of the traitor, Polyneices, whose body lies rotting, pecked at by birds, and eaten by dogs. That Creon would insist on such a decree reveals the tyrant's disregard for human ties of love and his dismissal of the human right to decency and dignity. Creon also violates the higher law, the 'divinely established order of things, . . . a sense of the larger sphere of which the polis and every human creation my be a part.' (Segal, 1966:

81) In making the law, Creon is attempting to save the polis from treachery, but in his limited vision he fails to conceive of an order beyond that of the polis, an order which requires honor for the dead, including traitors. In sum, Creon as representative of the tyrant's law, represents the following: one voice giving orders in the city, the creation of a law which degrades human love and decency; and blindness to an order higher than that of the polis.

Opposite Creon is Antigone, acting in reverence to the laws of the gods in a deed which violates Creon's edict. Antigone represents the higher moral law, which is also the law of human love. 'To live humanly, in Sophocles' terms, is to know fully the conditions of man's existence; and this means to accept the gods who, in their limitless, ageless power, *are* these conditions, the unbending realities of the universe.' (Segal, 1966: 85) Antigone's humanity compels her to bury her brother. Paradoxically, this human sensitivity makes Antigone a representative of the divine law. That code of law includes reverence to the gods through human rituals. Antigone's ritual of burying her brother is an assertion of her connection to him. Ultimately she can only assert her relation to him by 'shaking her entire being, her life.' (Segal, 1966: 62) The code of law she represents includes this willingness to sacrifice life for harmony with the higher order. Antigone, herself, is the sign of this law, and we come to understand the sign and what it stands for through her actions. We perceive that she is an agent through which the higher law manifests itself.

Faced with only these two extremes, Creon and Antigone, the audience would probably reject Creon entirely and embrace Antigone's heroism unconditionally. But Antigone's action represents and affront not only to Creon, but also to the polis. It threatens to undermine the law of the polis, and if Sophocles were to give Antigone unequivocal support, he might appear to advocate anarchy, which he does not do. Democritus' view that 'affairs of state and their proper conduct are the supreme consideration' (Procope, 1989: 325) is one that Sophocles shares. He strengthens the presence and importance of law abiding community by establishing the chorus in *Antigone*. This group of elders, loyal and patriotic, grounds the play in a framework of respect for law and the polis. The chorus demonstrates a balanced counterpoint to Creon. Loyal to leadership and to the polis, they also practiced reverence to the gods. They have no axe to grind, no position to prove themselves worthy of. They show sympathy for Antigone throughout the play and call her death sentence into question. Nevertheless, as Antigone prepares to go to death they repeat their conviction that 'strength lives in established law.' (Fitzgerald, 1947: 486) Thematically, the chorus is necessary as a representative of the established law of the community. Their faith in the importance of the polis is essential. Creon, the tyrant, will pass, but the ideal of the polis, strengthened by citizens ruled by common laws, is, as Democritus said, the 'supreme consideration.'

The framework of law and order in which the chorus grounds the play is established early. Their first entrance is a patriotic celebration of the 'beautiful morning of victory' for Thebes, in which Eteocles has triumphed, killing Polyneices. Their first response to Creon, upon hearing his decree is this, 'If that is your will, Creon, son of Menoiceus, you have the right to enforce it. We are yours.' (Fitzgerald, 1947: 465) Their choral ode, following the news of Polyneices' burial, almost echoes the orator, Democritus: 'When the laws are kept, how proudly his city stands! When the laws are broken, what of his city them?' (Fitzgerald, 1947: 466) The presence of such a chorus lifts the tragedy above a personal quarrel between a vengeful and arrogant man and his brave niece. The chorus' faith in law and order and their importance as members of the polis community bring the story to a conflict of laws and ideas. To understand how the chorus functions in this way it is interesting to imagine what the play would have been if, instead of Theban elders, Sophocles had made a chorus of young widows of the fallen rebel army. Such a chorus would have heightened the unresponsiveness of Creon's stance and exaggerated the cruelty of his edict. If Sophocles had only wanted to enlist sympathy for a wronged Antigone he might have chosen to do that. Instead he balances the play with the rational and sympathetic, yet ultimately law abiding group of elders. The audience cannot get carried away with sympathy for Antigone. It must remember 'the supreme consideration,' the polis.

After the entrance extolling Thebes' victory, the chorus demonstrates quick accord with Creon, the ruler of the state, when he announces his edict. Their response is 'We are yours', upon hearing the atrocious edict. Kitto says of their endorsement of Creon's right to make this law that 'Ordinary Greek sentiment would certainly reject this as political theory; it was, indeed, the reason why tyranny was hated, that the tyrant claimed to impose what laws he willed, without regard for traditional restraints.' (Kitto, 151) What function does the chorus' tacit acceptance of the edict serve? For one thing, it preserves the chorus' lives. Faced with a king who threatens death to all who break the law they prudently support it. If we interpret them as a symbol of the community, we can look at the nature of their action as descriptive of the community they represent. Their effusive endorsement strengthens their position as loyal councilors to the king and establishes them as a constitutional body working politically within the framework of the laws of the state and its ruler. Their primary focus is not preserving the sacred inter-connections between human beings, but rather, self preservation and the preservation of the established community. The fact that they support a strong community will not prevent them later from questioning what Creon does. But their early demonstration of loyalty to the laws governing the polis allows them later to question Creon without risking their lives.

Occasions when the chorus raise questions or depart from Creon's line of thought demonstrate their fundamental decency and their awareness of the laws of God. The first occasion when they raise a point which departs from the ideas of the king is when the news of the burial is brought out. The chorus says, 'I have been wondering, King: can it be that the gods have done this thing?' (Fitzgerald, 1947: 467) Kitto calls attention to the importance of the line and the need to take it literally. He tells us that in this tragedy the Greek gods play major roles. The chorus' question plainly demonstrates their frank belief in the supernatural powers of the gods. Creon violently rejects their suggestion with, 'Stop! Must you doddering wrecks go out of your heads entirely?' (467) But their question has been raised and their faith in the gods introduced. This helps to establish the chorus' multi-faceted character: they are capable of attributing the covering of the body to the gods; at the same time they maintain that obedience to the state is the preeminent virtue of man. It seems that Sophocles has them sustain these two beliefs throughout, and the chorus does not realize (or at least does not speak plainly) until it is too late that it is Creon, not Antigone, who has broken the supreme laws.

Because their diplomacy early in the play has won the ear of Creon, when the opportunity arises for the chorus to intervene in the plot's events, they take an active and influential role. When Creon threatens to have Ismene put to death, the chorus' sharp question, 'These girls? You have sentenced them both?' (Fitzgerald, '947: 483) elicits Creon's prompt decision to let the girl go free. Had they not won his trust by patient loyalty, the likelihood that Creon would heed their counsel at this point is negligible. Through the chorus, the playwright shows that good people can make a difference. If they represent the law of the polis, the necessity for established community, they also demonstrate the potential influence that established community can have on the tyrant. When Teiresias states plainly the dreadful fate that is about to befall Creon, it is the chorus who urge him to free Antigone. Late though it is -- too late, for the lives of Antigone and Hiamon are doomed -- he does listen. The chorus has earned his trust, never threatening his authority. Their unthreatening position helps Creon to admit that he has erred. He confesses his mistake to the chorus, and when they advise him to free Antigone, he does so.

The chorus' relationship with Antigone serves thematic and dramatic functions. It illustrates the theme, the need to find balance between the laws of man and the laws of God. It does this in several ways. First, by responding sympathetically to Antigone the chorus proves that respectable men sympathize with her and are touched by her predicament. They respond to the individual in the circumstances, as Creon does not. Their heart-felt response is appropriate and human, in contrast to Creon's inhumane invulnerability. Through the chorus, we see the possibility for a flexible response to the burial of Polyneices. If no threat of punishment existed from Creon, this chorus might speak to have the law reversed or the punishment lightened.

The chorus' inability or unwillingness to speak boldly on behalf of Antigone, and the fact that, despite their sympathy, they cling to the idea that she acted wrongly gives an unrelieved tension to the drama. The dramatic tension throughout gives evidence that, while Sophocles finds these three archetypal symbols to represent three kinds of law, he never sacrifices human drama. His 'symbols' are living characters. They lack the detail of twentieth century realists' creations, but they have the fundamental needs and wants that drive human beings, and that make from drama and tragedy. The chorus cannot give in and say, 'Reverence is virtue and your act is worthy of all honors,' despite their sympathy for the girl. That would betray their primary ållegiance to the laws of the community, and would destroy dramatic tension. Sophocles has the chorus stand firm until after the tragic death of Haimon. 'Strength lies in established law.' (Fitzgerald, 1947: 486) they say, even as Antigone goes to her death. This unrelenting expression of faith in the importance of established laws accentuates the courage and extraordinary quality of Antigone's deed. In her courage to follow the instinctive, god-given law and bury her brother, Antigone not only defies Creon, but also challenges the entire establishment of law-abiding citizens. The chorus' continued criticism of Antigone is necessary to clarify the magnitude of the challenge that her act represents. She did not intend it as a political, only as a personal, action. Nevertheless, not only Creon but the very state is challenged by her disobedience to the law, and the fact that it is a bad law doesn't seem to matter.

II

Drama derives from choices which characters make, and the chorus' choice to remain compliant with Creon, despite sympathy for Antigone, contributes to the tragic events of the play and helps to clarify the basic conflict between these different kinds of law. Sophocles sets up an essential crux of the play when he makes the penalty for breaking the edict death. The responses to this penalty, first by Antigone, and then by the chorus, show profound contrast in their characters and point to a different choice which each of them makes. Antigone calls her 'crime' a holy act. This is opposite to the chorus' view that anyone who crossed Creon was 'crazy' (Fitzgerald, 1947: 465) The clear contrast between the two sets Antigone in a singular position. Her willingness to risk death is significant. By following the contrast we may learn something about this dramatic difference. This specific contrast between the chorus and Antigone in response to death is carried further. Confronting Creon's sentence, Antigone says, 'Can anyone living as I live, with evil all about me, think death less than a friend? This death of mine is of no importance; but if I had left my brother lying in death unburied, I should have suffered. Now, I do not.' (Fitzgerald, 1947: 473) The chorus ignores the legitimacy of Antigone's claim, and recalls her father, Oedipus' stubbornness: 'Like father, like daughter! Both headstrong, deaf to reason.' (Fitzgerald, 1947: 473) The crux of the theme lies in these different ways of looking at death. For Antigone, life without honor is the greater death, and what gives her the perspective to regard death as of no importance is her reverence for the laws of the gods. The members of the chorus invoke the gods in choral odes, acknowledge them as having had a hand in the burial, and refer to their eternal laws. But in fact, they do not reverence the gods' laws when to do so means death. Instead they persist in loyalty to Creon. The law-abiding chorus does not see the wisdom in Antigone's reverence for the gods' law. In their last exchange with her, their remark, 'Reverence is virtue but strength lives in the established law.' (Fitzgerald, 1947: 483) expresses where their essential allegiance lies.

Antigone represents the divine law of morality. In literature, it is usually words that signify meaning and through words the interpreter of a text arrives at an understanding of the text. In drama, the 'language' includes theatrical settings, lighting, sound and scenery. One can interpret setting as a code for meaning, invested with the power of symbol. In the theatrical language of the stage, the dawn setting of the play's opening is our first experience of the character, Antigone. Sophocles gives us the visual representation of dawn to introduce Antigone and the law of divine morality. He presents the striking image of the girl, stealing out of the palace with her sister, on the untrafficed stage, where stillness is palpable, so that devotion to the laws of divine morality can be practiced without the distractions of daily life. In the play, reverence for the divine law is represented through Antigone's very human act of decency and love. In other words, when we think of Divine law, we think of Antigone's deed. The image of the naked body of Polyneices, pecked at by birds, provides a physical, earthly motivation for Antigone's action. Burial of the decaying body becomes Sophocles' symbol for the earthly ritual of human love that is the working out of the Divine law. Sustaining the tension between the divine, felt in the staging of the dawn entrance of Antigone, and the earthly, symbolized by the decaying images of Polyneices' body, is the unique responsibility of Antigone. Her 'holy' deed is a practical, earthly, even 'dirty' duty.

Antigone receives support from other characters in the play. Ismene and Haimon support Antigone in following the moral law. Also, the common people, Haimon reports in the scene with Creon, support Antigone and believe that what she has done is honorable. In examining Ismene's position as an active supporter of Antigone's burial of Polyneices, one sees a character who moves from support of one law to another. Ismene's first stance is with Creon's law. In the opening scene, Ismene objects to Antigone's plan. She is not unaware of the gods' laws. 'They mean a great deal to me,' she says. She cites her own weakness and the inferior position of her sex as reasons that she cannot act with Antigone. But Ismene reverses her decision and changes her allegiance by the time she appears again. This time, called by Creon to explain her role in the burial, Ismene wishes to claim full participation with her sister. When Antigone refuses to accept her sister, Ismene answers, 'But I know now what you meant; and I am hereto join you, to take my share of the punishment.' (Fitzgerald, 1947: 467) Even more explicitly stating her resolve, she says, 'I want to die with you,' (Fitzgerald, *Id.*) and 'I too have a duty that I must discharge to the dead.' (467) Acknowledging the awesome power of the law of divine morality, Ismene admits, 'what do I care for life when you are dead?' (Fitzgerald, *Id.*) By changing to align herself with

Divine law Ismene clarifies the power of that law. Once contemplated, once acknowledged and recognized by characters willing to open themselves to the moral law, it compels individuals so powerfully that nothing -- not fear, not the laws of man, not life itself -- can interfere with the individual's commitment to the law. The beauty and attraction inherent in following divine law takes Ismene beyond mere acceptance of punishment. She actively desires a share in the honor that ensues from following the law. Her words, 'I want to die with you,' attest to the overriding attraction and beauty of carrying out the moral law.

Haimon is another character who aligns himself with the gods' morality. He sacrifices his secure position as the tyrant's son for the more compelling role of Antigone's beloved. As such, he is another aspect of the code of the moral law, and another image of how human interconnections reflect compliance with the Divine. Haimon's place in harmony with the Divine requires sacrifice on his part. He sacrifices his father's blessing in order to stay true to Antigone.

Creon's long address to Haimon demonstrates the position Haimon is rejecting: 'subordinate everything else, my son, to your father's will. That is what a man prays for, that he may get sons attentive and dutiful in his house.' (Fitzgerald, 1947: 479) Haimon rejects Creon and gives his complete support to Antigone. He tries to dissuade Creon from his plan to kill Antigone. The moral law drives Haimon, but again, it is not a theoretical religious scruple, but a human matter of relationship and love. Haimon's relationship with Antigone is in harmony with the divine moral law. It seems that human happiness can only insue from being in harmony with the moral laws. Human relationships, like the one between Antigone and Haimon, and human decency, like Antigone's burial of her brother are signs of harmony with the divine moral law. Antigone, Haimon, and Ismene know that without this harmony with the higher law there will be no happiness in their lives so they embrace death gladly, finding harmony with the moral laws only through death.

III

Faced with the tyrant's law, the moral law, and the law of the community, each individual faces profound questions about his or her responsibility. If the citizen acts with the interest of the community as his primary concern, will he or she choose unconditional support for the ruler, or unwavering reverence to the laws of the gods? In *Antigone* the chorus supports Creon and upholds his edict. The consequences that follow from their compliance with the law are the deaths of Antigone, Haimon, and Euridice -- all tragic events that could have been avoided if all had remained in harmony with the divine moral law. Sophocles offers no easy alternative to the chorus' compliance with Creon. Their suggestion early in the play that the gods had intervened in the burial elicits such wrath from Creon that it is clear that his response to opposition is intolerance. He threatens any who contradict his edict with death. Contemporary examples in the twentieth century of uprisings in Iraq and Lithuania illustrate the violence with which tyrannical leadership can silence opposition. The citizens are faced with the choice: life without honor, or death. In the play, Antigone follows the eternal laws of the gods, takes the moral choice, and her action is motivated by love. It is no remote scruple that compels her, but a natural response to an indecent situation. She acts alone, though she is supported and joined by Haimon and later, Ismene. To envision a state comprised of citizens propelled by moral law, as Antigone is, creates a compelling vision of a moral land that is rarely realized. Sophocles' representatives of the community, the chorus, do not act with Antigone. Self preservation and interest in keeping the polis the primary consideration prevent these citizens from challenging tyranny. The tyrant's threat of force suppresses action in all but those most reverent to the laws of God and most attuned to the interconnections between human beings. Yet God's law, in the play, asks only decency. Kitto claims *Antigone* is a religious play, and religious faith perplexes logical analysis. To second guess divine action is to play the role of Creon, and commit the worst offense of man, arrogance. Dismissal of the power of the divine is Creon's downfall. The chorus' final line is 'Wisdom lies in submission to the gods.' (Fitzgerald, 1947: 499)

The audience, too, is a character in the play. Sophocles wrote at a time when tyranny was rampant in Greece and the question was how could decent but not particularly heroic people respond to tyranny. If Sophocles' -- and our -- greatest admiration is for Antigone and her sister and beloved, he shows us, through the chorus, a way people not blessed -- or cursed -- with heroism can survive and take action to right the affairs of a state suffering under tyranny.

ENDNOTES

1. Martha Kemper is Assistant Professor of Theater Arts at Penn State.

REFERENCES

Else, Gerald, F., 1963, *Aristotle's Poetics*, Cambridge: Harvard University Press.

Kitto, H.D.F., *Form and Meaning in Drama*, London: Metheun.

Procope, J.F., 1989, 'On Politics and the Care of the Soul,' *Classical Quarterly*, 39, 307-331.

Segal, Paul, 1966, 'Sophocles' Praise of Man and the Conflicts of the Antigone,' *Sophocles: A Collection of Critical Essays*, Thomas Woodward, ed., Englewood Cliffs: Prentice, 62-85.

Sophocles, 1947, *Antigone*, Dudley Fitts and Robert Fitzgerald, trans., *Greek Plays in Modern Translation*, New York: Harcourt, Brace, Javonovich, 455-499.

Woodward, Thomas, 1966, Introduction, *Sophocles: A Collection of Critical Essays*, Thomas Woodward, ed., Englewood Cliffs: Prentice.

Chapter 10

Pragmatism, Utopic Constructions and Legal Myths: A Glance at Durkheim's View of Peirce's *Method* of Semiotics as Related to Legal Norms

Roberta Kevelson[1]

I

It has been my assumption, underlying the position I take with respect to the semiotic investigation of law and legal matters, that Peirce's pragmatic method and his theory of signs afford a dynamic conceptual foundation of doing legal semiotics. The main distinction between a Peircean approach and the Greimasian structural linguistic model is that the latter, in my understanding, is primarily concerned with relations between states whereas the Peircean functional approach focuses on the dynamics of changing stages of development in ideas, legal and otherwise, by regarding semiotics as a process of change and transformation.

The Greimasian method could be said to correspond with one of two major strains of utopic vision, while the Peircean method corresponds with the alternative method. These two modes of regarding utopic vision are the most general that a vastly ramified and unwieldy notion of utopic thought has evoked in this last quarter of the twentieth century. The first presupposes a finite universe; the second presupposes an endless universe. In this paper I will focus on that utopic mode which illuminates and discloses the Peircean theory of signs, especially in connection with discovery of emergence of new social values, and the role of law in creating, producing and legitimizing emergent social norms and values.

It is in this sense that law serves to ground a normative Ethics and also a normative Aesthetics. This 'Esthetics', in Peirce's thought, functions for semiotic inquiry as a referential 'science of value.'

It is especially from Durkheim, in his posthumously published lectures on pragmatism and sociology of 1914, that we find implications of the two notions of utopic vision, mentioned above, sharply distinguished. By understanding that the utopic vision is an ideal vision of reality we have in the very idea of 'reality' two modes of utopic vision opposed and in conflict.[2] E.g., a static reality, is one which is 'immutable in time and space' (Durkheim, 4th Lecture, in Alcock, 1955:21-28). This Reality is an extension of logical absolutes: of Truth, Perfection, Beginnings and Ends, and of the concept of Finiteness of the world. It is prioristic and is bedfellow to all varieties of Positive Law, I suggest.

But the notion of reality which was held as a leading principle by Peirce and the pragmatists, and also by the Legal Realists who followed Peirce, is never ready-made nor is it ever finished. Not only does mankind create and continue to create Reality, since reality is merely another name for what we know thus far about our world and what we can exchange in a meaningful way about this world, but Reality is also the sum total of *resemblances* mankind creates to represent this open-ended design even as it becomes its own interpretant sign of itself. Such a pragmatic approach to reality begins within experience, however primitive, of some elemental notion of 'The Real,' and then evolves from itself in connection with all genuine novelty which comes to happen. Reality thus creates itself more real, i.e., more *multidimensionally* real. I will return to Durkheim's notion of a primitive ideal as a lawlike ideal, and the way pragmatism interprets the evolution of simple into complex law.

It is precisely in this sense that Durkheim speaks of the normative function of law as an evolving social myth that carries forward a utopic vision of the social culture of which it is the referent and which mirrors *it*. Law, no less than artworks from this point of view, fulfills an aesthetic function in society. Each variety of law and of legal order produces and creates a different respective aesthetics for the society it serves. The term 'aesthetics' used herein Peirce's sense, stands on not reverent if norms and/or values for evolving cultures and societies. In the beginning there was custom and social experience -- the rich, the vague, and the chaotically possible -- which, as it evolved and became differentiated into special functions, became a backdrop for interacting social systems, e.g. for law, for economics, for art, for all the human sciences. But it is the normativity of law, i.e., its quality and main characteristic, which results in its becoming the primary channel and code by means of which a dialogue on human values takes place and continues *ad infinitum.*

This paper is heuristic. It explores some complications for legal semiotics which Durkheim's indebtedness to Peircean semiotics makes clear. It also attempts to connect a pragmatic, pluralistic concept of utopic reality with problems in international law, on unlawful peace and on just war, for example. Indeed, the paper concludes on these confusions.

But it is the *purpose* of utopic inquiry to disorient a dominant ideology of any given political and social system. In other words, a utopic perspective from a Peircean point of view is a critical perspective on dominant idea systems or system of signs. Yet it is incorrect, according to Marin and others (Marin, 1984), to regard utopic constructions as political constructions. They are not. A utopic construction is an aesthetic construction. It is a challenge to an existing habit of thought. It attempts to dislodge a habit of thought, since the ideology which in power has come to be perceived as flawed and invalid, (Marin, 1984:195ff). Thus the utopic and the general or 'conventionalized' social structures are dialogic and interactional structures, I suggest.

Utopics, or the creating of social values in Marin's sense, is a form of spatial play. In Peirce's lexicon, spatial play corresponds to the discovery, via semiotic phenomenology, of a Quality abstracted from its customary ground. Such Quality in Peirce's phenomenology is the forerunner of the Iconic sign function. The iconic sign conjunction is an initial visual representation of the *idea* of anything, where idea is regarded as a plan of an action. The visual, space-relational stage of an idea is therefore that idea in its initial utopic mode. In Common Law concepts of Place and Real Property have served as correspondences of this spatial relational aspect of social structures regulated and referent to law.

It is fair to say that that mode of utopic action which is exemplified by the pragmatic construction of new reality is, from a Peircean position, a prophetic anticipation of what is in vanguard research explorations called the study of complex systems. This new direction of inquiry is interdisciplinary, semiotically allied, and is concerned with understanding and explaining how systems may continue to regenerate, to create themselves, to reconstitute themselves in ongoing and dynamic manner.[3] E.g. the Santa Fe Institute is a major locus for the study of complex systems at present. The key word is *recreate*, where the emphasis is not upon restoring to a former state, but rather upon a systemic and dynamic utilization of itself, plus whatever resource it draws into dialogue with itself as an instrument for *Becoming*. This was the Realists' view of the growth of open legal systems as well. In this regard it was Dewey who left the pragmatic legacy to law (Dewey, 1939/1972:42-44).

II

Perhaps Dewey's *Quest for Certainty* and Peirce's descriptions of people's methods of attaining certainty in his early and seminal 'Fixation of Belief' paper are ways that pragmatism has taken to correct a fatal flaw in all previous utopic ventures. Utopia was earlier regarded as a means of securing ideal and certain beliefs in sociolegal orders and of anchoring such beliefs to sociolegal institutional structures which, as kinds or architectonic or architectural structures, depict leading cultural values in spatial relations and then *graphically* verify such values over time. So in this manner Continental hermeneutics have recently come to connect architectural art with social value (Habermas, 1989).

Peirce also, in a little known manuscript, has called attention to significant periods in human history, particularly in western history, when the emergence of new and dominant ideology was signalled by the creation of new styles in architecture, such that architectural construction is said to represent emergence of a new value in its initial and iconic manifestation.

One such period, according to Peirce, was around 1200 A.D., marked by the introduction of Gothic architecture. It opened up large space he says, and utilized a redefinition of such space by its preference for the oblong over the square. Peirce says that this emergence of a new ideology was among the most creative and most significant in the history of human thought, and it should be interpreted as a response to the jeremiads of the 10th century and the prophetic nihilism which that 10th century expressed as its hallmark or symbolic characteristic (Mss 1228, 1229).

The utopic impulse is traditionally not only a rejection of the actual world as it is, but is also a projection of an ideal world as perfectible, and realizable *in time*. The idea of a realization of utopic vision in time is a modern interpretation of the 'nowhere and nowhen' time-space locus of ideal culture prior to the 19th century. This modification of utopic vision grounds the ideal in an evolutionary context, and places the ideal in the realm of the possible, according to pragmatism, however, (J.C. Davis in Alexander and Gill, 1984:1-18).

By the time that Peirce began to develop his notions of pragmatism at the end of the 19th century, the ideology of sociology became a means of bringing about utopic visions into active, actual human society. From this perspective the utopic vision became not *alternative* to reality but extension of a malleable and reconstructible real world, (Bauman, 1976:9-17). From this perspective the utopic projection is likened to invention, i.e., to a reforming and adaptation of the actual rather than to a counter, parallel and fantastic mode of human existence. Even science fiction as a literary genre becomes closer to this utopic notion of invention that to the idea of a genuinely novel creation of human culture, growing itself.

Indeed, what happened around the time that Peirce began to develop his ideas of the pragmatic method, i.e., the method of semiotics from which *our* legal semiotics is derived, the idea of utopia has itself evolved and become differentiated into at least two main strains: one became an idealistic extension of otherworldliness and theological perfectibility -- a closed universe of thought or self-enclosed uroborically defined space -- of the nature of religious socialism.

On the topic of religious socialism, for example, Buber describes varieties of marxist utopianism. An other alternative path is of an open-ended, experimentalist nature, resembling a complex network of interacting communities which, as a whole, functions like a pluralistic system of signs, open and evolving, (Buber, 1949:38,39,141). Buber does not here directly speak of Peirce or of semiotics. But he does stress the *experimental* nature of ideas and growth and development of systems of thought in a Peircean manner. He describes, in fact, the continuity of confrontation between State and Individual such that the Absolute

State and the Absolute Individual, as the focal structure of confrontation in the law through the 12th century changes and becomes instead, as an evolving idea, a sovereign State with citizens as *attributes or properties*, (Buber, *id.*).

The great revolutions of the United States and of France were fought to reassert the relationary structure between State and Individual as between equivalents and conjuncts; but the earlier emphasis on certainty and the possibility of realizing the utopic quest became, in the words of anarchists such as Kropotkin, *misinterpretations*.

According to Buber, the utopic quest should be that which emphasizes openness and noncertainty, i.e., indeterminism. The goals of a free and growing society should not be goals which derive from or which aim toward the restatement of absolutes. The 'best' utopia should represent a society in which 'the fullest development of individuality combined with the highest development of free association in all its aspects, in all possible degrees and for all conceivable purposes: an ever-changing association bearing in itself the elements of its own duration and taking on the forms which at any moment best correspond to the manifold endeavors of all', (Buber, 1949:43).

The idea of an idea infinitely evolving, i.e., an inquiry which is never completed (as Peirce held) is what Kropotkin views as utopic; he says that 'We conceive the structure of society to be something that is never finally constituted' (cited in Buber, id.).

In refuting the existing order of all forms of social organization the anarchists were not calling for anarchy but rather for ad hoc norms and ad hoc institutions such that government with all its various modes *could* be desirable, and no particular government or its aspects *could* become dominant and absolutely authoritative. Self-government *means* self-organizing, i.e., the ability of a system to regulate and to restructure itself in a self-corrective and cybernetically creative manner. This Anarchistic view is indeed the way in which Peirce understands semiotic processes to be actively operative in the development of all thought. The capacity to doubt is the capacity for self-correction. Real doubt, based on the perception of new, i.e., genuinely new, factors in one's world, asks that inquiry on all topical question be reopened and that the creation of the Real -- the *signification* of the Real -- be resumed.

This is precisely how Peirce's method of pragmatism was understood by Durkheim when it first appeared in the 19th century 'How to Make our Ideas Clear.' It is this seminal essay, translated the year after its publication in English in the United States into the French piece, which so profoundly affected Durkheim's ides throughout his life that it led him to say that *the law which derives from custom in any given culture becomes, for that culture, a normative and a living myth.*

The Law, then, is like an evolving idea of a utopia continually changing. The Law, *as* norm, becomes the mirror for society and not the other way, where social structure and social value are mirrored *by* the law. The Law *acts* as an absolute, where no absolute *actually exists*.[4]

Durkheim credits pragmatism with having first recognized this turnabout in the law-society dialogue. Pragmatism lets Truth go, and invests in its stead the normaltivity of the Law. Thus, in Durkheim's interpretation of pragmatism, it is the law which provides the ground of value in an evolving and open and indeterminate pluralistic society. (Durkheim, 'Pragmatism and Sociology,' 1914/1955, 1983 edition, referred to in this paper.)

According to Durkheim, primitive societies are characteristically like the *quality* or primitive stage of an idea or thought; both are undifferentiated in its parts, and both present in a Bergsonian sense, appearances of undividedness. They are *iconic*. Our ideas of anything of life, of individual people, of social organizations -- all these present themselves to our understanding as a unity, 'a concentration, in which nothing is properly speaking outside the other parts,' (Durkheim, 1914/1955:94).

This is precisely what Peirce means by a Quality. Quality is that first stage in the phenomenological protosemiotic investigation when we attempt to prescind, abstract or isolate, a quality from its customary ground, from its *contextual* relation which we have formed as a habit of our thought.

Peirce points out that other approaches to phenomenology attempt to identify ultimate and indecomposable things, conceived as rudimentary and atomic phenomena. But, Peirce says, this is a contradiction in terms since if something is indecomposable then we could not discuss it in terms of its connections or relations with other 'indecomposable' phenomena for to do so would require that we speak of definitions, of attributes of predications, of parts which are *not* decomposable into more primitive parts. Thus the phenomenology which prepares us for semiotic analysis can and should attempt only to analyze *parts of the process of change*, since by considering the phenomenon of 'change' we are not speaking of indecomposable phenomena by merely of modes of relation which describe and represent change. In this focus on constituents of social culture -- i.e., art, law and indeed all the sub-topics of the Human Sciences -- we want to look at modes of individualization, of cell-splitting and of differentiation. For to differentiate is not only to break into parts, but it is also to constitute new meaning at the same time, since processes *are* significant. The process whereby signification grows is *Semiosis*.

In Durkheim's twentieth lecture on pragmatism and sociology he concludes his review and commentary of pragmatism, which he rightly credits Peirce with inventing, with the observation that the real is not only that which actually exists in the world, but also that the real filters through us and is known to us only by our ideas *of* the real. This Reality in its primitive stage, i.e., that stage which corresponds to Peirce's perceived Firstness of ideas or Representation of Real, is a fusion of all the possible categories of human understanding which exist and which evolve to exist at a later time, says Durkheim. Thus, what we *mean* at the occasion of inquiry into anything is through interpretation of the implications with other categories of thought and meaning that we hold also at that time and which act as a repository of a confused admixture of what we already know about the subject in focus. We have and hold an empty slot in the structures of our cognitions for all that is *not* known *but which may become known.* This slot is what Peirce calls an 'imaginary': a slot for genuine novelty and for our perception of such novelty. Peirce adapts this notion here from Hamiltonian mathematics (Kevelson, 1987).

With respect to later stages of our inquiry of any object of inquiry, Durkheim says the Reality of such an object may come to be viewed as a complex, multidimensional, multilevelled, pluralistic system of interrelating significance. But at an elemental stage -- that stage of anything real which precedes analysis, 'the primitive form of any reality is a concentration of all kinds of energies, undivided in the sense that they are only various aspects of one and the same thing. Evolution consists of a gradual separation of all these functions which were originally indistinct,' (Durkheim, *id.*).

Durkheim goes on to say that just as the secular and the scientific have separated, and just as art and religion are now separate universes of discourse, morality and law also are no longer part of a parent ritual; they were weaned from a common mother myth, and they have grown apart, (Durkheim, above, 94, 95).

Durkheim understood Peirce far too well to misconstrue his pragmatism: he knew that Peirce, James, Dewey, Schiller, for examples, never held that social categories of art, law, morality, science, religion were inherently part of a primitive idea which merely needed to *unfold* its reality. Evolution is not the unfolding of an immanent reality. It is the making, creating, continuous splicing and transforming of that which is known thus far in to unique, irreversible and unrepeatable aspects of the Real, becoming more Real.

Whatever it is that any utopic vision began as from the pragmatic viewpoint it evolves, since all ideas evolve *through inquiry*. Whatever value a particular utopic view brings forward is transformed in the process of being carried further. It is such value that the law in society develops also, as it carries forward its utopic quest.

In this sense Durkheim correctly understood Peirce's view, namely that the aesthetic function is a norm-creating function, and that the law is a norm-bearer no less than are works of art. A semiotic dialogue evolves as a more developed mode of interrelation between law and art and science and morality and religion and myth; these elements are con-fused in every *primitive* manifestation of Reality. The relation survives but the *mode* of relationship changes. Primitive modes of interrelations among these social categories do not remain at primitive stages of con-fusion. And it is our task as legal semioticians to understand the changing nature and *process* of these relations. In point, we are attempting to show that *our* reality of The Law at the end of our 20th century is still interconnected with ideas of art, morality, science, myth, etc. But modes of interconnection are today transformed and present interrelations need to be rediscovered, disclosed, described, and above all, *need to be utilized.*

III

The notion of practical use needs to be closely looked at since we find that although Durkheim has correctly understood the pragmatist position on the Truth as a useful instrument, in James' and especially in Royce's writings, he seems not to have grasped the function of myth in the *Peircean* pragmatic discourse. According to Durkheim, the activity of practical action should be sharply distinguished from the activity of speculating. He assigns under activities of speculating, playing, dreaming, and myth-making, (Durkheim, above, 76). Yet it is the imbrication of the play function with consequential action, especially in intervals between perceived changes of phenomena, that we see *traces* of play manifest as consequences of play activity. In this sense Peirce says that all ideas are consequential, thereby attributing to deliberate transformation and development of thought a consequential function, i.e., a practical role. Similarly, evolution of utopic vision, i.e., transformation of the ideal into teleological and realizable goals, is akin to but not identical with the myth-making process.

Durkheim says in this context and elsewhere that pragmatism comes along as a corrective at a time in human development, and in the development of human societies as a whole, when the failure of social action, lived as distinct from mythological activity, had done great damage and had created rifts between the ideal and the real in social value structures. As long as the ideal of the utopic was regarded as a structure of beliefs which is distinct from livable 'instruments of action' the schism between secular and sacred, between mind and body, between noumena and phenomena, would continue to split and fragment a holistic possibility of human society. For the era preceding pragmatism, Durkheim says, myths had 'no essentially practical character' (Durkheim, above, 76). Especially in primitive societies, i.e., *our* Reality of the primitive, myths are merely 'objects of belief. They are not merely poetic forms. They are also groupings or communities of representations aimed at explaining the world. They are systems of ideas whose function is essentially speculative' (Durkheim, above, 76).

Durkheim's point is that knowledge is, according to pragmatism, a plan of action. Myth-making and consequential myths as primitive forms of knowledge should be regarded as plans of action, too.

This is indeed what Peirce understands. He attributes to semiosis namely the process of complexity as it is evolving and becoming, even as pluralistic, differentiated ideas also grow and evolve. Emergent new aspects of thought are in dialogic relation with old and known aspects of idea. Ideas are continua. Structurally, this relation corresponds with constructions of all discovery processes, and constituent parts of all thought co-mingle the vague and the determined, the known and the new. In Dewey's sense the indeterminate situation is always the meeting of surprising fact with settled opinion, such that new situations need to be created as amalgam of both parts, and then put into the service of society.

The history of every idea corresponds with the history of all other social institutions, according to Durkheim. Just as alchemy is the forerunner of modern science, there are indeterminate situations when the discourse is nothing less that dialogue between the more primitive and the more advanced and complex. 'Speculation and practice were . . . intermingled in the very early stages' of all the human sciences. (Durkheim, above, 77).

Durkheim is less critical of Peirce's thought than of the pragmatism of James, of Dewey and of Schiller. Yet he has not had contact with the bulk of Peirce's unpublished work. He correctly notes, with Peirce: We think 'because of doubt.' We doubt because we are capable of perceiving genuinely new and surprising facts. New beliefs, or what we take as a myth-function of beliefs, leads to action in the world, since while a belief or a myth does not directly produce action or directly change the world it is our ability to predict and to anticipate the possible effects of acting on our beliefs which is, in effect, the *meaning of our beliefs*. These beliefs become represented as *law*, i.e., as living mythic norms.

Recall, as early as 1879 Durkheim first became acquainted with Peirce's semiotics, as earlier mentioned, in the French translation of 'How to Make our Ideas Clear', in *Revue Philosophique*, under the title '*Comment rendre nos idees claires.*' We know from Durkheim's own words that he kept close contact with Peirce's development of thought as late as James', *The Will To Believe*, in the new edition of 1911. Durkheim speaks, also, of the French translation of James' *The Meaning Of Truth*, (1895), which appears as *L'Idee De Verite*, (1913), a year before Peirce's death. Durkheim has indeed, with astounding fidelity to the growth and dispersement of the idea of pragmatism, kept close watch on Peirce long past Peirce's death, in 1914. Durkheim understood the *core* of pragmatism, namely that what we mean by truth is never a copy of a *given* reality, but is always a human invention, a sign, and an interpretation of knowledge which, at any given time in the evolutionary process of an idea stands *as* the reality of that idea (Durkheim, 1955:37). What Peirce calls a 'verisimilitude' is a 'simulation' in modern studies of complex systems and their evolutions.

Whatever we take the effects or consequences of an idea to be and to become is nothing other than the meaning of the object of these beliefs. It is the outcome of the thought that validates and gives meaning to the object. An object that has no by-product or effect upon the world remains absent of meaning. It may well be a significant absence, i.e., a Zero Sign or logical possibility which may yet become taken up at a later time and realized. But possibilities are not endowed with an infinite possibility. Rather, like seeds in a package, if not used and planted and cultivated they simply lose whatever potentially they had previously carried.

Durkheim is particularly taken with the pragmatist notion that the past doesn't die, that logical possibilities don't disappear, that all ideas of which consequences were imagined leave behind as existent *traces* of what they were, what they meant, what they could *possibly* mean. (Durkheim, 1955:79).

As noted, Durkheim first became acquainted with Peirce's theory of semiotics and his method of pragmatism in 1879, and his writings refers to Peirce's work thereafter. His own great opus on *The Division of Labor in Society* was first published in 1893; a second edition came out in 1902 and a third in 1907 and a fourth in 1911. I mention these dates because they dovetail with some of Peirce's most important thought which developed and came together in greater and more comprehensive revisions at corresponding dates. In this classic text of Durkheim's there are no direct references to the pragmatists; yet there are clear and marked uses of *law* as a prototypical system of normative and aesthetic function in society. This work has profound allusory connections to the pragmatists.

Durkheim devotes, in fact, a central and pivotal chapter of this work to the topic of interactivity and cross-reference between legal contracts and the idea of social cohesion. He develops the notion that as labor relations between increasingly more differentiated, i.e., less primitive and more complex, the idea of contract emerges and it, too, undergoes this process of becoming more complex and more differentiated. Durkheim calls attention to the fact that laws governing private property may be regarded as corresponding or isomorphic with the visceral system of the social organism. (Durkheim, 1983/1933:206).

This correspondence strongly parallels Peirce's much earlier observation which identifies the character of the indexical function in his theory of signs with the visceral structure in human beings. Both are characterized by a structure of opposition. In this sense the Quality of existence, experienced existence, is marked by agonistic, dramatistic, adversarial and oppositional interactional sign-function. The law, as I have argued elsewhere, is such a predominating indexical sign function. (Kevelson, 1988). As a social sign, it mediates between an expanded logic and a normative aesthetics. A theory of law mediates between actual legal and normative rules for conduct, i.e., Ethics, which depends upon a normative Aesthetics or Value-referent.

What is especially important for our purposes here is Durkheim's account of how the primitive notion of contract in law has evolved so that this contractual relation, as legal idea, has continued to become increasingly complex and to become differentiated into ideas for new discourse. Law creates new legal discourse. We as investigators become partners in this creative project.

It is the structure of contract, as dialogic and interactive structure, which is prototypical of the law as dispute between two parties mediated by a third, i.e., by law as official mediational actor. This dyad plus mediator is Peirce's triadic relationship in semiotics of all kinds.

Further, all meaning evolves consensually according to Peirce; it is the result of agreement and not of any empirical correspondence between an idea and a phenomenal 'thing.' Thus contractual relationships are the basis of social community and are the core structures in Law's complex system as well.

Durkheim correctly points out that parties may and do contract outside the law and do indeed contract in opposition to the law of the land: in such cases they are *lawless*. But the law stands in the background as context even though its role of mediator is replaced or represented by a 'higher law' or a *not-law* mediator. I will return to this point with respect to the notions of just and unjust wars which conclude the following and final section of this paper.

The idea of legal contract has evolved to include the notion of impossible contract, i.e., has become oxymoronic and even paradoxical. Yet the idea of 'Contract' still represents its previous stage as bona fide agreement based on trust, on faith, and on promises which terminate in mutual performance of both parties, as predicted. The contract is still central in law, even as Zero-Sign Contract.

To carry this notion a bit further: the idea of contract law is an expression of a particular type of utopic vision, namely that which is grounded in pragmatism and semiotics and is an instrument for carrying forward aesthetic functions. Contract, even in default, represents a value upon which societies build as toward a goal or ideal or model. This aesthetic function, from the pluralistic perspective of semiotics and pragmatism, is not uniform across the societies of human-kind. But as with any idea which evolves and grows, it too has differentiated into various forms. Primitive ideas of trust and contract and interaction are not sufficient. They do not permit us to say that we can reverse the process of semiotic development of ideas and get back to the idea in its simple and primitive state. We cannot grow asymmetrically. They evolve in the direction of emergent novelty, of complexity and of pluralistic diversity.

Durkheim knew this. It is essential for us to revise our understanding of the semiotic structure of social myths, with which he is so closely connected, in the light of a clear influence of Peircean pragmatics and semiotics upon his thought. Similarly, our inquiry into problems that directly pertain to legal semiotics could be enhanced and enriched by this reinterpretation of Durkheim, and especially of his notion of contractual relations and of contract law as an instrument for the realizing of utopian ideals in practical life. Contract Law in this light is instrumental as a new Reality.

Durkheim says that 'From this point of view, the law of contract appears in an entirely different light. It is no longer simply a useful complement of individual conventions; it is their fundamental norm. Imposing itself upon us with the authority of traditional experience, it constitutes the foundation of our contractual relations . . . . The law of contracts exercises over us a regulative force of the greatest importance since it determines what we ought to do and what we can require.' (Durkheim, 1893:214-15).

The idea of contract law has consequences upon our world. It is our understanding of such consequences that result in the meaning of the idea of contract-law. It is our acting upon those consequences which brings the mythic function of contract law into play. It is the utopic vision of a community interacting *as* community which has resulted in the pragmatic aspect of an open-ended and evolving utopic plan.

Durkheim's discussion of contract law seems closely connected with my interpretation of the Peircean semiotics view of contract (Kevelson, 1988, 1990). It is hard not to assert the direct influence of pragmatism on Durkheim's though, although traditional scholars of Durkheim are largely opposed to this connection.

Durkheim says that 'contract-law is that which determines the juridical consequences of our acts that we have not determined,' (Durkheim, 1893:214). The idea determines, from Firstness (which is free) to Secondness (as oppositional and fact-like function) to Thirdness (at which stage the idea has become a symbolic function) which transforms representation in to a convention.

In other words, the possibilities that attach to symbolic aspects of the idea of contract law act upon those who carry out this idea into actual practice in everyday life, such that contractual relations are never arbitrary but are results of values which have become, as ideas, institutionalized, conventionalized and established in the structure of the society in which they are functions. Contractual relations, according to this view, are not altogether free actions but are *verisimilitudes* or representations of the *idea* of contract law. 'We co-operate because we wish to, but our voluntary co-operation creates duties for us that we did not desire,' says Durkheim, (Durkheim, 1893:214).

Thus, the claim I wish to make is that the law, as based on contract-law, is a utopic *type of instrument* for interactive and genuine community structures.

IV

What we take from Durkheim, then, is a new interpretation of the Peircean semiotic dictum which holds that all knowledge has its source in experience, i.e., that experience constructed as opposition and interaction is our primary teacher. It is this opposition or agonistic structure which provides, *as experience*, primitive foundations of the idea of contract law. But it is the idea of contract-law, as symbolic complex sign, which provides a referential norm for our contractual relations in everyday life, including those which fall outside the domain of the law and those which are deliberately lawless or *nonlaw* with respect to a *codified* legal contract regarded as *legal norm*.

Violation of the law, just as violation of the norms, may be seen as creative artwork, as emergent qualities against a backdrop of customary context. Doubt raises qualities for new inquiry and investigation. Doubt furthers the growth of ideas, even of ideas it rejects.

In Durkheim's sense, 'a contract is not sufficient unto itself, but is possibly only thanks to a regulation of the contract which is originally social,' (Durkheim 1892:215).

A semiotic inquiry should appropriately turn back the world of experience for verification. It must check itself as idea against an actual experiential context. Its proof is in the eating.

I conclude here with an attempt to connect some notions explored above, on interrelations between myth, utopic vision, pragmatism and legal contract from a semiotics point of view with a glance or two at the notion of 'just war.'

War, it may be argued, is merely a further development of contractual relation. But some contractual relations are lawful and some, it is suggested, are not lawful. Some wars are just, (which is different from lawful), i.e. some wars are moral, and some are not moral. And yet a nonmoral war may be a lawful war; a moral contract may be nonlawful.

It is especially when we deal with current problems of contractual relations in Private International Law, or Conflicts of Law, that a legal semiotics approach may help in unraveling some of the tangles which have become part of the idea of contract law, just as ideal and primitive notions have been spun out and developed on other ideals and ideas.

Let us regard the utopic function in law, including international law, as a set of active principles which are canonesque, and which are referential in those legal cultures which ascribe to allegedly moral rules and prioristic notions of the good and the right. In the case of war and peace in the western world, it becomes increasingly difficult to extricate the myth of honorable war, as in the Trojan war, from the utopic quest, as in the Crusades. Further, extensions of the idea of a lawful peace, i.e., periods of overt amicability and open contractual relations such as in trade, diplomacy, exchanges of all kinds, are utopically-structured as *approximate* realizations of transcultural values and goals.

But there are also examples of lawless peace as well as of lawful peace, e.g., where nations interact with one another even though this interaction violates conventional norms of community that hold throughout globally unified cultures of other nation states. E.g. the Axis powers in World War II may be regarded as examples within such federation of lawless peace among *those* nations. Any treaty which is honored among nations is a sign of trust among them. Even limited trust is a kind of contract which established a bond or agreement, and need not refer to a shared set of ethical norms or moral mandates.

These problems and related distinctions between notions of just and unjust have been rarely examined from a semiotics perspective. Some inquiries, however, are in the nature of semiotic inquiries even though they are not self-identified as such. For example, Eugene Rostow examined distinctions between lawful and unlawful war and peace in a now-memorable discussion on the crisis in international law at the end of the critical nineteen-sixties.

Rostow asks, from whence comes any global acceptance among the nation states that war is ever a lawful act, an act grounded in ideal, transnational and utopian beliefs, in ideological commitments that cut across individual boundaries of nation states and definitions of sociolegal cultures, that war is the continuation of legal acts and expresses legitimate human values, (Rostow, 1968). Quite the contrary, Rostow says.

He argues that it is the utopic vision of 19th century American free enterprise which held that a lawful peace may be sustained *without* extending to force and to lawful war, (Rostow, 1968:39, 125). According to Rostow's view, Americans continue into the end of the 20th century to be deluded into believing that world peace will come to pass providing everyone follow the same moral right principles. Näively, he suggests, it is asserted that there is absolute right and good even in the face of all evidence to the contrary which shows that right and good are relativistic and pluralistic in this country and probably globally, and that the same war at one and the same time could be viewed by one and the same sociolegal culture as both lawful and unlawful, as just and unjust. Further, nonwar is neither a lawful peace nor a nonlawful peace, but is a different idea entirely.

Nonwar is a different utopian vision than is the vision of war. War and peace are two different *utopic* views.[5]

Rostow says that modern Americans are like latter-day Rousseauans who maintain that so-called creative toys will produce creative citizens, and that enlightened criminal justice procedures will produce rehabilitated and useful citizens, and that peace will reign on earth if we are in deed and in our contractual relations nonbelligerent. *The old Eden will be restored if we revive the primitive aspect of our old utopian ideas.* The old utopian notion, says Rostow, is of a harmony in which all are free and no one's freedom interferes with the freedom of others, (1968:39). This utopic vision is self-destructive, and is insidiously so.

This utopian ideal, he insists, should have no place in international law and international politics since it is wrong-headed: it holds that Peace is the norm and War is the abnorm.

Rather, Rostow says, the opposite is closer to what most people act on. What people act on and what they profess become opposed, he suggests, because the inappropriate utopic vision has been permitted to be dominant. In this dominant vision it is peace which, as norm, is said to correspond with moral good, and war, wrongly viewed as the opposite of peace rather than as another idea in relation with the idea of Peace, is seen as morally not-good, i.e., immoral.

Rostow notes that it is an 'illusion that law can prevail without force, either within societies or in the society of nations,' and the belief in this illusion is the belief in an inappropriate utopia, (Rostow, 1968:125). Similarly, according to Peirce, belief in an inappropriate ideal which has consequences in the world and in the reality we make of the world, is *not ethical.*

Rostow uses the notion of utopic function only in a pejorative sense, failing to distinguish, as Durkheim *has* distinguished, between appropriate and inappropriate kinds of utopic visions or plans of action. According to Rostow, 'law cannot be imposed . . . by force alone.' Rather, he goes on, 'in societies of consent law must be sustained by public force backing the general will . . . (and) In international society (law) is inconceivable without the rational and agreed control of force.' (Rostow, *id.*).

Finally, in ending this inquiry, I want to regard utopic vision in contractual relations, i.e., in particular legal cultures as well as in international legal cultures, as a valency or directional channel for evolving and transmitting belief in the force of contractual will-power.

When Simone Weil's *The Iliad As A Poem Of Force* became talismanic for the new wave of the 1960's it triggered off a wish to return to Nowhere and to Nowhen, i.e., to a primitive elemental and undeveloped stage in the history of the idea of utopia. Utopia is the plan. Myths which tell utopic designs and plots are manifold, as competing explanations for contractual relations in law and community as a whole.

I conclude this paper with a reference intended to keep some questions open. I want to touch upon some definitions of law referred to by Hirst in his recent *On Law And Ideology*, (1979).

Here Hirst examines the idea of social relations as imaginary or utopic relations, i.e., as ideology which is *not* grounded in experience, he suggests.[6] He introduces in this study an approach to the function of law in society which is a semiotics in aim, (but not so labelled). Here Hirst turns our attention to Pashukanis' thesis which holds that 'Law is a realm of equivalent subjects in contest,' (Hirst, 1979:156-57) and further, that all legal functions including that of legal persons are but extensions and tokens of commodity forms. It is law, finally, which is that process that links legal relates whether they are human or goods or commodities or subjects of any kind. It is from this point of view that the process of law creates a process of change in social value. It is law as nexus-in-flux which becomes instrumental in bringing about changes in the status of contractual relations and thus effects changes in the meaning and force of beliefs for community-wide plans of action. Law is not, from this perspective, merely a blueprint of action: Law is action acting.

Hirst and Pashukanis, like Peirce and Durkheim and to a large extent also like Rostow, have found their way back to Locke and to the notion of legal subject as a discursive device, i.e., a sign, an instrument and even a strategy for producing new knowledge and new reality, (Hirst, 161).[7]

ENDNOTES

1. Roberta Kevelson is Director of The Center for Semiotic Research in Law, Government and Economics, and is Distinguished Professor of Philosophy at Penn State.

2. If we choose to say, as I do, that although traditional utopic idealogy presupposed ideal conditions for human societies where the idea of 'ideal' referred to perfectible organizations, i.e., some notion of a closed system and to the process of repairing damage by existential accident and circumstance, the idea of a new utopic ideology may be extended. Thus, a utopic society may transform and extend previous notions of Utopia. In this sense an ideal society may no longer be viewed as a state, or a static organization, but rather as a self-organizing human community.

3. The older idea of utopia as a static society presupposes that it may be explained and described by structural analysis, such as we find in nonPeircean approaches to legal semiotics. By contrast, a functional approach such as Peirce suggests for legal semiotics has to do with dynamics, with evolution, and changes in complex systems. From this perspective a predominant social value is inseparable from change and evolutionary transformation of all interdependent parts of any system into greater complexity and hence into more meaning and reality.

   I suggest in this paper that by having come into close contact with Peirce's writings on pragmatism and semiotics, Durkheim at least warmly entertained an idea of social utopias as ideal social systems, and therefore as aesthetically marked for social referent values.

4. See Kevelson, 1987, especially Chapter Five on Peirce's theory of the evolution of ideas as a dynamic and nonfinite process.

5. Rostow points to an especially important distinction between force and coercion. It is essential to investigate the desirability of force, of power, of valency, i.e., of such terms which may be included under the general heading of rhetorical persuasion, since it is the

purpose of communicative interaction in general and of Speech Acts in Law in particular to bring about consequential or meaningful purposes of thought. Peirce speaks of the 'continuum predicate' -- with reference to legal procedure -- as an assertion, the consequence of which reaches effectually into the future. See Kevelson, 1987, 69-82.

6. Hirst's thesis emphasizes the point made here, namely that a utopically-structured legal myth which is not grounded in transaction and dialogue is not qualitatively comparable with a Promise in Law (in Atiyah's sense above), and neither is it of the same character as a Contract in law. Rather it is of the nature of a wish and is not an Index or semiotic sign-function which does lead to real results in actual human society.

7. Max Fisch, especially, points up Peirce's return in his late years to a 'physicalism' which has its origins in Locke, just as Peirce's entire approach to modern semiotics takes its cue from Locke's *Essay*. See Fisch's introduction to Volume III of the *Writings of Charles S. Peirce.*

REFERENCES

Alexander, Peter and Roger Gill, eds., 1984, *Utopias*, London:Gerald Duckworth & Co., Ltd.

Atiyah, Patrick S., 1981, *Promises, Morals and Law,* Oxford: Clarendon Press.

Bauman, Zygmont, 1976, *Socialism: The Active Utopia,* London: George Allen & Unwin Ltd.

Bloch, Ernst, 1974/1988, *The Utopian Function of Art and Literature,* J. Zipes and F. Mecklenberg, eds., Cambridge, Mass.: M.I.T. Press.

Boas, George, 1959, *The Inquiring Mind*, LaSalle, Ill.: Open Court Pub. Co.

Dasqupta, P., 1988, *Trust as a Commodity*, Giambetta, Diego, ed., 49-72.

Dewey, John, 1939/1972, *Theory of Valuation,* Chicago: University of Chicago Press.

Durkheim, Emile, 1955/1983, *Pragmatism and Sociology,* J. Allcock, ed., J.C. Whitehouse, trans., from 1914 Lectures. See also Harper edition, K.H. Wolff, ed., 1960.

Durkheim Emile, 1893/1933/1964, *The Division of Labor in Society,* G. Simpson, trans., New York: Free Press.

Edelman, Murray, 1967, *The Symbolic Uses of Politics,* Urbane, Ill.: University of Illinois Press.

Fuller, R. Buckminister, 1968, *Operating Manual for Spaceship Earth,* London & Amsterdam: Feffer & Simons, Inc.

Goodwin, Barbara, 1984, in Alexander and Gill, *Economics and Social Innovation in Utopia,* 69-84.

Hacking, Ian, 1990, *The Taming of Chance,* Cambridge: Cambridge University Press

Hayek, Frederick, A., 1960, *The Constitution of Liberty*, Chicago: University of Chicago Press.

Hirst, Paul, 1979, *On Law and Ideology*, London: MacMilan Press, Ltd.

Hobbes, Thomas, 1662-1679/1971, *A Dialogue Between a Philosopher and a Student on the Common Laws of England*, J. Cropsey, ed., Chicago: University of Chicago Press.

Kevelson, Roberta, 1987, *Charles S. Peirce's Method of Methods*, Amsterdam: John Benjamins.

_____, 1988, *The Law as a System of Signs*, New York: Plenum Publishing Co.

_____, 1990, *Peirce, Praxis, Paradox: The Image, The Conflict, The Law,* Berlin: Mouton de Gruyter.

_____, 1992, in preparation, *Peirce's Esthetics,* New York: Peter Lang Publishers.

Luhman, N. Klas, 1988, *Familiarity, Confidence, Trust*, in Gambeltz, ed., 94-108.

Marin, Louis, 1984, *Utopica: Spatial Play*, R. A. Ullrath, trans., New Jersey: Humanities Press.

Mumford, Lewis, 1922/1950, *The Story of Utopias,* New York: Viking Press.

Peirce, Charles S., 1967, Microfilm edition of 30 reels of unpublished manuscripts, with annotated catalogue by R. Robins, M.I.T. Press

_____, 1931-35; 1958, *Collected Papers*, Vols 1-8, Ch. Hartshorne, A. Burks, P. Weiss, eds., Cambridge, Mass: Harvard University Press.

_____, 1982, 1984, 1986, 1990, *Writings of Charles Sanders Peirce*, Vols. 1-4, M. Fisch, Ch. Kloesel, et al, eds., Bloomington: Indiana University Press.

Rostow, Eugene, 1986, *Law, Power and the Pursuit of Peace*, Lincoln: University of Nebraska Press.

Shapiro, Michael, 1991, *The Sense of Change: Language as History*, Bloomington: Indiana University Press.

Smith, Joseph Wayne, 1986, *Reason, Science and Paradox,* London: Croom Helm.

Chapter 11

The Metaphysics of Punishing

Jay Knaack[1]

I

Most anyone interested in the problems of punishment sooner or later encounters the modern dispute between retributivists and utilitarians. Indeed, for many this provides a primary introduction and formal understanding of the entire problem. Readers and listeners, however, may find themselves tugged now one way and now another, and finally confronted with a haze of paradoxes, abandon the subject altogether. This is because retributivists and utilitarians are sometimes interested in the grounds for culpability, and are sometimes interested in the proper nature of penalties, which invariably become blurred. Also, each theory emphasizes but one aspect of those many considerations which contribute to culpability, which is absurd; intentionality in the case of retributivists, and harmful consequences in the case of utilitarians. Pointing out the shortcomings in each others' theories and the possibility of supporting tyrannical practices, they are both forced to endlessly modify their own. Others yet may interpret the two theories as involving substantially differing views of the grounds for culpability and the nature of punishment, related to differing views about the nature of persons, society, justice and politics. They may therefore be simply inclined to confirm one position or the other, and dismiss the non-preferred theory as misguided or extremist.

Now punishing and rewarding are everyday problems in the family, schools, business, sports, law and etc. It is probably deceptive to suppose any one simplified theory like retributivism or utilitarianism can accommodate (explain and justify) all of the forms and problems of culpability and punishment. Theoretical disputes of this nature therefore can be viewed as simply irrelevant (Harding and Ireland, 1989), and cut off from their historical bases in penal reform (Newman, 1978), where we find that neither theory by itself is entirely practical, acceptable, or operational. So we are left to consider whether the theoretical dispute reflects or duplicates more mundane features of penal reasoning and practice: displacement, regression and diversion. These last features, I suggest, require futher exploration, particularly in view of the fact that both theories about the principles of punishing contain political theories or disguised political agendas. In this case they can be interpreted as forms of utopian rhetoric or apologetics.

For example, retributivists, who claim punishment applies only to the guilty without any reference to extrinsic social or political aims, are often viewed as making a presumption in favor of individual liberty, liability, and desert over any demands of political or social necessity. Utilitarians, who claim that punishments should be administered only for the sake of some beneficial consequences, are viewed as making a presumption in favor of utility or the social good over individual liberty. For many, they entail two differing views of justice and the social order. The idea is that retributivism is more congenial to minimal state interference in the liberty of individuals to construct their own social relations. Utilitarianism is supposedly more congenial to an active and responsible state role in the construction of social relations.

On this level, how the theories and arguments are interpreted depend a great deal upon how various arguments are weighted, juxtaposed and constructed, and upon what examples and counter examples, or situations are used. Quite often, what promises to be a juridical science turns into political polemics.

This introduces two further related considerations. If the practice of punishment is taken to indicate, confirm, and symbolize, however loosely, status and power relations that exist in society, then offering differing rationales for punishments that exist may amount to little more than apologetics or a sign of frustration about the institution of punishment itself. Because of this, some view punishment as a regrettable fact about social life that cannot be given any rational justification. Others view it as a necessity that can be given a wide variety of justifications. Hence, we are left with the problem of trying to decide upon what constitutes a justification.

II

Newman (1978) provides considerable insight into the genesis of the problem. We should consider that punishment emerged as a distinctly modern problem for reflection when the individual came to be viewed as detached from religion, class, hierarchy and the state, and also in fact removed from the possibility of creating simple (or more primitive) constructions of equal desert, compensation (composition) or atonement. Hence, retributivism and utilitarianism, offering simple, straightforward and objective theories of compensation, gained possession of center stage. But as it turns out, neither can offer a satisfactory theory of just compensation acceptable in practice. The attempt, most notably made by Bentham, entails nothing less than creating an exhaustive schedule of degrees of culpability, damage and corresponding penalties, using what appear to be objective measures of net material utility, (which turn out to be exceedingly elusive).

Let us suppose, for example, that a retributivist claims that the primary consideration in punishing is to repay in kind an intentional infringement of a law. Let us suppose a utilitarian claims that the primary consideration in punishing is the realization of some good consequences, for example, respect for law. Are we therefore to be committed to upholding one truism or the other? What would be gained?

According to Harding and Ireland (1989), in practice punishment may have an astronomical number of forms and functions, as well as a tremendous number of motives and intentions in its application. In practice, punishments can have unintended consequences as well as consequences differing from those intended. For example, utilitarian intentions may conceal retributivist motives, and retributivist intentions may conceal utilitarian motives. Retributivist policies may have utilitarian consequences, and so forth. But in practice, it is impossible to distinguish retributive and utilitarian aims, (1989: 91).

Commenting on the dispute, these authors say:

> 'a cursory view of the writing conveys more than anything else a sense of argumentative virtuosity generated by academic ritual. If an uninformed reader, plunged into the middle of this debate, were to inquire 'what does it matter, anyway?' he would have to work quite hard to extrapolate a clear answer to that simple but important question. Indeed, much of the writing in this area is self-consciously prefaced by references to difficulties and obscurities.' (1989: 62).

III

I shall presently examine reasons for this either/or dichotomy between retributivists and utilitarians. We have already seen that they can be interpreted as concealing, or espousing, political agendas. According to Harding and Ireland (1989: 23), theorists are prone to place extreme cases of criminal (legal) culpability at the center of their arguments and suppose they address the problem of punishment globally, which would explain why the death penalty, as well as specters of political tyranny so often figure in the dispute. Choosing such examples, however, lead one to suppose the state alone is responsible for punishing and maintaining social order. Quoting from Michael Ignatieff (Harding and Ireland, 1989: 26), that crimes which the state punishes ought to be interpreted as the tip of an iceberg, they argue that legal forms of punishment are merely a small aspect of punishments that pervade a society as a whole. A somewhat similar point is made by Newman who attributes modern theory to anxiety over the role of the modern state. Newman, it will be recalled, claims that modern theory is detached from history; Harding and Ireland consider it detached from society. Hence, we should consider punishment in its wider historical and social context. Global truisms and assumptions about the role of the state, in other words, can effectively keep us from coming to grips with the problems.

From a wider view, punishment can be seen as an important part of the processes of interpersonal interaction. From cradle to grave, many forms of punishment serve processes of habituation or socialization. The family, schools, and all institutions employ a wide variety of sanctions and punishments. Punishment may consist of denials, or denied rewards, ostracism, verbal and physical coercion, shaming and shunning, and the denial of privileges. Indeed, almost any punishment will consist in more than one thing, intention or consequence. In other words, there are many social factors that influence law.

In view of this, theoretical decisions about what are to count as serious offenses warranting legal sanctions as opposed to informal sanctions are themselves arbitrary (Harding and Ireland, 1989: 85).

Let us now look at the theories. Briefly, and in general, retributivists rest their case upon the justice of proportionately equal compensation. Punishment is good for its own sake and restores a balance or is demanded by social reciprocity. In the hands of the state, punishment can be impersonal and a result of due process so that it is not a matter of private revenge. Also, the person punished must have willingly committed an infraction of a known and legitimately-made law. This view has been heavily criticized.

According to Newman, the idea of retribution is founded upon the idea of compensation between equals, or equal compensation for injury. However, the modern state is not an equal to the offender (Newman, 1978: 6-7). Rarely, if ever, is strict retribution allowed or carried out. Furthermore, today people are not in positions of social equality, and therefore retributivists are faced with the problem of the just distribution of punishment. Retributivists who claim that punishment is deserved because a law was broken, may ignore the possibility of mitigating circumstances. Also, retributivits may ignore questioning whether a law is just or not, or ignore the fact that laws are social conventions that single out classes of actions and persons in many different ways, placing some at disadvantages in some situations and at an advantage in others.

Utilitarian theory was devised, like retributivism, as a reform for arbitrary judicial practices, particularly the use of subjective elements in sentencing and prescribing punishments. Utilitarians do not claim that crime automatically calls for punishment, but that punishment is an evil in itself and ought to be administered for some good. In the classical utilitarian view, sanctions are necessary to maintain social order. Punishments should not be administered simply to inflict suffering, but only if it is to some greater or lesser degree useful in preventing crime. Hence, the disutility of punishment should be weighed against the amount of possible good that could result in order to deter or prevent crime.

As retributivists have pointed out, the emphasis on deterrence or prevention can upset justice in straightforward retribution, and devalue individual autonomy and responsibility. Utilitarians, on the other hand, claim that retribution merely for the sake of retribution, and without reference to any foreseeable consequences, can make punishment appear to be little more than an excuse for vengeance, or simply arbitrary. But social research suggests there is much more to the story. According to Harding and Ireland:

> An act acquires its social meaning from the way in which it is perceived. Those involved in an instance of punishment, the punisher, the punished, and other people (who may be split into a greater or fewer number of discrete subgroups) may conceivably all view the infliction of unpleasantness differently and may all ascribe a different 'purpose' to the same social fact. To the observing scientist it may be difficult to select any one of these interpretations as being the 'correct' one. (1989: 94).

Therefore, for example, to claim that the aim of punishment is to deter, as a utilitarian might argue, ignores the fact that actual deterrence may depend upon a number of variables. Some people will be deterred while others will not be depending upon motivation and perceptions of the law. To claim that the aim of punishment is to simply correct an imbalance or restore reciprocity as a retributivist might say will also depend upon a wide range of variables: the sort of law broken, circumstances, consequences, situations of the actors and so forth.

Actually both retributivists and utilitarians tend to assume that law and its administration will be ideally just in order to make others assume their own schemes are just. However, according to Newman, retributivists when pressed for some rationale for retribution, turn to utilitarian justifications. Utilitarians, according to Newman, largely rationalize obedience to the state. Utilitarians also presuppose the sense of retribution which makes sense of their own theory. But of course, utilitarians can claim that retributivists presuppose a sense of utility and disutility which makes sense of their own theory.

Therefore, we are left with the paradox that utilitarian theories conflict with the sense of retributive justice, while retributive theories conflict with the sense that punishment should be administered for some good reason other than simple retribution. This leads us to consider just why these two views of punishment are separated. Are retributivists champions of individual liberty, responsibility, and rationality, and the utilitarians champions of the social good? According to Newman, the retributivist and utilitarian responses to punishment are not new: they are, in fact, the oldest responses to punishment imaginable. Furthermore, we can locate parallels to these two responses in early childhood (Piaget, 1932).

IV

Piaget noted in many interviews with children that they are prone to be more harsh in assigning punishments to others on a reflective level than they would to themselves when told stories about hypothetical wrongdoing. They also exhibited a moral lag; they tended to apply very elementary reasons for punishing which they themselves had outgrown: for example, someone should be punished or deserves to be punished because they broke a rule or disobeyed their parent, or because something bad happened, or in order to keep the culprit from doing it again, regardless of considerations of intentions or the justice of the rules. These forms of elementary objectivism Piaget calls 'moral realism.' Similar reactions can be observed in adults. If utilitarianism and retributivism are interpreted in this narrow reductionistic sense, emphasizing consequences or rule breaking out of the many factors that can and do contribute to degrees of culpability and the assignment of appropriate punishments, they could be considered to exhibit a similar theoretical lag or regression.

The separation in penal theory between intentions and consequences can be seen most clearly in the works of Jeremy Bentham (1780, 1789; 1816, 1824) and Immanuel Kant (1785; 1797). Both objected to sentencing practices based upon what they called "sentiment." Both were evidently elaborating upon and reacting to the work of Beccaria (1764). Bentham seemed to be reacting to a wide range of incoherent practices and excessive punishments, preferring alternatives in legal and social reform. Bentham claimed that punishment is an evil which, if necessary, should be justified by resulting in some good. Kant seemed to think that utilitarian schemes would allow too little punishment, resulting in disrespect for law and personal responsibility and the use of punishments for social ends irrelevant to personal liability. Bentham contended that sanctions are necessary to curb egotistic tendencies and to assure compliance with practices that produce social and private goods. Hence, punishment, like all laws and social policies which curtail liberty, should be based upon a calculus of material benefits: the greatest happiness principle.

Kant maintained that people are, or, can be governed by reason or universal dictates of duty over and above the temptations of self-love or utility. The social order is founded upon self-willed commitment and obedience to universal and objective law. Principled behavior should not be influenced by feeling. Only good intentions to follow the dictates of duty, not personal desires for particular consequences, count in the consideration of which principles are truly right. According to Kant, principled behavior produces a kingdom of rational beings, or an enlightened regime of understanding that is above personal desire. Warning against the pitfalls of utilitarian thought, he claimed that only the laws of retribution can determine proper punishment; all other standards fluctuate and are mixed. Bentham claimed that appeals to universal reason, natural laws, or extra legal rights, are also suspect, and are ultimately subjective being based upon insupportable intuitions. Intuitions can serve to disguise other motives for punishment, and ignore the social and personal consequences of punishment and laws.

Therefore, retributivists may claim, following Kant, that their theory protects personal autonomy and freedom of choice. People should not be punished for social purposes. Considerations of consequences are suspect since they allow punishment for purposes extrinsic to justice in retribution. Individuals must be assumed to be adults who can follow reason on their own and be strictly self-responsible and therefore can be made to suffer in kind for disobedience. Utilitarians, following Bentham, may claim that good intentions to follow universal laws are suspect. So long as behavior is based in principles that are held to be universally correct without reference to social harms or benefits, it may disguise purposes extrinsic to or contrary to the social good. Theories of rational duty may also create thoughtless compliance to rules. In reply, retributivists claim that utilitarians advocate manipulating individuals by the use of threats to ensure uniform social compliance. Utilitarians, on the other hand, claim that justice in retribution is a disguise for revenge.

However, it has been argued that utilitarians presuppose a sense of retribution in order to make sense of their own theory. Retributivism, on the other hand, is inseparable in theory from such social sounding aims as preserving respect for common law or restoring social order. Now are these theories by themselves, in some pure and ideal world of their own, even improvements over some other world in which sentencing and punishment are absolutely arbitrary? If a utilitarian might allow scapegoating and the punishment of the innocent for social purposes, as retributivists claim, the retributivist would allow people to be at liberty to follow and enforce the letter of laws regardless of consequences, and would enforce retribution whether just or not as utilitarians claim. Does the dialogue between these two theories sharpen our senses of justice, or does it merely provide the illusion that one or the other must be correct?

It could be argued that retributivists' distrust any imposition of punitive sanctions upon individuals for the sake of objective sounding social purposes. Utilitarians, we could say, distrust moral idealism rooted in abstract theories of freedom. But, in fact, if punishment does not work out as either may claim it should in their own ideal scheme, they can blame each other for it. Since intentions and consequences are usually inseparable in practice, retributivists can say that the problem with punishment is the influence of utilitarian thinking; that considerations of social consequences upset justice. The utilitarian can say the problem is due to the influence of narrow retributivist thinking which can also be unjust. Supposedly, each theory must remain pure and uncontaminated by the other in order to remain objectively pure and just. Since both believe they are right and the problem of punishment can be resolved, they can blame each other for its lack of resolution. This is because, in fact, each theory will be contaminated (and should be contaminated in the broader interest of justice) by the other.

V

In conclusion we find that the two theories, for various historical reasons, are heritages of reform movements to make determinations of guilt and punishment objective. One emphasizes willful rule infraction, the other measureable consequences. Their objective solutions for assigning just reparations however, may be too wide or too narrow depending upon how equal retribution and measures of utility are defined. Both theories are considerably more sophisticated responses to punishment than one may find in children, yet one can note parallels with adolescent moral realism.

The assignment of guilt and punishment in mature practice usually does and should account for intentions and consequences, as well as circumstances, motives, foreseeable and unforseeable consequences, character, situation, knowledge, justice of the rules and applicability of rules, and etc. To suppose that an objective science of compensation can be developed upon mere payment in kind, or measures of utility, therefore, exhibit something like a theoretical lag, or regression. The habit of partisans of the two theories to blame the other side for the failures of penal justice, and their recourse to political rhetoric, seem to be forms of displacement. Together, they can result in a diversion from the problems of practice.

ENDNOTES

1. Jay Knaack is Associate Professor of Philosphy and Religious Studies at the University of West Florida.

REFERENCES

Beccaria, C. B., 1764/1963, 1984, *Dei delitti e delle pene,* English Trans. by Henry Paolucci, *An Essay on Crimes and Punishments*, Indianapolis: Bobbs Merrill.

Bentham, Jeremy, 1780, 1789/1948, *Introduction to the Principles of Morals and Legislation*, Reprint of the 1823 edition, New York: Hafner Publishing Co.

_____, 1816, 1824/1973, *Book of Fallacies*, Reprinted in *Bentham's Political Thought*, 228-256, Bhikhu Parekh, ed., New York: Harper & Row Publishers.

Harding, Christopher and Richard W. Ireland, 1989, *Punishment-Rhetoric, Rule and Practice*, London: Routledge.

Kant, Immanuel, 1785/1948, *Grundlegung zur Metaphysik der Sitten*, English Trans. by H. J. Paton, *Groundwork of the Metaphysic of Morals*, New York: Harper & Row.

_____, 1797/1965, *Metaphysische Anfangsgründe der Rechtslehre, Part I of Die Metaphysik der Sitten*, English Trans. by John Ladd, *The Metaphysical Elements of Justice*, Indianapolis: Bobbs-Merrill.

Newman, Graeme, 1978, *The Punishment Response*, Philadelphia: J.B. Lippincott Company.

Piaget, Jean, 1932/1965, *Le Jugement moral chez l'enfant*, English Trans. by Marjorie Gabin, *The Moral Judgment of the Child*, New York: The Free Press.

Chapter 12
Semiosis as Ritual

J. Ralph Lindgren[1]

'...[I]f ritual is the cradle of language,
metaphor is the law of its life.' (Langer, 1942: 125)

I

Why study the history of ideas? Umberto Eco, at the beginning of his treatment of Porphyry, observed that 'every revisitation of the history of signs is fruitful, because it helps to discover the remote origins of some contemporary theoretical 'camp.''(Eco, 1984: 46) To this I would add that it can often also enrich the insights and techniques of contemporary semiotics.

In this essay I revisit the early Pythagoreans who flourished from the 6th to the 4th centuries B. C. E. I select them because theirs is among the oldest living traditions to consciously focus on systems of signs as the ultimate basis of meaning. I do so in the hope of promoting reciprocal advantage for both classical scholarship and semiotics. In particular I hope to motivate the hypothesis signalled in the essay's title.

On this tour I intend to travel light, deploying very few of the devices of modern semiotics. I do this both to keep the analysis comprehensible and to permit any discoveries to be applicable to the maximum range of 'contemporary theoretical camps.' Following Peirce, Morris and Eco I understand signs as anything that can be taken by someone as standing for anything else and semiosis as a metaphoric rather than as an encoding process. (See, for example, Eco, 1984: 43, 88)

II

The central feature of early Pythagorean doctrine[2] was captured by Aristotle: 'they supposed the elements of numbers to be the elements of all things and the whole heaven to be a *harmonia* and a number.'(Aristotle, *Metap*. I, 5. 986 a 1-3) Three applications of that doctrine were made -- to music, to nature, and to morals. As to the application of number to music, Guthrie gave the following account.

> Until Hellenistic times . . . there was no such thing as harmony in our sense. *Harmonia* meant (a) tuning, (b) scale and (c) octave, and classical Greek music was melodic, without the use of chords. In calling certain intervals concordant, therefore, the contemporaries of Pythagoras referred to melodic progression. The essential point, however, is that the three intervals of octave, fourth and fifth were regarded as primary, as the elements out of which any musical scale or composition was built. To Pythagoras went the credit of perceiving that this basic framework depended on fixed numerical ratios 1:2 (octave), 3:2 (fifth), 4:3 (fourth). (Guthrie, 1962: 223)

The doctrine was applied to nature in two stage: the one showing how number is generated from limit and the unlimited; the other showing how bodies are generated from number.[3] Number, for the Pythagoreans, has its origin in fundamental opposition, most often expressed in the form of a table of opposites headed by the contraries 'limit' and 'the unlimited.'[4] The most common derivation of odd and even, the basic elements of number, from limit and the unlimited proceeds through the intervention of another pair of opposites, *viz.*, square and oblong.[5] The first number generated in this way is the unit. While opinions differ about the status of the unit in relation to the other numbers, i.e., whether the it stands (as Plato urged) outside the number series or is part of it, its role in their generation is clear. When added to an odd or an even number it produces the opposite.

The Pythagorean account of the generation of bodies from numbers is often referred to as the 'fluxion theory'. The unit is a dimensionless point, for dimension is the interval between units. Dimension appears when the unit is successively added to itself. With two the dimension is a line, with three a surface (triangle), with four a solid body (pyramid). (Cornford, 1957: 8-13; Guthrie, 1962: 263-4)

The result of applying number to the whole of nature was the representation of it as an ordered and beautiful cosmos. Two aspects of Pythagorean cosmology are remarkable even in our day. One is that it displaced the earth from the center of the universe. (Guthrie, 1962: 282-3) The other, 'the harmony of the spheres' doctrine. Reasoning that: (a) the motion of celestial, just as terrestrial bodies, produces sound; (b) the pitch of their sounds, like that of terrestrial sounds, is determined by the ratios of their intervals; and (c) their intervals replicate that of the harmonic scale; they concluded that the heavens are filled with harmonious music. (Aristotle, *De Caelo* II, 9. 290 b 12-24)

The Pythagoreans asserted that everything is number, even such conventional realities as marriage and such moral characteristics as justice. There was apparently wide disagreement about just what the number of these realities are, some asserting that the number of marriage is 5, some 3, others still 10.

Similarly, whereas there was agreement that justice is the square number, they disagreed about what that number is. (Guthrie, 1962: 303-4)

Pythagorean doctrine has consistently provoked exasperation in its readers. Exasperation seems the appropriate sentiment for such doctrines as 'things themselves are numbers', the 'harmony of the spheres' and 'justice is the square number' because such statements are quite obviously false. Marriage, justice, Jupiter, this paper, myself, simply ARE NOT numbers. For many that is the end of the matter. Others wonder if there is not perhaps more to it. A clue lies in a remark by Cornford:

> . . . if a man says that 'Justice is the square number' he cannot mean that Justice is a plane figure composed of four unit-points; obviously he means that the square figure is a symbol which represents or embodies the nature of fairness, just as when an honest man was called 'four-square without reproach', no one imagined that his figure really had four corners.' (Cornford, 1957: 26)

The clue here lies in Cornford's proposal that the Pythagorean doctrine is metaphorical. Like what is said of the honest man, it is literally false, but nevertheless admits of an interpretation, although of an unconventional kind. The thought that Pythagorean doctrine proposes one of the great root metaphors of the ages is not novel. (Pepper, 1942 and Collingwood, 1945) Before it can be developed, we need to clarify what is involved in the metaphorical process and to identify the competencies needed to test the hypothesis.

III

The traditional view until about fifty years ago was that metaphor is an elliptical simile useful for stylistic, rhetorical, and didactic purposes, but which can be literally paraphrased without any loss of cognitive content. Since then a small library on the metaphorical process, rich in interdisciplinary research, has appeared. (Lindgren, 1989) Several general themes are now well established. Metaphors are not completely paraphrasable, nor is their function limited to figurative speech. Metaphor pervades not only all discourse, but all thought and action as well. (Johnson, 1981: 42-4) Although at first regarded as a purely verbal transfer[6], the metaphorical process is now thought to be manifested wherever one domain is treated in terms of another. (Lakoff and Turner, 1989)

On the new understanding, metaphor inevitably involves putting dedicated tokens to unconventional uses, e.g., 'Mary is a peach.' At the same time, the main use of metaphor is not to inform, but to urge hearers to regard its subject in other than conventional ways.[7] Even so, metaphors must retain some linkage to a common ground if at least some hearers are to be able to distinguish them from lies. Accordingly, a certain tension between the metaphoric act and its context is a characteristic feature of metaphor. (Johnson, 1981: 23)

Consider one of Eco's examples, 'the tooth of the mountain.' There the nouns (tooth and peak) are substitutable because in this context they both express a common meaning (sharpened form). But there is more to it than that. Metaphor is not elliptical simile. Besides having something in common the substituted nouns also stand in opposition. The peak of the mountain is not part of a living organism. A tooth does not afford a habitat for alpine flora. For metaphors to 'work' the tension between shared common features and opposition of differences must be balanced so that, at least for some competent interpreters, neither overwhelms the other.

There are, of course, no recipes for accomplishing that balance. As Eco observed:

> No algorithm exists for the metaphor . . . . The success of a metaphor is a function of the sociocultural format of interpreting subjects' encyclopedia. In this perspective, metaphors are produced solely on the basis of a rich cultural framework, on the basis, that is, of a universe of content that is already organized into networks and interpretants . . . whose format . . . derives from the metaphorical production and interpretation the opportunity to restructure itself into new nodes of similarity and dissimilarity. (Eco, 1984: 127)

The reward to be gained from working through Eco's scholastic prose is an appreciation of the competence required for producing, recognizing and interpreting metaphors. As Eco points out, success in the use of metaphor depends upon mutual participation in a rich and shared heritage upon which the metaphorical activity draws. Some terms are substitutable in selected contexts for at least a subset of competent language users because those terms are already contiguous in the activity of the culture or sub-culture in which the metaphor has currency. 'Swans figuratively represent beautiful women, not mainly (or perhaps at all) because they resemble one another, but primarily because of the association conjured up by *Swan Lake* and its many variants, in which references to the two are juxtaposed.' (Cooper, 1986: 21)

Eco's image of an encyclopedia conveys one of his key premises, *viz.*, that metaphor presupposes metonymy.[8] The terms in a metaphor are not transferrable because one is included in the definition of the other. Metaphors are not grounded in a cultural dictionary. Rather, they are transferrable because the terms are already juxtaposed in a larger cultural context available to speaker and hearer alike.

In discussing these metonymic foundations Eco emphasizes the cognitive role of metaphor.[9] This emphasis prompts him to represent the shared context in which the substitutable terms are already contiguous as an encyclopedia, as a set of information, beliefs and modes of inference. As speakers draw upon already juxtaposed terms in their cultural encyclopedia, interpreters require access to that same collection of lore if they are even to identify metaphorical utterances. Thus, as Eco observes, a metaphor is recognizable only 'when its metonymic foundation is immediately (or only after mediation) evident.' (Eco, 1979: 82)

Emphasis upon the cognitive role of metaphor serves to focus attention on those ranges of metaphor that most closely approximate conventional usage in communication and conceptual manipulations. That focus, however, tends to distract attention from the tension that we noted above is a characteristic feature of metaphor. That leads us to suspect that the cognitive role does not exhaust the metaphoric process.

Another role of metaphor has been recently remarked, an affective role. One clue to the existence of that other dimension is the familiar power which metaphor holds to persuade. (Lakoff and Turner, 1989: 663-5, 89, 181-85) Ted Cohen observed that the use of metaphor has a bonding effect. The exchange between those who direct metaphors to others and those who respond to them builds on and reinforces the intimacy of community.

> There is a unique way in which the maker and appreciator of a metaphor are drawn closer to one another. Three aspects are involved: (1) the speaker issues a kind of concealed invitation; (2) the hearer expends a special effort to accept the invitation; and (3) this transaction constitutes the acknowledgement of a community. (Cohen, 1978: 6)

David Cooper took that proposal a step further. Interpretation of a metaphorical expression often, if not invariably, involves understanding why a more conventional utterance would have been less appropriate. Knowing why 'he didn't just come right out and say it' is part of appreciating a metaphorical performance. Consider a dead metaphor from street talk: 'Joe is a bad dude'. Access to the lore of the street, the sub-cultural encyclopedia of information, beliefs and modes of inference in common use there, although sufficient up to a point in decoding the jargon, is not enough to appreciate why so convoluted an expression is apposite. Why 'bad' and 'dude' both reverse conventional usage remains obscure until one appreciates it as an expression of rebellion against the regime by those moved by a passionate need to establish their self-esteem in the face of a recognition that they are trapped in an underclass. In addition to access to cultural lore, appreciation of metaphor requires sympathy with the moods and attitudes, the affective orientation shared by the speaker and competent hearers. As Cooper put it:

> . . . the very fact of uttering a metaphor instead of something more explicit presupposes -- justifiably or not -- a further intimacy. The intimacy in question is constituted by the attitude and viewpoint which the speaker must take his audience to share (or appreciate) if his use of the metaphor is 'justified.' (Cooper, 1986: 163)

Metaphoric expression relies on metonymy, both cognitive and affective. Amended in this way, Eco's approach to metaphor affords an approach to Pythagorean doctrine that may enable us to appreciate it as meaningful. To do so we must access, as best we can, both the cultural lore and the affective orientation which enabled the early Pythagoreans to produce, identify and interpret that doctrine.

IV

Plato pointed out that what distinguished the Pythagoreans among their contemporaries was not their doctrine, but their way of life. (Plato, *Rep*. X, 600b) Unlike those in the Homeric tradition who emphasized fate and admonished people to know and keep to their place in the order of things, to 'think mortal thoughts,' the Pythagoreans emphasized assimilation to the divine, and admonished people to follow a life of purification. (Cornford, 1912: 181-4) The Pythagorean way of life is perhaps best appreciated in comparison with other assimilationist ways of life, in particular with that of the Eleusians and Orphics which preceded it and that of the Platonists which succeeded it. What distinguishes each of these is the manner in which purification is accomplished.

The Eleusian Mysteries[10] were focused upon the initiation ritual. 'The general idea of an initiation ritual,' Walter Burkert explained, 'is generally taken to be that of death and rebirth.' (Burkert, 1987a: 99) He went on to identify its remote origin.

> The aboriginal institution of animal sacrifice, with the inevitable antinomy of killing and eating -- life presupposing death, and rising from its counterpart -- is enacted by playing out antitheses of renunciation and fulfillment, mourning and rejoicing, searching and finding, the fast and the feast. Mysteries evidently take part in this more general rhythm. (Burkert, 1987a: 111)

The Eleusian initiation rite included public ceremonies consisting of festivals and processions, song and dance in unusual attire, fasting and sleepless nights, followed by secret ceremonies at specially designated sites which featured unusual geographic formations. The secret ceremonies included three types of observances. First there were the 'things recited', oral statements expressing deep truths about the gods, including the myth of Demeter and Persephone. Next there were the 'things shown', objects that were previously concealed from view, that gave special embodiment to the gods. These 'symbols' included such objects as wine and a head of grain. Finally, there were the 'things performed', the liturgical drama. This included doning masks and special costumes and partaking in a communal feast. Once these observances were completed the initiates were joyously received by those previously initiated, the *mystai,* into the fold of immortals. (Meyer, 1987: 1-14)

Examination of these details, however thorough, does not reveal the Eleusinian mode of purification. A fragmentary observation attributed to Aristotle is helpful in this connection and applies with equal force to other assimilationist ways of life. '. . . Aristotle claims that those who are being initiated are not to learn anything but to experience something and be put into a certain condition ....' (F 15 R (Synesius, Dio 48A)) Purification is not achieved by being exposed to objects (natural or supernatural) or sets of utterances (sacred or profane). Purification, i.e., assimilation with the gods, is the condition that initiates experience in performing these rituals.

Drawing on the accounts of sympathetic ancient authors, Burkert was able to supply what he called 'a framework for empathy, if not for understanding what mysteries may have meant to participants.' (Burkert, 1987a: 93) The experience was patterned by ritual linkage of opposites, culminating in a joyous new synthesis. Participants moved between light and darkness, famine and feast, solitude and community, terror and happiness. Established patterns of perception, affiliation and sense of self fell away as participants were prompted to reach out for a different orientation. Receptive participants were thereupon introduced into a new way of seeing the world and themselves in it through the vehicle of the secret observances -- the things recited, shown and performed -- which new orientation was immediately reinforced by the jubilant chorus of *mystai*.

Burkert cites a report of Proclus as coming closest to a faithful report of what an experience of the mysteries was like.

> They cause sympathy of the souls with the ritual [things performed] . . . so that some of the initiands are stricken with panic, being filled with divine awe; others assimilate themselves to the holy symbols [things shown], leave their identity, become at home with the gods, and experience divine possession. . . . [*S]ympatheia* of souls and rituals, some form of resonance which does not come in every case but which, once it is there, will deeply move and even shatter the constructs of reality. (Burkert, 1987a: 114)

For the Eleusinians, purification was an experience of personal rebirth, renewal and transformation, attained mainly through liturgical drama. For them, purification was a status which, once attained through initiation, endured without further attention. The Orphics transformed these Mysteries by introducing an emphasis on literacy into the ritual, thereby reforming the character of purification. (Burkert, 1985: 297)

With the Orphics the 'things recited' merged with the 'things shown' and written texts containing the complex mythical doctrine became the privileged embodiment of the gods, the central 'symbols' of the cult. This change transformed the 'things performed', the liturgical drama, into a lifetime practice. As humans were shown as composites of the divine and the earthly, assimilation with the gods could be accomplished only through a lifelong effort at liberation. For the Orphics, although purification began with initiation, it continued into their lives outside the sacred precincts. Initiation, mastery of liturgical texts and observance of dietary taboos were among the most common practices associated with the Orphic way of life. (Guthrie, 1935: 194-205 and Burkert, 1985: 301)

The Orphics sought the same consummation as had the Eleusinians, *viz.*, union with the divine by means of what Proclus called 'sympathy of the souls with the ritual', but they transformed the ritual, making it a more of a literary exercise, and extended it from an episodic to a lifelong experience. The Pythagoreans, in turn, transformed Orphic practice. (Guthrie, 1962: 182) In doing so much was retained. Purification was still a lifelong liturgical drama. Dietary taboos and other forms of ritual purity also distinguished them from their countrymen. They continued to lay supreme emphasis upon mastery of the liturgical text.

The Pythagoreans were distinguished from the Orphics in two ways. First, they held that the divine presence, whether in the liturgical texts, the soul or the cosmos, consists in its quantitative not it's literary meaning, in number and proportion rather than narrative. For them poetry and music were important preliminaries for the ultimate assimilation to the divine in the study of mathematics.[11]

The second feature that distinguished the Pythagoreans from the Orphics followed from the first. As the divine IS the quantitative relations which constitute the deepest meanings of the cosmos, the self and the liturgical text, union with those relationships IS the highest form of purification. After elaborate preparations, including years of silence, poverty and fasting, Pythagorean initiates pursued studies, at first in music and astronomy and later in geometry and arithmetic. Pythagoras referred to these studies as the love of wisdom, *philosophia.* 'For Pythagoras then the purification and salvation of the soul depended not merely, as in the mystery cults, on initiation and ritual purity, but on *philosophia* . . . .' (Guthrie, 1962: 205)

The similarity between Plato and the Pythagoreans has often been remarked.[12] With Plato we find the same quest for union with the supreme principle of the cosmos. Both emphasized the crucial importance of mathematics in achieving that union. Both promoted a way of life that prepared their followers for that union. Both schooled their neophytes 'first through images, then through symbols, and then by the direct revelation of (mystical) truth.' (Dillon, 1976: 258)

For both 'the acquisition of knowledge partook more of the character of a religious initiation than of mere instruction or research.' (Guthrie, 1962: 214)

The fundamental difference between Plato and the Pythagoreans is that 'Plato's philosophy is a metaphysic of transcendent, [whereas] the Pythagorean philosophy is a metaphysic of immanent order.' (DeVogel, 1966: 197) For the Pythagoreans the divine IS order discernable IN the cosmos and can be formulated in terms of mathematical relations. For the Pythagoreans the study of mathematics IS union with the divine principle immanent within the cosmos. For Plato the divine principle transcends the cosmos and the study of mathematics is still part of the preliminary preparation for the final union accomplished only through another, dialectical, process terminating in the vision of the forms.

Following an amended version of Eco's approach to metaphor, we have taken a closer look at the lore and affective orientation of the early Pythagoreans and found that it sheds useful light on their otherwise opaque doctrine of number and harmony. We can now appreciate that their doctrine was imbedded in what is for us an unconventional pragmatic context from which it appears to have derived its primary sense and motivation. This renewed appreciation illustrates how classical scholarship can be enriched by semiotic insights. The next section shows how semiotics can be enriched by insights of classical scholarship.

V

Until relatively recently religious observances generally, and ancient cults in particular, were approached exclusively from a cognitivist perspective. From that perspective what is known is regarded as primitive and what is done is treated as behavior scripted by knowledge. That orientation traditionally gave primacy to mythology over ritual. When viewed in that light ancient cults are represented simply as a pattern of responses to unusual spiritual beliefs.

It is now widely allowed that the cognitivist approach does little to illuminate the significance of ancient cults and perhaps religious observances generally. The renewed appreciation of the significance of the ancient mysteries resulted in large part from a change in the perspective from which they are viewed. Over the past two centuries the cognitive orientation has been increasingly displaced by various forms of non-cognitivism, an approach that gives primacy to practice over knowledge, to ritual over mythology. For some this shift takes on stark proportions. Burkert called it a 'Copernican Revolution.' 'Ideas do not produce ritual; rather, ritual itself produces and shapes ideas, or even experience and emotion.' (Burkert, 1983: 27-8) On this view '. . . we should not presuppose that people perform religious acts because they believe, but rather that they believe because they have learned to perform religious acts, or even more plausibly, that they act in the accepted way, whether they believe or not.' (Burkert, 1987b: 156) In implementing this non-cognitivist orientation Burkert drew heavily on the work of Konrad Lorenz and through him the literature on animal communication.

Ritualization occupies a central position in the field of animal communication.[13] Serious discussions of such ceremonial patterns of animal behavior as courtship are by now familiar. The process by which those behavioral patterns evolved and are sustained, the process of ritualization, is not so well known. Stripped of the unworkable functionalist assumptions associated with the work of Huxley and Lorenz, that process is perhaps best understood as the evolutionary modification of behavior to serve communication.

Consider the following schema. Animal A engages in a fixed sequence of behavior beginning with (1) simultaneously opening its mouth and staring at animal B and ending with (2) biting animal B. Individual B's may react in a variety of ways. Those that retreat in response to (1) have a clear survival advantage over and so are more likely to be represented in subsequent generations than are those that do so only in response to (2). In this way natural selection favors animals that respond to (1) as a threat. Similarly, individual A's that are more successful in bringing about the retreat of B's without undertaking the risks associated with (2) have a survival advantage over their less successful counterparts. As embellishments that exaggerate threatening displays increase the likelihood of such success, natural selection favors exaggerated behavior such as prolonging the stare, exposing the teeth, and vocalizing loudly. (Barash, 1982: 206-7).

We have now seen how a non-cognitivist approach to ritual sheds fresh and useful light on communication. It is a short step to recognizing that it also illuminates metaphor as well. Communication is understood from a non-cognitivist perspective, not as the transfer of encoded messages, but as the coordination of stereotyped display and response patterns. It is that coordination which affords the metonymic foundations of metaphor, both the collection of lore and the affective orientation that effective metaphoric performances presuppose. Ritualization supplies the cognitive metonymy supposed by metaphor, what Eco called our cultural encyclopedias. It affords the juxtaposition of otherwise unrelated sights, sounds, moves, etc. It also affords the affective metonymy supposed by metaphor as well. Bonding, for example, has consistently been found to be a characteristic feature of animal communication.

> Lorenz's standard example is the triumph ceremony of a pair of graylags, consisting in common aggression against a nonexistent interloper; by triumphant cries, these geese assure each other of their friendship and solidarity. (Burkert, 1979: 36-7)

> . . . [R]itual actions performed in common are communicative in function, and virtually constitute the identity of the group. (Burkert, 1979: 46-48)

Semiotics can benefit from the foregoing discussions, however, not only by an enriched appreciation of metaphor, but more centrally still. The hypothesis that this paper seeks to motivate for semioticians is that the process of semiosis itself is better appreciated from a non-cognitivist than from a cognitivist perspective. Concretely, semiosis is better seen as a ritualization than as an encoding process.

This hypothesis can perhaps best be unpacked by reference to one aspect of the semiotic doctrines of C. S. Peirce. Peirce comes to mind here because there is little room for doubt that he approached semiotics from a cognitivist perspective. One dualism remains ultimately unresolved for Peirce. In his view 'dynamic' and 'sign action', causality and semiosis, are irreducible. The semiosic process is sharply distinguished from causal processes by its triadic structure, the central feature of which is reference.[14]

While the cognitivist approach in semiotics illuminates a wide range of symbolic behavior, as Eco's discussion of metaphor shows, it sheds little useful light on semiosis itself. As an example, consider Tom Sebeok's attempt to extend the scope of Peircean semiotics to 'zoosemiotics.' For him, as for Peirce, communication involves the production, exchange and deciphering of encoded messages. Extending that notion led Sebeok to an implausible account of animal communication drawn mainly from the phenomenological speculations of Jakob von Uexkull, which account succeeds only in further mystifying both animal communications and semiosis. (Sebeok, 1972, 1986; also see: Deely, 1990)

A non-cognitivist approach would overcome the unresolved dualism between causal and semiotic action. As in religion studies, it would give primacy to ritualization. We have already seen how ritualization affords both the cognitive lore and the affective bonding requisite to metaphoric expression. That shows its promise for other semiotic processes. From a non-congitivist perspective semiosis would be seen as embracing both diadic and triadic relationships, indeed the latter would be envisaged as a special case of the former under specific evolutionary circumstances. The view commended here is that semiosis is always diadic, but sometimes is triadic as well. A distinction that Cooper introduced in his discussion of metaphor may help clarify this proposal.

Cooper observed that speaking poetically and acting metaphorically should not be confused with producing and interpreting poems and metaphors. One can do the former without doing the latter. (Cooper, 1986: 137; also see Johnson, 1981: 43) The same can be said more generally about acting symbolically. One can act symbolically without producing or interpreting signs. Composers of music and dance perhaps best exemplify what Langer called connotation without denotation. (Langer, 1942: 118-19) Although performers might be excused for recalling Mozart only the source of the score that they interpret, that is not a satisfactory key to viewing Mozart's activity. Here again, changing the primary role from cognition to action shows us that one can, as Mozart presumably did, compose music without producing a score for someone else to interpret.

The reverse, however, in not the case. Poems result only from acting poetically, metaphors only from acting metaphorically and music only from composing. More generally, signs systems result only from semiosis. But, and here is the point of Cooper's distinction for this essay, semiosis is not limited to nor should it be confused with the production and interpretation of sign. It is often a free standing process. Although semiosis always manifests diadic relationships, it does not invariably generate artifacts that have the properties of sign systems, in particular the tell-tale triadic relationships. This was established in the earlier discussion of animal communication, which showed how stereotyped display and response patterns are coordinated without the benefit of denotation, reference and referring tokens.

If, as the title of this essay suggests, ritual captures the distinctive features of semiosis, and ritual is regarded as more primitive than the encoding and decoding of artifact, then referring, the special feature of symbolic behavior and sign systems generally, can best be regarded as a special form of ritual, as a language game, whose evolutionary history can perhaps be traced. But that is a project for another occasion.

ENDNOTES

1. J. Ralph Lindgren is Professor of Philosophy at Lehigh University.

2. The best general treatment of the early Pythagoreans is still Guthrie, 1962: 146-340.

3. I follow Cornford, 1957: 13, in dismissing Guthrie's third stage, 1962: 239, because the distinction between physical objects and geometrical solids seems foreign to the Pythagorean perspective. As Aristotle reported, for them things ARE numbers.

4. The Table of Opposites was recorded by Aristotle, *Metap*. I, 5. 986 a 22-26:

limit	unlimited	resting	moving
odd	even	straight	curved
one	plurality	light	darkness
right	left	good	bad
male	female	square	oblong

5. Imagine that a carpenter's square is used to sort (limit) a field of points (unlimited). The array takes a square shape and the carpenters' square encloses an odd number of points. Were the carpenter's square shortened on one axis, the shape of the array would be rectangular (oblong) and the altered carpenter's square would enclose an even number of points. Aristotle, *Physics* III, 4. 203 a 10-16.

6. 'Metaphor consists in giving the thing a name that belongs to something else; the transference being either from genus to species, or from species to genus, or from species to species, or on grounds of analogy.' Aristotle, *Poetics* 21. 1457 b 7-9.

7. '. . . [A] metaphor provokes or invites a certain view of its subject rather than saying it straight out in a commonplace. . . .' Davidson, 1984: 261.

8. In Eco's use 'metonymy is spoken of as a 'substitution of two terms for each other according to a relation of contiguity.'' Eco, 1984: 90.

9. Metaphor is often defined by this cognitive role, for example, '. . . [T]o provide a perspective from which to gain an understanding of that which is metaphorically portrayed.' Kittay, 1987: 13-14.

10. 'Mysteries are a form of personal religion, depending on a private decision and aiming at some form of salvation through closeness to the divine.' Burkert, 1987a: 12.

11. Two explanations are given for how Pythagoras first happened to invest mathematics with pivotal importance. The dominant legend has him discovering that musical harmony can be expressed in terms of number and ratios and then generalizing that discovery to the entire cosmos. Porphyry, who flourished during the 3d century C.E., is the earliest extant source for this story. Guthrie mentioned another account of much more ancient origin, one that seems more plausible and not inconsistent with the traditional account.

> Aristoxenus, the friend of fourth-century Pythagoreans, wrote in his treatise on arithmetic that Pythagoras derived his enthusiasm for the study of number from its practical application in commerce. This is by no means an improbable supposition. The impact of monetary economy, as a comparatively recent phenomenon, on a thoughtful citizen of mercantile Samos might well have been to implant the idea that the one constant factor by which things were related was the quantitative. A fixed numerical value in drachmas or minas may 'represent' things as widely different in quality as a pair of oxen, a cargo of wheat and a gold drinking-cup. Guthrie, 1962: 221-2. Also see pp. 176-8.

12. For a brief review of these similarities together with supporting authorities, see: C. J. DeVogel, 1966: 192-7.

13. Julian Huxley initiated the modern study of animal communication and inaugurated the use of the expression 'ritualization.' Huxley, 1923.

14. 'It is important to understand what I mean by *semiosis*. All dynamical action, or action of brute force, physical or psychical, either takes place between two subjects or at any rate is a resultant of such actions between pairs. But by 'semiosis' I mean, on the contrary, an action, or influence, which is, or involves, a cooperation of *three* subjects,

such as a sign, its object, and its interpretant, this tri-relative influence not being in any way resolvable into actions between pairs.' Peirce *CP* 5.484; See also: *CP* 2.227-9, 2.247-9. 5.473. 5.488. A number of modern commentators deemphasize this dualism. See, for example, Fisch, 1986 359-60 and Colapietro, 1989, Chapter 1.

REFERENCES

Barash, David, 1982, *Sociobiology and Behavior*, 2d Ed. New York: Elsevier.

Burkert, Walter, 1979, *Structure and History in Greek Mythology and Ritual*, Berkeley: University of California Press.

_____, 1983, *Homo Necans*, Berkeley: University of California Press.

_____, 1985, *Greek Religion: Archaic and Classical*, London: Basil Blackwell.

_____, 1987a, *Ancient Mystery Cults*, Cambridge: Harvard University Press.

_____, 1987b, "The Problem of Killing", in *Violent Origins*, R. G. Hamerton-Kelly, ed., Stanford: Stanford University Press.

Cohen, Ted, 1978, "Metaphor and the Cultivation of Intimacy", in S. Sacks, ed., *On Metaphor*, Chicago: University of Chicago Press.

Colapietro, Vincent M., 1989, *Peirce's Approach to the Self*, New York: State University of New York Press.

Collingwood, R.G., 1945, *The Idea of Nature*, London: Clarendon Press.

Cooper, David, 1986, *Metaphor*, London: Basil Blackwell.

Cornford, F. M., 1912, *From Religion to Philosophy: A Study in the Origins of Western Speculation*, New York: Harper & Bros.

_____, 1957, *Plato and Parmenides*, Liberal Arts Press.

Davidson, Donald, 1984, "What Metaphors Mean," In *Inquiries into Truth and Interpretation*, London: Clarendon Press.

Deely, John, 1990, *Basics of Semiotics*, Bloomington: University of Indiana Press.

Dillon, John, 1976, "Image, Symbol and Analogy: Three Basic Concepts of Neoplatonic Allegorical Exegesis," in *The Significance of Neoplatonism*, R. B. Harris, ed., International Society for Neoplatonic Studies.

Eco, Umberto, 1979, *The Role of the Reader*, Bloomington: Indiana University Press.

_____, 1984, *Semiotics and the Philosophy of Language*, Bloomington: Indiana University Press.

Fisch, Max, 1986, *Peirce, Semeiotic and Pragmatism*, K. Ketner and Charles Kloesel, eds., Bloomington: Indiana University Press.

Guthrie, W.K.C., 1935, *Orpheus and Greek Religion*, Methuen & Co.

_____, 1962, *A History of Greek Philosophy*, Vol. I, Cambridge: Cambridge University Press.

Huxley, Julian S., 1923, "Courtship Activities in the red-throated diver (Colymbus stellatus); together with a discussion of the evolution of courtship in birds," *Journal of the Linnaen Society of London* 35:253-92.

Johnson, Mark, 1981, *Philosophical Perspectives on Metaphor*, Minneapolis: University of Minnesota Press.

Kevelson, Roberta, 1988, *The Law as a System of Signs*, New York: Plenum Press.

Kittay, Eva, 1987, *Metaphor: Its Cognitive Force and Linguistic Structure*, London: Clarendon Press.

Lakoff, George, and Mark Turner, 1989 *More than Cool Reason*, Chicago: University of Chicago Press.

Langer, Susanne K., 1942, *Philosophy in a New Key*, Cambridge: Harvard University Press.

Lindgren, J. Ralph, 1989, "The Pervasiveness of Metaphor: Privacy and the Supposed Independence of Legislation and Adjudication," in R. Kevelson, ed., *Law and Semiotics*, Vol. 3, New York: Plenum Press.

Meyer, Marvin W., 1987, "Introduction," in *The Ancient Mysteries: A Source Book*, M. Meyer ed., New York: Harper & Row.

Pepper, Steven, 1942, *World Hypotheses*, Berkeley: University of California Press.

Sebeok, Thomas, 1972, *Perspectives in Zoosemiotics*, Amsterdam: Mouton.

_____, 1986, "The Evolution of Communication and the Origin of Language," in *I Think I Am a Verb: More Contributions to the Doctrine of Signs*, New York: Plenum Press, 10-16.

Vogel, C.J. de, 1966, *Pythagoras and Early Pythagoreanism*, VanGorcum & Co.

Chapter 13

Expanding Boundaries: Law and Economics as Creative Discourse

Robin Paul Malloy[1]

I

Introduction

As we enter the last decade of the twentieth century many changes are taking place in our society. Law and legal institutions are no exception and they, too, have been under continual transformation. In particular, the focus of this article is on the transformation in legal discourse concerning the relationship between law and economics. In essence, I will argue that a new conception of law and economics has emerged and that this new conception will be the dominant understanding of law and economics to survive into the next century.

Fundamentally, the new discourse of law and economics is a comparative undertaking that links economic and legal methods to no particular political or economic ideology.[2] At the same time, it is a discourse that recognizes that one's personal understanding of law is inevitably linked to one's ideological opinions concerning economic relationships. It is the struggle between competing ideological visions of the proper relationship between law and economics which stimulates the process of our legal evolution. The competing and conflicting foci of the legal economic marketplace are the metaphorical and ideological struggles of alternative visions of the 'good' and, 'just' society. These alternative visions are informed by first principle beliefs in basic ideological values concerning the understanding and the interpretation of the proper relationship between the individual, the community, and the state.[3]

In order to present a model of this new law and economics, as a creative process of legal economic discourse, I will build on earlier work where I distinguished between what I mean by 'law and economics' and the more traditional, more limited, and less useful, 'economic analysis of law.'[4]

II

A Model of Law and Economics

In this part of the article I will set out a model of law and economics as a creative process. In doing this I will first briefly describe a traditional view of law as an autonomous discipline. Second, I will briefly describe the developmental foundation of an economic analysis of law. Finally, I will describe my view of law and economics as a creative and evolutionary process. In the context of discussing creative law and economics I will address the conflict between communitarian and individualist norms and the role that natural rights play in distinguishing between various alternative ideological forms of legal economic discourse.

A. Law As An Autonomous Discipline or the Myth of Law as Practiced

A traditional approach to law holds that law is an autonomous discipline.[5] Law, as such, is an independently coherent system of rules that, when properly understood, allow us to reach correct resolutions to difficult conflicts and problems. This view of law is a view that is consistent with the notion of law as a science -- a system of thought that can be learned, mastered, and applied in an organized, systematic, and objective fashion.

This traditional approach to law, while under attack from many sides, is still a dominant feature of legal education. Students are still taught to identify the legal rules in cases and if they don't get enough of them in class, they instinctively turn to any number of commercial publications that identify in clear and simple text the appropriate rules for each compartmentalized subject of the law school curriculum. Likewise, the bar examination that follows graduation from law school serves as the official guardian to the practice of law and embraces the idea of law as a system of rules with correct answers to difficult problems. This, of course, is increasingly the case when bar examinations, and more and more law school course examinations rely on the multiple choice test question format. Inherent in this format of testing is an implied confirmation that the rules of law lead to provably correct answers. I call this traditional approach to law, 'the myth of law as practiced.' The components of this myth can be visualized in a simple equation which I will then discuss: (Facts) + (issues) + (rules and proper form) + (precedent) + (rationale) = (correct answers) $\pm$ (human error)

Using this equation the lawyer and the legal system seek to apply an independent process of inquiring in an effort to reach the 'right' or proper result. This process requires the lawyer to proceed through a series of steps recognized as valued by the legal community and which, therefore, validate the legal discourse and the ultimate conclusion reached or suggested by the discourse. In this systematic process the lawyer learns to sift through the facts of a given relationship or transaction in order to identify and isolate the *relevant legal facts*. Every first year law student is instructed on the process of separating mere facts from relevant legal facts for it is ultimately only the relevant legal facts that will play a role in 'scientifically' leading us to the proper resolution of our legal problem. Sifting through the facts of a particular problem leads the skilled lawyer to a discovery of the *legal issues* raised by the facts. When these legal issues are identified the proper *rules* of law concerning substance, procedure and form must be applied. These rules presented in the proper (legally recognizable) form are applied to the issues and facts in order to correctly answer the legal question being confronted. Given a proper identification of the facts, issues, rules and forms applicable to the situation, the traditional lawyer's task is next to examine precedent for guidance on how to weigh the various input variables in the legal equation. By looking at precedent, the lawyer consults traditions and surveys prior legal determinations. This effort validates end-state determinations for the current controversy by linking their resolution to past historical tradition and previously accepted cultural norms. Finally, the lawyer and the judge, unlike the legislature, are expected to explain and justify their resolution of the legal controversy by offering a clear and persuasive *rationale* for their conclusions. The rationale must persuade the intended audience that all of the input variables have been properly attended to and that when so understood, the conclusion reached is both correct and inescapable. Thus, the conclusion or determination of the case or conflict is a correct legal decision. One party wins and another party loses as a result of an independent and objective appeal to legal reasoning.

Naturally, people are not infallible so that sometimes correct answers will not be reached. Sometimes human imperfection will lead to a misunderstanding or misapplication of the facts, law, etc. However, the traditional view holds that the lawyer should seek to perfect the ability to perform every input function of the equation in order to improve the likelihood of discovering the correct answer. The format of traditional legal discourse, therefore, incorporates the recognition of imperfection on the part of human actors, but in its structure and content it proclaims law as a system of legal revelation and defines our mission as the quest for independently correct answers to difficult questions founded in the perfection of a basic set of lawyering skills.

Even as a myth, this traditional model of law and the lawyering process is important. For, even as traditional notions of law come under increasing criticism the symbolic format of legal discourse seems well established. That is, we recognize legal discourse, as distinguished from sociology or poetry, by its traditional format even if the discourse being offered is critical and in complete contradiction to the 'scientific' notions of law as an autonomous discipline. Arguments based on marxist economics or neoclassical economics which seek to change the structure and content of legal discourse, seem first to require a symbolic format familiar to and deemed persuasive by current legal culture. Thus, alternative conversations about law tend to redefine the nature of relevant facts, issues, rules, forms, and precedents. They likewise seek to offer different sources as the rationale for decision making. This leads to a 'correct answer' validated in a new source of discourse. The structure of the discourse changes with the ideological meaning and perspective attached to the accepted format of legal conversation. The 'signs' of legal discourse may look familiar, therefore, but the structure and content of the format is remapped. The more informed critiques of law, in this context, acknowledge that, the idea of *correct answers* is inherently contingent and subjectively chosen.[6] Consequently, correct answers do not exist independent of accepted cultural values and norms.

B. Economic Analysis of Law -- The Myth of Two Mirrors

I will refer to the economic analysis of law, most notably promoted by Judge Richard Posner and his followers, as 'the myth of two mirrors.'[7] In the discourse of an economic analysis of law, the basic form of the traditional legal model is left undisturbed. The only significant variation to the traditional model is the assertion that the law, knowingly or unknowingly, is actually informed by economics. Thus, the science of law turns out to be the science of economics and correct legal answers are synonymous with correct economic decisions.

In the construct of an economic analysis of law the separate disciplines of law and economics are like two distinct mirrors facing one another. In this metaphorical representation one finds that law reflects economics while economics reflects law. For Judge Posner this means that the law, the common law at least, is basically a story of economic efficiency -- the law is efficient in economic terms. Likewise, as a normative claim, going beyond this mere descriptive claim, Posner argues that law should seek to be efficient -- that is, correct legal answers should be economically efficient answers.

This method of discourse seeks to translate the components of traditional legal argumentation into the language of economics. Economic methods can then be applied to legal situations in order to derive a 'truly scientific' resolution. By this process the law is unified and made systematically understandable as a process that can still reach correct answers even though the attainment of those correct answers requires a reference to a discourse beyond that of traditional law.

The economic analysis of law remains a myth (in this case a myth of two independent mirrors) primarily because it continues the discourse of a 'scientifically' independent method for reaching corrrect answers. The economic analysis of law is based on neoclassical economics which is rooted in a particular ideological view of the relationship between the individual, the community, and the state. Not surprisingly, the evolution of law and of neoclassical economics reflect similar values and norms because they evolved side by side in the transition from a feudal society, to a mercantilist society, to a capitalist society. Inasmuch as law and legal insitutions evolve as derivative of the economic ideology of those in power (an observation made by none other than Adam Smith) it is no surprise that the two systems of discourse are similar in the class of people they tend to favor. The objective of economic analysis of law is to maintain the traditional vision of law by circumventing the current criticism of law as an autonomous discipline. The economic analysis of law accomplishes this by joining in the growing chorus of voices proclaiming the myth of law as practiced but, unlike other critiques, it seeks to perpetuate the structure and content of that myth by substituting a new discourse of economics analysis for the discredited discourse of law as a autonomous discipline.

C. Law and Economics -- A Creative Process of Discovery

Unlike the proponents of an economic analysis of law, I have argued that law and economics is an abstract theory of relationships -- that is a creative process of discovery. Law and economics is a way of thinking about and talking about the relationship between the individual, the community, and the state. Economics, when properly understood, is not merely an attempt at setting out a science of individual and public choice. Rather, economics is fundamentally a method of discourse; a method of interaction which is ever changing, dynamic and creative. Law and economics is no more about finding the *correct scientific* answer to a legal or social problem than is traditional legal discourse about the correct legal answer. Law and economics is a system, a metaphorical and symbolic abstraction that defines legal economic discourse and which, through alternative ideologies, can lead to real and substantive changes in the structure and content of law.

The best way to proceed, at this point, is to set out, in diagrammatic form, a conception of law and economics as a creative process. I will then proceed to explain each part of the diagram in the hopes of providing some clarity or definition for this construct.

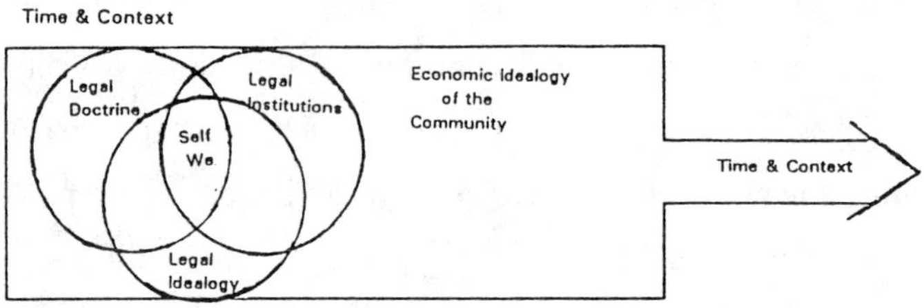

Diagram: Law and Economics as Creative Process

Economic Ideology of the Community: The general framework of law and economics is bounded by the ideological values and norms that are accepted and validated in any given community. This requires us to investigate the generally accepted ideological view point that informs a community's division of power concerning the choice making process and the allocation of scarce resources. One must examine the values, beliefs, and myths of a community in order to understand the community's perspective of the world around it.

From this viewpoint one can see that there is a vast difference between a society that internalizes free market capitalist norms and one that internalizes marxist communal norms. The allocation of power, the choice processes, and the distribution of scarce resources will be dramatically different. The difference will be reflected in a legal economic discourse that validates the norms, values, and beliefs, of the particular ideological viewpoint. Thus, institutions and relationships within the community will take on a structural form and substantive content that is reflective of the underlying economic ideology that supports any given view of the relationship between the individual, the community, and the state.

The major premise of this model is that one's understanding of law and legal institutions is derivative from one's views on the nature of economic relationships.

It is this derivative relationship to economics that makes legal economic discourse recognizable as something other than the discourse of sociology, psychology, poetry, or what have you. The format of legal economic discourse is distinct and it has recognizable boundaries within which competing arguments will be deemed persuasive or valid. No matter what its structure, however, legal economic discourse is always a conversation concerned with the allocation of power and resources. In this model the dominant economic ideology is always tentative and under pressure from other competing ideologies. Over time, competition and experience tend to have an evolutionary impact on the structure and content of legal economic discourse. Consequently, over time, community norms and values change as do community understanding and practice concerning law and legal institutions.

Time and Context: The entire conceptual framework of law and economics, as bounded by the economic ideology of the community, must be understood as contingently linked to historical, political, economic, social and cultural context. The idea of community is an idea that exists over time. In the context of time the process of law and economics is dynamic, creative, and always changing. Nothing is static. Context is important for it not only defines the nature of the problems faced but constrains the potential options for resolving them. Technological or political change, for instance, can have a dramatic impact on the context of community norms. Technological changes may create new problems (nuclear waste) while presenting solutions to old problems (replacing diminishing supplies of fossil fuels). Likewise, changes in political structure raise new possibilities that are related to the specific context -- Eastern Europe today is dramatically different than it was ten years ago.

Legal Doctrine: Legal doctrine is the formal law recognized as valid and persuasive at any given moment in time by a particular community. This includes the recognized values, policies, procedures, and practices which govern the formal set of legal justifications offered in support of the then current division of power and scarce resources. As underlying economic ideology changes it paves the way for an evolution in legal doctrine. Rules that once favored sellers such as caveat emptor are discarded and new doctrines emerge that favor consumers. Such changes may be justified on the rationale that market transactions do not work in the way previously accepted and consequently the previous legal rule or principal must give way to a new community understanding; a new community norm.

Legal Institutions: These are the formal institutions that are validated as and accountable for the handling of all matters considered legal matters. Institutional structures in the United States play an important function in our system of checks and balances. The scope and structure of legal institutions evolve over time and are contingent with respect to changing community norms. For instance, the dramatic growth in administrative agencies and administrative law under the New Deal was only possible in a context of tremendous change in the underlying ideology of the marketplace. In a similar way, new beliefs about the inappropriateness of our adversarial approach to law and social culture have opened the door to more arbitration and alternative dispute resolution systems.

Legal Ideology: By legal ideology I refer to the ideology that defines the role, purpose, or function of law within the community. This is the ideology that justifies what the law and legal actions are all about. The best way to understand this is to merely state five alternative legal ideologies. Each of the following ideologies are able to serve as a foundation for an entire superstructure of activity. The list is not meant to be all inclusive but rather serves as an illustration of the major thematic ideologies that one might identify from current debates.

1. Law is the search for the truth, (as in a criminal trial) and thus legal doctrine and institutions should aid in the discovery of truth.

2. Law is an independent and autonomous science or discipline and consequently legal doctrine and institutions should be understood as operating free of politics and economics. Law is not merely an exercise in political or economic power.

3. Law is completely indeterminate and contingent, therefore law is merely the politics of power. Law is, in other words, merely an exercise of political and economic power and those that control the exercise of these power sources control the law which legitimizes them.

4. Law is a reflection of economic science and ought to pursue the development of economically efficient doctrines and institutions. Thus, law should favor prior distributions of wealth and resources and all values can and ought to be quantified. There are no natural rights, only quantifiable rights and efficient outcomes.

5. Law is a derivative field of study that derives from one's first principle beliefs in economic philosophy and ideology. Thus, legal doctrine and legal institutions must be structured to support a legal economic discourse favorable to the subjective ideology of the promoter of any particular view of the proper relationship between the individual, the community, and the state.

Self/We: In the center of this entire dynamic process I have placed the 'self'/'we'. This serves as the fundamental referential sign or baseline for any model of law and economics. 'Self' as referential sign is an individualist philosophy and 'we' as referential sign is a communitarian philosophy. I believe that this comparative model of the relationship between law and economics can function equally well under either philosophical perspective. From my perspective, I place self at the center of this process because I believe we can only understand the world around us based on our own subjective life experience. While we, as individuals, live in community with each other, we are all biologically and environmentally unique. We see the world, we engage in discourse, we read text, etc. in a subjective manner. While one can argue that it is our interaction with others that gives us judgment about the world around us -- it is only our subjective and unique self that gives meaning to the world. When I read a text, when I listen to a conversation, I cannot know the exact meaning given to such discourse by its author. By accepted norms of interpretation I can usually come close, that is come up with an understanding shared by other readers or listeners. But, ultimately, like the multiple witnesses to an automobile accident that remember different things about the incident, each individual brings a unique and subjective perspective to the interpretation of the world around them.

In the creative process of law and economics, it is *experience* that anchors the self in this dynamic system, and it is through our interaction, by commission and omission, that we each effect, in some unique, all be it marginal way, the overall process of law and economics.

In contrast to the 'self' or individualist baseline philosophy, one could take a 'we' or communitarian approach to this entire model. Such an approach would make the community the key referential sign. This view would hold that we know ourselves only from interaction with others. It is a dialogic system of reference. Within the context of the overall model, however, the change in baseline reference point only changes the ideological perspective one brings to our study of law and economics. The process of creative discovery continues on its evolutionary path without regard to the choice of key referential sign. Regardless of the referential sign you use to approach this creative model of law and economics, you will observe the same *process* of interaction. It is, therefore, only the structure and content of legal economic discourse that changes based on the belief in any particular referential perspective. The *process* of creative evolution remains unchanged.

Concluding Comments on the Model: The concept of law and economics as a creative process is one that allows for a comparative and all encompassing view of economics. When understood as a form of discourse that channels our thinking about the proper relationship between the individual, the community, and the state, we begin to see that all forms of legal theory are concerned with the same fundamental problems of allocating scarce resources and the power of choice among competing notions of the good and just society. The constant conflict and competition between these alternative ideological views gives rise to a creative and spontaneous evolution of law and legal culture. The entire dynamic process itself is continually subject to outside pressure from other forms of discourse that have a way of gradually penetrating economic ideology, thus other social, political and cultural concepts are always at work transforming the structure and content of legal economic discourse.

III
Conclusion

The contingent nature of our legal evolution forces us to examine the creative process by which that evolution occurs. Proceeding by spontaneous interaction we experience a legal and social evolution that is the creative product of countless individual actors, incidents, surprises, and miscalculations. Within this ever changing legal landscape of dynamic interaction is a continuous struggle for ideological dominance by competing theories of the good and just society. Each ideological theory promotes a particular world view and each possesses its own appropriate, therefore validating, form of discourse. And, the form of discourse is important for it serves a channelling function for social conversation that ultimately has a substantive impact on the evolution of our community.

ENDNOTES

1. Robin Paul Malloy is a Professor of Law and Economics and Associate Dean for Research at the Syracuse University College of Law. This volume acknowledges author's copyright.

2. R. Malloy, 1990, *Law and Economics: A Comparative Approach to Theory and Practice*, hereinafter Malloy, *Law and Economics*; R. Malloy, 1991, *Planning for Serfdom-Legal Economic Discourse and Downtown Development.*

3. Malloy, *Law and Economics*, *supra* note 2.

4. *Id.* at Chapter 1.

5. Posner, 1986, "The Decline of Law as an Autonomous Discipline," *Harv. L.R., 761.*

6. R. Kevelson, 1988, *Law as a System of Signs*, 49-56, 273-86.

7. See generally, R. Posner, 1986, *Economic Analysis of Law*, 1st ed. 1972; R. Posner, 1983, *The Economics of Justice*; Malloy, 1990, "Is Law and Economics Moral? - Humanistic Economics and a Classical Liberat Critique of Posner's Economic Analysis," 24 *Val. Univ. L.R.* 147; Malloy, 1990, "The Limits of "Science" in Legal Discourse - A Reply to Posner," 24 *Val. Univ. L.R.* 175; Malloy, 1988, "Invisible Hand or Sleight of Hand? Adam Smith, Richard Posner, and the Philosophy of Law and Economics," 36 *Kan. L.R.* 209; Malloy, 1988, "The Merits of the Smithian Critique: A Final Word on Smith and Posner," 36 *Kan. L.R.* 266.

Chapter 14

Inadequate Stories

Andrew W. McThenia, Jr.[1]

I

We live in a culture and an age attuned to images of success and freedom from boundaries. Yet who among us has not come face to face with the reality that we inhabit a world that is ours to understand only a little and to control hardly at all?[2] When we confront these truths about the world and when our vision of life is overtaken by darkness, we wonder if daylight will ever return. Where do we turn in those times to avoid shrinking into despair?

Experience suggests that to get through those dark nights, we have to come to terms with the 'contraries' in life. How is it that we come to find power in weakness and strength in surrender? To learn to take on and at the same time to let go?[3] How do we make sense of the paradoxical nature of life which seems so often to be revealed only at moments of near despair?

Many times, of course, we do not because we will not trust either ourselves or the dark. We have not paid enough attention to the stories that would give us courage to wrestle with the Other in the darkness, and like Jacob, hang on for dear life in order to give the struggle time to result in blessing.[4] If we do hang on long enough to face defeat, it is at those moments while we are on the ground combing through the ashes of our lives that we are most likely to encounter the unexpected pale new growth of hope.

We all order our lives by labeling, highlighting, censoring, or ignoring the messy facts we encounter as we muddle along so that we can have some more or less coherent account of who we are. We hope that the stories we construct are true or are at least adequate for coming to terms with life. However, in a world fraught with uncertainty, one thing we must surrender if we are to find a way of going on when we can see only our own experience is the presupposition that we have some special access to the truth about that experience.[5] That is not very comforting, but I think it is true nonetheless; because as humans we have an almost unerring capacity for self-deception and that condition leaves us vulnerable to the seduction of evil.[6]

On occasion we are given glimpses of ourselves, which would otherwise remain hidden, by looking at the stories of others who are themselves struggling to make sense of life. Reflecting on and reacting to the stories of those others can tell us a good deal about what we have been doing with our own lives.[7] But to come to any real knowing, we have to be willing to push beyond the more passive question: What does the story say *to* me? and allow ourselves to enter the realm of the story and ask the deeper question: What does the story say *about* me? That is simple, but it is not simplistic. Nor is it easy. It requires an openness, a giving up of a search for some authoritative interpretation. It requires that we wait, and let the story itself, in its *own* voice, speak the questions that are important.[8]

While we may not know what The Truth is, or what a true story is, or even how to live in truth, we do know that some stories are more adequate than others for coming to terms with life.[9] It is my basic thesis that any account of life which does not take cognizance of the reality of evil as an essential part of the human condition is both inadequate and dangerous. Until and unless we can accept the darkness in our own hearts we will be enslaved to it. Yet so often we construct stories which deny that which the ancient and sacred texts of our culture attest --

the systemic, immensely inventive, seductive, and persistent nature of evil in the world. We are, all of us, related to Cain[10], and the capacity for evil still runs deep in our family. Yet we spend a major portion of our lives trying to distance ourselves from our wandering kinsman by pointing to our own goodness and uprightness.

That I think is our sin -- our all too human goodness which depends on the lack of it in others.[11] What is particularly diabolical is our inability or unwillingness to see that in the very act of drawing lines to separate and protect us and our rectitude from the evil of our neighbor, we also isolate ourselves from our neighbor's goodness.[12] Moral progress, according to Richard Rorty, is in the direction of greater human solidarity. And, he continues, solidarity is '. . . the ability to think of people wildly different from ourselves as included in the range of 'us'.'[13] Because we isolate ourselves in the act of affirming our own goodness, we are left vulnerable and often unable to resist the seductive pull of evil.

The tragic example of Mr. Thompson, the protagonist in Katherine Anne Porter's powerful novella *Noon Wine*,[14] is instructive. *Noon Wine* is a story of despair in which Thompson's life ends in suicide because he cannot tell a story which acknowledges his own complicity with evil. His was a tragedy of inadequate self-awareness. In this story, which is set in rural Texas around the turn of the century, Thompson, a law-abiding farmer, kills a stranger, Homer T. Hatch. Thompson is indicted for murder, tried, and ultimately acquitted on the grounds of self-defense. But he cannot put it to rest. He travels the countryside telling his version of the events leading to the killing of Hatch. The text probes Mr. Thompson's character as it is revealed to himself and to others. He has no perspective on his desperate need to justify his way of life; and that ultimately drove him to violence, first against Hatch, and finally against himself. By killing himself, Thompson was attempting to kill the truth -- a truth he was unwilling or unable to tell.

Noon Wine is compact, yet so many different meanings radiate from it. Each turn gives a strikingly different insight and draws the reader deeper into mystery and into a confrontation with the banality of evil. In this essay I want to turn the story over once again, probe its meanings and think about the adequacy of Mr. Thompson's story -- as well as my own.

II

As the story opens we are introduced to a proud but slothful Mr. Thompson whose life is '. . . going steadily downhill.'[15] The opening paragraph has a visitor coming through a gate '. . . sunk so firmly on its broken hinges no one thought of trying to close it.'[16]

Thompson was a man of severely limited vision. His view of himself was determined by what others thought of him and his notion of how life should be lived was defined by static roles. 'Slopping hogs was hired man's work . . . Killing hogs was a job for the boss, but scraping them and cutting them up was for the hired man . . . and . . . woman's proper work was dressing meat . . . .'[17] Those others in his life weren't persons but images he had created to make his life better. His description of his wife is revealing. He had fallen in love with 'a popular Sunday school teacher'[18] and he had expected her to do the major chores on the place, but she '. . . had simply gone down on him early.'[19] And when others failed to live up to his expectations, he used those failures to justify his own inadequacies. He would '. . . sit for hours worrying about it . . .' wondering 'what . . . [he] could do, handicapped as he was.'[20]

Through the broken gate a stranger appeared out of nowhere looking for work. He was Mr. Helton and he seemed to have no past and no real connection with the present. He never looked at Mr. Thompson, but he 'didn't seem to be looking anywhere else'[21] either. After a brief but one-sided negotiation, he and Mr. Thompson struck a deal and Mr. Helton went to work as a farm hand.

Although he lived on the Thompson place and ate with the family, he remained an outsider and something of a mystery. He was truly '. . . a stranger in a strange land.'[22] His only communication was deep within himself, perhaps in another world, and was through his lonely and incessant harmonica music.

Mr. Helton literally transformed the place. He repaired the fallen down buildings, fixed the broken gate, and generally took charge of the farm. There was no job too large for him. He was, in effect, an angel coming into Thompson's world and transforming it but all the while remaining untouched by it. While Mr. Thompson was sometimes contemptuous of Helton, 'he never gave way to those feelings [since] he knew a good thing when he had it.'[23] As the years passed, Mr. Helton, who never was a part of the Thompson family, became its 'hope and prop'.[24]

Life on the farm went on. One day, some nine years later, another stranger appeared looking for Mr. Helton. He was Mr. Homer T. Hatch, a bounty hunter. Hatch told Mr. Thompson that Helton was a violent man who had killed his brother with a pitch fork and was an escapee from a North Dakota hospital for the criminally insane. He, Hatch, had come to take Mr. Helton back to North Dakota.

Hatch was righteously evil, a man who worked within the law and safely defined himself by it. '. . . Homer T. Hatch is my name and America is my nation . . . .'[25] '. . . I'm for law and order . . . .'[26] He appealed to Mr. Thompson's shadow side, his pride, to assist him in the return of Helton to North

Dakota. '. . . I counted on your being a respectable man and helping me out to see that justice is done . . . . It won't look very good to your neighbors that you was harbring [sic] an escaped lunatic who killed his own brother, and then you refused to give him up. It will look mighty funny.'[27]

Hatch asked Thompson to help him overpower Helton so he could handcuff him and take him back to North Dakota. Thompson was seriously threatened. On the one hand Helton was his angel, '. . . the best standby a man ever had,' but he didn't want Hatch telling his neighbors that he was helping a lunatic evade the law. He yelled to Hatch to get off his land. Hatch stepped back and dared him on. At that point Helton appeared and stepped between Thompson and Hatch, prepared to defend Mr. Thompson. Hatch moved toward Helton and Thompson took an ax and smashed Hatch's skull. Helton, frightened, fled like a wild animal. He was subsequently captured by the local sheriff and died from wounds inflicted during the attempt to subdue him.

Mr. Thompson could not piece the events of the killing together. He thought he saw Hatch stab Helton, '. . . he saw the blade going into Mr. Helton's stomach . . . .'[28] When his wife, who had not seen the incident, appeared he told her that Hatch had killed Helton. She pointed out that Helton was running away. When Helton was finally captured, he did not have any stab wounds.

Mr. Thompson was charged with murder and was defended by a lawyer, Mr. Burleigh. Burleigh constructed a theory of self-defense, but he had some strange notions of self-defense. He told Thompson: '. . . about how his own father in the old days had shot and killed a man just for setting foot inside his gate when he told him not to. 'Sure, I shot the scoundrel,' said Mr. Burleigh's father, 'in self-defense: I told him I'd shoot him if he set his foot in my yard, and he did, and I did.' There had been bad blood between them for years, Mr. Burleigh said, and his father had waited a long time to catch the other fellow in the wrong, and when he did he certainly made the most of his opportunity.'[29]

He told Thompson 'that stranger hadn't any right coming to your house on such an errand. Why hell . . . that wasn't even manslaughter you committed.'[30] Mr. Burleigh knew his community well and he knew that the community would be suspicious of a stranger who came on another's land in any event. That is true in spades if the stranger is on a nasty mission. Burleigh knew in effect he could put the dead Hatch on trial. While Burleigh's notions of self-defense hardly accord with the written law, he was correct in his assessment of the community norm.

Burleigh's strategy was effective and Thompson was acquitted, but he remained extremely dissatisfied. He never got a chance to tell his story. 'At the trial they hadn't let him talk. They just asked questions and he answered yes or no, and they never did get to the core of the matter.'[31]

He was confused. He had not intended to kill Hatch and it had all happened so unexpectedly. He thought he had seen a knife go into Helton's stomach, but there was not a scratch on him. He knew he had an axe in his hand and remembered lifting it, but he couldn't remember hitting Hatch. He wanted to keep Hatch from harming Helton, but he hadn't intended to kill. He thought that the trial should have been about these matters. He wanted some formal sort of vindication. However, the trial was about Hatch, or more precisely, it was about some social rules -- about what is proper conduct when a stranger comes on one's land on a nasty mission.

The latter half of the story is about Thompson's attempt to come to terms with the events surrounding the Hatch killing. Mr. Thompson was a man possessed. For a while he kept dropping into Burleigh's office to talk about what a scoundrel Hatch had been. But Burleigh really didn't want to listen and finally

Thompson stopped going there. He then began a pilgrimage, travelling throughout the countryside to the homes of neighbors and strangers alike insisting that they listen to his version of the events surrounding the Hatch killing. He even took his wife along as a corroborating witness. While she dutifully and on cue would say that the killing was as Mr. Thompson described it to his audience, she smoldered, knowing she had accommodated one more lie in her victim-like life. She secretly considered her husband a murderer who ruined her sons' lives.

Of course his life did not get better; his neighbors didn't really listen, and the more he attempted to justify himself, the greater their disbelief became. Finally, in despair, he took a shotgun, walked to the far end of his field and killed himself. Immediately, before he took his life he made one final effort to come to terms with his history. He took a pencil and wrote:

> 'Before Almighty God, the great judge of all before who I am about to appear, I do hereby solemnly swear that I did not take the life of Mr. Homer T. Hatch on purpose. It was done in the defense of Mr. Helton. I did not aim to hit him with the ax but only to keep him off Mr. Helton. He aimed a blow at Mr. Helton who was not looking for it. It was my belief at the time that Mr. Hatch would of taken the life of Mr. Helton if I did not interfere . . . . If I had been in Mr. Helton's place he would of done the same thing for me. I still think I done the only thing there was to do. My wife --' [32]

Then he paused for a moment, crossed out the words 'my wife', and continued:

> 'It was Mr. Homer T. Hatch who came to do wrong to a harmless man. He caused all this trouble and he deserved to die. But I am sorry it was me who had to kill him.'[33]

III

Part of the genius of *Noon Wine* is that Ms. Porter draws us ever so skillfully into Mr. Thompson's world of alienation and loneliness. Even as he writes his suicide note, she has him offer ambiguous accounts of the Hatch killing. In the concluding paragraph of the story he describes the killing alternatively; first, as being in defense of Helton, and finally as driven by his hatred toward Hatch. We know that the latter version is closer to the truth than the former. But we are left wondering how to resolve the ambiguity and puzzled about this hatred of Hatch. To offer a fuller account of the killing and to understand Thompson requires that we walk in his shoes. And I think that is precisely what the author wants us to do. She invites the reader to construct an alternative account of Thompson's actions. Whether we can craft a more adequate and less ambiguous account is not at all clear.

If we accept her invitation, we have to read more closely[34] and explore the hints, which we have picked up on first reading, that there is something about Thompson's character which Hatch grasped almost immediately but which may still elude us.[35] On that reading, we see how closely intertwined Thompson and Hatch really are.

We know that Hatch is evil, almost comically so. He is a caricature of the red-neck racist, the arrogant patriot who drapes himself in the flag. Evil in the person of Hatch operates under the protective arm of the law. Hatch defines himself as one who believes in law and order, and that is his moral compass. Because he has defined his world in that way, he knows just how vulnerable Thompson is to the same charge. Hatch understands Thompson better than Thompson understands himself. That, I think, is why Thompson took such an intense dislike to Hatch. He retold Thompson's story without permission and in that retelling exposed to Mr. Thompson just how inadequate his chosen story was. Hatch denuded and humiliated him by twisting every description of reality which Thompson offered. Thompson's pride, his view of himself, was rendered meaningless by Hatch. Most, perhaps all of us, want to be accepted on our own terms. To be redescribed by another, particularly when that other has not asked permission, is finally humiliating.[36]

We as readers can safely distance ourselves from Hatch's rather comical evil. Yet when we see how close he is to Thompson, the smile fades, and we begin to get uncomfortable. How different are the two characters? Hatch wrapped himself in the flag and stood safely on the side of law and order. Thompson's definition of himself was more genteel, but was equally abstract. His 'feeling for the appearance of things' was the center of his character. The story Thompson chose for himself was inadequate for a host of reasons. His was a world of sharp dichotomies and hierarchies -- we/they, good/bad, manly/unmanly -- a world of rigidity with clearly marked boundaries. And those boundaries were carefully drawn to affirm his own righteousness. Thompson lived firmly within that conception of righteousness and with such insistence that any challenge to it was a threat to his entire world. He had so succumbed to a single view of life that he had no response other than violence when the inadequacy of his story was exposed by Hatch.

Thompson really was a man divided against himself. While he sought to justify his own righteousness, he never knew the self he was defending. On some level Thompson knew that he killed Hatch because he saw the loss of Helton as the loss of his own identity as a successful farmer. Helton was all that stood between him and the malaise of failure. Helton had become 'the hope and prop' of his life. When that prop was threatened, he was left with no hope. Helton was not a person in Thompson's eyes, but a machine of salvation, the one thing which stood between him and the darkness of despair. Hatch pointed out to Thompson just how fragile his world was, how false his chosen story really was. Given the world view Thompson had carved out for himself, there was really no way out except to silence Hatch. If he ran Hatch off and Hatch spread the story among his neighbors, Thompson would be destroyed. If he turned Mr. Helton over to Hatch, he lost his 'hope and prop,' that which allowed him to hold his head high, his image of himself as a successful farmer.

Thompson's story makes clear how powerful single-minded thinking is, and how we can deceive ourselves into making it a conviction. His story also shows how violence is practiced by those who live inside such a vision -- how they are forced to be violent by the power of deception to protect it. The more he sought to affirm his righteousness, the less chance he had to live anything close to a righteous life. The more he feared the truth, the more he distanced himself from it.

One way to test the adequacy of a story is whether it will accommodate another or an alternative story without a need for violence. The violent killing of Hatch was an attempt to kill the truth. His own suicide was a violent escape from facing the inadequacy of his life. The ultimate irony in Thompson's suicide was his attempt to take on yet another story which further mocks the truth: the stance of a defiant victim -- 'I had to kill myself to make you believe me.'

IV

Let me pause for a moment, take stock of where I think I have been and then rather quickly conclude. I said at the outset of this essay that we all order our lives by that which is the dominant sound in those lives -- '. . . the sound of story.'[37] I suggested that we could not depend on having any special access to truth about our own experiences because of our infallible ability to deceive ourselves. One way to see beyond ourselves is through the stories of others.

Ms. Porter took us on a journey with Mr. Thompson to a distant field as he tried to tell his story. I think that it is here that the author speaks to us as readers. She offers alternative accounts of Thompson's story, allowing us to draw on own conclusions. She also offers us two challenges. The first is, of course, to make sense of Thompson's actions. The second is to reconsider our own positions in the world as we struggle with Thompson's story. It is in this act that we as readers are affirmed as potential 'thous' (to use the imagery of Martin Buber)[38]) whose participation in the story is essential to give the text meaning. In our efforts to understand the story, we begin to see how similar Hatch and Thompson were. That may help us understand Thompson. But that in itself is insufficient to help us make sense of our own stories. To determine more about ourselves we have to see not only the connections between Hatch and Thompson but those between Thompson and ourselves.

It is after all not the Homer T. Hatches of the world we need to be worried about, but the Thompsons and those who would seek to be good only for themselves. As Karl Barth said, 'the devil is not as abhorrent and wicked as we like to think . . . his 'you shall be as gods'. . . does not suggest a depraved figure but one who is very respectable and eminent and religious and moral . . .'[39] That I think is what Eli Weisel means when he talks about the 'banality of evil.' It is the sort of evil Walker Percy is describing when he says that 'tenderness is the first disguise of the murderer and it always leads to the gas chamber'. When we succumb to the temptation to be good only for ourselves we are inevitably left in a position of drawing lines, of separating sheep from goats, rich from poor, good from bad, and dark from light. So long as we draw lines, so long as we define our goodness by someone else's lack of it, we will with consummate skill put ourselves on the safe side of righteousness. And we will remain firmly in the grasp of evil. Evil is single minded and cannot see that everything in life is at least two-sided.

Perhaps by now we are beyond the text and into the texture of our own lives. If so, and if we begin to get some glimmer of insight into ourselves we may see in ourselves something of Thompson. We might ask how distant is Thompson's story from our own? To what extent do we too seek to 'lay hold of goodness and roll it up and represent it in ourselves . . . and make goodness an instrument of our pride?'[40] The story then becomes a mirror for our own truth. But because we are who we are -- that is, humans who resist confrontation that will radically threaten us -- we have already censored what we will permit ourselves to see. While our goal is to gain some new insight, we most likely gain only a 'temporary stay against confusion.' Can we engage on a deeper level which goes beyond our own preshaped version of truth?

That brings me back to the challenges that Ms. Porter has offered us. How could Thompson have told a more adequate or true story? By being silent. By not trying any more. And what can we say to the implicit challenge to understand our own lives? If we really allow ourselves to be transported into the darkness at the far end of Thompson's field where we too can smell the metallic odor of his shotgun, our insight into his despair deepens and we feel the seductive tug of evil to which we are all so vulnerable when we are isolated and howlingly alone. How would we, looking at the wreckage of our lives and finally accepting that things really are as bad as they seem, resist the temptation to one more assertion of the will, which is what pulling the trigger represents? How would we, instead of pulling the trigger, embrace the brokenness of our lives and realize that perserving the illusion of innocence is no longer important? How would we surrender; let go and endure reality, rather than trying any longer to control it? I think we would have to let go of our world view that we can either understand such moments on our own terms or talk about them by using the labeling capacity of our language. The most transformative of stories are those that point beyond language to the mystery that is beyond the mind's capacity to describe. So too we must take on silence and listen for that still, small voice which says 'Be still and know that I am God.'[41]

ENDNOTES

1. Andrew W. McThenia is Professor of Law, Washington and Lee University. My deepest appreciation goes to all those participants in the Fifth International Roundtable on Law and Semiotics held in April of 1991. I am particularly grateful for the comments of Roberta Kevelson, Denis Brion, David Caudill and Emily Hardigan. Also I want to thank my research assistant Julie Barbo for her help.

2. R. Unger, 1984, *Passion: An Essay on Personality*, 95.

3. H. Fingarette, 1984, *Human Nature, Human Ordeals*, The Inaugural Romanell Phi Beta Kappa Lectures, 1.

4. Genesis 32:22-32.

5. Code, 1986, "Stories People Tell," 16 *N.M. L. Rev.* 599, 600.

6. H. Fingarette, 1969, *Self-Deception*; S. Hauerwas, 1977, *Truthfulness and Tragedy: Further Investigation in Christian Ethics*, Ch. 5.

7. R. Rorty, 1989, *Contingency, Irony and Solidarity*, 141.

8. Shapiro, 1987, *Let It Heal: Storytelling and Healing in Judaism*, Paper delivered at the Third Annual Conference on Christianity and Buddhism, Berkeley, California, August.

9. Lorraine Code suggests that while we may not be able to know the truth, we can with some certainty when stories are false: 'There are true stories, if perhaps not True Ones.' Code, 1986, "Stories People Tell," 16 *N.M. L. Rev.* 599, 605. *See* B. Jackson, 1988, *Law, Fact and Narrative Coherence*,161-174, 193, proposing a concept of integrity as an alternative to the concept of truth. To "live in truth" in a democratic society, Robin

West claims, requires at a minimum that we challenge hierarchally created ideologies by challenging our own world view. West, 1990, "Forward: Taking Freedom Seriously," 104 *Harv. L. Rev.* 43, 67. For Stanley Fish the search for truth is futile. Quoting Milton he says that "[t]hose few who wish to restore Truth's lovely form go constantly 'up and down gathering up limb by limb' as they can find them. 'We have not yet found them all,' . . . allowing us for a moment the prospect of a task almost complete, a task within our abilities to accomplish; but then he takes that prospect away with these chilling words: 'Nor shall ever do, till her Master's second coming.' Fish, 1988, "Unger and Milton," *Duke Law Journal* 975, 992.

10. Genesis 4.

11. K. Barth, 1981, *Ethics,* G. Bromiley, trans., 338. Martha Minow has written a wonderful book which delves deeply into this whole problem of line drawing and separating ourselves from others. She points out that the more powerful we are, the less able we are to see that the world coincides with our view of it precisely because we have shaped it in accordance with that view. The more marginal we feel in the world, the more likely we are to glimpse a contrast between another's perception of reality and our own. Learning to take the perspective of another is an opening wedge for an alternative to traditional treatment of difference. M. Minow, 1990, *Making All The Difference*, 379-380.

12. *Id.*

13. Rorty, *supra*, note 7 at 92.

14. In *The Collected Stories of Katherine Anne Porter*, 1965, Harcourt Brace & World, 222-268. Page references to the text are from this volume. I first encountered *Noon Wine* some eight years ago. My friend and colleague, L. H. LaRue and I have talked about the story often. Another friend, James P. White joined a couple of those conversations. He has written an insightful essay on the story which is included in his volume, *Heracles' Bow*, Ch. 8, 1985.

15. *Id.*, 234.

16. *Id.*, 222.

17. *Id.*, 233.

18. *Id.*, 234.

19. *Id.*, 234.

20. *Id.*, 234.

21. *Id.*, 223.

22. *Id.*, 231.

23. *Id.*, 235.

24. *Id.*, 241.

25. *Id.*, 244.

26. *Id.*, 253.

27. *Id.*, 255.

28. *Id.*, 255.

29. *Id.*, 260.

30. *Id.*, 260.

31. *Id.*, 261.

32. *Id.*, 268.

33. *Id.*

34. Shapiro, *supra* note 8, at 21.

35. *Id.*

36. Rorty, *supra* note 7, at 89-90. The best way to cause people long-lasting pain is to humiliate them by making that which seems central to them look futile or worthless.

37. R. Price, 1978, *A Palpable God*, 3.

38. M. Buber, 1970, *I and Thou*, W. Kaufman trans.

39. Barth, *supra* note 11, at 339.

40. *Id.*

41. Psalm 46:10. See also Hartigan, 1991, "The Power of Language Beyond Words: Law as Invitation," 26 *Harvard Civil Rights-Civil Liberties Law Rev.* . . . 67, (1991). ' . . . the best place of gestation for what remains beyond the reach of words, but enters the spoken from time to time, is a clarity not of reason alone but of the whole person. Perhaps it even requires prayer . . . .'

Chapter 15

Mob or People, Riot or Insurrection: Was There a Revolution in Massachusetts in November 1747?

William Pencak[1]

I

Early American law is an ideal field for semiotic inquiry. In British North America, inconsistent enforcement of both English and local authority combined with diverse, rapidly growing colonial societies to create a fluid legal environment. Conflict of laws, creation of new law, and improvised behavior to fill legal gaps were norms rather than exceptions.[2] The United States Constitution, which provided a framework for various actors to share power in uncertain degrees which could change over time, marked the codification of two centuries of colonial legal experience. I have argued elsewhere that Charles S. Peirce -- who knew such prominent American jurists as Judges Joseph Story and Oliver Wendell Holmes -- may have been influenced in his semiotic theory by American law.[3] Instead of law, or truth, being a given or absolute, it was the constantly changing product of a community of inquirers. By extension, then, American law and society were from the beginning inherently innovative and revolutionary: societies in which common folk and local authority enjoyed more leeway than elsewhere were bound to develop novel legal codes to fit new contexts. These would of course be interpreted quite differently by English and American communities.

Here, I wish to illustrate the manner in which colonial law lends itself to semiotic analysis. I will focus on a dramatic historical event, a turning point in American legal history semiotically defined, but largely unknown except to scholars. From November 17 to 20, 1747, Boston was in turmoil as a crowd seized British naval officers as hostages to compel the release of men impressed into the British navy by Commodore Charles Knowles hence the action is known as the "Knowles Riot". This event invites semiotic reflection on several levels.

1) Conflict over which law justified impressment or resistance thereto created what Peirce would consider a situation ripe for anancastic or cataclysmic evolution.[4] The inability of competing legal codes and of legitimate, customary ways of reconciling differences among them to resolve the issue led to a situation which hovered on the brink of revolution and war. Only the tact of Massachusetts Governor William Shirley in orchestrating an elaborate charade to play down the riot, as a lower-class tumult abhorred by respectable Bostonians, prevented bloodshed. He thereby not only postponed an American Revolution by thirty years, but effectively hid the brief revolution which may have in fact taken place.

2) Nevertheless, the unprecedented scope of the riot did lead to theoretical innovation. Some of the rioters advanced the English Revolution of 1688 as an interpretant for the events in Boston, which they argued were parallel. To legitimate the riot, King James II, who fled in the face of William of Orange's forces, became an interpretant for Governor Shirley, who briefly left Massachusetts or did he? -- see below during the riot. Also, English doctrines of natural rights were applied for the first time in an American setting to bolster violent resistance to authority. Thus, the Knowles Riot becomes the hidden interpretant for the American Revolution. It laid on the table, so to speak, the ideology which could be dusted off and reapplied to analogous situations where governments violating men's natural rights compelled them to defend themselves.

The connection becomes even more meaningful when we realize that the principal theorist who defended the Knowles Riot in a revolutionary manner was the young Samuel Adams, one of the American Revolution's prime movers.

3) Multiple interpretations of the Knowles Riot developed almost immediately so the actors involved could justify their behavior to the audiences they wished. Some of the arguments concerned whether the event was a 'riot' or an 'insurrection'; whether it was perpetrated by a 'low-lived mob' or 'the people' specifically 'the sober sort, who dared to express a due sense of their injuries' and whether the governor 'deserted or abdicated' by leaving the province. If so, did that put the people in a 'State of Nature' where they could take new measures to defend themselves, as Thomas Hobbes argued in *Leviathan* or did a people remaining in civil society continue to be represented through the Massachusetts legislature to borrow from John Locke in *The Second Treatise of Government*. On a variety of levels, the riot created the problem of how the people could be represented and the government maintained in a potentially anarchic situation, where traditional arrangements among various laws and authorities had broken down.

Impressment of sailors was perhaps the biggest legal mess in the American colonies. First, there was never an Act of Parliament specifically authorizing impressment in the colonies, although as of 1707 there was one forbidding it. But then Americans and Englishmen disagreed as to whether that law expired in 1713 when Queen Anne's War The War of the Spanish Succession in Europe came to an end. To complicate matters, a new law of 1746, passed the year before the Boston riot, exempted only the West Indies whose absentee sugar magnates sat in Parliament and influenced it considerably from impressment.[5] Commodore Knowles referred to this law as an 'indulgence,' illustrating the official English perception that only favor exempted inhabitants of the empire from impressment.[6]

Further complications: Massachusetts's charter forbade the enlistment of inhabitants outside the province without their consent, but Governor Shirley and the Council, the upper house of the legislature, had worked out a deal with naval captains which authorized impressment of non-Massachusetts seamen only on incoming vessels outgoing vessels would have to recruit new crews and their perishable cargoes might spoil.[7] To top it all off, colonials frequently abetted British sailors in deserting from the navy onto lucrative merchant and privateering vessels even in wartime. This in turn gave naval captains a legitimate if not a legal case for impressment: unless the colonies would help end desertion, the officers would fill their crews with colonials. Knowles' press began as a search for deserters.[8] So was impressment legal or illegal, legitimate or illegitimate, and did parliamentary, colonial, customary, -- or if all these failed, natural -- law apply?

The Boston Town Meeting, for its part, threw it all together in 1746 by claiming that impressment was 'arbitrary and illegal': it violated 'the Magna Carta, the Charter of the province, and an act of Parliament,' thereby denying the Governor and the Council the right to override such a prestigious panaoply of precedent by authorizing impressment.[9] But all this legal talk was moot for two reasons: a impressment was recognized as necessary for defense in England, and thus no one there was likely to respond to colonial complaints that the same practice prevailed in America; and b the naval captains could sail their ships out of colonial harbors; short of firing on the very ships which protected colonial shipping and shores in wartime, what could the people do?[10]

They could resist the press gangs themselves forcibly: in 1745 two Massachusetts combat veterans of the Louisbourg campaign had been killed in a melee with a press gang. The gang's leaders, subject to provincial as well as military law while within a province's boundaries, were in jail at the time of the

Knowles Riot awaiting the King's pleasure on their conviction by a local jury. But before the Knowles Riot resistance meant precisely this: slugging it out with the press gang and either winning or losing.[11] Knowles's monumental press of November 17, 1747, which took in between forty-six and hundreds of men and was made either only on shore or also on land the accounts differ provoked the Bostonians to new steps.[12]

These new steps were: first, seizing all the British officers who were ashore when the press was instituted, and holding them as hostages pending the release of the impressed men. Clearly, Knowles did not expect this or he would have recalled the officers to their ships: in other words, he did not expect resistance to transcend its usual, 'legitimate' channels. Second, the crowd demonstrated in front of Governor Shirley's house, accused him of instigating the press, and roughed up a sheriff and deputy sheriff who ordered them to disperse. They also burned a barge they thought belonged to the royal navy in fact a Scotsman who was part of the mob owned it. Third, they marched on the State House, whereupon the assembly which sat downstairs dispersed; members of the Council upstairs held them off with guns as Shirley spoke to them. He then left for Castle William, an island in Boston Harbor where the fleet could protect him, either to show his resentment of the mob, because he was afraid of it, or to negotiate with Knowles for the release of all concerned again, the accounts differ. The different reasons advanced in different sources for Shirley's departure led to the problem of whether he had in fact left Massachusetts.[13] If so, had he thereby 'deserted' or 'abdicated' the government, as Speaker of the House of Representatives Thomas Hutchinson wrote some of the 'higher spirits' had begun to suggest as the riot continued.[14]

Now 'desertion' or 'abdication' meant only one thing to eighteenth century Anglo-Americans. That was the legal excuse Parliament used after-the-fact to justify overthrowing King James II during the Glorious Revolution of 1688-89.

Of course James did no such thing: he lost his nerve in the face of an army commanded by his successor William III, which the very people who accused him of abdicating had invited to attack him.[15] Had he resisted with his forces, there would have been bloodshed. Historian J.G.A. Pocock in fact has recently argued that technically William can be considered victor in a civil war in which two armies faced each other but in which combat was 'gloriously' avoided.[16]

Now it may be argued that precisely the same thing happened in Massachusetts. Leaving to one side the question as to why Shirley did leave, the fact remains that Commodore Knowles threatened to bombard the town if his officers were not unconditionally released. 'By God I'll see now if the King's Government is not as good as a Mob,' Knowles exclaimed.[17] For him the legal issue simplified down to a mob setting itself against the government. Knowles then offered Shirley 200 marines to quell the riot after the governor had talked him out of firing on Boston.[18] On the other hand, there were some in Boston who preferred resistance to compromise or surrender. The *Independent Advertiser*, a newspaper founded shortly after the riot for the specific purpose of protesting against the press, Governor Shirley, and the unsuccessful war, maintained: 'Are we in so weak a condition. . . to be in danger from two or three fifty-gun ships? And would not His Excellency, could he have answered it [Knowles's threat], have acted a more soldierly part, and told the insulting Commodore, that if he offered to advance upon the town in a hostile manner, he should advance at his peril.'[19] For three days there was a stand-off in Boston between a royal military force and a town determined to defy it.

By advancing the possibility that Shirley had deserted or abdicated, the town's 'higher spirits' offered the Revolution of 1688 as an interpretant for current events. Having done so, they pursued the parallel further. *The Independent Advertiser* implicitly compared Governor Shirley's conduct with that of James II on three counts. Just as James had tried to establish Roman Catholicism in Anglican England, Shirley's efforts on behalf of the Church of England -- to which he belonged and which was then building the King's Chapel in Boston which still stands -- ironically became evidence of 'Popish' encroachments in a Puritan society which tended to view Anglicanism and Romanism as nearly synonymous. On January 25, 1748, *The Advertiser* debunked 'Popish Countries' where 'it is public spirit to build and beautify churches at the expense of the poor people.' On July 17, 1749, William Bollan, Shirley's son-in-law, and the province's agent in England, was criticized for failing to oppose a plan to install an Anglican bishop in America, 'which might be likely to disturb this people in the enjoyment of their inviolable liberties.' Second, *The Advertiser* linked Shirley with James through his supposed efforts to corrupt the people and their representatives through distribution of government jobs to 'tools'. With elections for the Assembly impending in May 1748, the newspaper urged on May 2 that the voters 'resent the insolence of those who by money, or by treats, or by smiles, would bribe you.' The July 4 issue attacked 'governors in general, who may by romantic but in perquisites profitable expeditions, depopulate the country.' Third, on August 29, *The Advertiser* brought together charges of corruption and Popery with another of the traits popularly attributed to James II: Shirley had permitted trade with the French in Canada to flourish under flags of truce, thereby, like James, revealing a secret dependence on England's great enemy.

If Massachusetts's governor could be branded as a reborn James II, the next step was to justify resistance to his rule as following in the tradition of Englishmen who made the Glorious Revolution. Here, however, Massachusetts went beyond England. Parliament bent over backwards *not* to use John Locke's *Second Treatise of Government* to show that James's 'desertion' had left England without a legitimate legislature Parliament and therefore free to reconstitute a new government. Rather, to apply a standard all could agree upon -- especially Tories who favored a strong, independent monarch -- Parliament simply declared that James's absence meant the throne passed to his heir, his daughter Mary, whose husband William made a logical co-ruler.[20] Both society and government remained otherwise intact.

Early American historians usually stress Locke's ideas, especially as mediated through the radical *Independent Whig* which published 'Cato's Letters' in the 1720s and 30s, as having a critical influence on the ideology of eighteenth century colonials. However, *The Independent Advertiser*'s inspiration came from Thomas Hobbes, not John Locke. It is Hobbes who insists in Chapter 21 of *Leviathan* that 'the right men have by nature to protect themselves, when none else can protect them, can by no covenant be relinquished.' 'The obligation of subjects to the sovereign, is understood to last as long, and no longer, than the power lasteth, by which he is able to protect them.'[21] Similarly, *The Independent Advertiser* insisted not only on Shirley's 'abdication,' but that government's failure to protect people's lives, liberties, and estates by allowing them to be dragged off to sea, created a dissolution of government which permitted them to take the remedy of the State of Nature: that is, self-defense. *The Advertiser* wrote:

> That they have a natural right to defend themselves in cases where no effectual defense is to be had from laws is indisputable. Indeed, wherever a sufficient remedy is legally provided against an evil, the people may undoubtedly be confined to that remedy. But where there is none, those who, in other respects are members of society, in this respect are really in a state of nature, and of consequence have an undoubted right to use the powers belonging to that state.

In a situation such as the Knowles Riot, John Locke's *Second Treatise of Government* would have maintained a very different position. If either through the tyranny or neglect of a prince, or the infringements of the legislature, 'there is no longer the administration of justice for the securing of men's rights, nor any remaining power within the community to direct the force to provide for the necessities of the public, there certainly is no *government* left,' but 'society can never by the fault of another lose the native and original right it has to preserve itself' [my emphasis].[22]

Why did *The Independent Advertiser* deny the continued existence of Massachusetts not merely as a government, but as a society? Speculation alone is possible, but it seems sensible to argue that while all of Massachusetts opposed impressment, *The Advertiser* represented a minority who objected to more than 'illegal' press. It also sought to de-legitimize a legislature fairly elected by the people which had cooperated with the governor in suppporting a war *The Advertiser* considered disastrous.

Thus Hobbes, not Locke, was needed. Locke would have maintained that the institutional framework of Massachusetts remained intact, that its local and provincial legislatures could have *represented* society. But for Adams and *The Advertiser* they had betrayed their own people. The legislature sat but could do nothing; the governor was absent. No effective representation of the people in society existed which could defend them -- except the mob.

The mob thus became a newly constituted people, assuming the powers of a newly covenanted society in the Hobbesian sense. *The Advertiser's* issue of February 8, the paper termed the protestors 'an assembly of the people.' Its final number December 5, 1749, branded as a 'scandalous misrepresentation' those who 'used terms of contempt' and 'invidiously represented as a rude, low-lived mob' the 'sober sort' of people, 'bullied with threatenings and mischiefs,' who were forced out of desperation to defend themselves. As *The Advertiser* went out of existence, it explicitly drew the connection that Massachusetts in 1747 had followed in the footsteps of England in 1688:

> That mob spirit -- that inimical disposition to government -- that sedition so much complained of in this paper, by those who could not avoid complaining, is the very soul and spirit of Revolution principles.

'Revolution principles,' of course, governed England in the years after 1688. Few would deny that American colonists shared the rights of Englishmen who rose en masse to oust a tyrannical ruler. But by arguing in 1747 that the Glorious Revolution was not merely a one-time event to be celebrated, with its principles embodied in the status quo, Massachusetts's 'higher spirits' fused Revolution principles and natural rights as a defense for resistance for the first time in American history. When the impasse over what laws governed impressment was broken by crowd violence and threats of military suppression, Samuel Adams and his cohorts on *The Independent Advertiser* insisted that the Revolution of 1688 in England served as the most adequate interpretant for Americans whose provincial laws could not defend them against conflicting imperial statutes and policy. Just as conflicting laws over impressment served as actors in the struggle of American and British interests, the great riot of 1747 was a moment of chaos which permitted new concepts of law to become actors that would later justify the founding of the American nation. The subtle substitution by *The Advertiser* of Hobbes rather than the more frequently cited Locke illustrates the uniquely revolutionary -- in the sense of novel -- nature of the incident. While at the time of the American Revolution the colonies -- except for Pennsylvania and New York -- would not deny the representative character of their provincial legislatures -- the

Massachusetts radicals of 1747 repudiated both British and domestic political institutions.

That America did not have a revolution in 1747 owes much to Governor Shirley's intelligent mediation of the crisis, and the willingness of Boston's leaders -- fearful of bombardment by the navy and being branded as traitors on the one hand and of popular unrest on the other -- to follow his lead. In a nutshell, Shirley instructed Massachusetts to blame the riot on 'foreign seamen, servants, negroes, and other persons of mean and vile condition' and to express 'the utmost abhorrence of such illegal criminal proceedings.'[23] When he so instructed the Boston Town Meeting and the Massachusetts legislature, Shirley in fact blamed the riot on 'some ill-minded inhabitants and persons of influence. . . who had secretly countenanced and encouraged it.' But he was reluctant 'at fixing a lasting brand upon the town for their failure' to stop the riot, and most anxious that 'we shall not appear to act with zeal or even in earnest' in punishing the rioters and preventing such tumults in the future.[24] So a cover-up was launched: Shirley wrote to England accusing 'strangers, chiefly Scotch' for instigating the mob, a particularly appropriate scapegoat as England had recently crushed a rebellion at Culloden.[25] Boston and Massachusetts duly passed laws to prevent illegal assemblies, and found twelve ringleaders -- obscure people who were probably foreign sailors -- to punish for the disorder. Only three were convicted, however, and none served more than two months in jail. And in what amounted to a symbolic reinstitution of government, the militia -- that is, all adult males between sixteen and sixty -- turned out to escort Shirley back 'to his house with as great a parade as when he first assumed the government.'[26]

But it was all a farce. The militia had refused to turn out to suppress the riot -- probably, given the size of the crowd, because many of its members were part of the protest.[27] The assembly adjourned before the mob reached the State

House, its members in all probability melting into the crowd, as its speaker -- ironically, future arch-loyalist and Governor Thomas Hutchinson -- in effect spoke for the mob, urging Shirley to use his best endeavors to get the impressed sailors released.[28] As the impasse continued from November 17 to 20, neither the legislature nor Boston Town Meeting would condemn the mob nor call out the militia, but awaited the outcome of Shirley's negotiations with Knowles. Given both bodies' repeated protests against impressment, and the fact that both sat while the riot continued, it is clear they were in sympathy with the rioters' demands, even if they feared what the crowd might do. But what clinches the complicity of both town and provincial authorities is Shirley's correct assumption that when he told them he could get nowhere with Knowles, they would immediately follow his orders to stop the riot, welcome him back with full military pomp, blame the riot on marginal people, pass ordinances against further tumults, and locate and punish some ringleaders.[29]

The Independent Advertiser objected to these deceptions. Instead of condemning a 'mob,' the paper praised 'an assembly of the people.' Similarly, Shirley himself termed the 'riot' an 'insurrection,' a much stronger term suggesting intent to overthrow the government, in his letter to the town.[30] Knowles, whose officers were humiliated in a 'ridiculous procession,' also used the term 'insurrection.' He noted that the members of the legislature were 'stoned and forced to fly out of the courthouse' hence, government was briefly overthrown, and in general 'no riot was ever carried to a more insolent extent.'[31] *The Advertiser* all but equated the riot with England's Glorious Revolution. But given the overwhelming force an England at war could bring to bear had the 'insurrection' proceeded further, and the fact that colonial suffering during King George's War had been largely limited to Massachusetts, it was clear to most Bostonians that nothing could be gained by continued protest.

Governor Shirley did more than orchestrate a charade to hide the true nature of the Knowles Riot. The language of camouflage has been the language of historical discourse describing the riot. Historians have either accepted at face value the notion that obscure folks made the riot and were opposed by their betters, or else argued that even if there was unity, the riot followed in the tradition of quasi-legitimate crowds which in colonial times sensibly protested grievances using intelligent, limited amounts of force.[32] No one was killed or seriously injured in the Knowles Riot -- ultimately Knowles released some of the impressed men when his officers were safely returned. But for three days Bostonians supported by the town meeting and province legislature held British officers hostage in the face of a Commodore who would have assaulted the town had not Governor Shirley, either driven or voluntarily absent from his post to negotiate with Knowles, talked him out of it. As Samuel Adams realized, Boston faced Shirley and Knowles much as William faced James in 1688. This was an implication from which Boston's leaders withdrew. Thus they participated in the cover-up that denies the riot its due as a three-day revolution in American political and legal history, when the 'mob' became an 'assembly of the people' and 'natural rights' became the means whereby a 'riot' could be justified as an 'insurrection' based on 'revolution principles.' These symbols of protest would be revived during the American Revolution, which thereby renders the Knowles Riot a neglected interpretant for the greater struggle of the 1760s and 70s, a mediating sign between two revolutions.

ENDNOTES

1. William Pencak is Professor of History at Penn State.

2. For the variety of early American law, see especially Stanley N. Katz, "The Problem of a Colonial Legal History," in Jack P. Greene and J.R. Pole, eds., *Colonial British America*, 1984, Baltimore, 457-490, and works cited in the notes.

3. William Pencak, "The United States Constitution: A Semiotic Interpretation," in Roberta Kevelson, 1988, ed., *Law and Semiotics, I,* New York, 311-340.

4. Peirce discusses anancastic evolution in "Evolutionary Love," which appears in volume 6, paragraphs 290-314, *Collected Papers of Charles Sanders Peirce, 1931-1958,* Charles Hartshorne, Paul Weiss, and Arthur W. Burks, eds. Cambridge.

5. Dora Mae Clark, 1931, "The Impressment of Seamen in the American Colonies," in *Essays in Colonial History Presented to Charles McLean Andrews by His Students* New Haven, 198-215.

6. Charles Knowles to Admiralty, January 18, 1748, Admiralty Records, London West Indies. I am grateful to Prof. Daniel Baugh of Cornell University for sharing this document from his forthcoming collection of naval records with me.

7. George A. Wood, 1920, *William Shirley: Governor of Massachusetts, 1741-1756,* New York, 384.

8. Knowles to Admiralty, January 18, 1748; Clark, "Impressment"; John Lax and William Pencak, 1976, "The Knowles Riot and the Crisis of the 1740s in Massachusetts," *Perspectives in American History* 10, 163-214, esp. 176-177, 184-185.

9. *Journals of the House of Representatives of Massachusetts Bay,* 1919-1989, Boston, vol. 22, 212-213; Boston Town Meeting Records in *Boston Records Commissioners Reports,* 1876-1902, Boston, vol. 14, 85.

10. For earlier incidents, including one of 1702 when Lieutenant-Governor Thomas Povey *did* threaten to fire on a warship, see Lax and Pencak, "Knowles Riot," 171-177.

11. Wood, Shirley, 385; *House Journals* vol. 22, 204-205; William Shirley to Lords of Trade, December 1, 1747, *Correspondence of William Shirley,* 1912, C.H. Lincoln, ed., New York, vol. 1, 416.

12. Lax and Pencak, "Knowles Riot," 186-187, present the various estimates and accounts.

13. *Id.*, 185-196 for an account of the riot itself.

14. Thomas Hutchinson, 1936, *History of the Colony and Province of Massachusetts Bay,* Cambridge, vol. 2, 332-333.

15. See Thomas Slaughter, 1981, "'Abdicate' and 'Contract' in the Glorious Revolution," *The Historical Journal* 24, 323-337.

16. J.G.A. Pocock, 1988, "The Fourth English Civil War: Dissolution, Desertion, and Alternative Histories in the Glorious Revolution," *Government and Opposition*, 151-166.

17. Depositions in libel trial of *Knowles v. Douglass*, Suffolk Files 312, Group No. 65,550, Suffolk County Courthouse, Boston, depositions nos. 10, 17, 18, 22, 26.

18. William Shirley to Josiah Willard, November 19, 1747, in Shirley, *Correspondence,* vol. 1, 408.

19. *The Independent Advertiser*, February 8, 1748, copies in American Antiquarian Society imprint series of early American newspapers.

20. J.P. Kenyon, 1977, *Revolution Principles: The Politics of Party, 1689-1720*, London, 12-13, 200.

21. For the reception of Cato's letters in the colonies, see David L. Jacobson, 1965, *The English Libertarian Heritage,* Indianapolis, New York, and Kansas City, xlvii-liv. Hobbes is not usually discussed as an antecedent of the American Revolution except as a forerunner of Locke, an omission which the analysis below suggests may need rethinking. Citation from Thomas Hobbes, 1950, *Leviathan,* New York and London: Everyman's Library, 187.

22. John Locke, 1952, *The Second Treatise of Government,* New York: Liberal Arts Press, paragraphs 219-222.

23. Published in *The Boston Weekly Post-Boy,* December 14, 1747; *House Journals,* vol. 24, 212-214; *Boston Records,* vol. 14, 127.

24. *The Boston Weekly Post-Boy,* December 14, 1747; Knowles to Admiralty, January 17, 1748 also mentions "secret abettors" of the mob.

25. Shirley to Lords of Trade, Shirley, *Correspondence,* vol. 1, 416.

26. Superior Court of Judicature Records, 1747-1749, 87, Suffolk County Courthouse, Boston; Lax and Pencak, "Knowles Riot," 199. Hutchinson, *History,* vol. 2, 333.

27. Shirley's orders to the General Court and its Committee of War, November 17, 1747, Wendell Family Papers, Massachusetts Historical Society.

28. Shirley to Lords of Trade, Shirley, *Correspondence*, vol. 1, 414-415.

29. Shirley to Willard, *Correspondenc*e vol. 1, 408-409.

30. *Boston Weekly Post-Boy*, December 14, 1747.

31. Knowles to Admiralty, January 18, 1748.

32. Jesse Lemisch, 1968, "Jack Tar in the Streets: Merchant Seamen in the Politics of Revolutionary America," *William and Mary Quarterly*, 3rd ser. 25, 371-407, esp. 387, 393, argues for class conflict; Pauline Maier, 1972, *From Resistance to Revolution: Colonial Radicals and the Development of American Opposition to Britain, 1765-1776,* New York, 3-26, argues for orderly, quasi-legitimate mobs.

The author thanks the members of the Folger Shakespeare Library Seminar in British Political Thought for Spring, 1990, especially the directors J.G.A. Pocock, Lois Schwoerer, and Gordon Schochet, for stimulating me to rethink the Knowles Riot's significance. Robert Ginsberg and Virginia Black called my attention to the critical fact that *The Independent Advertiser* was arguing a Hobbesian rather than a Lockean case.

Chapter 16

Creating a Vocabulary and a Conceptual Ordering Device for Conferring Appropriate Rights in Information: The Challenge for Law

Michael D. Pendleton[1]

I

The Challenge for Law

Alternatives to Property for Accommodating the Interests of Global Innovators, Competitors and Consumers with Appropriate Legal Rights in Information.

Aspects of rights to exclude others or to guarantee rights of access to the products of scientific research and its application in the form of technology and the various forms of engineering and the marketing of such 'products' and indeed marketing generally are all the subject of legal regulation but there is no such thing as a comprehensive law in relation to these areas. Legal regulation of these areas is ad hoc and piecemeal. To a large extent this is because legal systems have yet to take to full cognisance of the fact that all such matters share the common characteristic of being valuable commercial information. Where regulation exists it is in the form of property rights in the particular form of the information. The central characteristic inherent in science and technology and marketing is that they involve aspects of information.

For the purposes of illustration consider the area of telecommunications. Information is obviously inherent in telecommunications; the method of telecommunication such as the apparatus, the system, the kind of hardware and software employed, as well as what is communicated utilizing such a method, eg. medical information on a medical database. Yet at the present time the law of the United States of America and the British Commonwealth and the Civil law of Europe, South America, Japan and China to a large extent all reject information per se as property. There is of course a degree of protection in the form of intellectual property law and various *sui generis* rights but no jurisdiction that I am aware of really has a full blown information law on which any comprehensive telecommunications law would have to be predicated. Copyright law, an area of law of crucial importance for protecting telecommunications systems is, for example, the subject of intense debate on whether to protect the 'look and feel,' more usually meaning user interface (though sometimes used to refer to the structure of the program) of software, and if so how to maintain the traditional stricture that copyright does not protect ideas only the form of their expression. The reason for this neglect may well be that at the present time certain forms of telecommunication are sufficiently technically complex to make plagiarism and unauthorized accessing only a marginal problem. A high level of support facilities are also necessary at the present time. But I wonder how long this will continue. At the present time widespread plagiarism of materials by photocopying is not a problem in China because there are relatively few photocopying machines in the country. The cost of paper there suitable for photocopying makes it cheaper to have a book printed than to photocopy it. Of course this was the situation at one time in the West, (remember the dearth of photocopying machines and their unreliability and expense) but note what has happened, not only with photocopying machines but also sound and video cassettes, software and various other information mediums. Will this not become the case with all forms of technology in the long run? Should this become the case, as I suspect it will, a great challenge lies ahead for national and international law because of the conflicting interests involved in something as valuable and important as information of which technology (and telecommunications is but one small part) is just one application.

The following is a sketch of the nature of the challenge. A central thesis is that property may not be an appropriate legal device for accommodating the often conflicting interests of innovators in the fields of science, technology, and marketing, their competitors and the general public. An alternative legal device for ordering rights in information is explored. The more difficult and troubling problems of North/South dialogue and the demands of developing countries can not be addressed here.

This paper proceeds by addressing some preliminary definitional matters followed by a description of the present law of intellectual property and its relation to information. This is followed by an identification of relevant interest groups. The next section of the paper concerns itself with the adequacy of property based concepts to balance the rights of the relevant interest groups. Finally a suggestion of a rights based, as opposed to property based, information law is explored.

II

A Vocabulary of Information Products

A. Definitional Problems

Law is preoccupied by its very nature, at least in traditional jurisprudential theory, with the meaning of words, rules and definitions. It is therefore necessary to attempt to define the aspects of information we are concerned with. Take the technology example again. The word 'telecommunications' may comprehend systems for domestic and international communications involving an element of technology, often high technology, as well as the information carried on such systems. Thus, automated data bases, interactive services, and cable and satellite television are obvious embodiments of such systems. Although such an analysis seems self evident it is important because law has application to both the contents of communication and the method of communicating. Laws governing defamation, sedition, secrecy, obscenity, proportion of national programme content in television broadcasts all govern the content of communications, sometimes irrespective of the form of communication and sometimes depending on the form of the communication. Laws which seek to protect from plagiarism such things as television broadcasts, data bases, compact disc's, new forms of satellite dish aerials, and software only come into play depending on the exact medium of communication. If a different medium is utilized the plagiarist may often avoid such laws. For example some jurisdictions have decided that their laws governing literary copyright protect software while others have reached the opposite conclusion.

B. A Tentative Definition -- Science, Technology, Marketing and Intellectual Property: Information as a Product of the Intellect and the Vocabulary of Information Products

All of patent law concerns products of the intellect or mind, as does many parts of copyright, registered design and trade secret law. The residue, as well as the law concerning trade reputation and goodwill (trademarks and the law of passing off/unfair competition merchandising and sponsorship rights, inter alia) may be regarded as information which is equally a product of the intellect -- though in the case of trade reputation and goodwill with the qualification that the information must be effectively disseminated, often through the expenditure of money. Though different to the former products of the mind which largely take the form of ideas and knowledge they can be comfortably accommodated under the more generic category information. Professor W.R. Cornish writes:[2]

> Intellectual property protects applications of ideas and information that are of commercial value.

Moreover many of the new forms of intellectual property such as computer software or the so called *sui generis* forms such as semiconductor chip topography legislation can with equal accuracy be described as forms of information.[3]

It goes without saying that the products of science, technology and marketing are the result of substantial investments of labor, skill, effort and capital. Unlike tangible property which can be physically possessed and protected by fences, guards and ferocious dogs it is rarely possible in the long term to safeguard such things from unauthorized use and misappropriation (technical devices to exclude pirate receiving stations or hackers are often only one step ahead of their quarry, if that). Inevitably the task of preventing unauthorized use and misappropriation falls upon the law. The relevant area of law is primarily intellectual property law, i.e., patent, trademark, copyright, design, trade secret and unfair competition law. Certain newly created so called *sui generis* areas of law also have application as does the criminal law. The new technologies have forced substantial changes on this area of the law. In the past it was concerned with such relatively straight forward matters like brand names, books, sheet music, inventions, designs and trade secrets. Now it is under pressure to embrace such desperate matters as software, silicon chip topography, satellite and cable transmissions and various kinds of electronic eaves dropping.

III

Relevant Interest Groups

In my view the difficulty the law faces in these areas (and in most areas involving restricting and granting access to valuable commercial information) is to strike a balance between the claims of three competing interest groups.

1) Firstly, there are the interests of the devisers of the information;
2) Secondly, there are the interests of her or his competitors;
3) Thirdly, there are the interests of end users or consumers of the information.

Listening to industry lobbies it is evident they often assume that the issue of legal rights can be solved merely by protecting the first interest group. But this is clearly impractical as well as unjust. Cornish's words are again apposite.

> No country favors conferring on the creator of an idea a perpetual monopoly in it against imitators. The political and economic implications of such a privilege would be remarkable. Instead a set of limited forms of protection are fashioned against some types of exploitation by others. The *root issue* to which we constantly return is whether the *balance* achieved by this approach is broadly appropriate to the economic needs of the country and to the *prevailing sense of what is just*.[4]

Rarely will the claims of the above interest groups coincide. The devisor wants maximum protection for her technology and data transmissions. A competitor wants less protection so that he can gain access to the information in order to be in a position to compete with the devisor. However, few serious competitors will advocate no legal protection as this would mean that if they become successful competitors they also will receive no protection for their own information products. End users or consumers, on the other hand, will sometimes argue for no legal protection of communications technology and especially of data transmissions as they clearly want access to the information at minimal cost. They rarely think of the possible inferior quality services or the long term implications of a denial of such legal protection to industry as a whole -- one such outcome being the curtailment of information production for want of profitability.

Every legal system must inevitably face these questions and decide where to draw the balance in the best interests of their own jurisdictions. Of course there are additional factors in the equation. Some of these include obligations under existing multilateral or bilateral treaties and business comity. More recently there is the risk of trade sanctions from economically powerful trade partners who might be aggrieved by what they perceive as insufficient legal protection for their own nationals technology. Witness the recent elevation of intellectual property as a trade issue in the Uruguay round of GATT, designated 'Trade Related Intellectual Property Issues' or TRIPS. Usually, however, these additional factors merely demonstrate the fact that at the international level certain jurisdictions see their national interests as primarily those of devisor, competitor or end user. Jurisdictions, usually highly developed economically and technologically, which see their interests as predominately corresponding with those of initial devisers may tend to have very strong legal protection and to advocate that position to other jurisdictions. Those jurisdictions that see their interests as primarily end users or consumers, often economically and technologically under developed or developing nations, may have no legal protection and may advocate such a position for other jurisdictions. Frequently such attitudes are in reality a demand for aid from more economically developed territories. Those jurisdictions which see themselves as end users and potential competitors with the initial devisers of information such as new technology may tend to possess and to advocate laws which attempt to strike a balance between restricting access to the technology and defining under what circumstances access is permitted. It is submitted that this latter approach represents the most sensible compromise for all interest groups or jurisdiction whether they be primarily initial devisers, competitors or end users. Initial devisers and end users, whether as individuals or as nations, are not likely to remain in their respective positions in the long term. Initial devisers and end users, whether as individuals or as nations, are not likely to remain in their respective positions in the long term. Initial devisers will soon face competition and all conventional economic wisdom suggests this is beneficial. End users will similarly develop to the point where they are capable of and desire to compete. Some protection, albeit perhaps minimal, will be necessary to safeguard the investment of the fledgling competitors from wholesale misappropriation.

IV

Legal Doctrinal Concepts for Regulating Rights in Information: Property Rights in Information

D. F. Libling argues that the basis of proprietary rights in law generally is the expenditure of time, effort, labor and money and therefore the creation of valuable information so brought about should vest in the creator property rights to commercially exploit the information. This result, he argues, not only should be the case but is the case under the present Anglo-Australian law once certain hard cases have been explained (which he seeks to do)[5]. According to Libling those cases which have denied property rights to the creators of valuable commercial information brought into being through the expenditure of time, effort, labor or money were wrongly decided, given a Dworkonian assumption that law does not consist of the decided cases per se but rather of principles of which the cases are evidence.

> The courts have recognized property in the goodwill of a business -- a recognition in the main limited to the context of passing off actions -- and have protected and recognized property in such intangibles as trade reputation, news, 'know how', literary and musical compositions, film rights, advertising value of a name, and the name of a town. To classify those decisions as being the 'ticker - tape' cases, the 'collected knowledge' cases, the cases on the tort of passing off, the copyright cases and the cases under Taxation and Bankruptcy Acts and to ignore the underlying recognition of property is to assert that the common law is a barren desert of isolated decision, unwatered by principle. (118).

. . .

It will be argued below that this conclusion, even conceding the Dworkonian principles thesis, is not sustainable particularly in the light of recent cases and legislative trends. Moreover it will be argued that there are ethical reasons why property rights should not automatically attach to valuable information brought about by the expenditure of time, effort, labor, or money (or more accurately why property rights in the Hohfeldian sense should not always attach to the creator *vis a vis* certain categories of other persons).

V

The Doctrinal Basis of the Nature and Function of Property in Intangibles

There is of course a wealth of scholarship concerning the nature and function of property not only in the area of law and jurisprudence but also in many of the social sciences. Property as a concept has been extensively analyzed and defined. The literature adopts different frames of reference in discussing property. Often depending on their discipline, various authors adopt sociological, economic, political philosophical, analytical jurisprudential, or ethical among many available perspectives (or any individual theory within the former categories).

At first sight the property rights in intellectual property appear familiar. The following quotation is a useful summary of some of the points raised in the literature.

> Property is today best understood in terms of relational equities: Property rights are the sanctioned behavioral relations among men that arise from the existence of goods and pertain to their use. These relations specify the norms of behavior with respect to 'goods' -- something which utility with satisfaction to a person -- that each and every person must observe in his daily interaction with others, at least without bearing some cost as a result of non-observance. Hence the prevailing system of property rights in a community is the sum of the economic and social relations, with respect to scarce resources, in which individual members stand to each other.[6]

But this Hohfeldian approach to property is not without difficulty in the area of intellectual property. As Roger Cotterrel points out:

> The name given to the 'bundle of rights' identified in some property claims, for example 'copyright' or 'patent' or 'trademark', is the only name we use to refer to the asset protected, whereas in more traditional property forms we could distinguish, for example, the estate in land from the land itself. But there remains an apparent need - if we are to continue to think in terms of property in these

cases - for a focus of entitlement, an identifiable asset around which rights can crystallize.[7]

Sometimes it is not easy to see how this is to be done. According to Anglo-American law, copyright protects not ideas but the form of their expression, yet it may often be hard to separate the latter from the former, or to identify unambiguously the relevant form -- as, for example, in protection of computer software. It is often said that is the labor embodied in the creation which founds the right of protection but English copyright law has tended to provide protection for the commercial entrepreneur rather than the creator as such, given the absence of any clear concept of 'authors right' of the continental type. Thus it seems most appropriate to treat the *result* of the labor as being protected. But what exactly is this? German writers describe it as 'the fabric of the work determined by its substance and its form'. The complex nature of creativity and originality has to be explored, since what is actually being protected is the embodiment of ideas.

Certainly, in many cases this causes no problems. Earlier English law found no difficulty in manipulating extremely nebulous property forms. Only when we seek to *generalize* about the nature of property and related areas can serious problems arise, for English courts have understandably been reluctant to adopt a general principle that something as hard to define as knowledge itself can be considered property. But as technological or marketing ideas, design innovation and state of the art techniques, trademarks, market information and many kinds of data resources, etc., are recognized as increasingly important forms of *wealth* in contemporary societies -- often more

> important than the material things which have been the traditional focus of property law and which are now increasingly produced by means of, or are dependent on, these modern forms of wealth -- the future of property law as a coherent field of doctrine may depend on its capacity to analyze them convincingly as (objects of) property. One problem seems to be to define clearly the proprietary interest protected in such a way as both to facilitate and *justify* the protection to be provided by law. As will appear, this problem is ultimately not so much a technical -- legal one as a social one.

Cotterrell could with equal justification have said it is an ethical or social justice problem.

A similar point is made by Arnold Weinrib in *Information and Property*:[8]

> The fact that property is a conclusionary term does not help us to decide in what circumstances property rights should be awarded. That requires some conception of the function of property, which has long been a matter of dispute. The justifications that have been offered for the existence of property rights, and the views as to their proper scope, are many and varied. For our purposes (an examination of confidential information as the resource, information, and its relation to property) we need not examine such staples as the labor theory of property acquisition, or the view that property is an essential element of political liberty. While these views may lend some general support to the argument, in what follows we will limit ourselves to a less controversial instrumental view or property rights. Our social institutions exist to further certain ends: if property rights are assigned, the expectation must be that such an assignment will achieve a more desirable result than would otherwise be the case.

> The law of property is thus purposive. In economic terms, the protection of property rights serves as an incentive to encourage conduct desirable by regulating the actions of others in relation to that protected interest. For example, statutory copyright provisions give authors a proprietary interest in their work so as to permit a return to labor that could otherwise easily be appropriated . . . .[9]
>
> It should come as no surprise that if property originated in considerations of utility . . . its instances from time to time should deserve constant re-examination as to their continued conformity to new wants and the new circumstances of the changing society'. The process of adaptation has been continuous. The increase in state regulation over many forms of property interest is one aspect of this evolution. Another aspect is the expansion of the sorts of valuable interests the courts have been willing to recognize as property. And as our society continues to evolve, new interests will continue to arise with a claim to property protection. Recognizing the instrumental nature of property does not yield any easy answers as to whether or not property rights should be assigned. It does, however, inform us about the kinds of question we should be asking when new situations arise involving the potential assignment of property rights.

VI

Is Property the Most Appropriate Legal Ordering Device?

Various far from radical writers have suggested that the legal device of property is no longer appropriate for structuring rights in information in the way that the present law of intellectual property does. A Canadian law professor, Grant

Hammond, is concerned to illustrate that information is not necessarily a private good. He states:

> It is entirely possible that western legal systems have too much concern of creation of the stock of knowledge and too little concern with usage and access. One explanation for such imbalance has already been hinted at: Anglo-American law has a tradition of formal ordering through the ascription of extended property rights and it is more convenient to adapt existing rules and procedures than to think anew. (R. Grant Hammond, 1981, 'Quantum Physics, Econometric Models and Property Rights to Information,' 27 *McGill Law Journal*)

Hammond is not advocating the abolition of private property or pursuing a politically radical agenda. All that he is suggesting is that the law must adequately balance the interests of competitors and consumers with those of the creators of the information.

A similar point is made by the English academic Allison Coleman ('Trade Secrets and the Criminal Law in Canada', 1988, 1 *European Intellectual Property Review* 15):

> The increase in the economic importance of information as a commodity in its own right has given added impetus to the search for an appropriate conceptual base for the determination of the entitlement to prevent the unauthorized use of the dissemination of information, and it has been strongly argued that regulation via many of the traditional concepts of property law are inappropriate to intangibles, such as trade secrets.

Do information rights in the products of science, technology and marketing make more sense than property rights? How is the legal ordering device for the ascription of rights and duties to be framed? How do we develop a vocabulary to deal with information which is neither capable of physical possession but in which there is a societal demand to create exclusive or semi exclusive rights to deny access to that information by third parties? These questions have yet to be addressed by national and international law. Some of the parameters for such a discussion are dealt with in this paper.

ENDNOTES

1. Michael Pendleton is Professor of Law at the School of Economics, Commerce and Law, Murdoch University, Australia.

2. W.R. Cornish, 1981, *Intellectual Property; Patents Copyright Trademarks and Allied Rights*, London: Sweet and Maxwell, 2.

3. For a view which differs more in emphasis, particularly as to selection of a classifying differentia (but which might concede the genus -- information) refer to Leslie Melville, author of *Forms and Agreements on Intellectual Property*, who argues that the common unifying theme of intellectual property is activities; 'It is my view that intellectual property generally is concerned in principle with activities which have some commercial significance.' A Law of Activities -- the Choice of Words and their Limiting Effect, 1982, *EIPR* 63. Some support for such a law of activities can also be found in Cornish:

   > 'All intellectual property consists in the exclusive right to perform some defined activity, in the main productive or commercial,' *Intellectual Property*, 21.

4. Cornish, *Intellectual Property*, 6, my emphasis.

5. D.F. Libling, 1978, 'The Concept of Property: Property in Intangibles', 94 *LQR* 103.

6. R. Grant Hammond, 1981, 'Quantum Physics, Econometric Models and Property Rights to Information, *McGill Law Journal*, Vol. 27, 53.

7. 'The Law of Property and Legal Theory,' p. 88, my emphasis, in *Legal Theory and Common Law*, William Twining, ed., 1986, Basil Blackwell.

8. 1988, 38 *University of Toronto Law Journal* 117, 121.

9. The ease of appropriation is peculiar to intellectual property. One thing which is immediately apparent from the property analogy to the intangible property rights in

intellectual property are physical dissimilarities. For example, physical possession of intellectual property is not generally possible and where it can it does not have the same usefulness as does in relation to tangible property. Many kinds of intellectual property can be reproduced in multiple copies at low cost and intellectual property rarely depreciates with use. In fact it is usually only when intellectual property is used that misappropriation by others is possible.

Chapter 17

The Semiotics of Justice: Readings Across the Boundaries Between Law, Ethics and Politics

Michel Rosenfeld[1]

I

Justice is a multifaceted sign capable of depicting images of unity and social integration against unsettled backgrounds marked by discord and division. Depending on the particular circumstances involved, justice may be invoked to convey a picture of seemingly attainable social harmony or to underscore the failings of prevailing institutional arrangements. The sign of justice operates, moreover, at the interstices of religion, ethics, politics and law. Ideally, justice serves to bind together these different spheres of social interaction and to project normative accord across the various layers that make up the universe of social relations. In less than ideal conditions, on the other hand, justice can aspire to carve out an area of social compromise from the vast expanses mired in apparently irresolvable normative conflict.

Contemporary democracies are generally characterized by a lack of consensus concerning ethical and religious norms. At the same time, contemporary democracies are strongly committed to the rule of law, which makes for a sharp distinction between justice according to law and justice against or beyond law. Justice according to law is realized when each person is treated in conformity with his or her legal entitlement.[2] Justice against or beyond law, on the other hand, is the kind of justice that relies on such extra-legal criteria as ethical or religious norms and that makes it possible to claim that a law is unjust (even if it is scrupulously applied in strict compliance with the entitlements which it establishes).[3]

Justice according to law can be reconciled with justice beyond law under the aegis of natural law, which subordinates the positive law of humans to the higher law derived from God or Reason. But in the face of the deep divisions regarding ethical and religious values characteristic of contemporary societies, natural law rings hollow. One tempting alternative is for contemporaries to set their sights lower and to embrace legal positivism. Legal positivism severs law from ethics and religion and links a law's legitimacy to its pedigree. Legal positivism seems salutary in that it invites us to abandon the vain hope of finding any universally valid measure of justice beyond law. Instead, legal positivism offers us the more modest prospect of the relative justice of life under the rule of law.

For justice according to law to thrive independently from justice beyond law, it is imperative to maintain a firm boundary between law, ethics and politics. By carving out the sphere of law from those of ethics and politics, normative disputes concerning justice beyond law can apparently be prevented from spilling over into the legal arena, thus insulating the realm of justice according to law from fractional strife and parochialism. Accordingly, the legitimacy of modern law and the viability of justice according to law as independent from justice beyond law would appear to depend on the ability to keep law separate from ethics and politics. With this in mind, let us examine whether the images of justice that emerge in modern democracies are capable of sustaining a sufficient separation between law, ethics and politics to legitimate the autonomy of justice according to law.

Before proceeding any further, however, it must be stressed that in the last analysis, legal positivism cannot furnish the requisite support for the legitimation of justice according to law as independent from justice beyond law. As already noted, legal positivism ties the legitimacy of law to its pedigree. Such pedigree, moreover, appears to lead inevitably to the subjective values embodied in the will of a duly recognized sovereign. Indeed, whether the sovereign be an absolute monarch or a democratically elected legislature, the values injected into law through the expression of the sovereign's legislative will are bound to be merely subjective and legitimately contestable so long as some of the monarch's subjects or electoral or legislative minorities adhere to conflicting values. In other words, to the extent that no subjectively held value can be proven inherently superior to any other, and that legal positivism must necessarily rely on subjective values, legal positivism tends to reduce justice according to law to a virtually meaningless formality. If law must privilege certain subjective values over others, it is inherently unjust, and its equal application cannot make up for its arbitrarily unequal impact. Consistent with this, the legitimacy of an independent justice according to law requires elimination of law's dependence on subjective values. As we shall see, two contemporary theories of law, namely Luhmann's legal autopoiesis and Weinrib's new legal formalism seem to promote the independence of justice according to law without relying on subjective values for their validation. We will attempt to assess the potential of these theories, after concluding our examination of the role of justice as a communicative vehicle of social integration in the context of present day democracies.

II

The concept of justice can be said to revolve around two distinct unities: the unity among the subjects who may claim entitlement to justice -- to which we may refer as 'horizontal unity' -- and, the unity among the different normative levels at which justice may be prescribed, including, the religious, moral, political and legal levels -- to which we may refer as 'vertical unity.' One may further postulate that perfect justice occurs where there is both full horizontal and vertical unity. Moreover, in a state of perfect justice, justice is not likely to be an issue on anyone's mind, as there would be no interpersonal disputes or discrepancies among different normative levels.

The question of justice and the call for justice only arise in the face of some breakdown at least in horizontal unity. Indeed, even if vertical unity remains intact, one person could shatter horizontal unity by infringing upon another's entitlement. So long as only horizontal unity is breached, infringements of entitlement will give rise to calls for corrective or compensatory justice.[4] On the other hand, if vertical unity is also broken -- either because conflicting criteria of justice are suggested for different normative levels or because such clashing criteria are sought to be applied to the same normative level -- then questions of distributive justice[5] as well as of compensatory justice are likely to be raised. Questions of distributive justice are most obviously implicated when a breakdown of vertical unity is reflected at a single normative level. In that case, members of society clash over which, among competing criteria of distribution, ought to be used for purposes of allocating that society's benefits and burdens. Moreover, although perhaps less obvious, questions of distributive justice can also arise when the split in vertical unity cuts across different normative levels. Thus, for instance, distributive justice is at issue when acting in accordance with moral norms would lead to a different allocation of benefits and burdens than that which would result from the application of legal norms.[6]

Based on the contemplation of situations where no breach of vertical unity accompanies a departure from horizontal unity, it might be erroneously concluded that corrective justice can operate independently from distributive justice. Actually, any genuine measure of just compensation is parasitic on some norm of just distribution. For example, it is impossible to determine whether the proper measure of damages in a breach of contract case involving the breaching party's refusal to pay for goods received pursuant to the contract should be the agreed upon contract price, the market price for the goods involved, or some other price generally deemed to be 'just,' without relying on some conception of distributive justice. However, just as in the case of perfect justice there may be no awareness of justice as no one experiences a need to call for justice, where corrective justice is at stake in the context of unbroken vertical unity, the uncontroverted operation of distributive norms may well remain beyond the grasp of those concentrating on the pursuit of compensatory aims.

Law like justice can be viewed as becoming a matter of concern upon the dissolution of some mythic perfect unity. Modern legal systems, moreover, are the product of division among social groups and of conflicts that alienate the individual from the group. As Roberto Unger points out, modern legal systems prevalent in Western democracies are characterized by, among other things, group pluralism[7] and general rules of law that are universally applicable to all regardless of status or group affiliation[8] while prescribing duties and entitlements to individuals.[9] Furthermore, in Western democracies, the function of adjudication tends to be sharply separated from that of legislation,[10] with a view towards shielding the judicial resolution of legal disputes from the politics that inevitably surround the legislative process.

The advent of the market, which, as Max Weber has stated, is 'a relationship which transcends the boundaries of neighborhood, kinship group, or tribe,'[11] provides the key turning point towards the greater differentiation characteristic of modern legal systems. As recounted by Weber, economic scarcity prompted individuals to leave their own communities in order to exchange goods with strangers at market. In dealing with such strangers, however, individuals could not rely on the kinship rules that governed relationships within their own community, and therefore had to look to universally applicable laws capable of transcending the local biases of intra-communal norms.[12] In other words, interactions in non-communal spheres between strangers with different ethical and religious values require clearly differentiated laws that scrupulously avoid taking sides with respect to parochial issues or intruding upon intra-communal matters. This is paramount in order to alleviate the misgivings and reduce the uncertainties confronting those who must leave home and deal with strangers willing to trade on the market.

Given the twin aims of avoiding favoritism toward any particular parochial values and of fostering regularity and settled expectations regarding dealings in non-communal spheres, procedural rules loom as an especially apt vehicle for the institution of a highly differentiated set of laws designed to mediate interactions among strangers. Moreover, at least in the case of the *laissez faire* economic market, reliance on process oriented formal or procedural laws not only promotes greater certainty in non-communal dealings without trampling on substantive communal values, but also makes it possible directly to serve the aims of the market by codifying the rules of market competition. To the extent that lawful competition insures that market transactions collectively will promote the common good, the procedural laws that carve out the nature and scope of such competition at once foster substantive values in the non-communal spheres while presumably leaving intact pre-existing substantive values operative in particular communal spheres.[13]

It is important for laws designed to provide procedures for non-communal relationships to be differentiated from, and to avoid the appearance of depending on, communal norms. Accordingly, the formal, process-oriented and heavily procedural laws designed to facilitate non-communal exchanges must project an image of detachment from ethical and religious values -- an image that can be promoted through spreading of the belief that law itself can become completely independent from religion and ethics. Moreover, accompanying and reinforcing this image and the belief that sustains it, is of course, the perception -- buttressed by the sharp contrast between communal and non-communal dealings -- of a breakdown of vertical unity in the realm of justice, with justice according to law bearing little or no connection to justice beyond law. Thus, as communal dealings increasingly give way to non-communal dealings among strangers, from the standpoint of justice, both horizontal and vertical unity enter into a process of dissolution that seems headed towards a complete breakdown.

As it becomes apparently increasingly independent from other levels of justice, legal justice -- while retaining compensatory and distributive components -- tends to become primarily preoccupied with procedural matters. Procedural justice, like its distributive and compensatory counterparts, is a necessary but inconspicuous component of perfect justice. A call to justice, moreover, may concentrate exclusively on procedural justice even in the face of complete harmony regarding applicable criteria of compensatory and distributive justice. Thus, for instance, a dispute could arise on the subject of the best available procedure needed to implement an agreed upon criterion of compensatory justice. What is markedly different about contemporary legal justice, however, is the tendency to concentrate exclusively on procedural justice to the exclusion of the other forms of justice.

To better understand how procedural justice may acquire independence, it is useful to refer to the distinction made by Rawls between the two different types of procedures that might lead to the achievement of justice. The first requires both an independent criterion of justice to determine what would constitute a just compensation or distribution and a procedure to lead to the desired outcome as prescribed by the independent criterion. If the procedure guarantees the desired outcome then we have, in Rawls' terms 'perfect procedural justice;'[14] if it does not, then we have 'imperfect procedural justice.'[15] On the other hand, the second type of procedure, 'pure procedural justice' does not require an independent criterion of (distributive or compensatory) justice for its validity.[16] In this context, the outcome is supposed to be just, provided only that the relevant procedure was properly followed.[17]

Modern law's greater concern with question of procedure is most probably, in part, due to the fact that strangers tend to be suspicious of one another. As non-communal dealings occur in settings without established customs and traditions governing interactions, matters of procedure seem bound to leap to the forefront. More importantly, however, the independent law applicable to non-communal spheres, which is cut off from the ethical and religious norms operative in communal spheres, seems left with no more desirable path to justice than that of pure procedural justice. Indeed, where the adoption of any substantive criterion of justice would smack of parochialism, the pursuit of pure procedural justice looms as the best possible alternative.

To the extent that free market competition guarantees achievement of the common good, implementation of the laws needed to sustain the free market would produce pure procedural justice. Moreover, among the most important of these laws would be laws regarding contract formation designed to maximize freedom of contract.[18] Thus, assuming the existence of such laws, justice would require the enforcement of freely entered into contracts not because of the nature of the contractual terms involved, but because of the *fact* that the contractors had freely availed themselves of the rules of contract formation and freely agreed upon the terms of their mutual contractual obligations.

In sum, under optimal conditions and in the presence of a free market model of non-communal relationships, law acquires independence from other normative spheres, and its implementation is capable of producing pure procedural justice. Under these circumstances, moreover, justice beyond law has most likely become fragmented and largely cast away to a distant horizon. Justice according to law can then claim both independence and self-sufficiency inasmuch as it generates pure procedural justice.

As the market tends to become all-encompassing and local communities recede towards the vanishing point, justice according to law tends to dwarf justice beyond law and pure procedural justice becomes increasingly sweeping. At the logical culmination of this process, it would appear that law would achieve complete independence and that justice according to law relying on pure procedural justice would occupy the entire domain of justice, rendering justice beyond law completely superfluous. In reality, however, this state of affairs is impossible to realize for at least two principal reasons. First, the expulsion of ethical and religious values from the market is only possible so long as these values can find an outlet for expression in local communities that remain beyond the reach of the market. Thus, while economic exchanges take place among strangers, religious and ethical activities can remain largely confined to local communities among one's family and kinship groups. Relationships among strangers can be sustained to the extent that they are complemented by strong communal bonds. If local communities were to give complete way to market relationships, however, then all inter-subjective relationships would be among strangers, and individuals would risk losing all sense of identity unless they could find a way to forge ethical or religious bonds with the strangers they encounter on the market. In short, either ethical and religious concerns are confined to communal spheres that remain beyond the market or they are bound to irrupt on the market for the lack of any other available outlet.

The second principal reason why justice according to law can never come to occupy the entire domain of justice is that market competition is never perfect -- and, even if perfect competition could be achieved in the economic sense, the market would still fail automatically to promote a universally acceptable conception of the common good. Moreover, to the extent that unfettered economic competition must be curbed for the common good or public welfare, one must look beyond the market and justice according to law to find legal norms that will prove just and efficacious. So long as the public welfare is perceived as requiring that market relationships be curbed rather than eliminated, justice according to law and pure procedural justice are certain to retain legitimacy within a part of the domain encompassed by justice. The remainder of that domain, however, will call for justice beyond law (and laws embodying norms derived form the latter kind of justice). For example, let us assume that unlimited freedom of contract is deemed unjust insofar as it fosters exploitation of the weak by the powerful, but that the limitation of freedom of contract through the implementation of minimum wage and maximum work hours legislation would suffice to prevent exploitation in labor relations. Under these circumstances, a labor contract would be just, in part because its terms satisfied the minimum wage, maximum hours laws, and beyond that, because of the fact that the contractors freely mutually agreed to enter into it. Furthermore, the minimum wage maximum hours laws would not be just in themselves, but only in reference to some expression of justice beyond law which would itself have to be legitimated in term of adherence to certain extra-legal norms -- e.g., it is unethical or contrary to religious dogma to exploit human beings. Inasmuch as the labor contract is just because of the fact of agreement, there is room left for pure procedural justice. But since the determination on *how much* room ought to be left for pure procedural justice requires recourse to justice beyond law, in the last analysis, the legitimacy of pure procedural justice also depends on extra-legal norms.

There is no fixed point at which communal concerns spill over unto an expanding market sphere, nor is there a clear line dividing what ought to be left to the free market from what should be placed beyond its reach. There is also no set prescription concerning how the emerging community of strangers might find a suitable equilibrium between seeking to transform market relationships from within and attempting to circumscribe them through confrontation with non-market norms. All those issues are the subject of an ongoing dynamic process which involves confrontation as well as accommodation, and which is therefore likely to produce numerous boundary shifts. One thing, however, does remain constant throughout the unfolding of this process: the presence of justice beyond law. Although it has become prey to fragmentation and to seemingly irresolvable internal clashes, justice beyond law is either present implicitly or as the antagonist from which justice according to law seeks to wrest an independent existence.

Even though justice according to law cannot come to occupy the entire domain of justice, there are certain conceptions of law that purport to keep the concerns of justice beyond law out of the sphere of legal relations without having to fall back on purely subjective values. Moreover, these conceptions of law seek to legitimate the expulsion of justice beyond law from the realm of law through the delimitation of sharp boundaries between law, ethics and politics. Chief among those conceptions is Niklas Luhmann's theory of law as an autopoietic system that is self-referential and normatively closed.

III

The cornerstones of legal autopoiesis are: a conception of law in particular, and society in general, as networks of communication; the existence of a degree of social complexity that calls for a high level of functional differentiation; the generation of conflict as a means towards the creation and application of legal norms; self-referentiality and circularity; the legal (sub)system's normative closure combined with its cognitive openness towards other spheres of social interaction construed as the legal system's environment; and the independence of the legal system as a self-referential network of (legal) communications from the intentions of the persons who engage in legal discourse.

As Gunther Teubner emphasizes, legal systems are not born autopoietic; they can evolve towards greater self-referentiality and thus become autopoietic.[19] Moreover, the crucial moment in the evolution from an allopoietic to an autopoietic legal system is the 'central shift from 'external' societal mechanisms of evolution to 'internal' legal mechanisms. . . in the sense that *external mechanisms can only have a 'modulating' effect on legal developments while the evolutionary primacy passes over to internal structural determination*'.[20] On the other hand, as Luhmannn makes clear, the principal task of law is to stabilize expectations.[21] Now, in the context of a fully normatively integrated community where the vertical unity of justice remains intact, the stability of expectations would seem clearly better served by an allopoietic legal system firmly anchored on a well established and largely uncontroverted set of extra-legal norms. In the face of a breakdown of justice beyond law, on the contrary, the contest among extra-legal norms is bound to have a distabilizing effect, and accordingly law may be better poised to buttress settled expectations by turning 'inward' and drawing upon its own processes and elements.

The combination of the dissolution of the vertical unity of justice and the increasing need to deal with strangers in non-communal settings creates a strong need for an autonomous legal system. On the one hand, the lack of vertical unity of justice makes it impossible convincingly or authoritatively to reconcile law with any available extra-legal norms. On the other hand, because interacting strangers lack commonly shared extra-legal norms, it is imperative that they adopt some means of regulation which can stand independently from existing extra-legal norms. Moreover, this means of regulation must generate, in the context of non-communal relationships, the kind of stability of expectations that is customary in normatively integrated communities.

Even if the sphere of non-communal interaction cannot be stabilized through recourse to ethical or religious norms, it does not logically follow that an autonomous legal system offers the only plausible avenue to the stabilization of expectations. Arguably, the sphere of non-communal interaction could also be stabilized through a process of political accommodation that avoided reliance on contested ethical or religious norms. Both autonomous legal and political systems would bring increased stability to non-communal spheres through the deployment of a communicative process. The political system, as understood here, would involve the accommodation of conflicting interests through series of ad hoc compromises among contending groups vying for power and influence in order to be in a better position to promote their own interests. Moreover, although political compromises would themselves be ad hoc, the political process in which they would be embedded could well unfold within a stable political structure -- such as, for example, a parliamentary democracy -- capable of lending firm support to important normative expectations.

For purposes of the present discussion, the principal difference between a legal and a political resolution of a conflict lies in that legal resolutions do not consist of ad hoc compromises, but rather of determinations involving the application of previously established (legal) normative rules, principles or standards.[22] In spite of this difference, however, the legal and political systems could be viewed as working in harmony, with law -- perhaps in the form of a constitution -- framing the structure of the political. At the same time, law could also be interpreted as complementing the ad hoc compromises of politics with the resolution of conflicts pursuant to previously set legal rules, standards or principles. Moreover, in view of the apparent complementarily of law and politics in this universe marked by the breakdown of the vertical unity of justice, it would seem that the fusion of law and politics rather than their uncoupling (with a view to establishing two autonomous social spheres) would be most likely to lead to a greater stabilization of expectations.

From the standpoint of autopoietic theory, however, the stabilization of expectations in a complex society with interweaving communal and non-communal spheres of interaction might be best achieved through a process of increasing functional differentiation that requires uncoupling the legal (sub)system from the political (sub)system. In the context of non-communal dealings among strangers, legal interaction would promote greater stabilization of expectations than would political interaction to the extent that the former would have less of an ad hoc nature than the latter. In other words, if people could predict their legitimate legal expectations with a higher degree of probability than their legitimate political expectations, then the operation of the two spheres as separate and independent from one another might well lead to greater overall stabilization of expectations than if both spheres operated in a closely integrated manner.[23]

Within the framework of an autopoietic conception of social systems, the autonomous legal subsystem would be distinguished from its political counterpart by its mode of functioning.[24] Each of these subsystems would provide a different mode of structuring communicative interaction between social actors. Moreover, to the extent that laws lack the 'ad hoc' quality of politics, they are susceptible of acquiring enough of a meaning of their own to allow them to escape from the full grasp of their proponents.[25] Accordingly, submission of conflicts to an autonomous legal system rather than to the political sphere should generally signal a retreat from the purely power based relationships in the hope of achieving more stable expectations. In the context of a complete differentiation between the legal and political spheres, the commitment of a class of conflicts to the self-contained normatively closed realm of law signifies presumably both a deferral and an equalization of power among the parties to the relevant conflicts. Power is deferred in as much as the would be winner of a present political resolution of an ongoing conflict submits to a previously established legal norm that leads to an anticipated but less favorable outcome of the conflict in question.[26] On the other hand, power is relatively equalized to the extent that a rational decision to commit a certain kind of conflict for resolution within the legal sphere implies a willing loss of power by the strongest members of society coupled with some gain in power for its weakest members. Ultimately, the equalization of power stemming from rational agreement to refer certain conflicts to an autonomous legal system may not be very different from the kind of equalization that would be achieved through a Hobbesian social contract.[27] There is, however, one key difference between a Hobbesian agreement and submission to an autonomous autopoietic legal system. In the latter case the very mediation provided by the autonomous legal system would insure against direct subordination to the will of any individual or group vested with the powers of the sovereign.

The order of autopoietic law must be contrasted to the disorder of unregulated non-communal social interaction. Bý producing order -- any order -- autopoietic law differentiates itself from the potential chaos of unregulated non-communal dealings, and insures a significant measure of stability in dealings between strangers. Furthermore, the presence of such stability results in a distribution of benefits and burdens that is arguably far preferable to and more just than, that which would emanate from chaos. Accordingly, the order established through the process of differentiation set in motion by autopoietic law secures at the very least what may be referred to as 'minimal distributive justice.'

While all legal systems presumably satisfy minimal distributive justice, autopoietic legal systems are supposed to do more. Indeed, legal autopoiesis is not only poised to wrest order out of disorder but also to furnish some kind of insurance through the use of normative closure to stabilize expectations of expectations.[28] To reduce complexity, social actors seek to achieve greater certainty concerning their expectations, and especially concerning their expectations of the expectations of others. The greater the certainty that a social actor has concerning the expectations of all concerned, the more insurance that actor has concerning the consequences of his or her dealings with others. Particularly when dealing with strangers in non-communal settings, however, *cognitive* expectations are subject to constant revision as they are likely to be frequently disappointed due to error or miscalculations.[29] In contrast, *normative* expectations can be stabilized counterfactually, with the consequence that they need not be revised even if they are disappointed.[30]

For example, if I happen to expect all my business appointments to be punctual, and they frequently happen to arrive late, I would be better off by revising my (cognitive) expectation in order to minimize the aggravation I experience as a result of counting on punctuality. On the other hand, if the law provides that those who buy goods must pay for them I need not revise my (normative) expectation that my customers should pay for the goods they buy, even if many of them fail to pay. So long as the law remains in force I am entitled to hold on to my normative expectation. Moreover, to the extent that the law provides remedies for the disappointment of legitimate normative expectations, it provides insurance to legal actors.[31] Finally, although this is not logically required, the stabilization of normative expectations through law is also likely to lead to a significant decrease in the fluctuation of cognitive expectations. Indeed, it seems reasonable to expect that in the long run a vast majority of people will tend to behave in conformity with their legal obligations.[32]

In a nutshell, the core function of legal communications, according to Luhmann's autopoietic theory, is to provide information concerning the meaning of events and, in particular, actions in relation to the binary code legal/illegal.[33] This information is not simply the product of the enactment and application of legal rules, but rather emerges from the circular interplay between rules and decisions.[34] Moreover, because the validation of legal norms hinges on a process of unfolding circularity,[35] neither the substantive values embodied in particular legal norms nor the intentions projected by actors engaged in the legal arena can in any direct or significant way inform determinations dependent on use of the binary code legal/illegal. This is merely a further elaboration of the notion of normative closure. On the other hand, the internally sealed circular interplay between legal rules and decisions by no means forecloses expanding (or for that matter shrinking) the domain of that which can be rendered legally meaningful through submission to the binary code legal/illegal. This seems to follow from the very notion of cognitive openness.

In the last analysis from the standpoint of a complex modern legal system, the binary code legal/illegal may be necessary but it is not sufficient to account for the normative characteristics of law, except in a trivial tautological sense. Even conceding that *ex post facto* every legal communication may be interpreted as having designated the actions to which it refers as being either legal or illegal,[36] legal practice can hardly nontrivially be reduced to the classification of actions as either legal or illegal.[37] Autopoietic law promotes the values of order, insurance and equalization relative to the ad hoc compromises of its political environment. These values are not, however, the only ones pursued by law as a distinct contemporary practice. For example, the contemporary movement towards the juridification of human rights and constitutional guarantees extends beyond mere order or insurance. Actually, such juridification often appears to open the legal system to contested conceptions of justice beyond law that transcend mere communalism inasmuch as they are specifically oriented towards the domain of non-communal interaction. Moreover, to the extent that constitutional jurisprudence wrestles with fundamental values associated with justice beyond law, it is more likely to undermine than to promote the kind of predictability necessary to provide insurance.[38]

In conclusion, the claim of normative closure does not seem to be justified in the case of law. As a matter of fact, in certain fields like constitutional law at least, it seems more accurate to describe law as a practice as being normatively open to the extra-legal norms that underly justice beyond law. Moreover, to the extent that contemporary law as a practice is not restricted to the exclusive pursuit of order, insurance and relative equalization, the autopoietic thesis seems defective as it unduly and arbitrarily narrows the domain of legitimate contemporary legal relationships.

IV

Ernest Weinrib's new legal formalism[39] seems, upon first impression, capable of maintaining a clear boundary between law, ethics and politics without displaying the same drawbacks as Luhmann's legal autopoiesis. Unlike Luhmann, Weinrib does not seek hermetically to seal off legal norms from their ethical and political counterparts. Instead, Weinrib acknowledges that moral and political values find their way into legal materials, but he claims that legal relations maintain their distinct identity by means of their adhesion to certain particular forms. These are the forms of justice, namely corrective and distributive justice. From the standpoint of the breakdown of the unity of justice discussed above, Weinrib's thesis can be characterized, in a nutshell, as defining legal relationships in the context of mature legal systems in terms of their intelligibility as instances of corrective or distributive justice under a view of these forms of justice as operating essentially independently from one another.

Reduced to its bare essentials, Weinrib's new legal formalism postulates that law remains distinct from politics to the extent that law's structure is intelligible as an internally coherent practice.[40] As Weinrib specifies, 'from a perspective internal to the law's content, formalism draws out the implications of a sophisticated legal system's tendency to coherence by making explicit the justificatory patterns to which the content of such a system must conform'.[41] In other words, in a mature legal system, interpretation -- reveals law's tendency towards internal coherence through the articulation of immanent links between the form and the content of particular juridical relationships.[42]

As already mentioned, the abstract forms that endow juridical relationships with meaning, according to Weinrib, are the forms of justice, namely corrective and distributive justice. Weinrib further indicates that these two forms of justice are irreducible, and that accordingly particular juridical relationships come either within the sweep of corrective justice or within that of distributive justice, but never within that of both.[43] Moreover, drawing upon Aristotle's insight, Weinrib emphasizes that, paradigmatically, the juridical relationships that embody the forms of justice are those 'that obtain between parties regarded as external to each other, each with separate interests of mine and thine'.[44] In other words, juridical relationships involve agents who are connected through external links as opposed to such internal interpersonal links as those forged through love or virtue.[45]

As understood by Weinrib, corrective justice involves the award of damages which simultaneously quantifies the wrongdoing of one party and the suffering of the other party in a bipolar (voluntary or involuntary) private transaction.[46] Moreover, under this view, all bilateral relationships characteristic of the private law of torts and contracts are ultimately intelligible in terms of the structure of corrective justice.[47] In other words, the legal universe carved out by juridical relationships intelligible in terms of corrective justice is one in which formally equal individual legal actors are initially placed side by side owing each other nothing but reciprocal negative duties (of non-interference).[48] The initial equilibrium maintained by a network of reciprocal negative duties which makes for purely external relationships among legal actors, however, is bound to become upset as individuals either seek the cooperation of others in the pursuit of self-interest (contract) or voluntarily or involuntarily interfere with others in the course of such pursuit (tort). Corrective justice, through the award of damages, undoes (erases), the positive entanglements of (unfulfilled) contracts and the interferences of torts, and thus purports to reestablish (re-inscribe) the initial equilibrium between purely externally linked equals.

Corrective justice, argues Weinrib, deals with the immediate relationship of person to person,[49] and is completely removed from politics,[50] as it merely seeks to restore the initial equilibrium between a doer and a sufferer regardless of the actual wealth, merit or virtue of the interacting legal actors.[51] Thus, it apparently makes no difference whether one is politically inclined to advance the interests of the wealthy or the poor, as there is only one legitimate way to resolve legal disputes arising under private law: that is, by commanding payment of the quantity of damages which corrective justice requires in order to restore the initial equality between doer and sufferer. Accordingly, as Weinrib sees it, the judicial task in the context of dispensing the quantitative equality mandated by corrective justice is limited to the specification of the actual damages required in the particular case to be adjudicated.[52]

In contrast to the quantitative equality of corrective justice, distributive justice, according to Weinrib, requires the implementation of proportional equality. Whereas corrective justice is concerned with the recovery of a status quo ante, distributive justice requires the allocation of the benefits and burdens of social cooperation in the proportions set by an applicable criterion of distribution.[53] Also, consistent with Weinrib's analysis, unlike corrective justice, distributive justice cannot be completely severed from politics. Indeed, settling on any given criterion of distribution for purposes of achieving proportional equality involves a political decision.[54] Thus, for example, whether certain benefits ought to be distributed equally in proportion to need or in proportion to merit depends not on anything inherent to law or to juridical relationships, but instead on some collective decision that remains extrinsic to law and that must draw, at least in part, on political considerations.

Although distributive justice cannot avoid politics, Weinrib maintains that the former is not thereby reducible to the latter.[55] Once a particular criterion of distribution has been selected, distributive justice requires that juridical relationships conform to the proportional equality mandated by that criterion.[56] Moreover, Weinrib also believes that inherent in the very notion of distributive justice there is a conception of personhood and of equality which constrains all legitimate juridical relationships falling within the scope of that form of justice.[57] The concept of personhood thus requires judges to make sure that people engaged in the relevant juridical relationships are not treated as things; the concept of equality, that each person be treated as an equal consistent with the dictates of the prevailing criterion of distribution.[58]

Distributive justice, particularly through its conception of personhood and equality, is supposed to preside, in Weinrib's formalist vision, over the domain of public law. On the one hand, Weinrib maintains that the notions of personhood and equality impose nonpolitical constraints on the legislative and administrative processes.[59] On the other hand, Weinrib argues, 'The positive law may give effect to the fundamental values of personhood and equality in a variety of ways: by incorporating them into the techniques for construing statutes, by elaborating notions of natural justice or fairness for administrative procedures or by enshrining specifications of personhood and equality into constitutional documents.'[60]

Corrective and distributive justice, as conceived by Weinrib, may be viewed as offering two distinct (and irreducible to politics) paths towards the reconciliation persons capable of engaging in mutually external relationships. Corrective justice promotes the minimal harmony of mutual non-interference through the spread of a quantitative equality that ritualistically effaces the encroachment of a wrongdoing self upon a suffering other.

Distributive justice, on the other hand, also aspires to promote mutual non-interference by defusing the conflict over the allocation of collectively generated benefits and burdens. By instituting proportional equality, distributive justice circumscribes an order within which each person can see him or herself as a moral equal who is treated as an end rather than merely as means by being given his or her due. Because each individual self is ascribed a dignified place within the order carved out by the proportional equality of distributive justice, moreover, the self can presumably renounce confrontation with the other as a means to secure the socially generated goods which self-respect and dignity require. Thus, distributive justice, much like corrective justice, tends towards a harmony of purely external relationships of non-interference between a self and another who have competing claims on the products of social cooperation.

Weinrib's new legal formalism is ultimately unacceptable to the extent that it rests on certain arbitrary and unwarranted premises. There are two basic flaws with the premises underlying Weinrib's formalist thesis. The first flaw, derives from Weinrib's elevation of one (among many possible) historically grounded and ideologically determined version of what is entailed by corrective and distributive justice as the universal and ahistorical essence of those forms of justice. Moreover, this flaw is particularly troublesome because it reveals that Weinrib's apparent depoliticization of the forms of justice is achieved through the privileging and enshrining of a particular ideological vision which is certainly subject to political debate. The second flaw stems from Weinrib's insistence on the existence of an unbridgeable gap between corrective and distributive justice, and from his assertion that corrective justice is concerned with immediate relationships among persons. Actually, as pointed out above, corrective justice is necessarily parasitic on some criterion of distributive justice. And, consistent with this, all relationships that come within the purview of corrective justice must already be mediated.

Weinrib makes the unwarranted assumptions that the domain of corrective justice must preside over a regime of purely negative rights and that distributive justice necessarily involves respect for Kantian notions of equality and personhood. Corrective justice can operate in the context of purely negative rights under certain particular historical and ideological circumstances, namely those associated with a free market economy.[61] Thus, private law shaped so as to afford the greatest possible legal protection to free market transactions would undoubtedly be primarily oriented towards the protection of the negative rights and freedoms best suited to promote the orderly proliferation of market exchanges. And, under those circumstances, corrective justice would be quite properly confined to 'undoing' the entanglements having resulted in infringements upon negative rights and freedoms. Nothing in corrective justice as a form of justice taken at the highest level of abstraction, however, precludes extending corrective justice to cover a regime of positive rights, or, in other words, a legal system in which private legal actors are charged with positive duties towards one another.

Corrective justice is necessarily backward looking, in that it must pick some point in the past and set it as a baseline. After selecting its baseline, corrective justice must compare the set of intersubjective relationships existing at the baseline and that which is in force at the subsequent time at which a claim for compensation arises. Corrective justice must also introduce a concept of 'disruption' pursuant to which it can distinguish between compensable and non-compensable deviations from the baseline. Weinrib seems to assume that if we seek to establish the baseline logically, by carrying corrective justice to its highest level of abstraction, we will all be lead by reason to the same point: a static universe of purely abstract egos who remain entirely independent from each other and who scrupulously refrain from interfering with one another as a consequence of their strict adherence to a regime of purely negative rights and duties. Moreover, for those who accept this point as providing a purely logically compelled -- and hence completely apolitical -- baseline, the definition of what should count as a compensable disruption becomes self-evident: any deviation from the status quo of the baseline that involves a violation of a negative right.

Logic alone, however, does not compel acceptance of the atomistic universe that Weinrib projects at the highest level of abstraction. Indeed, it hardly seems contradictory to contend that at the highest level of abstraction, persons are cleansed of their selfish individualistic concerns, and that they are mutually dedicated to the maintenance of social harmony and welfare within their community through the deployment of care, concern and an elaborate network of positive rights and duties. Within this communitarian vision, moreover the baseline would be one of solidarity and mutual assistance, and any deviation involving a violation of a positive duty would quite naturally qualify as a compensable disruption.

Neither Weinrib's atomistic vision nor its communitarian counterpart are in any sense logically compelled. Each of them figures as an orignary myth suited to buttress a particular ethical and political ideology. More generally, setting a baseline for corrective justice involves an irreducibly arbitrary -- i.e. political and ideological -- element.

As we have seen, Weinrib does concede, on the other hand, that distributive justice has a political component, but he insists that it nevertheless transcends politics to the extent that imposes a duty to abide by Kantian notions of personhood and equality. Unless one incorporates these Kantian notions tautologically in the very definition of distributive justice, however, there is no reason to assume that all plausible conceptions of distributive justice need include such Kantian notions. For example, there seems to be nothing contradictory about a feudalist conception of distributive justice, according to which person are inherently unequal depending on the social class into which they are born, according to which much greater dignity attaches to those born into aristocratic families than to commoners, and according to which distributions should be made unequally, with a disproportionate share of society's goods going to the members of the aristocracy. Once again Weinrib has taken one possible conception -- or in this case more precisely a class of possible conceptions -- of a form of justice and presented it as universally valid. But to the extent that distributive justice at the highest level of abstraction does not imply Kantian notions of personhood and equality, judicial protection of the latter is not likely to be apolitical in the sense that Weinrib intends.

V

Ultimately, both Weinrib's new legal formalism and Luhmann's legal autopoiesis fail to capture the full essence of contemporary legal relations. To a significant extent, this failure is due to the fact that modern legal systems can not successfully expel justice beyond law from their inner preccints. Because of the clash between values, the presence of justice beyond law may often be barely discernible, but it is nonetheless steadfast. In spite of their failures, however, both Weinrib's and Luhmann's theories do provide illuminating accounts of a fundamental tendency of modern law. That tendency does propel law towards formalism, proceduralism, self-referentiality and the vindication of justice according to law. But that tendency cannot be properly comprehended unless it is set against the equally powerful tendency to enlist legal communication and legal relationships in the struggle to reconstitute the lost unity of justice beyond law. The substantive driving force behind this attempt at reconstructing the unity of justice beyond law is pluralism. Pluralism, however, is deceptive; it embodies substantive values, but it presents itself as being primarily concerned with forms and procedures.

To understand the appeal of pluralism one must keep in mind that the fragmentation of justice beyond law makes for extra-legal norms that are highly contestable and that thus apparently lend but precarious support to the laws which they purport to justify. One way to strengthen that support and to seemingly reverse the process of fragmentation is for justice beyond law explicitly to embrace pluralism as the paramount extra-legal norm. In other words, instead of abandoning the sphere of justice beyond law to a hopeless contest among antagonistic extra-legal norms, one may adopt pluralism as the best means to introduce unity in the shaping of legal norms without sacrificing the diversity generated by the coexistence of antagonistic norms.

Commitment to pluralism also leads to formalism and proceduralism, (although not necessarily for the same reasons as devotion to market competition does). From the standpoint of a pluralistic philosophy, diversity and tolerance of different normative outlooks are fundamental values. Pluralism recognizes the importance of justice beyond law, but insists on maintaining a clear divide between it and justice according to law, in an effort to avoid privileging some sets of competing extra-legal norms over others. Accordingly, the formalism and proceduralism sought by pluralism are not meant to weaken or eliminate justice beyond law, but instead to infuse law with a measure of neutrality sufficient to permit a peaceful coexistence between diverse conceptions of justice beyond law. In short, pluralism seeks to maintain the differentiation of law from extra-legal norms, in order to insure as much as possible that law will not stand in the way of the pursuit of different conceptions of justice beyond law and of the common good. Although pluralism may be capable of encompassing several different conceptions of justice beyond law, it ultimately fails to promote a legal system that is genuinely neutral with respect to all extra-legal norms. Indeed, to avert self-contradiction and self-destruction, pluralism can only protect those sets of extra-legal norms that can peacefully coexist with competing norms.[62] Because of this, pluralism must sacrifice neutrality and privilege mutually compatible norms over incompatible ones. In the end, pluralism itself must be counted as a substantive value that informs a certain particular conception of justice beyond law. What is unique about pluralism is that it requires sustaining the divide between justice according to law and justice beyond law as part of its strategy towards the realization of its own conception of justice beyond law.

Weinrib's formalist conception of corrective justice and his vision of distributive justice based on Kantian constraints are highly compatible with pluralism's commitment to accommodate as many different conceptions of justice beyond law as possible. By presenting corrective justice as essentially formal and procedural and as being thoroughly apolitical one conveys the impression that the canons of legal compensation are neutral regarding all the competing conceptions of justice beyond law. Furthermore, the Kantian constraints concerning personhood and equality are also well suited to foster the pluralist creed that each person's conception of justice beyond law is in principle entitled to respect and that none of competing conceptions of justice beyond law should be considered to be inherently superior to the others.

Even more central to pluralism is that law, consistent with Luhmann's autopoietic theory, should aspire to be autonomous, self-referential and circular. Indeed, from a pluralist standpoint, modern law cannot simply consist of the emancipation and triumph of justice according to law in the face of some final collapse of justice beyond law. Instead, the ascendance of justice according to law is accompanied by a movement towards the reconstitution of justice beyond law.[63] More precisely, contemporary law appears to be the product of an ongoing clash between two contradictory drives: the drive towards autonomy and that towards the reestablishment of the vertical unity of justice.[64] One of the dynamic functions of contemporary legal actions and communications is continuously to produce sufficient normative differentiation to avert the dissolution of the legal sphere through absorption into the theologico-ethical or political sphere. On the other hand, clashing against this relentless pursuit of differentiation is contemporary law's insatiable need to work towards the recovery of the lost vertical unity of justice. Accordingly, the first of these two drives fuels contemporary law's tendency towards autopoiesis and autonomy while the second, on the contrary, pulls law away from autopoietic self-referentiality.

Contemporary law cannot genuinely resolve the tension between its conflicting tendencies without losing either its identity or its legitimacy.

Paradoxically, contemporary law is more likely to fulfill its role by seeking to maintain an equilibrium between its conflicting tendencies than striving to minimize contradiction through a disproportionate development of one of these basic tendencies at the expense of the other. Moreover, the unrelenting pursuit of such an equilibrium is essential because the function of contemporary law is not merely one of differentiation but also one of unification. Finally, the justification for contemporary law's simultaneous pursuit of both unification and differentiation is extrinsic rather than intrinsic to law. From a pluralist perspective, contemporary law's tendency towards autopoiesis may be justified as part of a larger whole, but only in terms of extra-legal norms. In other words, it is legitimate for law to turn inward, but only because that tends to promote the integration of law in the larger social matrix in accordance with extra-legal norms poised to permeate social life as a whole.

The paradox presented by contemporary law's turning inward as part of its bid to recover the vertical unity of justice can be unraveled by reference to the social forces that shape contemporary legal relationships. The function of these relationships is not simply to produce differentiation or, on the contrary, to foment the unification of legal and extra-legal norms. Instead, the function of contemporary law is to produce differentiation and promote unification *simultaneously* as prevailing circumstances make the possibility of reconciling legal norms and extra-legal values conditional on carving out a distinct sphere of differentiation.

The meaning of the movement towards legal autonomy is prone to being misinterpreted to the extent that law's turn inward is overdetermined and that the full reason for it is likely to remain dissimulated. Contemporary legal relationships are inscribed in a normative universe animated by the necessity to eliminate communal norms from the sphere of non-communal relationships, and to replace them with non-communal -- or more precisely, trans-communal -- norms. Accordingly, on the one hand, law must turn inward to escape from both the grasp of past parochialisms and from the temptations of future parochialisms.[65] But, on the other hand -- and this is much more likely to escape notice -- the law must also turn inward as a means to the reconstitution of justice beyond law consistent with the establishment of extra-legal norms with trans-communal appeal. At the very least, the differentiation produced by law's inward turn should serve as a communicative vehicle designed to dispel the notion that the extra-legal norms sought to be given trans-communal validity are but the old parochial norms bent on venturing beyond their legitimate territorial boundaries.[66] In the context of pluralism, however, the tendency towards legal autonomy plays a key role in, and is as an integral part of, the systematic task of reconstituting the normative unity of the domain of non-communal interaction. Indeed, without maintenance of the movement towards legal autonomy, there would be no room for the peaceful coexistence of the different value systems that are compatible with pluralism. In view of pluralism's normative aim to accommodate as many different value systems as are compatible with it, the tendency towards legal autonomy associated with it should be interpreted as part and parcel of the pluralist effort to reconstitute justice beyond law so as to legitimately empower it over non-communal relationships.

Any attempt to reconstitute justice beyond law from the standpoint of pluralism, however, seems ultimately bound to fail. Viewing communal extra-legal norms as first order norms, pluralism generates a second order of norms. These second order or trans-communal norms, moreover, are supposed to provide a unified normative framework for the reconstitution of justice beyond law. Within this framework, first order norms are not suppressed, but merely subordinated to second order norms. For some first order norms, subordination means displacement. For example, pluralism is compatible with the embrace of certain particular religious norms, provided that the latter are relegated to the private sphere. Furthermore, for other first order norms, subordination to second order pluralist norms means in effect elimination. Thus, for instance, crusading religions, and rigidly antipluralistic moral and political norms can be given no room in a normative universe sought to be unified under pluralist values.[67] Now, because pluralism cannot do without any first order norms -- indeed, pluralism is meaningless without at least some available choice among different first order norms -- and because it cannot accommodate all first order norms, any pluralist attempt at reconstituting justice beyond law is in some sense arbitrary in as much as it incorporates some first order norms while excluding others. In other words, pluralism cannot avoid making choices among competing first order norms in the course of its attempted reconstitution of justice beyond law. From the standpoint of the first order norms left out, however, pluralism's attempted reconstitution of justice beyond law cannot overcome the breakdown in the vertical unity of justice as it necessarily privileges some of the contending first order norms over others.

We are now in a position clearly to see the place of legal autonomy in pluralism's attempted reconstitution of justice beyond law in the face of the predominance of dealings among strangers. Legal autonomy plays both a negative and a positive role in such attempted reconstitution. The negative role consists in uprooting, and cutting loose from, first order extra-legal norms in order to overcome the obstacles interposed by communal parochialisms. If legal autonomy were exclusively used for purposes of performing this negative role, however, it would promote nihilism instead of furthering pluralism. To serve the aims of pluralism, therefore, legal autonomy must also contribute to the positive function of reintegrating uprooted first order norms under the legitimating aegis of hierarchically superior second order norms. But since these second order norms are ultimately extra-legal in nature (in other words, pluralism is not an inherently legal norm) legal autonomy's positive contribution must be indirect in nature. Specifically, legal autonomy's indirect positive contribution to pluralism consists in furnishing the space necessary for the reintroduction of first order norms as subordinated to second order norms. Finally, through the ceaseless concurrent pursuit of its positive and negative roles, the legal system oriented towards self-reference and autonomy tends to postpone pluralism's ultimate inevitable failure to recover the vertical unity of justice. Moreover, focus on the autonomous tendencies of the legal system contributes to the postponement in question by concealing, on the one hand, the nexus between pluralism and justice beyond law and, on the other, the fundamental asymmetry between the legal system's role in uprooting first order norms and its role in the reintroduction of such norms as subordinate to second order norms. Indeed, whereas for purposes of the legal system's uprooting function, all first order norms are equivalent, for purposes of their reintroduction as subordinate to second order norms, such first order norms are by no means all equal, as only some of them will in the end prove to be suitable.

VI

In light of the preceding analysis, there does not appear to be anything intrinsic to contemporary law which automatically sets it apart from ethics or politics. Contemporary law's drive towards formalism, proceduralism and autonomy is one of its fundamental tendencies, and law as a practice looms as distinct from the practice of politics or that of ethics. Although law as a practice cannot avoid incorporating norms derived from ethics or politics, it preserves its distinct identity through a dynamic process of differentiation. This process of legal differentiation is complex and multifaceted and it involves many different operations, such as the deployment of formal and procedural devices, the development and maintenance of a specialized discourse for legal communications, and the use of techniques of dissimulation to conceal the extra-legal norms that inform legal rules and standards.

Understood in the context of pluralism, contemporary law simultaneously aspires to the contradictory aims of finding complete justification in justice according to law and justice beyond law. Because justice according to law never succeeds in displacing justice beyond law, and because the full reconstitution of justice is impossible due to pluralism's need to exclude certain first order values, justice must always be deferred in the case of contemporary legal relations. In short, not only must contemporary law constantly struggle to maintain a distinct identity but it also seems condemned to engage in a relentless yet always ultimately unsuccessful pursuit of justice.

ENDNOTES

1. Michel Rosenfeld is Professor of Law, Cardozo School of Law, Yeshiva University. Portions of this paper are adapted from two articles respectively entitled "Deconstruction and Legal Interpretation: Conflict, Indeterminacy and the Temptations of the New Legal Formalism", 11 *Cardozo L. Rev.* 1211, 1990 and "Autopoiesis and Justice", 13 *Cardozo L. Rev.* - 1992, forthcoming.

2. Ch. Perelman, 1963, *The Idea of Justice and the Problem of Argument*, 9-10.

3. While the distinction between justice according to law and justice beyond law plays an important role in contemporary democracies, it dates back at least as far as ancient Greece, as evidenced by the clash between Antigone's divine justice and Creon's human justice in Sophocles' *Antigone*.

4. Compensatory justice "requires the transfer of goods from one subject to another in order to restore the equilibrium that existed between these two subjects prior to their voluntary or involuntary involvement in a transaction that results in a gain for the violator and a

loss for the victim." M. Rosenfeld, 1991, *Affirmative Action and Justice: A Philosophical and Constitutional Inquiry*, 32.

5. Distributive justice, understood broadly, refers to the equitable allocation of the benefits and burdens produced by, or subject to the control of, a society among its members, according to some normative criterion of distribution.

6. In some cases, a break in vertical unity may be viewed either as raising questions of distribution or questions of compensation, depending on the perspective from which the relevant break in vertical unity is apprehended. For example, what from the standpoint of religious law may look like a matter of allocating benefits and burdens -- or more precisely entitlements and obligations -- from the standpoint of a human law running counter to the above mentioned religious law, the same matter may well loom as raising issues of compensation for breach of legal obligations.

7. R. Unger, 1976, *Law in Modern Society* 66.

8. *Id.*, 69.

9. *Id.*, 83, 86.

10. E.g., U.S. Con. Articles I and III providing for separation between the legislative and judiciary powers of the United States.

11. M. Weber, 1968, *Economy and Society*, G. Roth and C. Wittish, eds., 637-38.

12. *Id.* See also, Münch, "Differentiation, Rationalization, Interpretation: The Emergence of Modern Society" in J. Alexander et al, eds., 1990, *Differentiation Theory and Social Change*, 441, 448-49.

13. Consistent with the economic views of Adam Smith, the morals of the market contrast with the morals of other spheres. In the market individuals are obligated to act out of self-love rather than altruism, as the invisible hand of the process of competition automatically leads those who act out of self-love (but not necessarily those who act out of altruism) to contribute to the common good. A. Smith, 1976, E. Canan, ed., *An Inquiry Into the Nature and Causes of the Wealth of Nations*, 477-78. For a more extended discussion of the relationship between the morals of the market and the morals of other spheres, see Rosenfeld, 1985, "Contract and Justice: The Relation between Classical Contract Law and Social Contract Theory," 70 *Iowa L. Rev.* 769, 875-77.

14. J. Rawls, 1971, *A Theory of Justice* 85.

15. *Id.* As and example of imperfect procedural justice Rawls mentions the criminal trial under the adversary system of justice. See *id.*

16. *Id.*, 86.

17. *Id.* Rawls suggests that gambling provides an example of pure procedural justice.

18. *Cf.* Unger, 1983, "The Critical Legal Studies Movement", 96 *Harv. L. Rev.* 561, 625. "A regime of contract is just another legal name for a market."

19. Teubner, 1987, "Evolution of Autopoietic Law" in G. Teubner, ed., *Autopoietic Law: A New Approach to Law and Society*, 217-41.

20. *Id.*, 232 (emphasis in original).

21. Luhmann, "The Unity of the Legal System," in G. Teubner, *supra* note 19, at 27.

22. To the extent that legal rules are indeterminate or that, as in the case of the common law, legal principles emerge piecemeal as a consequence of the judicial disposition of individual controversies, it may be argued that the legal system can also be characterized as involving many ad hoc determinations. Nevertheless, as the common law relies on legal precedent, and as even novel interpretations of indeterminate laws must necessarily refer to a previously set legal norms, all legal determinations can be interpreted as being communicatively structured as necessarily relating to some previously established legal rule, standard or principle.

23. It is conceivable, if the uncoupling of the legal system from the political system were to result in a much expanded political domain and a much shrunken legal domain, that sharp differentiation between the two domains would not lead to greater stabilization of expectations. There seems to be no reason, however, for the assumption that such and uncoupling would result in dramatic shifts in the relative sizes of the domains involved.

24. Luhmann, "Closure and Openness: On Reality in the World of Law", in G. Teubner. *supra* note 19, at 340 ff.

25. It may be objected that the absolute ruler can fare as well in both the legal and the political arena since he or she can simply repeal any law before any application of it that would place an unwanted constraint on him or her. In reply, one can point out that the unchecked use of repeated repeals of law at will results in ad hoc resolutions of legal conflicts which would be virtually indistinguishable from the ad hoc resolutions of political conflicts. Furthermore, government by decree issuing form an absolute ruler would not satisfy the conditions of a modern legal system.

26. Under these circumstances, power is deferred rather than simply lost to the extent that the party who has been a relative loser by having to settle in the legal rather than the political arena may have enough political clout to influence changes in legislation that are calculated to make him or her fare better in future legal conflicts.

27. According to Hobbes, in exchange for securing a right to life, the parties to the social contract would be willing to relinquish all their other rights to an absolute monarch. See T. Hobbes, 1978, B. Gert, ed., *The Citizen Philosophical Rudiments Concerning Government and Society*, 190, 234.

28. N. Luhmann, 1985, *A Sociological Theory of Law*, 31-40; N. Luhmann, 1990, *Essays on Self-Reference*, 15, 232-33.

29. Luhmann, "The Unity of the Legal System", in G. Teubner, *supra* note 19, at 19-20.

30. *Id.*

31. I may be uncertain that my customers will pay me, but if the law provides for damages in case of non-payment, I will, in most cases, be assured of payment for the goods I sell.

32. If, for example, I am fairly certain that failure to honor my contractual obligations will result in liability to pay damages, I am not likely to have any reasonable incentive to break my contracts. My expectation would therefore most likely be to honor my contracts, and my actual and potential fellow contractors would have grounds to be relatively secure in their (cognitive) expectations of my expectation.

33. N. Luhmann, *Essays on Self-Reference supra* note 28, at 229-32.

34. *Id.*, 231. In other words, rules are validated by the decisions that invent or elaborate them and (to complete the circle) decisions are validated by the rules that use them as the medium through which they acquire a more definite shape.

35. *Id.*

36. Hubert Rottleuthner has argued against this last proposition. As a counterexample,he refers to instances in which adultery while itself strictly speaking neither legal nor illegal may have important consequences for the determination of legal conflicts, such as in the case of divorce. Rottleuthner, 1989, "A Purified Sociology of Law: Niklas Luhmann On the Autonomy of the Legal System", 23 *Law and Society Review* 779, 792.

37. It may always be countered that while it may be socially useful or meaningful, anything beyond the autonomous and self-referential process of using the interplay of rules and decisions to communicate whether actions relating to conflicts are legal or illegal is not, strictly speaking, encompassed within the legal system. While such an argument may be defensible from a strictly logical or purely semantical point of view, nevertheless, due to its extreme reductionism, it projects a distorted image that does not capture the full richness of contemporary law as a practice.

38. As example of significantly unpredictable areas of constitutional interpretation involving fundamental values relating to justice beyond law one can mention substantive due process and equal protection rights under the United States Constitution. Concerning substantive due process e.g., *Griswold v. Connecticut* 381 U.S. 479, 1965; *Roe v. Wade* 410 U.S. 113, 1973; and *Bowers v. Hardwick* 478 U.S. 186, 1986. concerning equal protection, on the other hand, there is perhaps no greater unpredictability than in the affirmative action area. M. Rosenfeld, 1991, *supra* note 4, at Chapter VII; Rosenfeld, "Metro-Broadcasting v. FCC: Affirmative action At the Crossroads of Constitutional Liberty and Equality," 38 *U.C.L.A. L. Rev.*, 583.

39. Weinrib, 1988, presents his theory in an article entitled "Legal Formalism: On the Immanent Rationality of Law", 97 *Yale L.J.*, 949.

40. Weinrib, *supra* note 39, at 951.

41. *Id.*, 1014.

42. *Id.*, 1011.

43. *Id.*, 980, 984.

44. *Id.*, 977.

45. *Id.*

46. *Id.*, 978.

47. *Id.*

48. *Id.*, 999.

49. *Id.*, 988.

50. *Id.*, 994.

51. *Id.*, 997.

52. *Id.*, 993.

53. *Id.*, 988.

54. *Id.*, 989.

55. *Id.*, 990.

56. *Id.*, 991-92.

57. *Id.*

58. *Id.*

59. *Id.*, 991.

60. *Id.*

61. Brudner, 1990, "The Ideality of Difference: Toward Objectivity in Legal Interpretation", 11 *Cardozo L. Rev.*, 1133, 1178-81.

62. For example, religious diversity is only possible so long as the adherents to one religion are prepared to tolerate the expression of other religious beliefs and practices. Crusading religions that preach forced conversions and intolerance of the infidel could accordingly only be tolerated by pluralists at the risk of undermining religious diversity. At the very least, the protection of religious pluralism offers a more favorable environment for non-crusading religious than for their crusading counterparts. For a more extended discussion of the paradox produced as a consequence of toleration of the intolerant, see Rosenfeld, 1987, "Extremist Speech and the Paradox of Tolerance" (Book Review), 100 *Harv. L. Rev.*, 1457.

63. The tendency towards legal autonomy is manifested in, among other things, the proliferation of process based and procedural rules. Law's tendency towards extra-legal norms, on the other hand becomes apparent in legal doctrines that rely explicitly on extra-legal values. In American constitutional law, the interplay between these two tendencies is exemplified in the contrast between procedural and susbstantive due process rights under the fourteenth amendment's due process clause. The tendency towards extra-legal values, however, is not limited to public law. Several legal scholars, for example, have sought to account for contemporary contractual relationships in terms of extra-legal norms. E.g., G. Gilmore, 1974, *The Death of Contract*; P. Atiyah, 1979, *The Rise and Fall of Freedom of Contract*; I. Macneil, 1980, *The New Social Contract*; C. Fried, 1981, *Contract as Promise*.

64. The constitutional jurisprudence of due process provides a clear glimpse of this clash. Indeed, the interplay between procedural due process and substantive due process illustrates how the search for legal autonomy through the implementation of procedural due process collides with the recurring need to appeal to extra-legal norms through substantive due process. Not only has the recognition of substantive rights repeatedly prevented due process from becoming exclusively procedural, see e.g., *Lochner v. New York*, 198 U.S. 45, 1905 (due process implies certain fundamental economic rights); and *Griswold v. Connecticut*, 381 U.S. 479, 1965 (due process implies a fundamental right of privacy). But the very determination of purely procedural due process rights may often be impossible without reference to substantive rights grounded on fundamental extra-legal values. See, e.g., *Board of Regents v. Roth,* 408 U.S. 564, 1972; and *Paul v. Davis,* 424 U.S. 693, 1976 (determination of procedural due process rights depends on conceptions of liberty and property that are ultimately traceable to fundamental extra-legal norms).

65. As an example of such and inward turn, one may cite the evolution of the English and American law of contract between the eighteenth and nineteenth centuries. This evolution saw the replacement of substantive contract rules based on custom by process oriented rules relating both to contract formation and to the measure of damages. Moreover, the development and use of those process oriented rules not only permitted abandoning locally rooted past customs but also made it possible to shield contractual relationships from future intermeddling in the name of extra-legal norms. For a more extended discussion of this aspect of the evolution of contract law in the nineteenth century, Rosenfeld, *supra* note 13, at 821-27.

66. In other words, preservation of the tendency towards legal autonomy protects against relapses into communal factionalisms while reaching out for trans-communal extra-legal norms.

67. Arguably, crusading religions and antipluralistic ethical and political creeds could be *partly* accommodated in the normative universe of the pluralist. To the extent that antipluralist values are an essential and inseparable component of a given value system, however, partial accommodation could well be tantamount to outright rejection.

Chapter 18

Frege's Semiotics Sampled: The Sense and Reference of the Verb 'Own'

Floyd W. Rudmin[1]

I

Overview

This presentation will be unusual for two reasons. First, the focus will be on the semiotic aspects of the work of Gottlob Frege (1848-1925). Because modern semiotics, at least in North America, has almost exclusively seen its origins in the persons of Peirce and de Saussure, the genesis of semiotic ideas arising in other persons has tended to be overlooked. A prime candidate for re-consideration would be Gottlob Frege. His intellectual development, in gradations, from mathematics, to philosophy of mathematics, to semantics, to the philosophy of representation is a record of brilliance and isolation, of insight and perseverance. Although Frege never used the word 'semiotics' and has rarely, if ever, been counted in the history of semiotics, his work on the sign, reference, sense, and coloring of names and concepts is ripe for a retrospective appreciation.

Of particular importance here will be Frege's differentiation of 'sense' and 'reference'. The reference of a sign is the object or event to which it points. Frege's reference is akin to the contemporary semantic concept of extension. The sense of a sign is the way in which it points to, or marks the reference. In current semantic theory, sense is akin to the intension of a word, the criteria by which a word is applied and known. Frege's theory is most clear in the example of proper names. 'Venus' has the same reference as 'the morning star', but a different sense. They signify the same thing, but do so with different signs that direct us in different ways. Thus, 'Venus' and 'the morning star' have the same meaning, but also have different meanings.

The second reason that this presentation will be unusual is that it will present empirical data. Semiotics is typically a discursive enterprise, given to theory, to interpretation, or to enamoured displays of symbols and the play of language. Semiotics rarely consorts with data tabulation, statistical tests, and other devices of positivism. The present study takes an empirical, phenomenological approach to understanding the state-of-affairs signified by the verb 'own'. The research design was to have substantial numbers of people look at the ownership of property in a fresh way and to give an account of their perceptions. This was done by asking people to distinguish between the sense and reference of 'I own x'. To be more specific, they were asked to consider property for which they have little sense of ownership and on other objects which they did not own but for which there was some sense of ownership. They were then asked to express, in their own words, what is the sense of ownership.

The study in some small way tests Ackerman's (1977) argument that lay conceptions of property and ownership are indeed varied and complex, with criteria different from those in legal theory and practice. The referent of 'own' is ultimately a decision of a court of law. And the domain of what can be legally owned is much more proscribed than what the lay sense of that term encompasses. Indeed, people named numerous categories of objects which they own but for which they have little sense of owning. However, they named significantly more examples of things that they do not own but for which they have some sense of owning. Over 40 explanations of the sense of the concept 'to own' were described. Clearly, the semantics and semiotics of ownership are neither precise nor uniform for the entire community. Discussion of gender differences based on these same data are presented elsewhere (Rudmin, 1991a). For detailed evidence and discussion of differences between law students and other adults, see Rudmin (1991b).

II
Frege's Biography

Frege was born in 1848 in Germany. He studied at Jena and Gottingen, and taught mathematics at Jena for his entire career (Bynum, 1972). His personal life had many tragedies. When he was just a boy, his father died. His own children died young, as did his wife. He himself died in 1925 at the age of 77. Not much else is known of his personal life, though a last letter to his adopted son Alfred, says something of the degree to which he sunk his soul into his scholarship. About his unpublished papers, Frege wrote to his son:

> Do not despise these papers written by me. Even if they are not pure gold, there is gold in them. I believe that one day some of the things in them will be valued more highly than now. See to it that nothing is lost. In love, your father. There is a great deal of myself that I leave you in these papers. (Frege, quoted in Currie, 1982, p.3)

This letter also points to the degree to which his ideas were unappreciated in his own lifetime, a fate not dissimilar to that of Peirce.

Frege, like Wittgenstein, was 'discovered' by Bertrand Russell, at least discovered to be a revolutionary thinker. The young British philosopher had found a paradox in Frege's set theory calculus. Russell's Paradox is 'the class of all classes which are not members of themselves'. Thus, if it is not a member of itself, then it is; and if it is a member of itself, then it is not. The existence of this paradox was a great undoing for Frege's notational system. In 1967, Russell said of Frege's response to this paradox:

> As I think about acts of integrity and grace, I realise that there is nothing in my knowledge to compare with Frege's dedication to truth. His entire life's work was on the verge of completion, much of his work had been ignored to the benefit of men infinitely less capable, his second volume was about to be published, and upon finding that his fundamental assumption was in error, he responded with intellectual pleasure clearly submerging any feelings of personal disappointment. It was almost superhuman. (Russell, quoted in Heijenoort, 1967, p. 127)

Frege's writings, though not widely appreciated during his lifetime, had significant impact on several key personalities in modern philosophy. For example, Wittgenstein's *Tractatus* was powerfully influenced by Frege, as acknowledged in its preface. Indeed, it was Frege who recommended to Wittgenstein that he go to Cambridge to study with Russell (Bynum, 1972). Frege's most noted student was the positivist Rudolph Carnap, who said of Frege's lectures that they were 'the most fruitful inspiration I received' (Bynum, 1972, p. 8). Frege also maintained a long correspondence with Edmund Husserl and is in large part responsible for Husserl's turning away from psychologism.

Frege produced more than 40 publications over his career. But unfortunately, many of his unpublished papers were destroyed during World War II. Even into the early 1960's, most of his writings were untranslated and unavailable at major universities, even in German (Bynum, 1972). However, a

Frege renaissance began in the mid-1960's. By the 1970's, the corpus of his major works had been translated, and there was a rapidly building body of analysis and criticism on Frege. See Bynum and Bynum (1972) for a bibliography of primary and secondary references.

III

Frege's Semiotics

It is not possible to here give a full, or even an adequate, account of Frege's theory of representation and meaning. The objective here is to present just enough to entice, to point to the possibilities. This summary of Frege's theory of sense and reference is drawn from Frege's 1892 papers 'On Sense and Reference' and 'On Concept and Object' (Geach & Black, 1960), and from secondary analyses by Grossmann (1969), Thiel (1968), and Walker (1965).

Frege's initial motivation was to explain arithmetic. In doing this, he developed a notational system of logic and as a result is credited with being the inventor of logical functions and truth tables. Frege extended his analysis of mathematical expressions to encompass those in natural languages as well. Fundamental to this is Frege's world-view, which is remarkably close to modern lay conceptions. Namely, we experience and know a private inner world of sense impressions and cognitive processes, which engage real physical objects in the external world as well as logical objects, such as numbers. Contrary to the solipsism implicit in this world-view, we communicate with other private selves. Thus, for Frege, the representation and signifying necessary for communication are the core concerns.

For Frege, there are thoughts, ideas, and objects. Thoughts have existence prior to perception and are independent of the thinker. In thinking an idea, we grasp rather than produce a thought. Meaning and truth are the fundamental phenomena to be explained. This requires an analysis of expressions, since there can be no ideas without expression. Frege identifies four components of an expression:

A. Sign (Zeich)

The clearest examples of signs are proper names, for example, 'Aristotle', 'the capital of Germany', '4', or '2-squared'. An object's sense is expressed by the sign, and its reference is designated by the sign. One oject can have several signs, alluding to different properties and thus signifying the object in different ways. A sign has both a reference and a sense.

B. Reference (Bedeutung)

The reference is the object which the sign refers to or designates. For names, the reference is a physical or logical object. For concept words or functions, for example, 'a dog', 'the capital of ( )', or '( ) > ( )', the reference is the concept. For assertions, such as 'Kepler died in misery', or '2+2=3', the reference is the truth value.

C. Sense (Sinn)

The sense is the way the sign designates. It does not lead to all sided knowledge of the object because it alludes to selected properties of the object. But a comprehensive knowledge of the reference allows us to immediately say whether or not a given sense belongs to it. Sense carries the information. The expression '4=4' is tautological because the same sense is expressed in the subject and the predicate, whereas '4=2+2' is informational because the same referent is given a different sense. An expression is true if its sense is true.

D. Coloring (Faerbung)

This consists of subjective ideas and images. Frege was a major opponent of psychologism in mathematics and philosophy, and argued that the logical must be distinguished from the psychological and the subjective from the objective. Sign, sense, and reference are all logically necessary and objective. Coloring is the subjective, psychological residual.

In understanding sense and reference, it is important to bear in mind Frege's emphasis on the expression, the sentence. Sense and reference are only intelligible within the context of the expression. What a name contributes to the expression is its sense. The reference of a word is not to the idea to which the user connects the word, but to the sense of the sentence. A word may lack a corresponding image, and thus seem to have no sense and no referent, but these can only be found within the context of the expression. If a sentence has sense, then its parts must also have sense.

IV

Study of the Sense of Owning

Frege was a mathematician, and his use of the term 'sense' was exact and technical. When bringing that term into common language, and setting it in the context of empirical survey research in which it will be interpreted and responded to by a wide variety of people, 'sense' will certainly become inexact. Thus, in asking people to identify objects for which they have little sense of ownership, it is possible that they will be directed to Frege's 'colorings'. That is, they might list objects for which they do not register a subjective, ownership feeling. But as this becomes articulated and communicated in expressive form, it necessarily acquires the true Fregian sense. If someone asserts, 'I own my child', an appropriate response would be, 'What do you mean? In what sense?' An appropriate answer would be to articulate the semantic intension, or criteria by which 'own' is being used. If we had a complete understanding of the term 'own', we would not have to ask for clarification. Frege did acknowledge that a major problem with natural languages, as opposed to mathematics, is that different people can have a different sense for the same sign. Thus, semantics is both analytical and empirical. The purpose of this research is to contribute to a more complete understanding of the term 'own' by surveying the sense of that word within a large sample of people.

The sample consisted of 353 adults (over age 20) recruited in three settings: 121 were general public recruited in their cars while waiting at a ferry boat crossing; 105 were mature undergraduate students recruited in evening and summer session classes; and 127 were first-year law students. Mean ages were 42 for the public sample, 26 for the undergraduates, and 25 for the law students. Approximately half of the sample were women, half men.

The respondents were informed on the research consent form that they were being asked to 'help in an exploratory study of the meaning of ownership'. The task instructions were to 'List as many examples as you can of a) things that you do own but for which you feel little sense of ownership; b) things that you do not own but for which you feel a sense of ownership. Then referring to your exemplars if you wish, try to describe what your sense of ownership consists of.' Labelled columns of 14 lines each were provided for the exemplar listings and space was provided at the bottom of the form for the description of the sense of ownership. The order of appearance of the positive (do own but feel little sense of ownership) and negative (do not own but do feel a sense of ownership) exemplars were reversed on half of the forms, as were the corresponding report columns. Most people completed the form in 15 minutes or less.

To analyze these data, the responses were first grouped into common categories. In accordance with phenomenological principles of atheoretical descriptiveness, categorizing was done on a post-hoc basis, looking for 'natural' categories in the data. Other studies of possessions and property done in different cultures have adopted this practice (e.g. Beggan, 1991; Csikszentmihalyi & Rochberg-Halton, 1981; Dittmar, 1989; 1991; Furby, 1976; Kamptner, 1989; 1991; Rudmin & Berry, 1987; Schrader, 1966; Sherman & Newman, 1977). However, there is no consensus on a standard set of categories. For this study, the key words actually used by the respondents were first sorted alphabetically. Then synonymous groupings were combined, categories with few listings were merged to larger ones, and 52 categories of objects eventually emerged. These are listed in Table 1 in order of frequency of mention by the respondents.

Most respondents gave some qualified answers, such as 'my boyfriend's tapes', or 'borrowed things'. These qualifications were categorized and tabulated separately from the actual objects of ownership. Following the procedure just described, 21 categories of qualifiers emerged. These are listed in Table 2, again in order of frequency of mention.

The respondents' expressions of their sense of ownership were categorized in a similar fashion, with the eventual emergence of 45 categories. These are listed in Table 3 in order of frequency of mention. The categorization of the ownership objects, of the qualifying comments, and of the explanations of the sense of owning was done a second time using the same methods by a paid research assistant. Tests of replication using Cohen's kappa were statistically significant, with k=.85, k=.86, and k=.83 respectively for the three categorization schemes.

TABLE 1
PERCENT OF RESPONDENTS MENTIONING OBJECT CATEGORIES

	Owned But Lacks Sense of Owning	Not Owned But Has Sense of Owning		Owned But Lacks Sense of Owning	Not Owned But Has Sense of Owning
Residence	13%	48%	Sundries	7%	0%
Cars, Trucks	20%	25%	City, Region	0%	6%
Peopple	2%	25%	Toiletries	6%	0%
Parks, Lakes	1%	22%	Tools	3%	3%
Furniture	15%	8%	Utilities	2%	4%
Government Property	8%	14%	Body, Organs	4%	1%
Things, Stuff	10%	11%	Business	2%	3%
No Response	17%	4%	Education	4%	1%
Pets	9%	11%	Freedom	2%	3%
Clothes	16%	2%	Ideas, Thoughts	3%	2%
Personal Space	3%	13%	Personality, Self	3%	2%
Recreation Items	7%	7%	Emotions	1%	3%
Books	8%	5%	Life, Destiny	2%	2%
Nation	1%	11%	Partonized Places	1%	3%
TV, Stereo	8%	4%	Time	2%	2%
Institutions	1%	10%	Work Site	0%	4%
Environmen	2%	9%	Beliefs, Values	1%	2%
Roads, Walks	3%	8%	Culture, Art	1%	2%
Food, Drink	9%	1%	Health	1%	2%
Stocks, Bonds	8%	1%	ID Cards	1%	2%
Money	7%	2%	Jewelry	2%	1%
Rights, Vote	3%	6%	Miscellaneous	2%	1%
Job, Employment	3%	5%	Debts	1%	1%
Land	5%	3%	Name	1%	1%
Air, Sun	1%	6%	Trash	2%	0%
Family	0%	7%	View	0%	1%

TABLE 2
PERCENT OF RESPONDENTS MENTIONING QUALIFIERS

	Owned But Lacks Sense of Owning	Not Owned But Has Sense of Owning
Family's XXX	6%	39%
Public XXX	4%	14%
Friends' XXX	1%	14%
Rented XXX	0%	12%
Employer's XXX	2%	7%
Nearby XXX	1%	6%
Borrowed XXX	0%	6%
Former XXX	2%	3%
Mortgaged XXX	2%	3%
Shared XXX	3%	2%
Given XXX	2%	1%
Unimportant XXX	3%	0%
Paid For XXX	1%	1%
Temporary XXX	1%	1%
Found XXX	0%	1%
Societal XXX	0%	1%
Used XXX	1%	0%
Hidden XXX	0%	0%
Stolen XXX	0%	0%
Valuable XXX	0%	0%

TABLE 3
PERCENT OF RESPONDENTS MENTIONING CATEGORIES

	Sense of Owning		Sense of Owning
Control	26%	Pride	6%
Bought, Paid for	20%	Self	6%
Possess, Have	18%	Acquired	5%
Exclusive, Private	16%	Communal	5%
Use	16%	Family	5%
Responsible For	15%	Gift	5%
Right	15%	Intangibles	5%
Emotion, Attachment	14%	Tangible Tings	5%
Unrestrained	14%	Can Dispose Of	4%
Care For	11%	Keep	4%
Earn, Achieve	10%	No Ownership	4%
Legal Title	10%	Personal Meaning	4%
'Mine'	10%	Miscellaneous	4%
Familiar	9%	Accessible	3%
Clear, No Lein	8%	Claim	3%
Enjoy, Like	8%	Cognitive	3%
Need, Utility	8%	Can Share	2%
Permanent	8%	Degree, Priority	2%
No Response	8%	First	2%
Complete, Total	7%	Protect, Defend	2%
Value, Asset	7%	Not Disruptive	1%
Belong	6%	Want, Desire	1%
Made, Changed	6%		

V

Discussion of Results

The first result to note in the data shown in Table 1 is that there is a clear tendency to be expansive about ownership. That is, people can identify some criteria or sense of ownership for things that they do not own more readily than they can identify a lack of criteria or sense for things that they do own. For things not owned but for which there was some sense of ownership, people listed a mean of 3.5 examples, and 4% listed nothing. For things owned but with little sense of ownership, people listed a mean of 2.5 examples and 17% of the people listed nothing. These differences were statistically significant for the number of items listed ($t=-9.43$, $df=352$, $p<.001$) and for the amount of no response ($t=5.83$, $df=352$, $p<.001$). Even eliminating those respondents who had no response on either task, the mean number of items listed for things not owned was 4.1 and for things owned was 3.1. Again, this difference was statistically significant ($t=-6.47$, $df=280$, $p<.001$).

Several explanations are possible for this phenomenon of ownership expansiveness. First, in our society, disposal and dispossession of unwanted property is easier and more directly under the owner's control than is the acquisition of new property. With few exceptions, people can get rid of what they do not want to own, whereas the marketing forces in our society excite us to expect and presume eventual ownership of things that we cannot yet acquire. A second, more theoretical, explanation is that people would tend to refer to a relatively smaller set of criteria or qualities of owning for 'things owned' whereas they would refer to a larger set of criteria or qualities for 'things not owned'. The second task is an invitation to expand the set of criteria or qualities referred to. Finally, from the qualifiers listed in Table 2, it would seem that the force of affiliation is asymmetrical. We tend to presume ownership of the properties of our families, communities, and employers, but little sense loss of ownership from corresponding presumptions the other way.

A second important result is the sheer variety of 'things' that people listed as examplars. Of course, the common examples of real property and of chattels are there. But the third most frequently listed examplar was people of various sorts, including family members, work and school colleagues, and children, even other people's children. Various types of communal and common property were also noted, including parks and lakes, government property, institutions, and the environment. People also listed intangible possessions, including personal space, the nation, rights, education, freedom, ideas, personality, and life destiny. This extension of property and possessions beyond real estate and material chattels is not unusual in this type of research and has been reported in other studies, for example, Beggan (1991), Dittmar (1989; 1991), Furby (1976), Kamptner (1991), and Rudmin and Berry (1987). Law, by its traditional exclusion of these types of possessions from its property regimen, certainly designates ownership to a more proscribed and narrow set of phenomena than do the lay public.

Finally, the listing of explanations of 'owning' shown in Table 3 begins to indicate the extent of possible answers to the inquiry, 'In what sense do you own ( )?' These are the properties, or criteria, of ownership. Highest on the list is 'control'. Within political economic theory and within the social and behavioral sciences, control has been a major component of ownership (Rudmin, 1988). In her analysis of the origins of property, Furby (1980) argued that control is the primary motivation. However, it is also possible that control appeared as the pre-eminent criterion because the research task was focused on sense-reference discrepancies. We control many things that we do not own, and own many things that we do not control.

Other of the criteria in Table 3 are familiar to legal theory, including purchase, exclusivity, rights, etc. But criteria that are prominent in political economic theory were mentioned by the respondents rather infrequently. Only 8% mentioned 'need'. Only 6% mentioned 'made'. Only 2% mentioned 'first possession'. It may be that the sense of ownership has changed since classical political economic theory was articulated in the 16th, 17th, 18th, and 19th centuries. However, it may also be that those theories were spun with unusually narrow reference to what it means to 'own'.

Ownership clearly is not a simple concept. Respondents listed, on average, 4 criteria, and the total list is over 40 criteria. When someone makes the claim, 'I own ( )', it is indeed appropriate to reply, 'In what sense?' And this question must be answered before the truth or falsity of the claim can be assessed.

ACKNOWLEDGEMENTS

During preparation of this manuscript, funding support was provided by the Social Sciences and Humanities Research Council of Canada. Travel funding was provided by the Faculty of Law, Queen's University.

ENDNOTES

1. Floyd W. Rudmin is Canada Research Fellow, Faculty of Law and School of Business, Queen's University, Kingston, Ontario.

REFERENCES

Ackerman, B.A., 1977, *Private Property and the Constitution,* New Haven: Yale University Press.

Beggan, J.K., 1991, 'Using What You Own to Get What You Need: The Role of Possessions in Satisfying Control Motivation,' *Journal of Social Behavior and Personality,* 16 (6): 129-146.

Bynum, T.W., 1972, 'Life and Work of Gottlob Frege,' T.W. Bynum, ed., *Conceptual Notation and Related Articles*, 1-54, Oxford: Clarendon Press.

Bynum, T.W., and Bynum, A.W., 1972, 'A Frege Bibliography, 1873-1966,' T.W. Bynum, ed., *Conceptual Notation and Related Articles*, 239-287, Oxford: Clarendon Press.

Csikszentmihalyi, M., and Rochberg-Halton, E., 1981, *The Meaning of Things: Domestic Symbols of the Self*, Cambridge: Cambridge University Press.

Currie, G., 1982, *Frege: An Introduction to his Philosophy*, Sussex: Harvester Press.

Dittmar, H., 1989, 'Gender Identity-Related Meanings of Personal Possessions,' *British Journal of Social Psychology,* 28: 159-171.

_____, H., 1991, 'Meanings of Material Possessions as Reflections of Identity: Gender and Social-Material Position in Society,' *Journal of Social Behavior and Personality,* 6 (6): 165-186.

Frege, G., 1960, 'On Concept and Object,' P. Geach & M. Black, eds., *Translations from the Philosophical Writings of Gottlob Frege,* 42-55, Oxford: Blackwell, Originally published in 1892.

_____, G., 1960, 'On Sense and Reference,' P. Geach & M. Black, eds., *Translations from the Philosophical Writings of Gottlob Frege,* 56-78, Oxford: Blackwell, Originally published in 1892.

Furby, L., 1976, 'The Socialization of Possession and Ownership among Children in Three Cultural Groups: Israeli Kibbutz, Israeli City, and American,' S. Modgil and C. Modgil, eds., *Piagetian Research: Compilation and Commentary*, vol. 8, 95-127, Windsor, Berkshire, England: National Foundation for Educational Research.

_____, L., 1980, 'The Origins and Early Development of Possessive Behavior,' *Political Psychology*, 2: 30-42.

Geach, P., and Black, M., eds. 1960, *Translations from the Philosophical Writings of Gottlob Frege*, Oxford: Blackwell.

Grossmann, R., 1969, *Reflections on Frege's Philosophy*, Evanston, IL: Northwestern University Press.

Heijenoort, J. van, ed. 1967, *From Frege to Goedel*, Cambridge, MA: Harvard University Press.

Kamptner, N.L., 1989, 'Personal Possessions and their Meanings in Old-Age,' S. Spacapan and S. Oskamp, eds., *The Social Psychology of Aging*, 165-196, Newbury Park, CA: Sage.

Kamptner, N.L., 1991, 'Personal Possessions and their Meanings: A Life-Span Perspective,' *Journal of Social Behavior and Personality,* 6 (6): 209-228.

Rudmin, F.W., 1988, *Ownership as Interpersonal Dominance: A History and Three Studies of the Social Psychology of Property*, doctoral thesis, Queen's University, Kingston, Ontario.

_____, F.W., 1991a, 'Gender Differences in the Semantics of Ownership: Hazy Hints of a Feminist Theory of Property,' J.A. Costa, ed., *Proceedings on the Conference on Gender and Consumer Behavior, June 19-23, 1991, Salt Lake City,* 292-302, Salt Lake City: University of Utah Printing Service.

_____, F.W., 1991b, 'The Sense of Ownership: Survey of Property Exemplars and Meanings in Three Populations', unpublished manuscript.

_____, F.W., and Berry, J.W., 1987, 'The Semantics of Ownership: A Free-Recall Study of Property,' *Psychological Record*, 37: 257-268.

Schrader, A., 1966, *Die Soziale Bedeutung des Besitzes in der Modernen Konsumgesellschaft (The Social Meaning of Property in the Modern Consumer Society)*, Koeln & Opladen, Germany, Westdeutscher Verlag.

Sherman, E., and Newman, E.S., 1977, 'The Meaning of Cherished Personal Possessions for the Elderly,' *Aging and Human Development,* 8: 181-192.

Thiel, C., 1968, *Sense and Reference in Frege's Logic*, Dordrecht, Holland: D.Reidel Publishing.

Walker, J.D.B., 1965, *A Study of Frege,* Oxford: Basil Blackwell.

Chapter 19

A Sign of Itself

Paul Ryan[1]

I

Introduction

The phrase 'a Sign of itself' comes from Charles Peirce:

> But in order that anything should be a Sign it must "represent", as we say, something else called its *Object,* although the condition that a sign must be other than its Object is perhaps arbitrary, since if we insist upon it we must at least make an exception in the case of a Sign that is part of a Sign. Thus nothing prevents an actor who acts a character in an historical drama from carrying as a theatrical "property" the very relic that that article is supposed merely to represent, such as the crucifix that Bulwer's Richeleu holds up with such an effort in his defiance. On a map of an island laid down upon the soil of that island there must, under all ordinary circumstances, be some position, some point, marked or not, that represents *qua* place on the map the very same point *qua* place on the island . . . we shall, or should, ultimately reach *a Sign of itself* [my emphasis], containing its own explanation and those of all its significant parts: and according to this explanation each such part has some other part as its Object. (CP:2.230)

In this paper, I will present a 'Sign of itself' that, I believe, satisfies the intent of the above statement made by Peirce. For reasons that will become clear, I call this sign a relational circuit. I originated this circuit while working as an artist with video and reading Charles Peirce, Gregory Bateson and Warren

McCulloch. Over the past twelve years since I originated the relational circuit, it has proven as valuable to my art work as *contrapposto* to a Greek sculptor or perspective to a Renaissance painter.

I think the value of the circuit is evident in two art projects, both of which I have presented at the Museum of Modern Art. 1) A relational practice that works for three people the way T'ai Chi or Yoga works for an individual (Ryan, 1985). 2) A design for a television channel dedicated to monitoring the ecology of a particular region and developing consensus about how best to live there (Ryan, 1987). Both the practice and the television ecochannel use the relational circuit as a 'figure of regulation', and both use Peirce's phenomenological categories of firstness, secondness and thirdness. The ecochannel also uses the sixty-six fold semiotic array Peirce developed from his categories.

Of course, exposure in the art world does not insure that my claim to have originated a 'Sign of itself' is valid. I originated something. I think it is a sign of itself. Moreover, I think it constitutes the logic of relations that Peirce was after, but failed to get (Murphey, 1961) Is it really a sign of itself? Does it satisfy Peirce's quest for a relational logic? If so, why not argue on logical and scholarly grounds? Why cite the art world at all?

I cite the art world to indicate that I am talking as an artist to scholars. What I am presenting comes out of the phenomonological realm of firstness known as aesthetics. I arrived at the relational circuit by a process Peirce would call abduction. My process of abduction is documented in my video work and my writings (Ryan, 1969-1985, Sharp, 1981). It is the fruit of that abductive process that I am presenting. Whether or not my guess at the riddle constitutes the relational logic Peirce pursued is obviously a matter for Peirce scholars to decide.

My paper will continue in the following order.

II. Presentation of the Relational Circuit.

III. Characterization of the Circuit.

IV. Argumentation that the Circuit is a Sign of Itself.

  A. Consideration of Gödel's Proof

  B. Consideration of Peirce's Text

V. Discussion of the Circuit re Peirce's Philosophic Project.

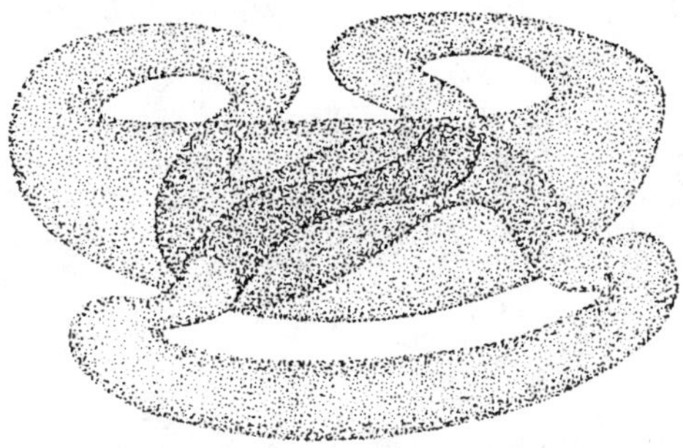

Figure 1. The Relational Circuit

illustrated by Michael Krieg

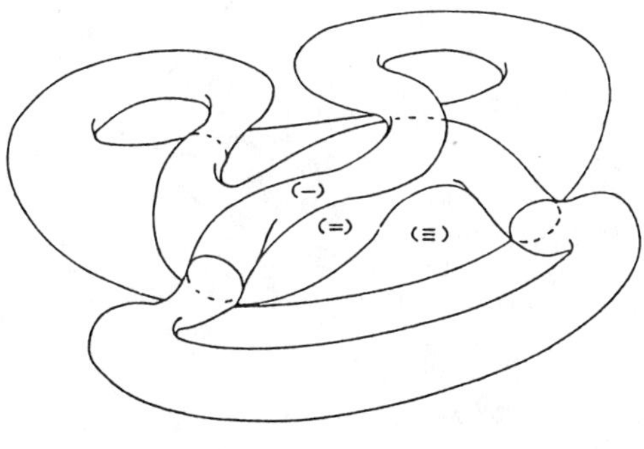

Figure 2. The Relational Circuit with Characterizations

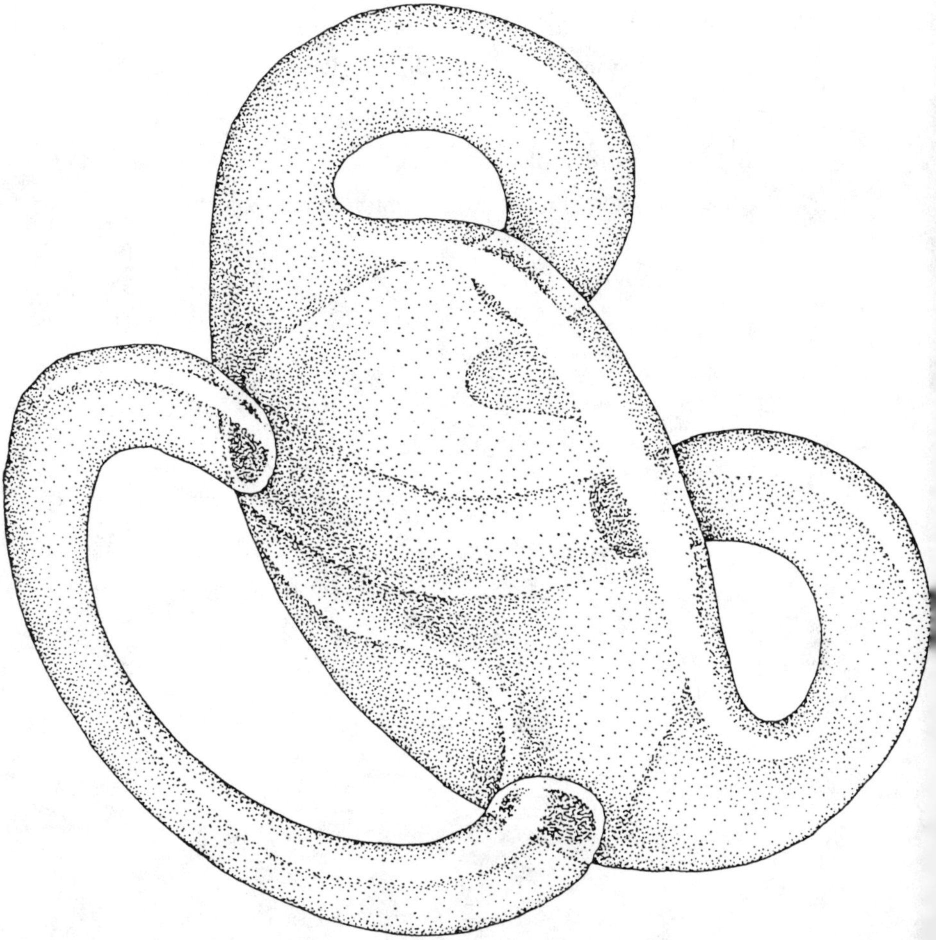

Figure 3.

illustrated by Gary Allen

II

Presentation of the relational circuit

The two dimensional drawing presented here (Figure 1) is a rendering of the three dimensional form I call a relational circuit. The second figure (Figure 2) repeats the form and includes parenthetical markings to expedite the characterization and argumentation that follows. These markings are not part of the form. The third figure (Figure 3) is an artistic illustration of the form.

Figure one results from taking the relations of positions and inclusion that obtain in the topology of a Klein bottle and developing these relations into a circuit. Respecting the circuit's debt to the klein bottle, I have sometimes called it a Kleinform. A Klein bottle has three related positions: a position neither contained nor containing (the neck of the bottle), a position containing another position (the body of the bottle), and a position contained (within the body of the body). In the Kleinform, these three related positions are developed into a six part circuit with three positions neither contained nor containing (- =), (= =), (≡ -),one position contained by two (-), one position that contains and is contained (=) and one position that contains two positions (≡). It took me seven years to develop the three-part Klein bottle into a form that satisfied the criteria for a circuit articulated below. Along the way, over a dozen attempts were discarded.

III

Characterization of the circuit

The statements that follow are based on observation of the form. In Peirce's language, these statements are abstractive observations (CP 2.231).

1. *One*

There is but a single form.

2. *Empty*

The form is empty. The emptiness itself constitutes the form.

3. *Continuous*

The form is a continuum. It is possible to move from within any part of the form to any other part without crossing a boundary.

4. *Bounded*

The form is bounded. The boundary limits the continuum.

5. *Infinite*

The continuum is infinite. The continuum returns to itself without end.

6. *Six-Part*

The form penetrates itself six times. This self penetration yields six different positions on the continuum. Each position is part of the continuum.

7. *Positional*

The differentiation in the form is structured according to differentiation of position on the continuum. In contrast to any statement of description, differentiation in the form does not correspond to the differentiation implicit in the subject/predicate structure of propositions. Hence, the form cannot be fully explained in any axiomatic system of propositions. The form is positional, not propositional.

8. *Unambiguous*

The six positions are unambiguous. There is but one position of firstness (-), but one position of secondness (=), and but one position of thirdness ($\underline{=}$). (For refined observation, thirdness can be described as the position surrounding secondness in which a stiff torus can be trapped. All the other positions are differentiated by the passage of the continuum through the thresholds created by the self penetration.) There is only one position on the continuum between firstness and secondness (- =), only one position on the continuum between thirdness and firstness (≡ -).

The naming of these positions is not arbitrary. Firstness is a compact, empty position,-- free of any other. Secondness has another part of the form passing through it, -- something it is up against, -- the position of firstness. Thirdness contains both secondness and firstness.

9. *Non-Identical*

No position in the form is identical with any other position. No two positions can be equated.

10. *Non-Orientable*

Assigned direction makes no difference in determining the relative positions in the form. This can be understood by contrasting the orientation involved in reading. As a reader, your eyes are moving from left to right, down the page of print that is in front of you. If you turn 180 degrees, what was in front of you is now behind you, what was on your left is now on your right. In the conventional understanding of position, if you change your orientation, you change your referencing system for position. In the form, changes in orientation make no difference in determining relative positions. The form has no center, no front and back, no left and right and no up and down. The six part differentiation of position holds regardless of orientation.

11. *Intransitive*

It is possible to understand each position in the continuum without going outside the bounds of the continuum. Each position in turn is explained by two other positions. The position of firstness is the position contained by secondness and thirdness. The position of secondness is contained by thirdness and contains firstness. Thirdness contains both secondness and firstness. Each of the 'in between' positions on the handles is explained by reference to two of the three positions of firstness, secondness and thirdness.

12. *Complete*

The form is complete. The term 'complete' is used here in two senses. i) Nothing outside the form is required to make it whole. By contrast, the series of natural numbers is always incomplete. One can always move toward completion by adding another number. Indeed, the sequence of natural numbers can be embedded in this six-part continuum in sets of six with remainders *ad infinitum.* ii) Nothing outside the form is required to understand its wholeness. The form consists of an empty continuum of six positions. Each position is explained in terms of the other positions in an intransitive way. The form has all the parts necessary to explain itself . No metalevel of explanation is required.

13. *Consistent*

The circuit is one continuum with six positions. There is no position which is also *not* a position. There is no position which is simultaneously another position, as in the case when two people face each other and what is on one person's right side is simultaneously on the other person's left side. Although secondness simultaneously contains and is contained, the reference for each relationship is unambiguous. The form is internally consistent.

14. *Relative*

The form is absolutely relative. The six positions are completely determined by each other. To move from one position to another position is to change relationship to every other position. A difference in position makes a difference in relationship.

15. *Non-Sequential*

While it is possible to move sequentially through all six positions, the positions themselves do not depend on sequence for their identity. The positions of firstness (F), secondness (S), and thirdness (T) are indifferent to sequence. You can outline the form on the floor and move through the continuum in any of the following sequences without altering the positions themselves. (For simplicity of explanation, I am omitting the in between positions). FST,TSF, STF, SFT, TFS, FTS. In the last example, FTS, what is indicated is that you can go from firstness to thirdness without passing through secondness. Firstness and thirdness are contiguous without reference to secondness. Relative position is detached from sequence.

16. *Irreducible*

The form cannot be reduced and maintain its characteristics. For example, the only possible reduction of the figure that remains bounded would be a four part form with one part containing another part and two parts uncontained (two handles). However, in such a reduction, the two parts uncontained could not be distinguished from one another without going outside the form and referencing the left and right hand side of the viewer. Such outside referencing would violate the non-orientable characteristic of the form.

17. *Non-compact*

The figure cannot be reduced to a ball and retain its identifying characteristics. Like the "hole" is integral to the identity of the torus, the three "holes in the handles" are integral to the identity of this form.

18. *Heterarchic*

Choices between positions within the form operate according to intransitive preference. That is to say, choices are not constrained by a hierarchy but can operate heterarchically. If I outline the form on the floor and stand in the position of firstness (-), I can move through an "inbetween" position (- =) to the position of secondness(=). But once in secondness I am not compelled to move to thirdness (≡), as if there was a fixed hierarchy of preference or choice. I can return to firstness (-). Any position in the form allows this pattern of intransitive preference. There are always two choices, and no choice compels an irreversible sequence of hierarchic choice.

19. *Self Corrective*

To say that the form is self corrective is to say that it is a circuit. This characteristic is not self evident by abstractive observation. Rather the ensemble of characteristics given above must be seen in terms of the criteria for a circuit. The format I will use to demonstrate that the form is a circuit proceeds as follows. I will state each criteria and then describe how the circuit satisfies that criteria by referring to the eighteen characteristics established above. The six criteria for a circuit, employed below were established by cybernetic theory and articulated by Gregory Bateson (1979: 89-129). Bateson regarded any entity that satisfied these criteria as a 'unit of mind.'

i) A mind is an aggregate of interacting parts or components.

The form has six parts or components.

ii) The interaction between parts is triggered by difference.

The form is relative. A difference in position makes a difference in relationship. Any interaction between parts takes place in terms of these positional differences. Hence interaction between parts is triggered by difference.

iii) Mental processes require collateral energy.

The form is empty. The form can be likened to a six part zero. It is empty of energy. Processing of differences in the form requires collateral energy.

iv) Mental processes require circular (or more complex) chains of determination.

The form is a continuum. The continuum is a circular chain determining unambiguous differences.

v) In mental process, the effects of differences are to be regarded as transforms (i.e., coded versions) of the difference which preceded them.

Each difference in position is, in effect, a transform from the preceding position or positions. This can be made clear by using the television ecochannel cited above as an example. If we map Peirce's semiotic understanding onto the positions in the relational circuit we get the following: the sign maps onto firstness, the object onto secondness and the interpretant onto thirdness. The television ecochannel provides programming (sign) about the ecology (object) for the people who live in that ecology (interpretants) so they will not destroy it (ground of the sign). Differences in the ecology (object, position of secondness) make differences in the programming (sign, position of firstness), which make differences in the interpretation of the ecology interpretant, position of thirdness), which in turn make differences in the ecology itself, (object, position of secondness). Each difference in position is, in effect, a transform from the preceding position.

vi) The description and classification of these processes of transformation disclose a hierarchy of logical types immanent in the phenomena.

While the heterarchic form itself cannot be subsumed by a hierarchy (Ryan:1980b), transformations in the form can be described so as to disclose a logical typing immanent in the form. Firstness is at a 'lower level' of logical typing than secondness. Secondness is at a 'lower level' than thirdness. Moving from 'level' to 'level' is a transformation of relationships.

Now that I have given an extensive characterization of the form and shown how it satisfies the criteria for a circuit, I will now argue that the relational circuit is a 'Sign of itself.'

IV

Argumentation that the circuit is a sign of itself

This section has two parts. The first part discusses the circuit in relation to Gödel's proof. The second part discusses the circuit in relation to the text from Peirce quoted at the beginning of this paper.

A. Consideration of Gödel's proof

Many mathematicians working to construct a complete and consistent logical system, a sign of itself, were discouraged by the publication of Gödel's proof (1931). Gödel proved that it is impossible to create a complete and consistent set of axioms. The relational circuit avoids being subsumed in the domain of Gödel's proof in two ways: 1) The form is positional, not propositional. 2) The relational circuit is topological, not arithmetic. Each way will be discussed in turn.

1) The form is positional, not propositional. (Characteristic #7, III above).

Peirce did develop the categories of firstness, secondness and thirdness in part from a study of the syllogism. Firstness corresponds to the term, secondness to the proposition and thirdness to the illative *if . . . then.* But firstness, secondness and thirdness are categorically more general than the structure of the syllogism. Hence it is possible to move from these general categories back to the structure of the syllogism and derive a conclusion that way.

However, this is derivative from the circuit itself. You must first derive the structure of the syllogism and then derive the conclusion. If you stay within the intransitive, heterarchic, relational circuit itself, you cannot reason through the relational circuit and arrive at a logical conclusion. As a non-propositional form, the relational circuit is also formally inconclusive. There is no way to preserve the necessary relationships of position *in* the circuit and simultaneously draw a necessary conclusion *from* the circuit. In my opinion, Peirce's definition of mathematics as the science of drawing necessary *conclusions*, rather than seeing math as drawing necessary *relations,* as a factor in his failure to develop 'a Sign of itself.'

Because there is no way to derive a conclusion from the circuit itself, this condition precludes the generation of an excludable contradictory proposition. If I understand it correctly, Gödel's proof exploits the possibility of generating an excludable contradictory proposition from and axiomatic system. If you decide not to generate the excludable proposition, the system in incomplete. If you decide to generate the contradictory proposition, the system is inconsistent. Therefore, any axiomatic system has inherent undecidability. It will wither be incomplete or inconsistent. By contrast, the relational circuit is a system that is both complete and consistent (Characteristics #12 and #13, III above).

Because the relational circuit is formally inconclusive, it does not mean that it cannot be used as a figure of regulation for making decisions. The circuit does not suspend you in perpetual undecidability. The brute facts of life do call for decisions. I have developed a procedure for decision making by consensus based on the circuit. The procedure is an extension of the relational practice (Ryan, 1980a, 1985). Briefly, the procedure works as follows. In a domain of decision making, each of three people, or multiples of three, takes a subdomain. For example, three editors each take a section of a magazine. Each editor is required to keep the other two informed of his/her decisions. If one of the other editors objects to a decision, convinces the third editor of the objection, and both of these editors convince a predetermined outside party to agree with their objection, these three can override the decision of the one. If these three cannot agree, then the original decision of the one stands. This procedure precludes two against one dynamics and preserves an intransitive heterarchy of decision making. Decisions develop from the dynamics of formalized relationships, not from syllogistic reasoning to conclusions. Of course, the formal relationships can, and should, include reasoned arguments.

2) The form is topological, not arithmetic.

Gödel's proof makes it clear that constructing a sign of itself from arithmetic units is impossible. The sign of itself presented here is not arithmetic, but topological. Topology is understood in the sense given the term by Riemann before the field was subsumed by algebra and set theory. For Riemann, topological study considered only relations of position and inclusion in continuous magnitudes. He explicitly excluded measurement. Subsequently, Peirce explicitly excluded magnitude.

While Peirce was able to free continuity from attributes of magnitude, he was not able to free the continuum from attributes of sequence. I see this as a major reason for his failure to arrive at a relational logic. As Murphey reports, Peirce burdened the ordinal numbers with both expressing relative position and exemplifying position (Murphey, 1961:284). This cannot be done without confusion. As long as the ordinals are arranged in a sequence of first, second, third, etc., there is no clear way to distinguish between each member of the series and the serial relationship. A confusing duality between relations of position and examples of position results. Placing firstness as an example in a position expressed as secondness is more confusing than the Abbott and Costello comedy routine "Who's on first?"

Sequential positioning is a consequence of orientation, i.e., assigned direction. The form presented above is non-orientable (Characteristic #10, III above), hence it is also non-sequential (Characteristic #13, III above). The confusing duality of position and example in the use of ordinal numbers is resolved. There is no need to hold a double sequence in mind. Examples can be sequenced through an empty continuum of 'ordinal' positions that do not depend on sequence. The positions obtain without orientation, hence without sequence. Once the mind is freed to think positionally without orientation a logic of relationships naturally ensues.

In concluding this section on Gödel, it can be noted that the logic of relationships inherent in the circuit is robust enough to generate a rich semiosis, as in the design for a television channel mentioned above (III, 19, v). This television channel makes use of Peirce's entire sixty-six fold sign classification system by mapping it into the relational circuit (Ryan, 1987:46-64, Sharp, 1981:17). As a formal system, the relational circuit combines cybernetics and semiotics. This is non-trivial, albeit non-axiomatic.

B. Consideration of Peirce's text

The relational circuit will now be discussed in relation to the text quoted at the beginning of this paper that call for a 'Sign of itself.' Of course, presenting argumentation in terms of one abbreviated text only begins the discussion of how the relational circuit relates to the body of Peirce's work. Indeed, by omitting the section of the text that I left out in the quote, I am omitting discussion of the realm of signs that are other than their object. This does not invalidate my basic argument. As demonstrated in the discussion of the ecochannel above (III, 19, v), signs that are other than their objects can be mapped into this 'Sign of itself.'

In the selected text, Peirce makes three points about a 'Sign of itself.' These three points will be reiterated with a discussion of how the relational circuit satisfies each point.

1) A sign need not be other than its object, a sign can be part of a sign.

The relational circuit is one continuum. There is not an 'other' object. All signing is *part with* this continuum. The phrase *part with* rather than *part of* is more appropriate for the intransitive character of the continuum. This sign does not designate something else. This sign shows itself.

2) 'The Sign of itself' will contain the explanation of all its significant parts. According to this explanation, each significant part will have some other significant part as its object.

Two characteristics of the relational circuit, unambiguousness (#8, III, above) and intransitivity (#11, III, above), insure this part to part explanation. The way Peirce words his statement seems to require that each part have but one other part as its explanation. In the intransitivity of explanation that obtains in the circuit, explanation does not take place in a one-to-one correspondence. Explaining position in this continuum requires that each explained position have not one, but two other parts to explain it. Any one part explanation would fall back on sequence: example, this part is the one that follows that part. Insisting on any one-to-one correspondence for explanation leads right back to the impossibility of working with arithmetic units. I do not think this two part explanation invalidates the relational circuit as a sign of itself, regardless of Peirce's text, since the intransitivity of explanation remains complete and consistent.

It can also be argued that this 'parts to part' explanation of positions, in terms of the intransitivity and unambiguousness of the form, is the only possible way to explain the positions *qua* positions. No other explanation of the relations of position and inclusion *within the form* appears possible. All other efforts reduce to the absurd. This argument is perhaps the weakest argument for taking the relational circuit as a sign of itself. Someone other than myself may be able to successfully imagine and argue another explanation of position. At the same time, it seems the *reductio ad absurdum* argument must be made in order to invite proper criticism.

3) Peirce also states that the 'Sign of itself' should contain its own explanation. I interpret this phrase, 'containing its own explanation,' to refer not to parts

explaining other parts, but to the Sign as a whole explaining itself as a whole.

Because the circuit has no more than six parts, it can contain its own explanation. Six is perceptible without counting (McCulloch, 1965:7). The whole form stays within this perceptible limit of six. Differences can be understood without arithmetic units. The perceiving mind can grasp this self differentiating form as a whole, without adding parts to parts. All that need be grasped are the six positions *qua* positions. To grasp the positions is to grasp the relations of position. The positions constitute the relations. To grasp the relations of position is to contain 'its own explanation.' All the form is, is relations of position. If you grasp the relations of position you have grasped the form itself.

In the Stoic term used by Warren McCulloch, I am describing a 'lekton,' an event in the mind like a fist in the hand (McCulloch, 1965:390-395). A fist holds all fingers. To grasp the form is to hold all six positions. If the form becomes an event in your mind, you prehend all the relations of position needed for explanation. You prehend the explanation of the form itself, as a whole.

In Peirce's terms, prehension of the circuit is firstness of thirdness. It is iconic of the whole.

V

Discussion of the circuit re Peirce's philosophical project

It may be useful to end this paper by attempting to state what prehension the relational circuit gives you in terms of Peirce's overall project. What is prehended when you prehend the relational circuit? What do you grasp when you grasp this icon?

The prehension gives you a continuum. Peirce argued that his entire philosphy was based on continuity, i.e., synechism (Murphey, 1961:379).

The prehension gives you correlated positions of firstness, secondness and thirdness. No position could maintain its identity without the others. Hence the icon gives you a non-degenerate grasp of firstness, secondness and thirdness. These are Peirce's prime categories. The indexical function derives from secondness. The interpretive function derives from thirdness. This icon is transparent to *any* indexical function, and any interpretive function that respects that indexing. Both the indexing and the interpreting are pictured in the icon. Using Peirce's terminology, I can say that this icon prescinds from indexing and interpretation, but it is not severed from these functions. Hence it is not degenerate. A supporting argument for non-degeneracy comes from cybernetics. Because the icon satisfies the criteria for a circuit, it is a 'unit of mind.' As a unit of mind it has thirdness, it combines differences in a non-degenerate way.

The prehension of this continuum of prime categories is given topologically, i.e., mathematically. This means that the prehension gives you the possibility of knowing whatever is knowable in the categories of firstness, secondness and thirdness. Peirce argued that there are no worlds which are not knowable in terms of these three categories. The categories provide a non-excluding approach to the infinitely cognizable world. *In the architectural theory set out by Peirce, the relational circuit is an icon of all knowable worlds.* As an icon that is a 'Sign of itself,' it is a figure of regulation for any open process of semiosis that 'explains itself by itself' (Eco, 1979:198).

ENDNOTES

1. Paul Ryan is an Artist, Educator, Ecologist and member of the *Earth Environmental Group* in New York City.

Permission to reprint obtained by author of the Department of Sociology and Anthropology of Purdue University.

REFERENCES

Bateson, Gregory, 1972, *Steps to an Ecology of Mind*, New York: Ballentine.

_____, 1979, *Mind and Nature*, New York: Dutton.

Eco, Umberto, 1979, *The Role of the Reader*, Bloomington: Indiana University Press.

Gödel, Kurt, 1931, On Formally Undecidable Propositions of Principia Mathematica and Related Systems, in *The Undecidable*, M. Davis., ed., 5-38, Hewlett, New York: Raven Press 1965.

McCulloch, Warren, 1965, *Embodiments of Mind*, Cambridge, MA: M.I.T. Press.

Murphey, Murray, 1961, *The Development of Peirce's Philosophy*, Cambridge, MA: Harvard University Press.

Peirce, Charles S., 1931-35, *Collected Papers*, C. Harthshorne and P. Weiss, eds., vols I-VI, Cambridge, MA: Harvard University Press.

Ryan, Paul, 1969, Everyman's Moebius Strip, Installation, TV As A Creative Medium Show, Howard Wise Gallery, NYC.

_____, 1970, Tender is the Tape II, alternate title, Media Primer, Videotape. Raindance Archives, NYC.

_____, 1974, *Cybernetics of the Sacred*, New York: Doubleday.

_____, 1976, Video Variations on Holy Week, one person show, Kitchen Performance Space, NYC.

_____, 1980a, Relationships, *Talking Wood* 1 (4), 44-55.

_____, 1980b, A Metalogue, *All Area #1* 1 (1), 47-69.

_____, 1985, A Ritual of Triadic Relationships, Videotape, Collection, Museum of Modern Art. NYC.

_____, 1987, Ecochannel Design, *Is Journal 2* (2), 46-64.

Sharp, Willoughby, 1981, 'From Teenage Monk to Video Bareback Rider,' Interview, *Video 81* 2 (1) 14-17.

Chapter 20

International Law, Liberal Democracy and Hostile Terrorist Activity

Michael Saltman[1]

I

When a liberal-democratic state ratifies international conventions on human rights, it probably does so with the best of intentions. At the same time, it is probably also fully aware that there are circumstances under which it will renege both on its own liberal ideology and its ratification of the conventions. This raises the question whether the ratification was merely a formal gesture indicating the sovereign state's affirmation of a generalized ideological position, or the acceptance of the convention's terms as binding legal principles. The implication of the latter alternative is that the recognition of the rights stipulated by the convention imposes a set of obligations on the agencies of the signatory party. The provisions of such international conventions tend to be clear, unequivocable and little given to the manipulations of legal casuistry. Article 5 of the Universal Declaration of Human Rights states quite simply that 'No one shall be subjected to torture or to cruel, inhuman or degrading treatment or punishment'. Article 3 of the European Convention of Human Rights essentially makes the same statement. The United Nations General Assembly not only ratified the Universal Declaration, but also added that 'all persons deprived of their liberty shall be treated with humanity and with respect for the inherent dignity of the human person'. This essay will pit a specific theory of rights, that of Dworkin, against the argumentation used by a judicial commission of inquiry that investigated the alleged abuse of human rights by a governmental agency.

The kernel of Dworkin's argument for taking rights seriously is contained in two ideas -- 'the first is the vague but powerful idea of human dignity . . . (and) the second is the more familiar idea of political equality' (Dworkin, 1973:219-20). From this Dworkin correctly concludes that governmental invasion of the rights associated with these ideas 'means treating a man as less than a man, or as less worthy of concern than other men. The institution of rights rests on the conviction that this is a grave social injustice, and that it is worth paying the cost in social policy or efficiency that is necessary to prevent it' (Dworkin, 220). These assertions presumably bear a universal or even absolute quality. Certainly, as a conceptual framework of reference for the analysis of civil rights issues in the United States immediately prior to 1970, when the article was first published, Dworkin's arguments are convincing. But in order to test the argument to its limits, it may prove worthwhile subjecting it to even more rigorous testing by looking at harder cases than those considered by Dworkin.

However serious the circumstances may have been in the United States during that period, their gravity was somewhat less than the conditions obtaining in Israel during the past 42 years. The contention here is that the example provided by Israel is empirically sounder for the purpose of subjecting Dworkin's ideas to the test of their possible limits. While America's involvement in South-East Asia was that of a massive war, there was little 'clear and present danger' either to America's physical existence or to the everyday security of its civilian populace as a consequence of that war. In comparison, the fact that successive Israeli governments, through their possible stupidity, incompetence or even for any other reason, have been one of the several contributory factors leading to the continuation of the Middle Eastern conflict, has little or no bearing on the reality that Israel faces clear and present dangers more so than other contemporary liberal democracies. It is the situation, rather than its causes, that provides the appropriate context for the examination of some of Dworkin's ideas.

This paper proposes to examine some of Dworkin's contentions in the light of the findings of a State of Israel Judicial Commission of Inquiry, the mandate of which was to examine the investigatory methods and procedures of the General Security Services (henceforth referred to as the 'GSS'). In addition, the Commission was also required to examine the GSS's suspected practice of submitting false evidence to the courts. The three-man commission, headed by Supreme Court Justice Landau, received its mandate from the government on 31.5.1987 and published its findings as the 'Landau Report on 30.10.1987, excluding from publication certain sections that were deemed secret. In essence, the report only deals 'by implication' with the rights of individuals suspected of terrorist activities or other breaches of national security. The report is geared primarily towards establishing the obligations of GSS investigators in lawfully carrying out their duties.

II

The main thrust of Dworkin's argument is directed to the examination of the individual's moral right to break a law that does not accord to his conscience. He examines the issue in the light of liberal and conservative political ideologies. In contrast, this paper formulates, specifically by implication, a different question, which, notwithstanding, remains within the same general framework of reference assumed by Dworkin. Having ratified international conventions on human rights, does the state have an obligation to uphold these rights in the face of Hostile Terrorist Activity (henceforth referred to as HTA) ? The actions, and their associated motivations, of persons in this general category are several -- ranging from terrorist actions aimed indiscriminately against a civilian population to non-violent civil disobedience against military rule (when Emergency Laws are in effect). Also included would be suspected acts of treason. Insofar as Israel is concerned, there is a common denominator in that all persons suspected of offences in these abovementioned categories will initially undergo the investigatory procedures of the GSS rather than the normal procedures of criminal investigation by the police. Within the former set of procedures there is a greater likelihood that the abridgement of most elementary rights will occur.

Returning to the broad abovementioned question, the moral stance taken in the ratification of the convention is neither a necessary or a sufficient condition for the conferral of validity on a right, unless the authority chooses to make it a necessary or sufficient condition. Against this, and following the contention of some of the Scandinavian Legal Realists, it can be assumed that a right has no objective standing in reality. A right is no more than a belief held by a person to the effect that he has a right. This belief is perhaps 'objectified' in judicial decisions. The Scandinavians point out the possibility that people may be obeying laws (that in turn confer rights) not only out of fear of sanctions that would be imposed in the event of their infraction, but also out of the sense that they feel a positive inner compulsion to obey a law, or respect a right, since they believe it to be commonsensical/reasonable/morally correct/mutually advantageous to do so. When Dworkin speaks of moral rights, it is understood in the present context as those rights that are perceived by people as bearing some sort of moral quality -- for example, rights that protect human dignity, or, possibly, political equality. This is different from, say, a right which gives me freedom of movement in the face of a green traffic light, which, if not moral, is at least reasonable or mutually advantageous.

Dworkin indicates at least two ways in which he considers that governments may not be taking rights seriously. The first 'recommends striking a balance between the rights of the individual and the demands of society at large' (Dworkin, 218). The second 'stipulates that once a right is recognized in clear cut cases, then the government should act to cut off that right only when some compelling reason is presented, some reason that is consistent with the suppositions on which the original right must be based' (Dworkin, 221). In either instance the government appears to be saying that it recognizes a basic right for its intrinsic ('moral' ?) value -- for example, out of consideration of human dignity or the acceptance of the principle of political equality. But at the same time it is also saying that there may be certain circumstances under which such a basic right has to be abridged. This would imply that the initial recognition of the right by the government was not really serious, if the original 'moral' consideration is to be overruled by practical circumstances. The government, of course would be hardly likely to refer to 'practical circumstances'. Instead it would prefer to formulate the issue as a conflict between moral issues, citing the moral right of other members of the society to enjoy, for example, security.

The conclusion then is that either a paradox has been created or that the government is not taking rights seriously. This means that any claim laid to being serious about rights, or alternatively an impasse out of the paradox, can only be achieved within the context of a given political ideology. In any case, it is the political ideology itself that gives birth to rights. Political ideologies themselves are no more than beliefs about the virtues of a given social order. If, as the Scandinavian Legal Realists claim, rights are also no more than beliefs, then these same rights are also justified by the belief system of a given political ideology. A committed fascist, morally bereft in the eyes of the liberal-democrat, may be utterly convinced that he is morally justified in confining individual rights to that which does not conflict with the interests of the State, arguing that such a belief provides the greatest possible benefit to society at large. Human dignity and political equality may only serve to hinder the high moral ideal of providing the greatest amount of benefit to the greatest number of people. Who, after all, could resist the idea of a Volkswagen for every worker ? The fascist, in his belief, has at least opted for a given direction, and from the outset does not recognize a priori the moral rights of individuals only with the view to suspend them when it is no longer convenient to recognize them. This last is the unhappy lot of the liberal-democrat, who not only languishes and anguishes with the paradox, but also, on occasions, has to recognize the seeds of fascism encroaching on his own deep-seated beliefs.

Dworkin describes situations designed to test a government's measure of seriousness in upholding moral rights. These situations include the right not to serve in the armed forces as an expression of conscience against killing, and the right to freedom of expression. He indicates a clear predisposition to the effect that the government has an obligation not to hedge these rights on the grounds of their social costs. The only concession that Dworkin makes toward the qualification of the right of free speech is what Holmes has termed 'clear and present danger'. Clear means the high degree of probability that something dangerous may occur, while present emphasizes the apparent immediacy of that occurrence. There remains, of course, a degree of uncertainty as to what might constitute danger, as a consequence of free speech. The doctrine of 'clear and present danger' will be discussed below in the comparative context of analogous doctrines, such as 'the defence of necessity' or the 'lesser evil doctrine'.

Any consideration of the rights issue in Israel has to take certain background factors into account. Since its inception in 1948 Israel has been in a state of conflict, often violent conflict, with both the Palestinians and the Arab states. At one and the same time Israel professes to be ideologically committed to the principles of liberal democracy and has ratified international conventions on human rights, yet its concerns and orientations are highly statist, nationalistic and militaristic in comparison with other contemporary liberal democracies. This peculiar combination of factors gives rise to ambiguous perceptions about moral rights held both by the branches of government and by public opinion. The situation of conflict produces dangers, real and imagined. The real dangers are those that actually take place, for example PLO armed attacks against military and civilian targets and violent insurrection (intifada) against military occupation and Jewish settlers in the occupied territories. The imagined dangers are what the politicians claim to be the foreseeable consequences of a given policy. This distinction ultimately becomes quite important in any consideration of the question of rights.

III

The issue to which this paper is addressed is within the general domain of the right to due process of law, with particular emphasis on the moral implications of brutal interrogatory practices. Any governmental invasion of this right could be rightfully construed as meaning, in Dworkin's terms, as treating a man as less than a man, or as less worthy of concern than other men. What is being specifically isolated for discussion is the interrogatory practices employed by the GSS investigating persons suspected of terrorist activities or other breaches of state security. A series of events that took place in Israel from 1984, culminating in the abovementioned Landau Report, has brought the whole issue to the forefront of both public and judicial attention.

The practices of the GSS came under initial judicial scrutiny in the light of a case, known as the 300 Bus case (Saltman & Rosenfeld, 1990). The case established, among other things, the fact that members of the GSS, including members of the GSS legal staff, had lied before judicial commissions of inquiry with reference to allegations that they had employed brutal interrogatory techniques. This conclusion led to the reopening of another case, known as the Nafsu case [PD 124/87] from which two additional facts emerged. The first was that the GSS had consistently submitted false evidence to the courts over a considerable length of time. Second, the GSS had employed improper investigatory procedures in order to obtain Nafsu's confession to the charges against him. Lieutenant Nafsu, a Circassian serving as a professional army officer, had been convicted by a court martial on the counts of treason and espionage in addition to some lesser charges. He had been accused of having communicated information about the IDF (Israel Defence Forces) to a senior PLO commander in southern Lebanon. He was convicted on the basis of his own admission to the charges and was sentenced to eighteen years imprisonment, loss of rank and expulsion from the army. His subsequent appeal to the Military Appeals court was denied.

In his appeal to the Military Appeals Court Nafsu claimed that he had not admitted to his guilt on his own free will. On the contrary, his compliance was extracted by means of a combination of of physical force and psychological pressure -- blows, kicks, being forced to stand for hours day and night in the prison courtyard and having to take freezing showers. Furthermore, he was threatened by his interrogators that both his wife and mother would also be arrested. The GSS personnel, in their appearance before the court, denied that any of this had taken place. The court accepted their testimony and rejected the appeal. As an immediate consequence of Nafsu's appeal to the Supreme Court, the GSS carried out an internal investigation and concluded that Nafsu's claims were correct and that the evidence submitted to the Military Court of Appeals by the GSS was false. Therefore, Nafsu had not admitted to the charges against him on his own free will. On the strength of this a plea-bargain arrangement was achieved. Nafsu admitted to a lesser charge, and the sentence on the major charges was quashed. (Nafsu had already served seven and a half years of the eighteen year sentence imposed on him, and the court assumed that damages would have to be paid to Nafsu by the authorities). The court criticized the methods employed by the GSS. In the wake of this case and the previous 300 Bus case, the Landau Commission was set up in order to examine GSS practices.

On the basis of the GSS's own internal self-investigation, the report establishes that what had happened to Nafsu had been standard practice for several years. The application of physical pressure on suspects and the subsequent denial of its application in the courts were both normative practices (Landau Report, Sec.2.5). The internal investigation, however, gives no indication as to any reservations held by the GSS as to the propriety of these actions. Quite to the contrary, the GSS witnesses, who appeared before the commission unabashedly justified the practices by virtue of necessity. The word 'necessity' is a crucial one, for it is not being used just in common parlance, but, as will be demonstrated below, it has a specific legal meaning.

The commission assumes, as a point of departure, that there has to be a fundamental difference between a regular police investigation of a crime and an investigation carried out by the GSS in regard to suspected acts of terrorism (Landau Report, Sec.2.18). The grounds for making this difference are laid out in the report by the specification of the distinctive characteristics of a terrorist. In Section 2.9 the report definitively states that the aim of the Palestine Liberation Organization is the destruction of the State of Israel by means of armed struggle (by citing paragraph 9 of the P.L.O. Charter). 'Armed struggle' is interpreted as 'acts of terror' in the Landau Report. 'For the purposes of the 'armed struggle' the organizations conduct acts of terror in the form of mass-murder in public places, such as the public transportation system, markets, open squares, cinemas and bathing sites' (Landau Report, Sec. 2.10). But for the more specific purposes of the report's ultimate conclusions, one aspect of the terrorist's training is singled out for consideration and that is his ability to withstand normal procedures of investigation and interrogation (Landau Report, Sec.2.15).

If we accept that the respective profiles of the common criminal and the terrorist are different, then this would necessarily have implications for the aims and methods of the authorities. The report states that within the domain of criminal activities it is the duty of the police to gather evidence, to achieve a conviction, to deter, punish and, perhaps, rehabilitate criminals as a final end. The functions of the GSS are to protect the State and its citizens against acts of terrorism, to gather information about terrorists and their organizations in order to foil acts of terrorism (Landau Report, Sec.2.18). Unless a terrorist is caught in the actual perpetration of a terrorist act, the most effective way of achieving his conviction, and more importantly, his removal, is by means of extracting his confession to the acts attributed to him. Of even more immediate concern is the possibility that the apprehended terrorist may also possess information of an imminently impending act of terror. Finally, it may also be assumed that he has additional information, the knowledge of which, if learned by the authorities, may prevent a terrorist act at some non-stipulated time in the future. Given these situations, what rights, moral or otherwise, have to be taken into account, if at all?

These are not hypothetically constructed dilemmas for the purpose of allowing intellectual debate on questions of moral philosophy. All the abovementioned issues occur on a regular, almost daily basis. The Landau Commission heard testimony from the GSS personnel, who were questioned specifically about their methods of interrogation and the perjured evidence they had submitted to the courts. Paragraph 12 of the Rules of Evidence 1971 states that 'the testimony of the accused's admission to his commission of a crime would only be acceptable when the prosecutor brought evidence as to the circumstances under which the admission had been made, and when the court regarded it as having been given freely and voluntarily'. This created two problems for the GSS investigators, who had to appear in pre-trial hearings in those instances when the accused retracted his admission on the grounds that he had made it under physical duress, and not voluntarily. The first problem was that the GSS had good reason not to disclose their methods, since such disclosure would only serve to assist future suspects in their resistance to investigation. This in turn led to the second problem, that of lying to the courts. For not only did they wish to prevent any disclosure of their methods, but it also became essential to lie in order to prevent the acquittal of the accused.

The Landau Commission's examination of GSS witnesses revealed the existence of ideological justifications for the illegal actions of members of the Service. The discovery and prevention of acts of terrorism had become a 'holy war' that justified any means taken. Cliched responses to questions, such as 'one cannot clean sewers without getting dirty' were common (Landau Report, Sec.2.40). Nor was it a question of the lower echelons in the Service making their own rules without the knowledge of their superiors. The ideology was acceptable at all levels. A certain measure of bitterness was reflected in the responses of several witnesses who claimed that the judiciary and the political functionaries were fully aware as to what was going on, and also 'constituted part of the game' (Landau Report, Sec.2.45). The legal staff of the GSS are singled out by the Commission for particular criticism. One of the legal advisors, in response to an investigator's statement that he had in fact used 'physical pressure' on a suspect, categorically ordered the investigator to conceal this fact from the court. The Commission, in commenting on this, expressed its disgust (Landau Report, Sec.2.51).

IV

The third section of the report addresses itself to the legal and moral aspects of the issue. In order to determine whether the interrogator is himself criminally liable for his actions, the report surveys both the existing laws and principles on the subject as well as examining a selection of relevant academic legal sources. The resulting discussion is both enigmatic and inconclusive, since it cannot reduce the moral problem to a legal formulation, while conversely it seems to be incapable of separating the legal issue from its moral context. The defence of necessity, the underlying idea of which is that a person finds himself in a situation where it is necessary to perform an act in order to prevent death or serious injury to himself or to another, is a legal principle. But it cannot be separated from the moral questions arising from it. Similarly, the Lesser Evil Defence demands an appraisal that cannot be divorced from moral considerations. Legal principles, legal terminology and legal language cannot gloss over the moral issues.

As distinct from the principles of International Law (see above), the responses of legal systems of sovereign states is characteristically utilitarian, a philosophical position to which Dworkin is so opposed. In practice, the outcome of 'balancing' between conflicting rights (in those hard cases involving fundamental rights) appears to give the edge to the public weal over the individual right. The Landau Report cites sources to support this contention. Zuckerman is quoted as follows:

> This is not to say that it is impossible to envisage situations where the organs of the state may excusably resort to torture. Where it is known that a bomb has been planted in a crowded building, it is perhaps justifiable to torture the suspect so that lives may be saved by discovering its location (1986:45).

But the members of the commission are quick to point out some of the obvious implications of this. 'The loosening of the leash..(can create a situation) . . . when each interrogator can make his own law by means of unrestrained and arbitrary force against a suspect . . . . The image of the State as one governed by the Rule of Law, as respecting civil rights, might be irreparably destroyed and will come to resemble those ruling powers that accord unlimited powers to their security services'. This is immediately followed by a set of conclusions, stated more as principles than as operative directives.

> First, the exaggerated use of pressure against a subject should be proscribed; pressure should not reach the level of physical torture . . . or the severe infringement of that degree of dignity that denies his very humanity. Second, the employment of less severe means should be balanced against the degree of the anticipated danger on the basis of the data known by the interrogator. Third, the permissible means of physical and psychological pressure at the disposal of the interrogator should be defined and limited in advance by obligatory directives . . . . (Landau Report, Sect.3.16).

In essence, these are the principles upon which the operative conclusions in Section 4 are based. The element of 'balancing' emerges quite clearly in the analysis. The members of the commission state categorically in Section 4.5 that if the aim of acts of terror is to negate the basic rights to life and limb of the citizenry, the perpetrators of these acts have no moral right to demand that the State should accord them the acceptable standards of civil rights. 'Despite this, the State and its agencies should maintain standards of humanitarian behaviour and human dignity towards terrorists in order to maintain the credo of the State itself, as a state ruled by law grounded in basic concepts of morality'. This leads to the most important statement of the report, which elicited most of the critical public reaction after its publication. The statement in Section 4.7 reads as follows:

> The means of pressure should concentrate mainly on non-violent psychological pressure in active and continuous interrogation, and the use of stratagems that would include deception. But when these do not achieve their aim, one should not abstain from the use of *moderate physical force*.

As to what constitutes 'moderate physical force', this is no longer a public issue, since the exact criteria are discussed in the secret portion of the Report in order to prevent the disclosure of GSS methods and techniques.

The Landau Commission found itself seriously dislocated between the poles of a moral commitment on the one hand, and the pragmatic considerations of national security on the other. Its exit from the impasse is tortuous and evasive. It assumed that if the use of physical violence against a suspect under interrogation is controlled by the law and used in moderation, then it meets the requirements of both the moral obligations of the state, and in particular the rule of law, and the security interests of the community at large. This approach did not convince the participants of a Symposium devoted specifically to an analysis of the report's content, to which the overall response of the participants was highly negative. Not one of the critical commentators in that symposium, however, chose to place his arguments within the context of Dworkin's contentions about taking rights seriously. Some of the arguments made, in my opinion, validate Dworkin's position on the subject.

Neither courts nor judicial inquiries constitute the arena where moral issues are to be debated. Legal institutions are concerned with the legality or illegality of actions and as such, any implications bearing moral implications are incidental. A judicial commission of inquiry, such as the Landau Commission in its search for justifications, may include 'the moral aspects' in its purview, which in fact it did. But the essence of its conclusions is to be found in the narrower interpretations of statutes. A significant portion of the commission's inquiry was devoted to the question whether the GSS personnel were criminally liable for their actions.

Section 22 of the Penal Law states:

> A person may be exempted from criminal responsibility for an act or omission if he can show that it was done or made in order to avoid consequences which could not otherwise be avoided and which would have inflicted grievous harm or injury on his person, honour or property or on the person or honour of others whom he was bound to protect or on property placed in his charge: Provided that he did no more than was reasonably necessary for that purpose and that the harm caused by him was not disproportionate to the harm avoided.

The defence of necessity, as a justification for what the commission ultimately deems legitimate in the use of 'moderate physical force', is not particularly convincing. If Dworkin concedes that clear and present danger is a justification for the abridgement of the right to free speech, why should not an analogy be drawn with the danger implicit in the idea of necessity? The danger in 'clear and present danger' is more easily definable than it is in the qualification of 'necessity'.

Several participants in the abovementioned symposium took issue with the commission on this very point. S.Z. Feller states:

> But there is an additional condition for 'necessity', and the Commission takes pains to rule it out. It is the demand for the 'immediacy' of the danger. Imminence is not merely a matter of time but also of the nature of the harm inherent in the possible realization of the danger, in terms of its specific materiality and quantitative dimensions (1989:205).

Similarly, A.Dershowitz writes, 'the necessity defence is by its very nature an emergency measure: it is not suited to situations which recur over long periods of time. This is especially so when the claimant to the benefit of the defence is a state agency (or its members)' (1989:197). M. Kremnitzer repeats Feller's contention more succinctly by saying that 'the Commission thus fails to distinguish between different dangers by their imminence and concreteness' (1989:232-33).

The justification in balancing evils one against the other is not a convincing argument. The commission makes this argument by citing a hypothetical situation, more remarkable for its gentility than for its representation of reality.

> To put it bluntly, the alternative is: are we to accept the offence of assault entailed in slapping a suspect's face, or threatening him, in order to induce him to talk and reveal a cache of explosive materials meant for use in carrying out an act of mass terror against a civilian population, and thereby prevent the greater evil which is about to occur. The answer is self-evident (Landau Report Sec.3.15).

It is hardly likely that the establishment of the Landau Commission was a response to complaints about 'face-slapping'. The Penal Law's designation of the necessity defence indeed supplies a criterion for the purpose of balancing evils. Section 22 stipulates that a person must show 'that the harm caused by him was not disproportionate to the harm avoided'. The moderate pressure allowed by the commission is clearly something more vicious than the slapping of a suspect's face, when balanced by the suspect's refusal to reveal an arm's cache, yet at the same time is not too vicious so as to violate his human dignity. Kremnitzer points out that the 'Commission itself states that the physical pressure exerted must not be such as to deprive a suspect of his human dignity' (1989:249). Given the nature of the variables at issue -- degree of physical pressure; scope of the act to be prevented; and what may constitute human dignity, all of which are difficult to quantify -- there is no way in which an objective scale for achieving a balance may be created. Any utilitarian approach not only produces morally questionable conclusions, but may also lead to logical inconsistencies.

The Landau Commission wanted the best of all worlds. It espoused the moral position that human dignity has to be preserved, but not at all costs. At the same time they justified the use of 'moderate physical pressure' on suspects by a formal, narrow and literal reading of the necessity defence. While it was not incumbent on them to do so, they failed to recognize the philosophical implications of their reasonings. They balanced 'evils' in the crudest of utilitarian terms and discarded their intuitive understandings of the moral issues at hand. Both the commission and its detractors in the subsequent symposium dug themselves a trap by pitting the moral issues against pragmatic considerations. The alternative framework of reference suggested by this paper is that of taking rights seriously. The reformulation of the question then is not whether the Landau Commission was morally bankrupt or not, but is rather one of whether it has taken fundamental rights seriously or not.

The taking of rights seriously is preconditioned, in Dworkin's terms, by making a distinction between what he terms background rights and institutional rights. Background rights are those 'that provide a justification for a decision by society in the abstract, and institutional rights . . . provide a justification for a decision by some particular and specified political institution' (Dworkin, 1975:1069-70). If the former are no more than abstract entities conforming possibly to general standards of morality, the latter are clearly highly concrete rights perceived in terms of the aims and actions of the institution itself. The Landau Commission paid more attention to the issue of background rights by pitting one set of generalized principles against another -- Necessity against Rule of Law; Necessity against Human Dignity -- rather than to the set of concrete rights and obligations with an institution such as the GSS. It is not surprising, then, that the commission arrived at such an indeterminate operative conclusion that gives licence to the GSS to employ moderate physical force. Had the commission focussed on the concrete aims and purposes of the institution, as well as on the alternative means of achieving them, it might have arrived at different operative conclusions. It is true that there is a secret addendum to the report, which may indeed provide detailed guidelines and criteria for the modus operandi of the GSS. But about this we shall never know and it is really not the point, since the bone of contention rests with the published statement about the use of moderate physical force, the indeterminacy of that statement and the potential interpretation of that indeterminacy by public officials.

The commission should have attempted to construct a principle whereby necessity is more rigidly defined. Such an attempt on its part would have indicated some measure of taking rights seriously. In the first place, as explained above, necessity can be qualified by its relative immediacy. An impending act of terrorism can be reasonably measured in hours, possibly even in days. Beyond this, any measurement in terms of weeks or months clearly reduces the justification of immediacy. Following this, the alternatives to physical force then become a function of the time available to the interrogators. Over time the psychological resistance of the suspect can be sapped without resorting to violence, mainly by tiring him. Furthermore it provides a period during which the suspect can also prove his innocence. The commission had not bothered to make a clear distinction between the prevention of a terrorist act and the need to obtain a conviction. As in any criminal investigation, the investigators have to search for evidence above and beyond what the suspect may choose to admit or deny. Violence is the lazy man's approach to criminal investigation. Not only is it an affront to human dignity, but neither does it necessarily lead to the truth. The Nafsu case substantiates this point. The commission points out, on the basis of testimony submitted by GSS personnel, that it is more difficult to gather evidence in instances of suspected terrorist activity than in a regular criminal investigation. This claim was uncritically accepted by the commission. The contrary argument is that the difficulties in obtaining corroborative evidence are not insurmountable for an efficient intelligence agency, even though it is easier to extract a confession by means of physical force.

The commission did not ask itself whether it was taking rights seriously as part of its mandate. Had this been its terms of reference, it would have been hard put to find the justification that it found in respect to the activities of the GSS. It is true that that the original mandate given to the commission by the Government did not refer to the issue of rights. The operative sentence of the mandate reads, 'To establish a Commission of Inquiry in accordance with Sec.1 of the Commissions of Inquiry Law, 1968, regarding the methods and procedures of the GSS on HTA , and the giving of testimony in court with these investigations. The Commission will make recommendations and proposals, *as it sees fit*, also regarding the appropriate methods and procedures concerning these investigations in the future, while taking into account the unique needs of the struggle against HTA' (italics mine). There is no stipulation in the mandate that would preclude the casting of the commission's analysis within the conceptual framework of rights and obligations. The words 'as it sees fit' denote the degrees of freedom available to the commission. But the commission opted not to do so. This was a judicial commission with the powers to recommend criminal proceedings against GSS personnel, who had broken the law (as determined by the commission itself) by lying to the courts. This raises the question whether the commission even took the law seriously.

V

Admittedly, the terms of reference raised in this paper are somewhat different from those of Dworkin. Dworkin's point of departure is in his question whether a person has a moral right to break a law when that law does not accord with his conscience. It is possible to twist the argument in this paper by claiming that certainly those GSS personnel, who appeared before the commission, felt that they had the moral right to do just this. In their minds they had the right to combat the evils of terrorism by any means at their disposal. But can such a right be upheld by a government? Presumably, a totalitarian government would have no problem in upholding it. But in line with liberal-democratic thought the Landau Commission condemned this attitude on the part of the GSS officers, but neither seriously nor unequivocally. For its conclusions were tempered with a degree of 'understanding', in addition to which no recommendations were made to instigate criminal proceedings against those who had so blatantly broken the law. If on the other hand, the commission considered the obligations of the GSS more seriously, it did not overextend itself by considering, as a related issue, the rights conferred by these obligations -- i.e. the rights of suspects. By ignoring the rights issue, the commission merely engaged in a masterful exercise of equivocation. By the same token (i.e. ignoring the rights issue) the criticism of some of the Commission's detractors, evoked in the abovementioned colloquium, remains muted in its formalism.

Fundamental rights are most seriously threatened by the idea of national security. In wartime, these rights are usually severely curtailed by Emergency Laws. Since war itself is an indignity, there is little sensitivity to the respect of human dignity at such a time and the correlated rights are not taken seriously. But even in times of peace, the idea of national security does not vanish. Certainly in Israel, and in other Middle Eastern countries, the 'peaceful' period between wars is merely the interval during which preparations are made for the next war. Violence is endemic to the area and sporadically occurs both in the form of acts of terrorism and Israeli military reprisals. The occupation of the West Bank and the Gaza Strip has caused the unremitting and escalating violence of both sides. This is precisely the type of situation in which any government that wishes to be seen as a government that takes rights seriously, has to take them seriously. The social and political costs of taking rights seriously under these circumstances are very high, but at the same time are indicative of the government's degree of seriousness. A government has also to take into account that a non-serious approach to fundamental human rights also has its high social and political costs in terms of the nature of the society that emerges under that condition. The government has to decide where the line of national security has to be drawn. For if it overextends the bounds of national security beyond clear and present dangers in order to justify the abridgement of fundamental rights, it is no longer even taking its own laws seriously. The final sentences of Dworkin's article effectively sums up the implications of not taking rights seriously. In addressing himself to the question whether the government respects the Law, he argues that 'it cannot do that if it neglects the one feature that distinguishes law from ordered brutality. If the Government does not take rights seriously, then it doesn't take the law seriously either' (Dworkin, 227).

Given the choice of formulating a problem as a 'duties and obligations' issue, as opposed to a 'rights' issue, opting for the former makes better political sense from the point of view of the authorities. While opting for the latter (i.e. the rights issue), there is a greater likelihood that governmental powers may be curtailed, since the contradictions between fundamental human rights and, what may be termed as the 'public interest' emerge clearly in the starkest of terms. The ratification of human rights' conventions by any government ought to indicate, at the very least, the necessity to examine the rights issue as a point of departure.The Landau commission addressed itself to the question of the duties and obligations of the GSS, as demanded in the government mandate to them. The terms of reference were the 'methods and procedures' of that agency. The relevancy of the incidents that triggered the establishment of the commission (i.e. the 300 Bus case and the Nafsu case) was incidental rather than central to the deliberations of the commission. The individuals, whose rights had been infringed upon by the existing 'methods and procedures', were not considered except in the sense of some infrequent and incidental references to general standards of morality. Certainly, a lesser dilemma is created by pitting vague and generalized standards of morality against the idea of the common weal, than by pitting the specific fundamental rights that serve to emphasize and highlight the contradictions. The most telling conclusion by far is that of the different social contexts (in the political sense) in which the utterances of international law are contrasted with the legal utterances of the sovereign state. The international community is not a constituency in the same sense as the citizens of a sovereign state. The international community of liberal democracies, as well as other states that ratify international conventions, voices its high moral aspirations in the form of international laws, for it is not beholden to any given defined constituency. But as demonstrated here, at the level of an individual state's constituency, there is a point beyond which circumstances will inevitably demand the use of different legal utterances.

ENDNOTES

1. Michael Saltman is Professor of Anthropology at the University of Haifa, Israel.

REFERENCES

Dershowitz, A.M., 1989, 'Is It Necessary to Apply 'Physical Pressure' to Terrorists -- and to Lie About It?,' *Israel Law Review*, Vol. 23, Nos. 2-3, 192-200.

Dworkin, R., 1973, 'Taking Rights Seriously', The New York Review of Books, 18 Dec. 1970; repr. in Simpson, A.W.B., *Oxford Essays in Jurisprudence*, Second Series, Oxford, Clarendon Press.

_____, 1975, 'Hard Cases', *Harvard Law Review* 88(6).

Feller, S.Z., 1989, 'Not Actual 'Necessity' but Possible Justification; Not 'Moderate Pressure' but Either 'Unlimited' or 'None at All',' *Israel Law Review*, Vol. 23, Nos. 2-3, 201-215

Kremnitzer, M., 1989, 'The Landau Commission Report - Was the Security Service Subordinated to the Law, or the Law to the 'Needs' of the Security Service?' *Israel Law Review*, Vol. 23, Nos. 2-3, 216-279.

Saltman, M. and H. Rosenfeld, 1990,'Rule of Law Versus Political Interest,' *Contemporary Crises*, Vol. 14, 1-22.

Zuckerman, A.S., 1986, 'The Right Against Self-Incrimination: An Obstacle to the Supervision of Interrogation,' *Law Quarterly Review*, January.

Chapter 21

Codification

William T. Scott[1]

I

Introduction

In law, medicine and health, religion, education, politics and even the quasi-professions such as estate agency, or the various forms of journalism, the constitutive role of communication is widely acknowledged, to the extent that many such occupational groups have devised and published the Codes of Conduct or Practice which this paper will discuss.

To claim a constitutive role for communication is consciously to borrow John Searle's well-known distinction between constitutive (generally obligatory) rules, which make an activity such as playing chess what it thereby is, and regulative (generally optional) rules which result in playing chess in a particular manner.

To take the example of medicine, the claim is that doctoring is not just helped by or dependent upon successful acts of communication, but that it is quite literally constituted by such acts. Consider the doctor-patient interview, studied by many. (See Byrne and Long, 1976; Ostwald, 1964; Pendleton and Hasler, 1983; Raffler-Engel, 1989) ('Interviews' of various sorts are central to most professional practitioners' relationship with clients and deserve a systematic, comprehensive study in their own right, for purposes of training at least).

Consider, also, symptomatology, the 'reading' of signs, a joint concern of semiotic/communication theory and of medical education since classical times. Psychiatry, even drug-preoccupied psychiatry, is overwhelmingly communicative.

To exemplify further from the field of medicine, there is great concern currently with issues of confidentiality, of truthfulness, of trustworthiness with regard to professional competence (and all the 'legal' consequences thereof). These cannot be understood unless we approach them with some sort of theory that addresses the communicational forms, the representational resources and practices for making and taking sense, that doctoring comprises.

Likewise, the criminal lawyer's work is, typically, concerned with what happened how and why, with reconstructing series of events as narratives, using all the forensic and rhetorical devices that we associate with the legal process. (See Lance Bennett and Feldman, 1981; Mellinkoff, 1963; Goodrich, 1987; Jackson, 1988). Evidence in the form of exhibits is that which supports a story by being -- not 'representing', if that term means 'something standing in for something else' -- part of what is being reconstructed, ie represented in sworn statements, cross examined oral evidence and so on. The distinction between bits of reality brought in to speak for themselves, and a surrounding representation of the rest of the reality that has been lost forever, is an important one that serves to underline the main point in hand at this stage. Less dramatic forms of legal work, such as the drafting of contracts, are no less semiotic and explicitly communicative.

Sermons, prayers, blessings, benedictions, confessions, absolutions, declarations of marriage, exorcisms and many other proper practices of the clergy extend what may have become a tedious demonstration of the initial claim that communicative acts constitute professional practice.

The list of specialized social functions we consider professions, some practices of some of which are briefly mentioned above, is certainly longer than that given. In many, the role of communication, while important, is not so fundamental as it is in those named in the opening paragraph here. A Chartered Civil Engineer for example, performs core professional duties that need to be taught/learned, that others may need to have explained or defended to them, that will be represented in plans, models, sets of calculations and so on, all of which are semiotic/communicative but which are not the motorway or sewage system that the engineer's expertise ultimately creates. By contrast, while the outcome of a successful doctor's efforts is some acceptable state of health, of the clergyman some state of grace, of the lawyer's some regulated state of personal/social relations, in each case the bulk of the work involves gaining and/or creating understanding, by means of communication.

II

Normal and Abnormal Communication

In order to approach the notion of professional codes regulating the essentially communicative practices, it is necessary first to identify more precisely what sort of 'communication' is usually going on. That can be done in a contrastive way by considering what might be the interpersonal counterpart to Habermas's conception (Habermas, 1984) of an idealized social order, one allowing full undistorted acts of communication by members. We will call this normal communication, and will focus upon the interpersonal dimension.

Normal communication operates on a set of assumptions held and conformed-to reciprocally by participants. From first principles of communication theory, the very normality of the practices about to be discussed renders them invisible and, conversely, foregrounds those instances where the normal operating assumptions are violated or suspended.

One assumption is that in spontaneous small group interaction, where participants are of reasonably similar age and status, all will have, in principle, equal access to 'the floor' or 'airtime.' Many variables to do with 'situation' in the general sense familiar from the work of sociolinguists (a combination of who is speaking with whom, in what cultural/organizational/ interpersonal context, about what) radically affect the contractual basis on which the interaction proceeds. However if we retain a focus on free, spontaneous exchanges between or among relative equals, taking that as the ideal/idealized basis for social relations, some underlying assumptions or terms in the contract may be teased out.

The notion of reciprocity, for example, much discussed by microsociologists, anthropologists and ethnographers extends beyond access to equal floortime (in principle), or co-operative rule-following in turn-taking, types of interruption/interjection and so on. (See Saville-Troike 1984; Fasold 1984 and 1990). As a general principle it calls for commitment to the idea that anything any participant can do by way of communicative behavior can be done by any other participant in the exchange.

The idealized nature of the notion 'normal communication' will be obvious when we consider the numerous exceptions or deviations from this general contractual term. In standard medical interviews, doctors usually ask the questions and only expect to be questioned at particular stages and in particular ways. They do not expect to be questioned in the sense of having their diagnoses and prescriptions debated. To return to the everyday from the professional context, the now large literature on gendered language, more generally the language habits forced-upon the powerless by the powerful (of which the professional-client relationship is a special case) gives cause for caution in our description of what constitutes normal communication, albeit idealized. We will return to these issues below.

Meanwhile, we will continue to explore some terms and assumptions within this notional contract. A common basic assumption, for example, is that we act freely in deciding how to behave in the company of others. The assumption unpacks into numerous related concepts, as difficult as they are indispensable if we are to conduct social lives far less examine that behavior in a scholarly way. The free agent is one who behaves intentionally and/or purposefully, i.e., who is conscious of freedom from duress or some other compulsion and is minded to behave in some chosen way in pursuit of some chosen goal. Consciousness, free-will, goal-creation and pursuit are classic problems (See Anscombe, 1979; Mackay in Hinde, ed, 1972; Scott, 1990, Ch 4; Parfit, 1984) which cannot be merely left to philosophers and which manifestly concern ordinary people in their dealings with other ordinary people quite apart from their dealings with people as embodiments of social power.

We may usefully dodge full-blown discussion by distinguishing what can be justified by objective argument and demonstration (e.g., that people, as opposed to machines, can behave intentionally) from what people believe about their and others' actions. Not only do they seem to believe that some actions flow from reasons rather than causes, but that other related notions such as responsibility and accountability are, to use an undervalued word in these matters, reasonable. Extreme determinists and other scorched-earthers who deny these capabilities in others and who therefore deny the very possibility of meaningful action (especially communicative action) doubtless mean what they say, which leaves them with a rather obvious problem no amount of negative-juggling of the sort displayed by the arch proponent of such modish notions, Stanley Fish (Fish, 1989; Introduction) can resolve.

Another aspect of the standard contract -- truth -- alarms even serious students of how meaning is made in social life. Sincerity is, however, not nearly so daunting as the concept of truth. Truth concerns relationships between words and facts while truthfulness or sincerity concerns relationships between words and their utterers. I can be sincere but mistaken. I can also be sincerely insincere, as when I sincerely advertise my partial withdrawal, at another level, from the sincerity clause in the contract and begin teasing, or indulge in sarcasm. White lies, the use of tact or some other form of euphemism, hyperbole and so on, raise related issues to do with what Grice referred to as the quality relationship between utterer and utterance. (See Grice, 1975). Candor is a different concept from that of sincerity. (See Scott, 1990 (b)).

Trust, of course, is heavily dependent on perceptions of truthfulness. In normal communication we typically settle for what is offered to us as the 'truth as believed' by someone. If they merely guess, hope or imagine what they tell us they will be the more trustworthy for telling us so. In the professional situation we may reasonably expect more, namely the truthful utterance of the truth as someone *knows* it to be, because they are appropriately knowledgeable. That body of knowledge embodies relevant facts and other information such as general principles. It also embodies knowledge of good practice, that is professional expertise and competence, the general framework of which are captured in the codes we will shortly examine.

Another working assumption of the contract for normal communicative behavior is brought out by the concern for knowledge about what is believed to be professional competence just noted. In ordinary social life, a basic competence is the ability to talk/listen so that what 'is meant' (literally; conventionally; by the utterer on the occasion of utterance; potentially under another interpretation) is in principle identifiable and held in play by the parties concerned. Thereafter, what we decide to mean and what we are taken as meaning is a matter for skilled negotiation and is, in the normal situation, heavily dependent on the co-operative goodwill of the other parties. As with all skills, some are better than others, attentiveness fluctuates and so on. Nonetheless, we routinely assume that others we encounter will know enough of the basic semiotic resource, talk, and be consciously conscientious enough in its use (both as speakers and listeners) to say/hear what is meant and mean/understand what is said.

Numerous other working assumptions on the basis of which we treat (with) one another through our semiotic resources deserve discussion, but perhaps enough has now been said to warrant a brief return to the skeptical view of normal communication alluded-to briefly earlier.

The right to participate in social life fully entails access to the contract just sketched. That access is earned at some cost, as children and apprentices of all sorts know.[2] It is also withheld or withdrawn from foreigners, fools, the deaf, mute, mentally-ill and otherwise disabled, indeed from many of the powerless and underprivileged. (Defensive and retaliating strategies such as prison argots, rhyming slang, the canting talk of criminals and vagabonds, backslang, satire, and silence itself, are of great linguistic and sociological interest in this context.)

The broad thrust of Critical Theory (now sufficiently important in academic discussion to have 'grown capitals') with regard to the sketch of normal communication above is that if it occurs at all it only occurs in a very few, atypical situations. Most of the time it would appear from these essentially pessimistic and even nihilistic writings, we wrestle with words and meanings in two senses: talk is a weapon by means of which we cannot help but carry on the power struggles of private and public life; it is also an overpowering influence on our thoughts (and indeed our capacity for thought) against which those of us who have glimpsed the walls of the prison struggle in vain.

That these ideas might be mutually incompatible, and independently incompatible with the groundrules of academic discourses through which they circulate so successfully matters little if 'contradiction' is regarded as the most desirable, indeed inevitable, condition of mental and social life. Since this presumably self-refers and therefore must be true and untrue simultaneously, we will proceed with the latter possibility and seek to resolve the apparent counter evidence to the view of normal communication given.

There is no suggestion that 'normal' means 'what most people experience most of the time'. There *is* the suggestion that most people expect to experience communication on this basis in certain circumstances which they will seek out and miss greatly if they are deprived of them. In this sense, normal communication is really normative, what should happen, and the idealization offered is also an ideal, something good to strive for, at least when it clearly matters a lot to one or other of the participants. (Without some statement of this ideal, of course, skeptical critical theorists are in no position to indict the practices they object-to). Ten minutes a month spent in this kind of interaction may nonetheless serve to identify the 'abnormality' of what a person may experience the rest of the time.

We argue that abnormal communication occurs when one or more of the principal assumptions constitutive of normal communication is altered, suspended or withdrawn, especially when this is done unilaterally and/or covertly. In the public domain Codes of Practice often make explicit, among much else, what are considered minimal standards with regard to professional communication with the client. As s result what is *not* on offer, if only for the fact that is not explicitly mentioned, should be evident. For example, as Bok points out in her excellent study *Lying*, (Bok, 1978) most American medical patients at least claim that they value honesty (frankness and completeness, rather than technical truthfulness) from doctors. However, none of the oaths and codes subscribed-to by these and other health professionals meets this desire. Related matters, such as confidentiality are usually catered-for, making silence on what is often referred to as 'the patient's right to know' (see the book of this title by G. McLean, 1989) the more noticeable. If, as the International Code for Nurses tells us, 'The nurse holds in confidence personal information and uses judgement in sharing that information' we might expect some converse commitment to disclosure where the patient's rights under the standard contract so require. Even allowing for the general problem of competence and effability picked up in Endnote 2, and other reasons why full information leading to informed consent might be impossible or undesirable, such a contractual basis for communication is clearly abnormal in the pejorative sense established above.

In increasingly litigious times, professionals are not only conscious of clients' rights to full and frank information, but also of their own vulnerability if this communicative action or inaction comes under scrutiny. All professionals make mistakes, more typically come to judgements unilaterally (or, at least, without fully informing clients and/or their advisors) on the basis of which debatable actions are taken, advice given and so on. Even sparing a client's feelings, attempting to be tactful or polite, using imprecise or misleading language, all of which fall short of lying by omission or commission, render the professional vulnerable.

Other pressures on professionals have contributed to the move towards public statements of Codes of Practice. The experience of working in teams or with other professionals creates need to demarcate, hence define, each participant's contribution. Legislature on data held within organizations forces staff to articulate tighter rules about information-handling generally, hence encroach on the essence of the professional-client relationship. The threat of legislature, for example against the 'excesses' of newspaper reporters, can precipitate self-regulating pronouncements from groups seeking to reassert, or assert the professionalism, of practitioners. (See Appendix 1). In the latter case, proto-professionals may advertise their emerging respectability by, among other devices such as the establishment of recognized qualifications, publishing Codes of Practice.

(In passing, note that the confidentiality issue for journalists concerns their obligation to remain silent in protecting the privacy of sources, along with an obligation to breach confidentiality where the publication of information is concerned. The right to, indeed compulsion to, silence, on specific matters at least, is an interesting aspect of the standard contract in normal communication. It is also enshrined in British rules of legal evidence, with controversial exceptions in the case of suspected terrorists. It is part of the American Constitution, in a very specific form. For some clients, such as school-children or psychiatric patients, the right to silence is obviously an inconvenience to the professional).

III
Codes

A. Rules and Regulations

These considerations bring us to the first of two senses of the term 'code' that need to be clarified. In this sense of the term, we are dealing with a set of precepts for action. Codification involves formalizing and systematizing members of the set, so that a finite and principled notation or vocabulary is established, that this is used consistently across the various statements making up the Code, and that these form a coherent set, in various senses of that term (e.g., that no internal contradictions appear). The law is seen by many as codified moral and reasonable practice, whether at the level of a Highway Code, at the level of a system such as the Code Napoleon or, even more abstractly, in the distilled essentials of any conceivable legal order, a level of idealization pursued by those seeking to ground particular legal orders in absolute, fundamental principles of any legal order.

In the context here, stressing communication, efforts such as those of Hohfeld (see Hohfeld, 1919) are interesting. He argued that all law exists for the ordering of human relationships, the essential concepts being Right, Duty, Privilege, Power, Immunity and Liability. These, in practice, relate to one another, as jural opposites (Immunity-Liability) or jural correlatives (Right-Duty), in an elegant pattern of fundamental requirements. Codifiers within particular jurisdictions may even dream of 'mechanical law', whereby all legislation would be grounded in some such basic principles and systematized to the point where each decision is transparently correct and necessary.

The emphasis on necessity, albeit thoroughly rationalized, is important. Even in less ambitious schemes designed to prescribe and proscribe (religious pronouncements such as The Ten Commandments, and the various catechisms; Declarations of Constitutional or Human Rights; Regulations and rule-statements of all sorts . . . .) the central concept is that of control, either willingly complied with or imposed and sustained by threats and rewards.

Many political and philosophical problems spring up when we consider the mechanisms and systems embedded in all cultures as a result of which instead of anything happening anyhow only certain things happen in certain ways. One key point for the communication specialist is that the pattern and predictability which rule-following behavior brings about makes for an intelligible and (a matter of great importance to those who benefit most from the order thereby created) a manageable world. Control, the imposition of order, is vastly more efficient and discreet if it is not directly coercive but exercised semiotically. By influencing the symbolic order the social order is also influenced, if the initial claim of this paper (that much of social life comprises semiotic action and reaction) holds.

By managing the managers through the systematic rule statements comprising codes of this sort the administered world envisaged by Weber is made possible. Professionals are agents licensed and legitimated to act on society's behalf, according to rules both general and specific, explicit and tacit, and who frequently disguise their personal identities the better to enact their roles in maintaining the social order. It is a person who says 'This court finds . . . .', who disappears behind the institutional subject of 'We wouldn't recommend . . . .', or 'One prefers in general to recommend . . . .,' or who otherwise disguises real agency with such devices as the dummy subject ('It is forbidden to') and many forms of nominalization, passivization, euphemization, or deletion.

Many of these transformations apply especially to verbs and their auxiliaries, such as 'shall' and 'will', as well as the so-called modal verbs expressive of freedom and constraint ('may', 'must'). Some codes, for example the Code For Nurses issued by the ICN in Geneva already quoted from, virtually avoid direct imperatives preferring a verb form (at least in English) of legendary flexibility, the present tense, *viz* 'The nurse carries personal responsibility for nursing practice . . . .' The unassertive formulation contrasts with others, notably those drafted by, or directed against, members of professions whose conduct is typically or irreducibly controversial. Journalists in Britain already had Codes of Conduct or Practice long before, in November 1989 and March 1990 first the Newspaper Editors' Association and then the Press Council respectively issued their two attempts at setting the profession in order, and reproduced here as Appendix 1. The former favors the no-nonsense 'will' verb form while the latter favors plain statement ('It is the duty . . .') or the 'should' form, as does the Calcutt

Committee's own Proposed Code of Practice for the Press. (See 'Calcutt' 1990, Section 13.6 and Appendices L, P, Q).

The examples quoted and many others (e.g., the Civil Service Pay and Conditions of Service Code, HMSO 1987) have the effects already noted, of controlling key agents of the social order thereby maintaining that order in an intelligible and manageable form.

However there is another sense of the term 'code', of interest to the communication specialist, which may move us beyond the rather sinister conception discussed so far.

B. A communication code is a two-fold phenomenon, a set of signs along with a set of rules for their organized use in constructing messages. The link with the previous discussion of the term code as 'precepts for action' is obvious in that both involve rules. However, in the former sense the rules *are* the code. They state, explicitly or implicitly, compelling and prohibiting action in the rigid and non-negotiable codes, suggesting or dissuading in general terms (cf. handy hints and rules of thumb) in the cases where optionality and some degree of latitude is permissible, or inevitable because the behavior being regulated is so complex that the agent's common sense judgement has to be relied upon. Acting within the spirit of the law when the letter of the law is non-obvious is a good illustration of the practical problems of judicial processes, which always stop well short of the extreme notion of mechanical law alluded to above (cf. the debate about 'original intent' on the part of those who drafted the American Constitution, which bedevils the American judicial system).

The rules, however incomplete and vague at points, are the code. Also, they are stated *in* another code, typically language, which is a code in this second sense we are now considering, beginning with the importance of rules.

That languages are rule-dependent systems is a truism so evident as to pass unnoticed, except when we detect deviations from the rules we expect to be used or when we attempt seriously to explicate the rules, as the sub-disciplines of linguistics try to do. (The fact that we notice breaches and breakdowns of linguistic and other communication-code rules, and are oblivious to the infinite output of users which is consistent with the rules illustrates a basic principle, once again, concerning the invisibility of the normal and conversely).

In the case of communication codes, we need to distinguish what might be called internal rules from external rules. Firstly, the signs a code deploys are not selected randomly or allocated to their individual significations randomly. The number system of arithmetic, for example, makes uses of a limited set of shapes, regulated combinations of which give the numbers which we traditionally (i.e., conventionally) link with values on a scale. In principle, these signifier-signified relationships are all arbitrary, as is the case with the words of our languages, but only in principle. Individuals are not free to reallocate the signifiers to the signifieds.

The main internal 'ruled for organized use' govern horizontal and vertical combinations of number and other functional signs, generating organized statements of the arithmetical code: 321 is not 123, 4/5 not 5/4 etc. At this level of pattern-forming, all combinations are meaningful, in arithmetic, which is not the case with language where ambiguity and incoherence can be created by the production of underegulated or irregular combinations. JOHN LOVES MARY is not MARY LOVES JOHN (cf. 321/123), as is clear from the syntactic rules of English, but JOHN MARY LOVES/LOVES MARY JOHN etc. are ambiguous/archaic (at least in the written form). OF THE OF IF OF is radically incoherent, eschewing as it does the basic rules of syntax. (The fact that someone can, with ingenuity and effort, make *some* sense of these rule-breaking structures in irrelevant).

Beyond the sentence what are sometimes called co-textual rules move us towards the category that has been called external rules, ie rules outwith the essential structure-forming internal rules of language. To know only the phonology syntax and semantics of a language is to fall far short of communicative competence, a concept which refers to the ability to use language (and other codes) appropriately. It comprises at least the following: *co-textual* rules (e.g., maintaining relevance to topic, consistency of style, genre characteristics, intertextuality in all its forms, etc.); and *contextual rules* (interpersonal considerations; anticipated conditions of reception up to and including the institutional and cultural settings in which the message will do the job intended for it . . . .

There is clearly a continuum here, from deeply internal rules out to rules of appropriate use in real situations, which are entirely social matters. It has nothing to do with arithmetic per se if we use to count the dead in a famine or the tons of food rotting in our warehouse any more than it is centrally important for language (or any particular language) that it can supply its users with fascist, racist, sexist, ageist, ablist, or whatever forms of talk.

This returns us to themes and issues raised earlier, which we may now address by considering two essential features of communication codes.

Firstly, the interlocking internal and external rule systems briefly sketched are generative, a mathematical property routinely demonstrated in the originality of even turgid or ill-considered utterances such as the present one, the author of which is fairly confident has never before been constructed just like this in the history of the language and the reader of which no doubt hopes never to encounter again, now that it is complete. A simple experiment would be for the reader to copy it out and wait for its next appearance, which is improbable to the vanishing point.

This amazing fact remains the most interesting feature of our richer communication codes. Their fecundity is boundless, not only in the behavior of the gifted but in the lives of ordinary people. Because what is coming next is underdetermined it is relatively interesting, which would not be the case in a mechanical universe. (First principles appear yet again). Because it is underdetermined it must be managed, mostly by ourselves as users who decide to speak or not; if so, to say this or that; if this, in this way or that, for theses purposes or those . . . etc.

However, what we come to mean can also be influenced by others, typically in the benign give-and-take of interpersonal influence as when we tease, use sarcasm, try to persuade, defend ourselves against misunderstanding by others and so on. The outright (ab)use of language as an instrument of power, by an individual performing that power semiotically ('I pronounce you . . . .') or more insidiously in the ideological pollution we absorb unnoticed in acquiring our mother tongues, should not obscure the normality of creativity or disable the potential we all possess for linguistic (and other) cunning.

This leads to the second major feature of communication codes, which is that they have to be used intentionally. Especially in codes where individual signifier-signified relationships are arbitrary (BIG is a little word: MINIATURE is quite a big word) and where in phrases and sentences it is always possible to say the same thing in different ways, different things in the same way, we normally have no choice but to make the choices listed above (to speak or not etc.). Note that 'to make the choices' is ambiguous, for creating the options from which we choose is choice of a different order from merely choosing from what is on offer. The already-noted fecundity of the communication codes all cultures possess, together with the arbitrariness that severs signifier and signified, code and massage, enable that potential. Meaning has to be meant.

For all of these reasons, normal communicative behavior is behavior for which we are more rather than less responsible and are so deemed by those within our semiotic range. A wink is not a blink (but may, mistakenly, be taken for one) and vice versa. Seeing to it that we make appropriate sense and are uptaken appropriately by others is routine business for us in societies where fully two-way interaction with others is still the norm. The encroachments of one way 'mass' media, and of professionals dependent upon our compliance in renegotiating the footing on which some exchanges barely worthy of the term take place (with or without published Codes for our reassurance or even the customer-relations training now imposed on public servants) should not deflect us from the most important and fundamental sense of the term 'code', sketched above and indispensable in meaningful social communication life.

In conclusion we should perhaps note a third sense of the word code. So-called 'secret codes' as used in the world of espionage or in computer security are special cases of the conditions that apply to any communication code. Given that there are no truly universal codes, any code that we use will be opaque to at least some of our potential audience. 'Encryption' whereby plain text is transformed according to rules, emerging in apparently scrambled bundles of the original signifiers, or in different signifiers altogether (cf. the huge strings of 1's and 0's that the machine language of computers deals in) merely systematizes what we all do when choosing to encode a message in text that is anything but plain to monoglot speakers of other languages. See the diagram in Endnote 2, which can also be applied to the variants and subcodes in use within a given language. Jargon, for example, is not usually widespread in a community, is usually restricted to certain sorts of topics, and is frequently used as a semi-secret code for the exclusion and/or intimidation of the uninitiated. This, of course, returns us to the central issues raised by the title of the paper.

This last sense of code is also in play, of course, when we hear of 'coded language' being used in political discourse. Some form of disguise is at work as a result of which plain and above-board text is reworked. The effect may be to by-pass, baffle or mislead unwanted decoders who may or may not be aware that another message exists within the signifying bundle. Often, unwanted are not the speaker's concern so much as unwanted decodings, or at least, decodings that he or she would rather not acknowledge were intended if challenged. Coded language, then, allows us to say what we want to say obliquely, while remaining free to deny the intent. Some of the saving graces of civilized social life, such as sarcasm and tact, belong here. They are examples of institutionalized withdrawal from the contract outlined above, as well as examples of how codes, in the second of our main senses, engender creativity even including their subversion by artful users mindful of what they are about.

ENDNOTES

1. William T. Scott is Professor of Communications at Glasgow Polytechnic, Scotland.

2. At some point in all our lives we are semiotically and otherwise culturally incompetent. Deliberate or unwitting exclusion of some potential participants by use of a language known only to some present, or by use of a sub-code of a language (eg jargon -- or dialect-laden speech) are examples of such disenfranchisement. The philosophical problem of ineffability raises similar issues.

   The general array of possibilities we all negotiate within can be summarized as follows, where A-B displays the proportion of members in a community familiar with a code/sub-code and C-D the range of topics that a code can readily accommodate. Plain or everyday speech would score high on both, (top-right) heraldry or some obscure bunch of mathematics low (bottom-left). Other positions on the two dimensional array raise equally interesting questions about the extent of our communicative and cultural competence, and about the relationship between the two.

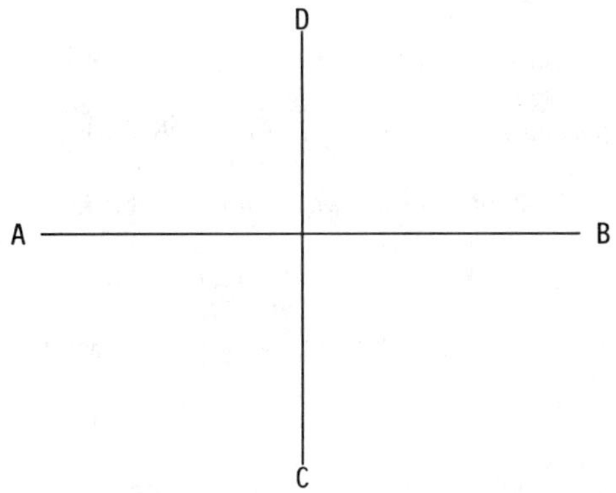

APPENDIX 1

In addition to the various codes of professional practice mentioned in the text here, and hence listed in the references, many others are freely available, indeed widely advertised. The Advertising Standards Authority encourages the public to send for its Code, entitled the British Code of Advertising Practice, which it enforces as publicly as possible.

The Broadcasting Bill of 1990 requires the Broadcasting Standards Council to devise, publish and enforce a Code of Practice, with particular regard to sensitive topics. (See the BBC's own current guidelines for factual programs, dealing with 86 categories of topic from 'accidents and disasters' to 'women.')

The Newspaper Editors Code of November 1987 is as follows:

> 'We, the editors of all Britain's national newspapers, declare our determination to defend the democratic right of the people to a Press free from government interference.

While pursuing our campaigns for a Freedom of Information Act and reform of libel and contempt law, we have also given due consideration to criticism of the Press in Parliament and by the public.

While supporting the Press Council, each individual national newspaper now accepts the need to improve its own methods of self-regulation, including procedures for dealing promptly and fairly with complaints.

Editors have agreed on a common code of practice and the establishment of systems of ombudsmen to take up complaints and breaches of the code. The ombudsmen's authority will be set out in formal terms of reference.

They will safeguard standards of accuracy, fairness and the conduct of journalists.

They will have the power to question journalists and editorial executives. They will have the right to require prompt publication of statements of correction and to have their findings published.

If a dispute cannot be settled in this way, the right to appeal to the Press Council, of course, remains.'

THE CODE

With variations, this is the Code adopted by national newspapers.

'RESPECT FOR PRIVACY: Intrusion into private lives should always have a public-interest justification.

OPPORTUNITY FOR REPLY: A fair opportunity for reply will be given when reasonably called for.

PROMPT CORRECTIONS: Mistakes will be corrected promptly and with appropriate prominence.

CONDUCT OF JOURNALISTS: Subject only to the existence of an over-riding public interest, information for publication will be obtained by straight-forward means. Similarly, newspapers will not authorize payment to criminals or to their families and associates to enable them to profit from crime.

RACE,COLOR: Irrelevant references to race, color and religion will be avoided.'

(*British Journalism Review*, Vol 1, No 2, 1990, p 49)

The Press Council's effort of March 1990 is:

1 ACCURACY -- It is the duty of newspapers not to publish deliberately or carelessly, inaccuracies or statements, designed to mislead, and to correct promptly and with due prominence, significant inaccuracies which they have published, or misleading statements for which they are responsible, apologizing for these where appropriate.

2 OPPORTUNITY TO REPLY -- It is the duty of newspapers to allow a fair opportunity for reply when reasonably called for.

3 PRIVACY -- Publishing material, or making inquiries about the private lives of individuals without their consent is not acceptable, unless these are in the public interest, overriding the right of privacy. The Press Council's
Declaration of Principle on Privacy should be observed.

4 COMMENT AND FACT -- Newspapers are free to be partisan, but they should distinguish between comment and fact. Conjecture should not be elevated into statements of fact.

5 SUBTERFUGE -- Newspapers and journalists serving them should use straightforward means to obtain information or pictures. Their use of subterfuge can be justified only to obtain material which ought to be published in the public interest and could not be obtained by other means.

6 PAYMENTS FOR ARTICLES -- Payments or offers of payment for stories, pictures, or information should not be made to witnesses or potential witnesses in current criminal proceedings, or to people engaged in crime or their associates, except where the material concerned ought to be published in the public interest, and the payment is necessary to enable this to be done. The Press Council's Declaration of Principle on Payment for Articles should be observed.

7 INTRUSION INTO GRIEF -- Newspapers and journalists serving them should in general avoid intruding into personal grief. Inquiries should be carried out with sympathy and discretion.

8 INNOCENT RELATIVES -- Newspapers should exercise care and discretion before identifying relatives of persons convicted or accused of crime, where the reference to them is not directly relevant to the matter reported.

9 INTERVIEWING CHILDREN -- Journalists should not normally interview a child under the age of 16 in the absence of, or without the consent of, the parent or other adult who is responsible for the child.

10 CHILDREN IN SEX CASES -- Save in exceptional circumstances, newspapers should not, even where the law permits it, identify children under the age of 16 as victims, witnesses, or defendants involved in cases concerning sexual offenses.

11 RAPE VICTIMS -- Newspapers should not identify victims of rape, or publish material likely to contribute to such identification.

12 PICTURES -- Newspapers should refrain from publishing pictures which needlessly exacerbate grief or cause distress.

13 RACE AND COLOR -- Newspapers should not publish material likely to encourage discrimination on grounds of race or color, and should avoid reference to people's race or color in prejudicial or pejorative contexts unless they are directly relevant to the story.

14 FINANCIAL JOURNALISM -- Journalists should not use for their own profit financial information they receive in advance of its general publication. The Press Council's Declaration of Principle on Financial Journalism should be observed.

15 HOSPITALS -- Journalists making inquiries at hospitals or similar institutions should identify themselves to a responsible official before entering, except in very rare cases, where information which ought to be disclosed could not otherwise be obtained.

16 CONFIDENTIAL SOURCES -- Journalists have an obligation to protect confidential sources of information.'

(*The Glasgow Herald*, 15.3.90)

The Police have operated since 1882 under a Police Code, which has been amended repeatedly. Revised Codes of Practice, within the English jurisdiction, for specific activities (e.g., identification parades; detention and interrogation; stop and search on the streets, etc.) will be published by the Home Office early in 1991. Meanwhile, the Association of Chief Police Officers, in collaboration with the Home Office and in response to considerable public disquiet about police methods, published the following during 1990.

> 'The purpose of the Police Service is to uphold the law fairly and firmly, to prevent crime, to pursue and bring to justice those who break the law, to keep the Queen's Peace, to protect, help and reassure the community, and to be seen to do all this with integrity, common sense and sound judgement.
>
> We must be compassionate, courteous and patient, acting without fear or favor or prejudice to the rights of others. We need to be professional, calm and restrained in the face of violence and apply only that force which is necessary to accomplish our lawful duty.
>
> We must strive to reduce the fears of the public and, so far as we can, to reflect their priorities in the action we take. We must respond to well-founded criticism with a willingness to change.'

The Department of Employment published a comprehensive code of Good Practice on the Employment of Disabled People, among many others from among the various categories of professionals active in our society.

REFERENCES

Anscombe, G.E.M., 1979, *Intention*, Oxford: Blackwell.

Bryne, P.S. and Long, B.E.C., 1976, *Doctors Talking to Patients*, London: HMSO

Dingwall, R. and Lewis, P. (eds), 1983, *Sociology Of The Professions: Lawyers, doctors and others*, London: Macmillan.

Fasold, R., 1984, *The Sociolinguistics of Society*, Oxford: Blackwell.

_____, 1990, *The Sociolinguistics of Language*, Oxford: Blackwell.

Fisch, Stanley, 1989, *Doing what Comes Naturally: Change, Rhetoric and the Practice of Theory in Literary and Legal Studies*, Oxford: Oxford University Press.

Goodrich, P., 1987, *Legal Discourse*, London: Macmillan.

Grice, H.P., 1975, 'Logic and Conversation' in *Syntax and Semantics*, 3, New York: Academic Press.

HMSO,1990, *The Civil Service Pay and Conditions Code*, London: House of Commons Treasury and Civil Service Committee Order paper number 2601, Session 1989-90.

HMSO, 1990, *Report of the Committee on Privacy and Related Matters*, 'The Calcutt Committee,' London: HMSO CM 1102, June 1990.

Hinde, R.A., ed., 1972, *Nonverbal Communication*, Cambridge: Cambridge University Press.

Hohfeld, W.N., 1964, *Fundamental Legal Conceptions*, Cook, M.W., ed., New Haven/London: Yale University Press.

Jackson, B.S., 1988, *Law, Fact and Narrative Coherence*, Liverpool: Deborah Charles Publications.

Lance, Bennett W. and Feldman, M.S., 1981, *Reconstructing Reality in the Courtroom*, London: Tavistock.

Mackay, D.M., 1972, 'Formal Analysis of Communicative Processes,' in Hinde, R.A. ed., *Nonverbal Communication*, Cambridge: Cambridge University Press.

McLean, S.A.M., 1989, *The Patient's Right to Know, Information, Disclosure, the Doctor and the Law*, Dartmouth: Gower.

Mellinkoff, D., *The Language of the Law*, Boston: Little, Brown.

Ostwald, P.F., 1964, 'How the Patient Communicates About Disease With the Doctor,' in Sebeok, T.A. et al, eds., *Approaches to Semiotics*, The Hague: Mouton.

Parfit, D., 1987/1984, *Reasons and Persons*, Oxford: Clarendon Press.

Pendleton, D.A. And Hasler, J.C., eds., 1983, *Doctor-Patient Communication*, New York, London: Academic Press.

Raffler-Engel, W.V., 1989, *Doctor-Patient Interaction*, Amsterdam: John Benjamins.

Saville-Troike, M., 1989, *The Ethnography of Communication*, Blackwell.

Scott, W.T., 1990, *The Possibility of Communication*, Berlin/New York: Mouton de Gruyter.

_____, 'Candor, Euphemism and the Professional-Client Relationship,' *International Journal for the Semiotics of Law*, III/9, 1990: 255-272.

Sebeok, T.A. et al, eds., 1964, *Approaches to Semiotics*, The Hague: Mouton.

United Kingdom Central Council For Nursing, Midwifery and Health Visiting, 1984, *Code of Professional Conduct*, London: 23 Portland Place, London W1N 3A1.

Chapter 22

A Semiotic Model of Economic Theory

Gordon E. Whitney[1]

I

Economics is a social science devoted to the analysis of the production and consumption of both goods and services with a view to guiding the process of choice used by the various controlling actors. Peircean semiotics is a method of representation of reality by means of an irreducibly triadic schema under the abstract categories he named: Firstness ('qualitative state of feelings'), Secondness ('the facts of actual events'), and Thirdness ('the rules which determine what could-be'). This triadic approach combines theory and practice in an attempt to form models of reality which include human actors whose behavior is not limited to what can be modeled formally, mechanically, or mathematically. The triadic model of economic actors includes informal as well as formal causes for action and allows for adaptive behavior which includes formation of habits deemed useful for the future.

When an individual or a unified community reflects on past experience, it forms for itself an abstraction of past Secondness known in philosophy as a 'form of life.' Royce did not use this phrase but he did adopt Peirce's irreducible triad when he wrote: 'Rights are defined . . . only in terms of duties. I have a right to my life because it gave me my sole opportunity to do my duty. It is an old teaching: rights and duties are correlative . . . of late unpopular.'[2] In triadic interpretation, 'Duties' as necessities are thirds, while 'Rights' as possibilities are firsts. The importance of economics for the application of law has been indicated by Malloy (1990) who also notes the effect of social philosophy on judicial decisions.

II

A Framework for Human Experience

All personal experience occurs within a 'framework' of incompletely interpreted prior experience and immediate context. Diverse human cultures establish distinctive forms of life so that what is observed as significant is conditioned by that culture as ways of acting, feeling, and thinking about experience. While each culture through its language and culture supplies the means of giving expression to experience, the framework of this experience, at its deepest level, is never expressed, indeed is inexpressible. Thus Charles Peirce argued against Descartes' concept of absolute doubt and against applying the 'law of contradiction' to human affairs, since our investigations must always start 'with mediate data, subject to error, and requiring correction' (CP 7.464). And while our skill in marking differences and likenesses enables us to conjecture new possibilities, 'The truth is there are no data' (CP 7.464), by which we understand that without both a framework of knowing and a theory of interpretation, no experience can be reported as an event of data.[3]

Since the framework of knowing is our starting point, we will characterize 'monadic knowing' as consisting of the raw data of experience placed against this framework. The existence of monadic knowing is not only inadequate, it is mythical. Since monadic knowing gives no insights, we see that philosophers are prone to utilize 'dyadic knowing' which includes the data of experience contained within a related theory of interpretation, both placed against a framework of knowing. Peirce's unique contribution to philosophy was the discovery that a triadic (or polyadic) theory of knowing was both necessary and sufficient. By a principle of triadic substitution a tetradic theory can always be reduced to a triadic one. Peirce through the logic of relations and through personal phenomenology arrived at his three categories of which secondness contains fact and experience, while thirdness and firstness are partitions of the traditional 'theory of knowing' or 'modes of being'. Firstness and thirdness can be seen as polarized vertically with respect to the sphere of action. On the upper side action is restricted, based on rules of habit and necessity; while from below action is open to possibility, creativity, freedom, and spontaneity all acting in response to context. Peircean action then is a resolution, in the immediacy of the present, of two polarized forces, characterized by the contrast between possibility and necessity.

III

Triadic Representation of the Hierarchy of Reality

M. Polanyi utilized a dyadic theory of knowing when he distinguished mental activity into focal and subsidiary awareness. However as he developed his own categories, he proposed that focal awareness occurs at a particular level in a hierarchy of physical reality and that every focal level exists under dual control: an upper level which exercises constraints from above and a lower level which provides an open system of possibilities. A standard example is the living cell which is constrained from below by the properties of molecules, and from above by the functions required of it in the context of life.[4]

S. Salthe has set forth an elaborate exposition of triadic modeling suited to evolutionary biology but general enough to be useful in both physical and social sciences. Salthe introduces a large number of terms which he uses with precision. We sketch the interrelationship of his more important terms: A *hierarchy* is to be distinguished from a *heterarchy* and is the basic unit of all analysis; any actual hierarchy is characterized by a *partial order* of its component parts; each hierarchy is representable by a series of ascending *basic triadic systems*, each consisting of a *functional hierarchy* of which the center of the triad is Polanyi's *focal level,* surrounded by *boundary conditions* which are polarized relative to the focal level, so that the upper level exercises *regulation* and the lower level *activation* relative to the focal level; events at the focal level are *actualities* which occur within an *input/output environment* and are manifest as an instance, which shows the purpose of the focal level; *processes* may be distinguished from *events* and both are manifestations of *immanent* and *emergent possibilities.* Salthe also draws on the metaphysics of J. Buchler and indirectly on Peirce. Buchler defines a *natural complex* as a concept created by interpretation of some aspect of reality within an *order*. The number of such orders is not limited and any complex may belong to many, according to the point of view of the interpreter. Every complex is subject to two fundamental properties: *prevalence* and *alescence,* which represent respectively 'stability of enduring existence,' and 'ability to change'. In Peircean terms these correspond to the 'regularities of thirdness,' and the 'spontaneity of firstness' respectively.[5]

Learning. All living things must adapt their behavior to the changing environment in order to survive. Two persons participating in different ways in an economic transaction may learn, from different perspectives, entirely different things as a by product of this exchange. Also F. Hayek has characterized the free market, as a process in which prices are allowed to change and these changes are information to suppliers and consumers who adapt their behavior accordingly. The market itself repeats continuously a learning or discovery process as it adapts price at a point in time to a balance between the forces of supply and demand. In terms of the triadic model, learning is a feedback process which takes two forms. A feedback signal which causes change is called *positive* and this signal itself is polarized so as to cause an increase or a decrease in the parameter being controlled, i.e. supply or demand. This positive feedback signal will apply primarily to triadic firstness as this is the factor which introduces change. A second kind of feedback signal is called *negative* and its character is to establish stability and to confirm rules previously learned. This negative feedback signal is an aspect of thirdness as a rule-following and rule-preserving system.

IV
The French Turn in Social Theory

Hayek has identified a major family or school of economic thought which is contrary to his own and which he feels needs to be identified and its error exposed, lest it lead nations into an economic ruin brought on by a totalitarian, centrally planned economy. He traces the origin of this school to the early writings of Rousseau, and to Rousseau's dependence on Descartes for philosophic inspiration. We deal with the Scottish school which opposed Rousseau in the next section.

Hayek traces the 'French Turn' in social theory to a departure from medieval social tradition. A late representative of this social tradition is Luis Molina (1535-1600), whose theory was that a law-abiding community prospers through a divine providence which permits a spontaneous order beneficial to all members. This social order develops slowly through incremental changes in tradition and in law. A similar emphasis on the need for and benefits of continuity of tradition within a community is found in Vico with his emphasis on the philosophic wisdom to be found in successful social practices and in the *sensus communis* which is best rendered 'consensus of the community.'[6] Such a consensus need not exist in legislation to have value which benefits the community. Like Hayek, and Peirce, Vico also opposed Descartes. These three all viewed Descartes as having taken a turn for philosophy which broke continuity with medieval tradition. The outcome of this turn ultimately was positivism on the one side and Marxist-communism on the other. Hayek provides a useful summary of this position:

> [French] rationalism [is] the doctrine which assumes that all institutions which benefit humanity have in the past and ought in the future to be invented in clear awareness of the desirable effects that they produce; . . . It is from this kind of social rationalism or constructivism that all modern socialism, planning and totalitarianism derives. This . . . 'social contract' view has no place for social theory proper . . . it demands that every action should be judged in full awareness of all its foreseeable results -- a view which in the last resort tends to dispense with all abstract rules and leads to the claim that man can achieve a desirable order of society by concretely arranging all its parts in full knowledge or all the relevant facts.[7]

To illustrate where authoritarian planning led England under the Labor Government around 1948, Hayek cites three books, whose titles alone confirm his position: *Ordeal by Planning* (1948), *The Socialist Tragedy* (1949), and *The Passing of Parliament* (1952). Additional confirmation of economic failure of the

'French Turn' is given by Eberstadt, whose work done in the 1970s was clearly prophetic. The patterns he describes have now led to the breakup of the European communist community and to the reunification of Germany.[8] The French turn has an associated theological doctrine. It denies or ignores the presence of sinful tendencies in man. It holds that reason is able to cure the disease of sin. It looks forward to an earthly utopia under a benevolent dictator. Indeed, democracy does not confer on its leaders the authority needed to carry out such a rational program of planning and control. Rousseau's new kind of social order is inherently totalitarian.

V

Spontaneous Economic Order

Hayek's study of the history of economic thought does not yield all negative results. For he aligns himself with those who extended the medieval concept of social continuity achieving incremental economic progress under divine providence. This is the school of Mandeville, Adam Smith, and Carl Menger. In history it includes Herder and in law, Savigny. For this school the growth of social order is a pattern similar to the way one cares for a garden. The soil cannot be forced by reason alone to produce, but the gardener applies certain rules learned from experience and tradition. He believes that a garden cared for in a certain way is more likely to flourish, while the actual outcome, is partly out of his control.

Applying this analogy to economics, we find that human beings tend to cooperate for their own mutual benefit. Now such cooperation has many preconditions and can be disrupted by such social unrest as leads to riots or war.

For social order to evolve for the mutual benefit of all community members, there must be a time of peace and there must be some force to establish lawful protection of what traditionally are termed 'private property and contracts.' As abundantly illustrated by Adam Smith, given a law-abiding society, with private property safe from war and riot, men tend to cooperate and benefit mutually from such cooperation. The development of a stable currency moves society to participate in a market-based economy where specialization and industrialization make the whole society, not just the sovereign, more wealthy. According to Smith this beneficial process of free trade, specialization and market economy, is not directed by some all knowing central planner but rather by the 'invisible hand' of divine providence. It became known as a system which was the result of human action, but 'not of human design.'

The need for men to be protected from one another by law is consistent with the Judeo-Christian tradition which affirmed the sinful tendencies of men. This tradition provided restraints for these tendencies and the initiative of the law abiding individual might be rewarded by prosperity. In Smith's time the protestant work ethic gave religious support to the free-market economy based on a new ideal type, one for which a secular vocation could be deemed a proper religious calling. This was a departure from pre-Reformation Catholic ideals where the highest calling for a religious person was to service within the church. The claim that capitalism has a religious basis may be too strong, but it is clear that the mainly protestant nations, Germany, Holland, England and America, did achieve a more rapid internal economic development than did the European Catholic states. Thus, protestantism seems to have fostered that kind of social order in which others not motivated at all by religion but rather by desire for personal gain could bring about an ever-increasing prosperity through a competitive market economy.[9]

VI

The Triadic Shape of Economic Actors

According to Peirce, all thought is by means of signs. Every sign exists only with a framework or ground which unlike the sign cannot be signified or expressed and which against Descartes must remain as a subsidiary form of knowing -- partly inexpressible. Yet, since human life is then a stream of signs, man himself may be viewed as a complex composite sign. Viewing man as a sign we are led to consider the triadic nature of such a sign. This leads to a reformulation of traditional faculty psychology, where man had a triadic nature consisting of the powers of reason, will and feeling (or cognition, volition and emotions). While this theory was based on the now-rejected theory that the soul was divisible into 'faculties', yet it is instructive to locate these traditional faculties within our new triadic categories. Since secondness, the sphere of action, is not a capability or a nature, no faculty is assigned to it. This leaves duties (thirds) and freedoms (firsts) as categories open for assignment. While not all cognition can be classified as mechanical, certainly some mental acts are patterned exactly as the mechanical following of a rule, as with the rules of addition. Other acts, like riding a bicycle, are formed by habit and effort (physical and mental) and follow rules which are based on skill not formal reason. That aspect of cognition which is formally understood can be classified as thirdness. However, this leaves volition and emotion, the aspects of the non-formal sources of one's personal 'form of life,' to be found in firstness.[10]

Buchler has introduced the idea of the contour or shape of his fundamental metaphysical object, the 'natural complex'. This contour exists within every 'order' in which interpretive analysis assigns a concept a 'location'. Such 'locations' include both personal opinions and scientific facts. Extending Buchler's concept of the 'contour' of a natural complex, we propose that the collection of three triadic categories be viewed as a visual object for the purpose of comparative concept formation. Since secondness (action) is a dependent category, it can be viewed as an infinitely thin border between firstness and thirdness, and can in this way be effectively omitted from consideration in assigning shape to human nature. Following Peirce's suggestion that every sign has a certain area of significance, and the area being visualized as a rectangle, we see thirdness as having both breadth and height above the focal level, and firstness having breadth and depth below it.[11] Consider, then, the triadic shapes of certain ideal types: dictator, serf, and product innovator, and for each of these we analyze internal and external relations.

Dictator. This ideal type is under no direct external authority. He may be by nature cruel or paternal but in neither case is this a role forced by external necessity, tradition or law. Thus, he has in his role a minimal zone of personal duties or rules and a maximal zone of personal freedoms. Montesquieu wisely observes the beneficial effects of religion on a dictator: 'A prince who loves and fears religion, is a lion who stoops to the hand that strokes [it, but] . . . he who has no religion at all is that terrible animal who perceives his liberty only when he tears in pieces and when he devours.' Hitler held to the ideal of the essential superiority of the Germanic race. Yet this ideal while freely chosen, through use became a habit, and eventually it became for him a mechanical principle of reasoning. It is primarily in initial choices that the dictator has reduced duties (thirds) and maximum freedoms (firsts).[12]

Serf. A serf as a triadic shape has the inverse profile of a dictator. He has a minimal zone of freedom and is subject to an external system of rules which exercise control over most of his form of life. Poverty is not the same as serfdom since it is not directly imposed as a system of rules which control behavior. Poverty reduces possibilities without increasing duties.

Product Innovator. We visualize this ideal type within a market economy. He is subject to the same rule system as other citizens. What characterizes this triadic shape is an expanded sphere of freedom and creativity relative to others (under the same legal constraints) who do not avail themselves of the opportunity for innovation. An innovator of a new product benefits both himself and others. He increases the available wealth in his society and thus increases for others their sphere of firstness. This is not the case with a dictator whose exercise of personal freedom brings no increase in the wealth or opportunities while his freedoms become constraints on the form of life of those under his rule. No social order is possible with a plurality of dictators within one society, and such a state will be at war with itself until one leader prevails.

In every society, the number of successful innovators will always be small. But the pattern of innovation is learned in a society by imitation. Planned or controlled societies minimize innovation and therefore do not build a pattern of tradition for the training of potential innovators. Not only will such societies fail to achieve relative wealth as a nation, but if they try to change to a free market economy, they will lack a layer of skilled innovators who can rapidly generate economic growth. In any change to a free economy, excessive layers of government officials will have to be dismantled with an associated disruption of the social order. In highly controlled economies the pattern of economic innovation which yields a personal reward, usually financial, is missing. Instead, innovative types learn how to make political progress by advancing within the ruling hierarchy, and not by a contribution to economic progress.

VII

Tocqueville's Ideal Society

In May 1831, Alexis de Tocqueville, age 25, arrived from France and began a 9 month tour of most of the then current states of the United States. Based on this visit, he authored his classic, *Democracy in America.* Being well aware of France's earlier 'Reign of Terror' and her own recurring difficulty in establishing a stable democracy, he admired America's institutions and form of life. His work issued warnings to both sides of the Atlantic, as to where the current strengths and weaknesses of the American institutions lay. He concluded that in America the active role of self interest could be successful only so long as it was formed and guided by a religious morality emphasizing 'Mutual solidarity over individual dominance.' So his summary: 'while physical circumstances of the United States have contributed to the maintenance of a democratic republic, laws have contributed more than those circumstances and mores (French: *moeurs*) more than laws' and 'an undermining [of] American mores is the most certain road to undermining the free institutions of the United States.'[13]

The best paraphrase of *moeurs* is the phrase 'habits of the heart' which should be understood as those notions, opinions and ideas that shape mental habits and as the sum of moral and intellectual dispositions of men in society. Mores also involve habits associated with religion, political participation and economic life. Following this theme Zubiri, noting that Tocqueville was a lifelong student of Pascal makes a connection between the two through the concept of the heart:

> In Pascal we are witness in part to one of the few fully realized attempts to apprehend philosophical concepts which are capable of encompassing some of the important dimensions of man. For example, his concept of 'heart,' so vague, is true but on account of

> its vagueness badly understood and poorly used. It does not mean blind sentiment as opposed to pure Cartesian reason, but the knowledge constitutive of the day-to-day and radical being of man.[14]

Relative to our own agenda, we should seek to classify Tocqueville's 'habits of the heart' with respect to firstness and thirdness. Peirce assigned habits to thirdness but in lectures on 'Vitally Important Topics' (CP 1.616-676) he warned against depending on reason rather than prior moral training in matters involving moral judgment. He notes that adultery or embezzlement when continuously reasoned upon could yield in reason an apparently logical case for doing that which the heart knows to be wrong.

We see 'habits of the heart' as a theme which needs to be assigned to both thirdness and firstness, since it carries with it ideas of both duty and freedom within a moral tradition. This can be done in two stages, first by defining a model of man in society as an outer triad. In such a triad, the society supplies all the formal rules of thirdness. The personal dimension then is restricted to firstness. Within this firstness we can impose another inner triad with an inner firstness and an inner thirdness. Before one acts, there is a two stage process of conflict resolution: first there is a resolution of tension present within the 'habits of the heart' (between reason and emotion) establishing for this case the immediate private desires; next a second stage of resolution between private desires and public restraints finally producing action. This final resolution occurs at the level of the outer triad.

Kukathas's Critique of Hayek. Kukathas has given an appreciative yet critical study of Hayek's political philosophy. He identifies Hayek's key contribution as recognizing the crucial error of rational constructionism (the school of Rousseau) as 'its refusal to see the limitations of reason', partly due to fallible knowledge of context. He seems to agree with Hayek that growth of constructivism leads toward a totalitarian society. Yet he claims that Hayek has fallen into a kind of error in methodology. Hayek assumes that Hume and Kant have the same program and support each other. While Rawls and Hare have explicitly tried to achieve a Hume/Kant reconciliation, the current philosophic consensus is that such an effort must fail and Kukathas suggests:

> Liberal theorists should turn away from their preoccupation with uncovering the Kantian foundations for liberalism, and look again to Hume. . . . [and] A society is more than . . . its contractual ties, it coheres because people share common beliefs and practices.[15]

We suggest that Hayek's recurring use of the term 'anti-rationalism' for his position is not an actual error but rather that his terminology is both inadequate and out of date. While rationalism may be triadic thirdness, the spontaneity of firstness is not equivalent to 'anti-rationalism.' We noted above that one essential characteristic of a person is 'habits of the heart.' As Pascal claimed: 'The heart has its reasons which reason cannot know.' We would suggest that Pascal's former reason is an instance of freedom and the latter a form of mechanical rules. While Kukathas's critique is significant, it can be answered by a Peircean restatement of Hayek's position. Reason (thirdness) and the sentiments and creativity of the heart (firstness) interact to produce the social order. This social order may be based on a law of love, a law of fair dealing, or a law of greed (see Peirce's essay 'Evolutionary Love,' CP 6.287-317). Under a 'law of fair dealing' each does his duty to benefit himself within the law and that contributes to that spontaneous order in which all benefit through specialization and sharing through trade and exchange. While under the 'law of greed,' by deliberate fraud or by border line dealing, some seek success at others expense. This in an extreme example was the pattern of Hitler's wars of unprovoked aggression and mass genocide. Here greed extended to a lust for international power which included wealth as one factor. For Peirce, 'the law of love' is the force of long term enduring change in human affairs. It is not merely the opposite of greed but is a force of change superior to greed and which subsumes it at a higher level. As a summary of his social philosophy Peirce in 1910 wrote:

> I am an old-fashioned christian, a believer in the efficacy of prayer, an opponent of female suffrage and universal male suffrage, in favor of letting business-methods develop with out the interference of law, a disbeliever in democracy.[16]

VIII

Natural Law as a Basis for Social Reform

Hamowy has supplied a social critique of Hayek's dependence on the 'spontaneous social order' noting: 'it militates against . . . reform. Thus sutee in India, the binding of feet in China, slavery in the southern states, all could claim the protective shield of tradition.'[17]

Hayek's model of freedom -- based on consensus which minimizes that form of coercion which comes from central planning -- is independent of the question of whether there will be social progress. It is consistent with Polanyi's idea that true progress requires both 'dwelling-in' and 'breaking-out-of' traditions. The 'breaking out' is relative to the 'dwelling-in' and is never total. The danger of the totalitarian myth according to Peirce, Hayek and Polanyi is two-fold: (1) the denial of an inexpressible framework of knowing and (2) the false promises of a social contract which rejects continuity with traditions and morals. Any reform must both destroy and create. To achieve more than it destroys, reform must be based on a wide consensus that includes the truth that man is capable of both good and evil.[18]

Slavery. Hamowy's claim that 'spontaneous social order' did not end slavery is not historically grounded. In England abolition came through a change of law, pioneered by religious leaders. In America, under Lincoln's leadership, the goal was achieved through a war which neither side wanted and at great cost to both sides. In both England and America, spontaneous social order was effective within the parties of the contest throughout the process of change. In totalitarian societies, abolition came even more slowly; as for example in Cuba. Spontaneous social order permits but does not force social reform which comes not from a profit motive alone but more from habits of the heart. Spontaneous social order does not force but it does permit a consciousness that human rights is a value to be sought.

Ghetto Social Problems. The large inner cities of America have deep problems of long duration which show no positive trend toward solution. The spontaneous social order found there does not bring increased prosperity because the preconditions of a stable order are absent. These societies are partly characterized by: underemployment, lawlessness, decaying housing, ineffective public education, lack of civic pride, and drug abuse. We note with Malloy, that housing is one factor in the economic matrix that locks these communities in a downward trend. He provides insight and documentation to show the negative effects on the community, of government interference with the free market supply of housing. Wise proposals have been made to reverse this trend by substituting a 'rent voucher' system for the current public housing programs. This would restore one factor in these economies toward a free market system. Building codes need also be studied, as to their possible negative effects on the poor.[19] Also, government-imposed minimum wage laws help to perpetuate underemployment in the inner city. A religious revival of basic morality would do much to reduce the lawlessness and the economic decline associated with it. Lawlessness is just one of the factors associated with a Gospel of Greed. These issues lie deep in personal firstness, in habits of individual hearts, and progress will only be found by imitating communities that have prospered by conforming more closely to the principles of natural law and to seek self-help from leadership that arises from within. Our point is not to give a quick solution for those problems, no one seems able to solve, but to indicate that a philosophy of how social order works is basic to any solution. Present welfare philosophy seems unable to break an unending cycle of poverty.

IX
Conclusions

The contributions to a philosophy for economics, and hence for social order from Peirce and Hayek have been found to support each other. A weakness in Hayek's approach was found to be that an 'anti-rational argument' is not a clear position. Our proposal is two fold: (1) To replace Hayek's dyadic opposition with a triadic model so as to reformulate his justification without rejecting his insights. (2) The breaking-out-of an existing social consensus may lead to progress, it may also lead to socialism and a decrease of freedom. Lasting progress must be: (a) incremental; (b) in conformity to natural law; (c) such as to give due recognition to man's imperfect nature and (d) protect all groups from criminal violence and from monopoly power based on greed in any area whether in business, in labor or in government.

ENDNOTES

1. Gordon Whitney now retired after a career as Member of Technical Staff, AT&T Bell Laboratories, is an independent scholar.

2. For background on Peirce's triadic categories, see Kevelson 1987, 6-28, and Whitney 1990 and 1991. The quotation is from Royce 1916, 1.

3. Citations for Peirce, 1931-1958; 8 vols., are in the form CP x.y for *Collected Papers* Vol. x and paragraph y.

4. Polanyi introduced his triadic model to counter the claim that the double helix DNA coding system provided a reductionist explanation to the phenomenon of life, 1962, 55; 1969, 225-239,.

5. Salthe, 1985; Buchler 1990. Dyke, 1987, offers nominalism as a critique of Salthe.

6. Hayek, 1960; 1967, 82-95. On Molina see Joyce 1948, and Hayek, 1967, 98. See also Vico 1709, and the interpretation of *sensus communis* by Gadamer 1975, 21.

7. Hayek, 1967, 85-86. Hayek, 1960, 55, n. 5, also cites Francis Lieber concurring in a 1848 essay, 1880, vol.1, 282.

8. Hayek, 1967, 216-228; Eberstadt, 1988.

9. Smith, 1776. On the practical effects of the doctrine of sin, see Hayek, 1960, 61; Weber, 1924; Tawney, 1947.

10. With respect to human faculties, firstness, intuition, emotion, will) and thirdness (mechanical reasoning) are distinguishable, yet interdependent. Different approaches to philosophy elevate one over the other but the tension between will and reason is best seen as irreducible.

11. On Peirce's concept of the depth and breadth of a sign see CP 2.409-413 and Kevelson 1987, 135-137. As with Weber, the ideal types analyzed below are types of individuals. Privately Manfred Pieck has suggested that collective groups, as corporations also have ideal types, but these are not direct analogues of individuals and need to be analyzed as a unified society with distinctive roles, internal network and external transactions.

12. Montesquieu, 1748, 54 of the Introduction to the 1977 edition.

13. Tocqueville, 1835, 305-8, 287.

14. X. Zubiri, 1981, *Nature, History, God*. University Press of America, 123.

15. Kukathas, 1989, 60, 206, viii, 215. Sometimes Hayek, 1967, 93, does assign Kant and Humbolt among those under Rousseau's influence.

16. The terms "Law of Love" and "Law of Greed" appear in Peirce as "Creative Love and "The Gospel of Greed respectively." For our presentation we have introduced the term "law" to emphasize that they are aspects of thirdness. The term "Law of Fair Dealing" is implied in Peirce's 1898 harvard Lectures: "Vitally Important Topics", CP 1.616-676. The Peirce quotation is from MS 645, cited by Kloesel, 1988, 15,; Peirce also used the analogy of a reliable and useful bridge as an model of a solid citizen fulfilling that duty which he was created to do; Pencak, 1991, has an analysis of Peirce as an historian that gives a significant exposition of Peirce's essay "Evolutionary Love." Pencak cautiously agrees with Peirce that history is punctuated by significant change called "Strides" separated by periods of little change termed periods of "Pause." For Peirce, the "Strides" are signs of significance and must be brought about by potentially great men whose greatness is a latent possibility which is brought to fruition by the tumult of a certain stage in history.

17. Hamowy, 1987, 35.

18. Polanyi, 1962, 195-202.

19. Malloy, 1990, 113-125.

REFERENCES

Buchler, Justus, 1990, *Metaphysics of Natural Complexes,* K. Wallace et al., eds., New York: SUNY Press, 1st ed., 1966.

Dyke, Charles, 1987, *The Evolutionary Dynamics of Complex Systems*, London: Oxford University Press.

Eberstadt, Nick, 1988, *The Poverty of Communism,* Transaction Books.

Gadamer, Hans-Georg, 1975, *Truth and Method,* New York: Crossroad.

Hamowy, Ronald, 1987, *The Scottish Enlightenment and the Theory of Spontaneous Order,* Champagne: Southern Illinois University Press.

Hayek, F. A., 1960, *The Constitution of Liberty*, Chicago: University of Chicago Press.

_____, 1967, *Studies in Philosophy, Politics and Economics*, Chicago: University of Chicago Press.

Joyce, W. S., 1948, *The Economics of Louis de Molina*, Unpublished thesis, Cambridge: Harvard University.

Kevelson, Roberta, 1987, *Charles S. Peirce's Method of Methods,* Amsterdam: John Benjamins.

Kloesel, Christian J. W., 1988, "Charles Peirce and Honoré de Clairefont," *Versus,* Bologna, 49, 5-18.

Kukathas, Chandran, 1989, *Hayek and Modern Liberalism*, London: Clarendon Press, Oxford University.

Lieber, F., 1880, *Miscellaneous Writings: Contributions to Political Science*, 2 vols.; New York: J.B. Lippincott Co.

Malloy, Robin, 1990, *Law and Economics*, St. Louis: West Publishing Co.

Montesquieu, 1748/1977, *The Spirit of the Laws*, D. W. Carrithers, ed., Berkeley University of California.

Peirce, Charles S., 1931-58, *Collected Papers*, 8 vols., C. Hartshorne et al., eds., Cambridge: Harvard University.

Pencak, William, 1991, "Charles Sanders Peirce, Historian and Semiotician," *Semiotica* 83, 311-332.

Polanyi, Michael, 1964, *Personal Knowledge*, 3rd ed., New York: Harper & Row, 1st ed. 1958.

_____, 1969, *Knowing and Being,* Chicago: University of Chicago Press.

Royce, Josiah, 1916/1967, *The Hope of the Great Community,* Books for Libraries.

Salthe, S. N., 1985, *Evolving Hierarchical Systems,* New York: Columbia University Press.

Smith, Adam, 1776/1937, *The Wealth of Nations,* E. Cannan, ed., Modern Library.

Tawney, R. H., 1947, *Religion and the Rise of Capitalism*, New American Library.

Tocqueville, A. de, 1835/1969, *Democracy in America*, J. P. Meyer, ed., New York: Doubleday.

Vico, G., 1709/1990, *On the Study Methods of Our Time*, D. P. Verene and E. Gianturco, eds., Ithaca: Cornell University Press.

Weber, Max, 1924/1947, *The Theory of Social and Economic Organizations,* T. Parsons, ed., Free Press.

Whitney, Gordon E., 1991, "The Place of Thirdness in Legal Reasoning," R. Kevelson, ed., *Peirce and Law,* New York and Berlin: Peter Lang, 203-220.

__________, 1991, "A Semiotic Approach to the Use of Analogy in Legal Reasoning," in R. Kevelson, ed., *Action and Agency: Proceeding of the Fourth International Round Table on Law and Semiotics,* April 1990, New York and Berlin: Peter Lang, 391-412.

Zubiri, Xavier, 1981, *Nature, History, God,* University Press of America.

Chapter 23

Registers of Legal Opinion

Eve Wilson[1]

Law, says the judge as he looks down his nose,
Speaking clearly and most severely,
Law is as you know I suppose,
Law is but let me explain it once more,
Law is The Law.

W. H. Auden "*Law like love*"

I

Semiotics and Linguistics

This paper looks at legal language as a social semiotic. It discusses judges' opinions: how they constitute a literary genre with a distinctive group style. The genre contains four different linguistic registers: descriptive, narrative, instructional, and persuasive. The registers are analysed using functional grammar; they can be distinguished by the different use they make of standard linguistic signs.

The study of semiotics was founded by Charles Sanders Peirce in about 1897:

> Logic, in its general sense, is, as I believe I have shown, only another name for *semiotic* (σημειωτικη), the quasi-necessary, or formal, doctrine of signs. (Peirce, CP 2:227)*

Peirce defined three types of sign:

> A sign is either an *icon*, an *index*, or a *symbol*. An *icon* is a sign which would possess the character which renders it significant, even though its object had no existence; such as a lead-pencil streak as representing a geometrical line. An *index* is a sign which would, at once, lose the character which makes it a sign if its object were removed, but would not lose that character if there were no interpretant. Such, for instance, is a piece of mould with a bullet-hole in it as sign of a shot; for without the shot there would have been no hole; but there is a hole there, whether anybody has the sense to attribute it to a shot or not. A *symbol* is a sign which would lose the character which renders it a sign if there were no interpretant. Such is any utterance of speech which signifies what it does only by virtue of its being understood to have that signification. (Peirce, CP 2:304)

The association with speech and language was strengthened in a fuller definition of indexes, for example:

> While demonstrative and personal pronouns are, as ordinarily used, "genuine indices," relative pronouns are "degenerate indices"; for though they may, accidentally and indirectly, refer to existing things, they directly refer, and need only refer, to the images in the mind which previous words have created, (Peirce, CP 2:305).

* *Attempt is made to designate Peirce references here in approximation of standard procedure. Editor's Note.*

However Peirce's theory remained general and logic-based and Ferdinand de Saussure is usually regarded as the man who established linguistics as a branch of semiotics -- although he used a term with more social connotations, semiology. The term was introduced in three courses in general linguistics taught between 1906 and 1911. Here, according to notes taken by his students, de Saussure said:

> *A Science that studies the life of signs within society* is conceivable; it would be a part of social psychology and consequently of general psychology; I shall call it semiology (from Greek *sëmeiôn* 'sign'). Semiology would show what constitutes signs, what laws govern them. Since the science does not yet exist, no one can say what it would be; but it has a right to existence, a place staked out in advance. Linguistics is only a part of the general science of semiology; the laws discovered by semiology will be applicable to linguistics, and the latter will circumscribe a well-defined area within the mass of anthropological facts, (Saussure, 1960:16).

Each term has extended its meaning to embrace the other and, today, both semiotics and semiology stand for an interdisciplinary study of signs.

The linguistic sign, as defined by de Saussure, liberated linguistics from the word and sentence boundaries of traditional language studies:

> Other sciences work with objects that are given in advance and that can then be considered from different viewpoints; but not linguistics . . . . Far from it being the object that antedates the viewpoint, it would seem that it is the viewpoint that creates the object; besides, nothing tells us in advance that one way of considering the fact in question takes precedence over the others or is in any way superior to them, (Saussure, 1960:8)

Although de Saussure did not in his own work push his definition to its logical boundaries, the definition implicitly recognises that the study of language can be analysed from many different perspectives, that there is no way of determining in advance which method of analysis is best, and that the unit of analysis may vary with the viewpoint. Hence, de Saussure's approach permits us to study language from many different viewpoints and to look for a semiotic system that represents each viewpoint. It is only a small step to see language as an integration of many different semiotic systems, which may be studied independently or together.

De Saussure saw language (langue) as independent of the individual:

> Language exists in the form of a sum of impressions deposited in the brain of each member of a community, almost like a dictionary of which identical copies have been distributed to each individual. Language exists in each individual, yet is common to all. Nor is it affected by the will of the depositaries. Its mode of existence is expressed by the formula:
>
> $1 + 1 + 1 + 1 \ldots = I$ (collective pattern) (Saussure, 1960:19)

However, he saw the use of language (parôle) as the sum of individual contributions or speech acts:

> Speaking is thus not a collective instrument; its manifestations are individual and momentary. In speaking there is only the sum of particular acts, as in the formula:
>
> $(1 + 1' + 1'' + 1''' \ldots)$ (Saussure, 1960:19)

Nevertheless, a set of contributions from one individual may frequently be distinguished from a set from another individual. It is this phenomenon that gives rise to the study of style, i.e. to the study of a writer's linguistic preferences or choices. Since style depends on the aggregation of linguistic acts, while being independent of any single act, it must be defined as variations in form that transcend content. This fits in well with Hendricks' extension to ideas of Hjelmslev and Barthes:

> Any system of signification consists of a plane of expression (E) and a plane of content (C); the signification coincides with the relation (R) of the two planes. A connoted system is a complex second-order system, with a first-order system as one component -- its plane of expression. In other words, a connoted system of signification is a system whose plane of expression is itself constituted by a signifying system, (Hendricks, 1976:5-6)

Therefore, a study of style must concentrate on the semiotic systems in linguistics that are independent of content.

II

Group Style

Individual choices are not the only factors that contribute to style. Frequently, style is influenced by the social context or purpose of the linguistic act. The speakers/writers are given incentives to efface themselves to meet the expectations of a specific audience. Viewed more positively, they are encouraged to use language in the way that their speech community feels appropriate to their purpose. Writers may be aware of constraints on their writing: they must please an employer, or they are writing for a specialist scientific journal. However, the adoption of a style is often unconscious: an intuitive employment of the language skills acquired by association with the peer group. As Sapir succinctly expresses it:

> No matter where we turn in the field of social behavior, men and women do what they do, and cannot help but do, not merely because they are built thus and so, or possess such and such differences of personality . . . , but very largely because they have found it easiest and aesthetically most satisfactory to pattern their conduct in accordance with more or less clearly organized forms of behavior which no one is individually responsible for . . . (Sapir, 1949:558)

Style in this context is *functional style* and may be described for a group of people in the total linguistic environment. It contrasts with *literary style*, which attempts to describe the systematic linguistic choices that distinguish a writer from his peer group. A writing community that shares the same functional style is equivalent to Greimas' *groupes sémiotiques* (Greimas, 1976:53). Many professions share a functional style and law is no exception. Jackson says:

> Within the legal system, a great variety of such groups exist, each characterised by its own set of semiotic features. For this purpose, even the differentiation between legislative, doctrinal and judicial functions proves too broad; within each of them, distinct *groupes sémiotiques* may be discerned, each with its own objectives, texts, and processes of semiosis. (Jackson, 1985:284)

Of the three main functional groups distinguished by Jackson, this paper concentrates on the *judicial* and considers only written texts, in particular, judgments from the All England law reports: (All England 1988).

III
Genre and Register

Law reports obviously constitute a textual *genre*: they are embedded in the same situation, namely a court hearing, and have the same structure. Structure consists of:

i) a set of obligatory elements

ii) a set of optional elements

iii) a set of rules about location and frequency of occurrence of the elements.

It is easy to appreciate the common structure of law reports because that structure is explicitly revealed through layout of the printed document, often aided by explicit headings. Thus, an All England law report has about fourteen components: *name, report reference, court, panel, hearing date, date of decision, catchwords, headnotes, introduction, counsel, judgment/opinion, disposition, solicitors/agents, reporter.*

The longest component is the judge's opinion; (there may be more than one). Although only an element of a law report a judge's opinion may be regarded as a semantic unit in its own right, and an instance of its own textual genre: *legal opinions.* If this is so, then we should be able to define a common structure for opinions using the occurrence and ordering of obligatory and optional elements. When giving an opinion, a judge performs four main tasks:

i) he describes the situation appertaining amongst the protagonists: he uses *descriptive* language.

ii) he gives an account of the events relevant to the court hearing: he uses *narrative* language.

iii) he elucidates the principles of law involved in coming to a decision: he uses *instructional* or *didactic* language.

iv) he reasons his way to a judgment: he uses *persuasive language.*

These are four different functions i.e. four different uses of language. The variation of language with use is known as *register*. The term was introduced by Reid (Reid, 1956), but has been extended and developed by other linguists. In 1978, Halliday succinctly defined register as *the clustering of semantic features according to situation type*: (Halliday, 1978:68). Halliday is saying that register can be described by a semantic semiotic and a social semiotic. Let us consider these in greater detail.

IV

A Social Semiotic: Situation of Context

Halliday's work on social semiotics extends the vision of Malinowski and Firth. The anthropologist and linguist Malinowski was the first researcher to develop the concept of a *context of situation* (Malinowski, 1923) to describe the social environment of a text, i.e. where it *comes to life* (Halliday, 1978:109). Malinowski's work was developed by his pupil Firth, who defined a more formal framework for the environmental description:

the participants, with rôles and status;

the verbal and non-verbal actions of the participants;

other relevant features of the situation;

the effects of the verbal action i.e. result. (Firth, 1950)

Since Firth there have been other extended frameworks to describe the situation of context, but today one of the most complete and widely accepted is Halliday's (Halliday, 1978, 1985). Halliday analysed the context of situation as a three dimensional complex:

i) field: the social action where text is embedded.

A court hearing to regulate social interaction through the legal system.

ii) tenor: the status and rôle of each participant; the relationship between the participants.

The judge addresses the community as prescribed by the community. (This is a mythological description if we envisage the *community* as the *general public*. Paterson (1982) has found that the primary audience of the Law Lords are fellow Law Lords and senior members of the Bar. However unsatisfactory this might be for an idealised view of society, it improves the semiotic analysis by providing a restricted and uniform *groupe sémiotique* in the Greimasian sense).

iii) mode: the function of the text in the situation.

It includes the text's symbolic organisation, status and rhetorical mode: eg an opinion written to uphold the institutional legal system and form part of the documentary records of the system. The text is also written to be read aloud, and composed rather than spontaneous. It is performative, (i.e. it realises a decision and has an outcome). It takes the form of an exposition containing narrative/descriptive, instructional and persuasive elements.

Now we will consider how these three fields of context are realised in the semantic system of the text.

V

A Semantic Semiotic: Linguistic Function

A semantic system in Halliday's sense is simply a classification of the linguistic functions of language. As de Saussure has made clear, the functions needed are frequently a product of the viewpoint adopted. For example, Malinowski, an anthropologist, in his study of the Kiriwinian language found the need for only two broad classes:

i) *pragmatic*, which can be split into *active* and *narrative*

ii) *magical*, used in cultural ceremonies or religion, (Malinowski, 1923).

Karl Bühler, as a psychologist, saw language in relation to the individual and had three categories, based on the three person categories of the verb system: *expressive* (first person), *conative* (second person) and *representative* (third person) (Bühler, 1934). One day a lawyer/linguist may well find a functional categorisation that is ideally suited to law. Meanwhile, Halliday's analysis will be adequate.

Halliday postulated four functions: *experiential* and *logical*, (which are sometimes grouped together as *ideational*), *interpersonal*, and *textual*.

The *ideational* function is used by writers to describe their culture and environment and to express their own experience of it. Halliday calls it *Language as reflection* (Halliday, 1985:20). The *experiential* component reveals the *field of discourse* through the words and word ordering at clause level; it is the *content* function of the language. The relationships between the clauses are revealed through the *logical* function as expressed in the paratactic and hypotactic relationships between clauses within the text (shown either below or above sentence level).

The *interpersonal* function is used by writers to reflect their participation in the situation, to give their views, to attempt to influence their audience. Halliday calls it *language as action* (Halliday, 1985:20). It realises the *tenor of discourse*.

The *textual* function enables the *ideational* and *interpersonal* functions by establishing relationships with:

i) what has been written before, and

ii) with the situation of context. It realises the *mode* of discourse.

Of course, none of these functions can operate at the semantic level in the discourse without being apparent in the lower level strata, i.e. in lexico-grammatical systems and, finally, in phonological systems.

VI

How Linguistic Functions are Realised

A. Experiential

The experiential function is largely realised through the system of *transitivity*. Transitivity performs the same function as the earlier case grammars of Charles Fillmore (Fillmore, 1968) and others. Fillmore extended the concept of case, familiar from European languages such as Latin, (which recognised six cases: *nominative, vocative, accusative, genitive, dative* and *ablative*). He wanted to extend analysis of language, at the sentence level, from the purely syntactic, where intra-sentence relationships are defined by their function in the linguistic metalanguage, i.e. as parts of speech: *noun, adjective, verb, preposition, determiner*. To help define function in terms of the semantics of English Filmore proposed six cases:

A: agentive	: animate instigator of action
I: instrumental	: inanimate force involved
D: dative	: animate being affected by action
F: factive	: objective resulting from action
L: locative	: location or orientation
O: objective	: everything else

Fillmore's cases were never accepted as standard: indeed, Fillmore himself later suggested an alternative set: but the principle was adopted by other linguists and features in augmented transition networks (e.g. Gus [Bobrow, 1977]) and transformational parsers (e.g. UCLA grammar [Stockwell, 1973]).

With the introduction of case, sentence constituents could be linked by relationships that were significant to the events described, i.e. the relationships were functional rather than syntactical. These relationships were defined by Halliday as transitivity:

> Transitivity specifies the different types of process that are recognised in the language, and the structures by which they are expressed. (Halliday, 1985:101)

Halliday recognises three major process types: *material*, *mental* and *relational*, which may be subdivided, and three subsidiary process types: *behavioural*, *verbal*, and *existential*: figure 1. A process is realised by a verbal group, and the participants are characterised by their rôles in the process: figure 2.

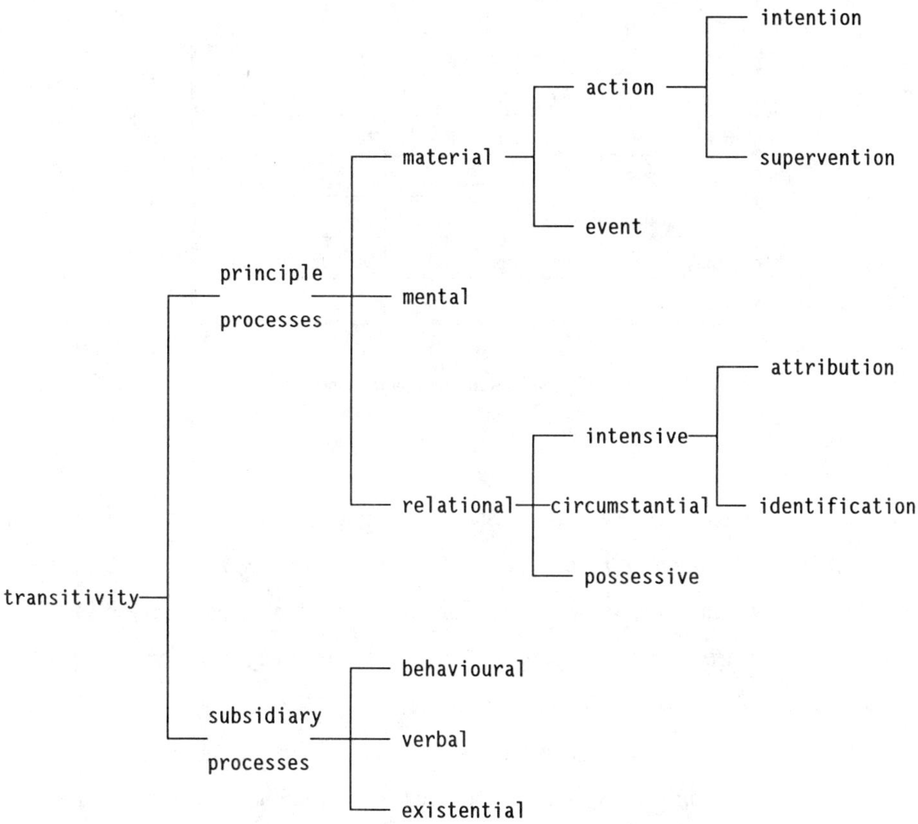

Figure 1. Transitivity system.

Process Type	Direct Participants	Other Participants
material	actor, goal	beneficiary, range
mental	sensor, phenomenon	range
relational	token, value	
attribution	carrier, attribute	beneficiary
identification	identified, identifier	
behavioural	behaviour	range
verbal	sayer, target	beneficiary, range
existential	existent	

Figure 2: Roles and participants

The circumstances surrounding the process are usually given by prepositional phrases. These, too, have a classification network containing seven main categories: *time*, *location*, *manner*, *cause*, *accompaniment*, *matter*, and *role*. Most of these can be subdivided: figure 3. Some example sentences analysed in terms of transitivity are shown in figure 4. Of course, Halliday's system is no more stable or definitive than Fillmore's; as he says:

> . . . transitivity in English . . . is in a state of considerable flux; . . . not something fixed and harmonious but something shifting, fluid and full of indeterminacies. (Halliday, 1978:116.)

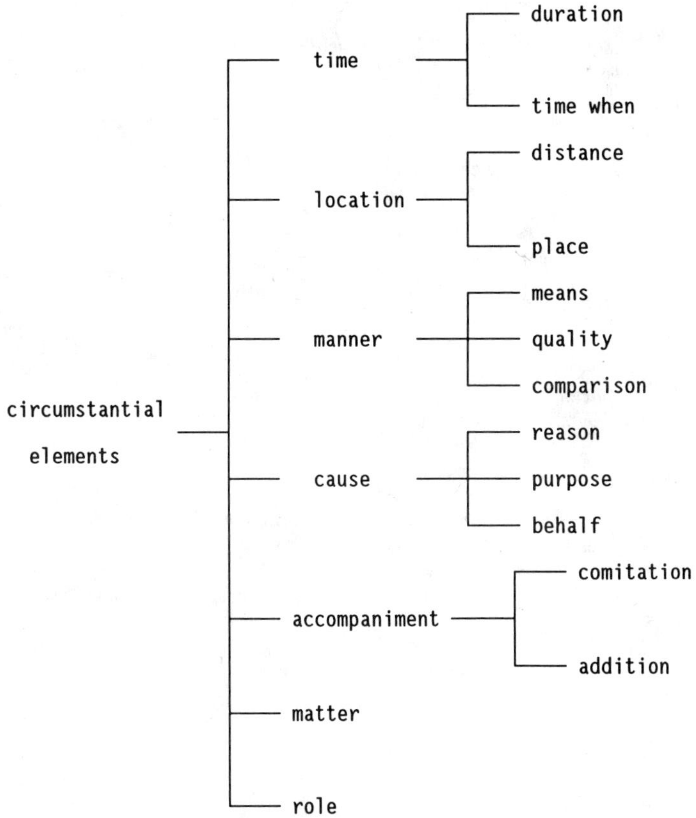

Figure 3. Circumstantial elements.

The woman	*cooked*	*her daughter*	*an evening meal*
actor	material process: action	beneficiary	goal
The neighbour	*heard*	*the burglar alarm*	*in the house*
senser	mental process: perception	phenomenon	circumstantial location place
I	*cannot accept*	*this view*	
senser	mental process: cognition	phenomenon	
The appellent	*is*	*Sean Joseph Wiseman*	
identifier	relational process: intensive	identifier	
The applicant	*was becoming*	*threatening*	
carrier	relational process: intensive	attribute	
She	*would have to share*	*a bedroom*	*with her two sisters*
behaver	behavioural process	range	circumstancial: accompaniment comitation
His wife	*damned*	*him*	*with faint praise*
sayer	verbal process	target	range
There are	*four bedrooms*		
process existential	existent		

Figure 4: Sentences analysed by transitivity

B. Interpersonal

The interpersonal function is largely realised through *mood* and *modality*. Mood exists in a sentence that contains both a subject and a finite verb; together, they realise the feature *indicative*. Sub-categories within indicative depend upon the order of subject and finite element, and the presence/absence of an explicit question word i.e. a WH-element. A fuller network is shown in figure 5. The finiteness is realised through a verbal operation which may be either *temporal* or *modal*: figure 6.

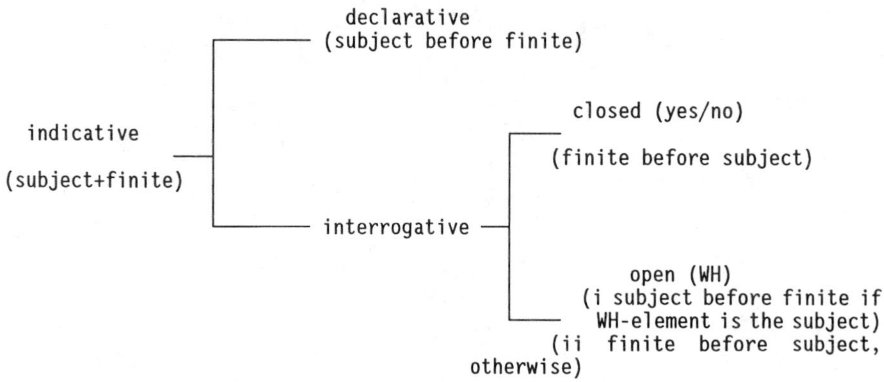

Figure 5: Indicative Network

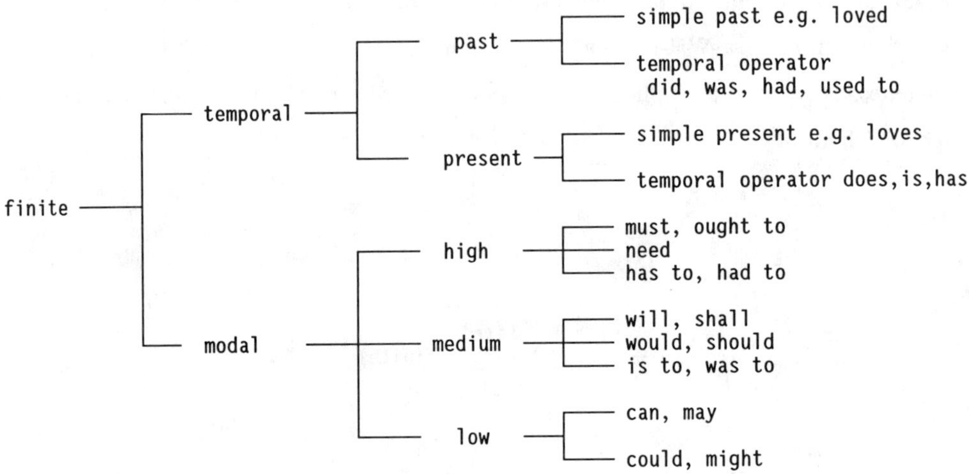

Figure 6: Finite network

The finite element is also subject to the *polarity* system:

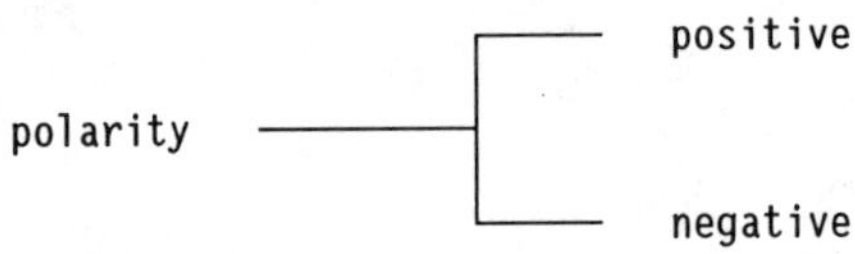

There are intermediate degrees of indeterminacy. Halliday distinguishes between propositions and proposals:

i) propositions, ie, statements and questions, which are subject to degrees of probability: *possibly*, *probably*, *certainly*
Degrees of unusuality: *sometimes*, *usually*, *always*. In statements, modality reflects the speaker's opinion; in questions it asks for the listener's opinion.

ii) proposals i.e. commands and offers. Commands are subject to degrees of obligation: *allowed to*, *supposed to*, *required to*. Offers are subject to degrees of inclination: *willing to*, *anxious to*, *determined to*.

Modality may also be *neutral* or *assessed*. Modality can be represented in different ways; the simplest of these ways can be summarized in the tables shown in figure 7.

Modality (Statements and Questions)				
	Probable	Possible	Virtually Certain	Certain
Neutral	*will*	*may*		*must (cannot)*
Tentative/ Deduced	*would*	*might*	*should, ought to*	*must (could not)*

Modulation (commands and offers)						
	Active		Passive			
			Permission			
	willing	*able*	*allowed*	*entitled*	*obliged*	*required*
Neutral	*will*	*can*	*can, may*	*can*		*must*
Hypothetical/ Tentative	*would*	*could*	*could, might*	*could*	*should, ought to*	

Figure 7: Modality and modulation

C. Textual

The two most important attributes for giving texture to a discourse are theme and *cohesion*.

Theme approximates to the traditional linguistic concept of topic in a sentence. The related notion of *comment*, i.e. the part of the clause where the theme is developed, is the *rheme*. Theme in English is realised by placing it first in the clause:

He	*cannot have seen the child*
theme	rheme

If such a placing constitutes a disturbance in the usual word order, then the theme is marked i.e. given prominence in the text:

Only at the last moment	*did he see the child*
marked theme	rheme

The marked theme highlights the importance of time at that point in the narrative. Structural analysis using theme and rheme can also operate over a sentence:

<table>
<tr><td>if</td><td>he</td><td>was not a trespasser</td><td>then</td><td>he</td><td>was a visitor</td></tr>
<tr><td>structural</td><td>topical</td><td></td><td>structural</td><td>topical</td><td></td></tr>
<tr><td colspan="2">theme 2</td><td>rheme 2</td><td colspan="2">theme 3</td><td>rheme 3</td></tr>
<tr><td colspan="3">theme 1</td><td colspan="3">rheme 1</td></tr>
</table>

In functional grammar, a sentence is more usually described as a *clause complex*. Clause interdependencies within the complex are often signalled by conjunctions, which form part of the cohesive function.

Cohesion is probably more difficult than theme to evaluate fully by automatic means. In addition to the easily recognised characteristics of conjunction, lexical collocation, and repetition, cohesion includes more intractable elements such as ellipses, exophoric reference, anaphoric reference and substitution. These last are not directly relevant to the concerns of this paper. Conjunction, as relevant to our purpose, features strongly in clause interdependencies and the logical function of the text; it is discussed below.

D. Logical

Logical relationships are often signalled through conjunctions used as explicit clause connectors. Within a clause complex, clauses are linked in two ways: through a *structural* relationship and through a *lexico-semantic* relationship.

Structural relationships

If the relationship between clauses is symmetrical and transitive, then the clauses have equal status in the clause complex i.e. they are *paratactic*. Otherwise, one clause is *dominant* or *primary* and the other is *dependent* or *secondary*; here the relationship is *hypotactic*.

Lexico-semantic relationships

There are two major categories: *expansion* and *projection*.

Expansion can take place in three different ways:

i) by *elaboration* i.e. by restating, clarifying or exemplifying.

ii) by *extension* i.e. by giving a new element, an alternative, or an exception.

iii) by *enhancement* i.e. by modifying with reference to time, manner, place, cause or condition.

Projection has two prevailing forms:

i) *location* i.e. directly (paratactic clause) or indirectly (hypotactic clause) reported speech; i.e. projected words.

ii) *idea* projected through a cognitive process: thought, belief, feeling; i.e. projected meaning.

Halliday has devised a notation to represent the structure of a clause complex (usually a sentence) using these relationships.

i) Paratactic clauses are numbered consecutively using an increasing sequence of digits: *1, 2, 3* ......

ii) Hypotactic clauses are denoted by Greek characters, α, β, γ ..... in order of increasing dependence.

iii) Every clause, except the first clause or primary clause in any sentence, has its lexico-semantic relationship represented by one of the following symbols:

=	elaboration
+	extension
*	enhancement
"	locution
'	idea

Examples of sentences analysed by these principles are shown in figure 8.

He said	*that he had been involved in a minor accident*	*and that a small part of his car had dropped off*	*so he had parked*	*and was running back*	*giving the appearance of jogging*	*but really looking for the small part*
α	"β1	β+2	*γ1	γ+2	*δ1	δ+2

a) α"β1β+2*γ1γ+2*δ1δ+2

I said	*"I'm not stopping you"*	*and let her out through the front door*
1	*"2*	**3*

b) 1"2*3

Figure 8: Analysis of clause relationships

Describing register

Judges' opinions constitute a literary genre with a regular structure:

- i description of situation
- ii narration of events
- iii exposition of the law
- iv justification of opinion

Each of these is written in a different *register* or represents a different *text type*. Each register uses a different mix of semantic options. It would be convenient if the sets of features which define register were discrete and mutually independent; unfortunately they, like the registers they represent, are fuzzy and overlapping. The most important attributes are summarised below:

Descriptive

Process types are mainly relational and existential.

Modality is infrequent.

Process participants have referents in the real world.

Clause complexes have few clauses. The clauses are usually paratactic and semantic relationships are frequently of expansion especially as elaboration or extension. There are many embedded clauses modifying nominal groups.

Circumstantial elements are frequently locational.

Narrative

Process types are mainly material.

Modality is infrequent.

Process participants have referents in the real world.

Clause complexes have few clauses. Both parataxis and hypotaxis occur and the semantic relationship is frequently one of expansion as enhancement; occasionally, projection through locution.

Circumstantial elements are predominantly temporal or causal.

Instructional

Process types are mixed.

Modularity more frequent than in descriptive or narrative text.

Process participants are divided between those with referents in the real world, and those with abstract or conceptual referents.

Clause complexes contain more clauses than complexes in descriptive or narrative text. The clauses are predominantly hypotactic. The semantic relationship is often one of projection either through locution or idea. Rhetorical questions often feature i.e. the discourse is problematised and then de-problematised.

Circumstantial elements contain many references to external authorities.

Persuasive

Process types are frequently cognitive.

Modality features strongly; tentative and hypothetical forms are often used.

Process participants often have abstract or conceptual referents; some process participants take the form of whole propositions. First person pronouns frequently occur in association with cognitive processes.

Clause complexes are longer and hypotactic relationships predominate. Semantic relationships are often those of projection through an idea or expansion as enhancement (frequently conditional).

Circumstantial elements are mainly causal, particularly conditional and concessive.

The next step was to decide what length of textual unit to work on. One possibility was simply to take fixed length blocks sequentially through the text which would have given equal sized chunks for comparison. However, it seemed more natural to use the paragraph, which is the logical unit of discourse in written text. This meant, of course, that paragraph size varied enormously and very short paragraphs could be indeterminate. So, too, could longer paragraphs. Not all clause complexes in a paragraph are of the same type: descriptive text can appear in any register; text that is instructional often includes sentences that are persuasive in form, and so on. Nevertheless, in a well-written text, paragraphs should be semantically cohesive: semantic cohesion is difficult to achieve if register varies continually within a unit of information.

VII
Conclusion

In all discourse it is important to be aware of the signs, often subtle, that signal when the speaker's language is not factual and certain but tentative, hypothetical, and persuasive; in legal argument it is of greater consequence. Any analysis which gives an indication of the degree of uncertainty in an opinion must interest linguists and lawyers alike. The next step is to attempt an automatic analysis to find numerical parameters, for each register, based on large volumes of text. This would act as a yardstick for future studies.

ENDNOTES

1. Eve Wilson is Professor of Linguistics at the Computing Laboratory of the University of Kent at Canterbury, England.

2. I should like to thank Mr. R. C. Saunders, University of Kent at Canterbury, for advice and comments on draft versions of the paper, and Ms. Christine Wilson for converting the final version into Wordperfect.

REFERENCES

All England law reports, 1988, Butterworth, London, Vol. 1.

Bobrow, D.G., 1977, "GUS: A Frame Driven Dialogue System", *Artificial Intelligence*, 8: 155-73.

Bühler, K., 1934, *Sprachtheorie: die Darstellungsfunktion der Sprache*, Fischer, Jena.

de Saussure, F., 1960, *Course in General Linguistics*, London: Peter Owen.

Fillmore, C., 1968, "The Case for Case", in *Universals in Linguistic Theory*, Holt, Rinehart and Winston, 1-90.

Firth, J.R., 1950, "Personality and Language in Society", in *The Sociological Review*, vol 42, 37-52.

Greimas, A.J., 1976, *Sémiotique et Sciences Sociales*, Paris: Editions du Seuil.

Halliday, M.A.K., 1978, *Language as Social Semiotic*, London: Edward Arnold.

_____, 1985, *An Introduction to Functional Grammar*, London: Edward Arnold.

Hendricks, W.O., 1976, *Grammars of Style and Styles of Grammar*, Amsterdam: North-Holland Publishing Company.

Jackson, B.S., 1985, *Semiotics and Legal Theory*, London: Routledge and Kegan Paul.

Malinowski, B., 1923, "The problem of meaning in primitive languages" in *The Meaning of meaning*, by C.K. Ogden and I.A. Richards, London: Kegan Paul.

Paterson, A.A., 1982, *The Law Lords*, London: MacMillan & SSRC.

Peirce, C.S., 1960, *The Collected Papers of Charles Sanders Peirce*, 8 vols., Cambridge, Mass.: Bellnap Press, *(New edition - Editor).*

Reid, T.B.W., 1956, "Linguistics, structuralism and philology", *Archivum Linguisticum*, Jackson, vol 8, 28-37.

Sapir, E., 1949, "The unconscious patterning of behavior in society", in *Selected Writings of Edward Sapir in Language, Culture and Personality*, D.G. Mandelbaum, ed., Berkeley: University of California Press.

Stockwell, R.P. et al, 1973, *The Major Syntactic Structures of English*, Englewood Cliffs, N.J.: Holt, Rinehart and Winston.

Chapter 24

Standing on Ceremonies: Legal Rituals, Regulative Rules and the Metaphysics of Jurisprudence*

Peter A. Winn[1]

I never stood on ceremonies, but now they fright me.

Shakespeare, *Julius Caesar,* Act 2, Scene 1.

I

According to traditional jurisprudence, legal formalities, ceremonies and rituals are not real. The reality of legal systems is the process of making rules, interpreting them, applying them to specific cases and sanctioning violations. Nearly every American law school graduate leaves school having learned some version of this jurisprudential metaphysics. Nearly very American lawyer ends up repressing this learning. If lawyers do not very quickly learn to respect, understand and master the forms, ceremonies and rituals of the law they not only will be wrong, they will be out of a job.

Under the traditional jurisprudential model, rules are either public or private. Public rules are set forth in statutes, regulations and judicial decisions; private rules are set forth in contracts, trusts and other documents. But whether public or private, rules reflect the intentions, purposes or policies of those who enact the legislation or draft the legal documents. Courts of law sanction violations of the rules and clarify their scope. Individuals adjust their behavior according to the rules. Legal behavior is a product of rational deliberation based on rules and sanctions, a type of ends-means rationality. Needless to say, legal rituals and ceremonies fit poorly into this model of the law.

Legal ritual may involve a ceremony, like the entry of a plea of guilty or the swearing of a jury; it may involve the execution of an instrument, like a will or a promissory note; or it may involve some combination of both the enactment of a ceremony and the execution of an instrument. But the effect of legal rituals turns not on the intentions of the participants, but on the definition of the ritual action itself. Ritual in general is interpersonal symbolic action, in which standardized forms of language and behavior are used to constitute and order human affairs and social institutions. Legal ritual is no different from religious ritual or other social rituals, except it takes place in contexts which are invested with special legal meanings, and which are the special province of the lawyer.

Legal rituals must be understood as things which are *done* not *said*. The execution of a will, the conveyance of real estate, the entry of a guilty plea, the enactment of a statute, the filing of a complaint or answer, the execution of a trust document, all are concrete events in time and space, transforming the social situation of the participant. This active transforming character of ritual is more important than its expressive character. Legal ritual may or may not actually express the intentions of the parties, but if the proper forms are observed, the legal transaction is completed. Strictly speaking, legal consequences do not 'follow' from the execution of a legal ritual; rather, the execution of the legal ritual *constitutes* the legally significant event. Legal ritual, then, involves the use of words not simply to communicate thoughts and intentions, but directly to create social events and institutions.

In the ritual use of language, words, rather than serving merely as messengers of thought, are themselves critical transforming acts. In a series of lectures, J. L. Austin called such utterances 'performatives.'[2] For example, the statement, 'I give and bequeath my watch to my brother,' accompanied by the handing over of the watch, is not a report of my intention; it is the very act of giving. In a marriage ceremony, the 'I do' is not a report of some inner state of mind; it is the act which creates the marriage. Likewise, 'I promise' is not a report of what I have done a moment before in my head; it is the very promise itself.[3] With the utterance of these words in the proper ceremonial context, the speaker alters his status in the network of obligations which constitute his world. Marriages, gifts and promises are all primarily symbolic *actions*, not merely expressions of thoughts or intentions.

With ritual, determinate social action takes place whatever specific thought or intention is associated with the ritual by the participant. To have undergone a marriage makes one married. Even if one was insincere and there was no intention at all to become married by virtue of the ceremony, one is still married. The marriage can sometimes be undone, but only by executing another ritual, that of annulment or divorce. Likewise, a promise, in exchange for valid consideration, creates a binding obligation of the person making the promise. The actual intentions of the promisor can be irrelevant to the creation of this obligation. If the promise was in fact made in exchange for valid consideration, but the promisor had no real intention to follow through with the promise, evidence of his lack of intention to be bound will not constitute a defense to an action against him to enforce the contract. The promise of a liar may be enforced against him even if the person to whom the promise was made reasonably believed that the liar had no intention of performing the contract. The ceremony of the contract -- the rituals of contractual formation -- make the obligation binding.

Legal rituals, especially legal instruments, are closely related to legal forms. A legal form is a fixed pattern of legally significant words which is consistently used to execute a specific legal ritual. Attorneys themselves usually model their forms on other forms from previous transactions or from models found in form books. Different names and factual information are inserted into the form, while the form itself recites the legally operative language. Many times, standardized commercial 'fill in the blanks' forms are used. Standard lease and real estate purchase forms are available from realtors' associations, standard promissory notes are available from banking associations, and standard construction contracts are available from the American Institute of Architects. The Blumberg legal form company of New York has a sales catalogue which lists 30 different forms for affidavits, 26 different forms for deeds, 42 forms for mortgages, 31 different types of contracts and several types of form for bills of sale. Blumberg sells a form kit for the creation of a corporation. It sells special forms for the entry of judgments, forms for writs of execution and release forms for the settlement of claims. Blumberg also sells form pleadings for New York City Court, New York Supreme Court, U.S. District Court and various courts of appeals.

Legal forms are seldom analyzed and rarely adjusted or altered. Used by large rich corporate law firms as well as by struggling solo practitioners, legal forms are rarely drafted from 'scratch.' Absent some official 'blessing,' lawyers are notoriously resistant to change the standard forms they use. The mechanical operation of a form causes it to continue to be used even if language in the form has not been scrutinized by a court. In some cases, after a court has ruled that a particular term of a form is unenforceable, the term continues to be found on the standard form in the industry.

Within the academic study of law, the widespread use of forms by practitioners is all but ignored. Law professors achieve academic success by studying judicial decisions and statutes; the law that they teach reflects this bias. In spite of the tremendous impact forms have on the actual practice of the law, no formal study has been conducted of modern form books. When addressed at all, legal academics consider the pervasive use of forms by practitioners an ugly little fact. Usually it is just not mentioned. Academics do not get tenure by publishing form books.

Legal forms, of course, are not themselves legal rituals, but are *used* in legal rituals. For instance, the execution of a promissory note, the conveyance of real property, the issuance of a writ, the execution of a will, the making of a residential lease, all may involve the use of a standard or customary form. But the form for the note does not itself create a negotiable instrument, the quitclaim does not itself convey real property, the writ of execution does not enforce a judgment, the realtors' lease form alone does not create a tenancy. Only when the form is used in the proper circumstances by the proper parties does the legal event which is the ritual come into existence. Until then, the form remains an inert set of marks on paper.

Legal rituals and legal forms should be sharply distinguished from legal rules, for they operate quite differently. A rule of law regulates pre-existing behavior and typically applies to more than one person on more than one occasion. A legal rule might require drivers to stay on the right side of the road or remain below a certain speed limit. One has a duty to learn the rule and act accordingly. If one's behavior is challenged, the rule is interpreted, and the behavior is examined to see whether it is within the scope of the rule. But the behavior exists apart from the rule regulating it, and if necessary the behavior can be described without reference to the regulative rule.

Rituals, on the other hand, have uniformity and structure, but not the same kind of uniformity and structure as a regulative rule. Rituals are governed by what the philosopher of language John Searle calls 'constitutive rules.'[4] Unlike regulative rules, constitutive rules create or define new forms of behavior. Constitutive rules are less like the rules of the road and more like the rules of a game. Searle gives the example of a constitutive rules of chess: 'a checkmate occurs when the king is attacked in such a way that no move will leave it unattacked.'[5] A constitutive legal rule might be, 'a will is a written declaration of a person over the age of eighteen disposing of his property at his death signed by that person and two attesting witnesses.' The rules of chess do not regulate an independently existing activity of playing chess; the rules of will making do not regulate an independently existing activity of will making. Without such rules, there would be no such activities. While driving on the right side of a road can be described without reference to any regulative rule, wills and chess playing could not exist without their constitutive rules.

Constitutive rules, then, create new forms of behavior. Searle calls the new forms of behavior created by constitutive rules 'institutional facts' as opposed to 'brute facts.'[6] Brute facts are statements about physical or mental events: statements such as, 'this stone is next to that stone,' 'bodies attract with a force inversely proportional to the square of the distance between them and directly proportional to the product of their mass,' and 'I have a pain.'[7] Institutional facts are statements about actions within social institutions: statements such as, 'Mr. Smith married Mr. Jones,' 'the Dodgers beat the Giants three to two in eleven innings,' 'Green was convicted of larceny' and 'Congress passed the Appropriations Bill.'[8] Statements about institutional facts cannot be reduced to physical or psychological events. Although institutional facts sometimes include 'brute' facts (for instance the marks of ink on paper making up a contract), these only count as part of an institutional fact if they occur in the context of a system of constitutive rules.

A regulative rule is properly evaluated in terms of its effectiveness in promoting the policy or achieving the purposes which it was intended to promote or achieve. For instance, the federal income tax deduction for home mortgage interest payments promotes the policy of encouraging individual home ownership in the United States. The rule works if more people buy their own homes because of the rule. The rule, 'no vehicles in the park,' achieves the purpose of keeping the park free for pedestrians. It works if the rule actually keeps cars out. Regulative rules look outward toward independent behavior and are evaluated in terms of how effectively they modify this behavior.

On the other hand, it makes little sense to analyze legal ceremonies and instruments in terms of independent purposes or policies. No one would seek to find an independent purpose for the rule of checkmate in chess. The rule is a matter of definition or convention. To attempt to find such a purpose confuses a constitutive rule with a regulative rule -- a category mistake. Constitutive rules in the law are no different from the constitutive rules of any other game. Nevertheless, legal academics continually try to understand legal rituals in terms of hypothetical purposes or policies.

Lon Fuller, in an attempt to find a purpose underlying the requirement of a seal in the execution of certain types of debt instruments, suggests that the seal performed a cautionary function:

> A formality may also perform a cautionary or deterrent function by acting as a check against inconsiderate action. The seal in its original form performed this function remarkably well. The affixing and impressing of a wax wafer -- symbol in the popular mind of legalism and weightiness -- was an excellent device for introducing the circumspective frame of mind appropriate in one pledging his future.[9]

On Fuller's reasoning, one could equally argue that the function of the rule of checkmate is to make chess players cautious about permitting their king to be exposed to danger. A good chess player does try to keep his king out of danger, but this is not the *purpose* of the rule. Fuller confuses a constitutive rule with a regulative rule, but constitutive rules do not have determinate purposes or policies. To understand the legal ritual of a debt instrument under seal one must place it in the context of the English civil pleading system, the legal game, so to speak, in which the constitutive rule of the seal played a role. In the old English pleading system, against an action, or lawsuit, brought on a sealed instrument the defendant could not plead *non debet,* i.e., he could not deny he owed the money.[10] The only plea available to him was *non est factum suum*, it is not my deed or seal.[11] However, if a defendant made the plea of *non est factum suum* and a jury found that the sealed instrument was indeed the defendant's, the defendant was sent to prison for making the plea.[12]

Fuller cites no historical or scientific study to support his assertion that the seal caused people using it to be 'cautious.' Of course, whatever such a study might show, we would still feel that people using sealed instruments *should* be cautious, for the same reason that we believe a good chess player should be cautious about exposing his king to attack. We think people should know the rules of the game, but this does not mean the ritual of a seal magically produces in us some independent psychological state of mind. In general, if people tend to be cautious with legal rituals, it is because they have a basic understanding of the institutional structure in which the rituals play a role; if they lack this understanding, they may execute the rituals without much reflection or concern.

Another purpose often given for legal rituals is that of serving as evidence of a transaction. For instance, the requirement that a gift be 'handed over' to be valid is sometimes explained by saying that the 'handing over' ritual serves an evidentiary function. According to this argument, the delivery of the donor and acceptance by the donee serves to prove the intention of the donor to give the gift and the intention of the donee to accept it.[13] The problem with this type of argument is that what is presented as 'evidence' of an intention to make a gift and to receive it is none other than the legally significant event itself. The ritual of 'handing over' involved in a gift giving is simply part of the legal and conventional meaning of a 'gift.'[14] The 'evidentiary' explanation of ritual purports to refer to the concept of proof at trial, but the actual mechanics of forensic proof do not reference 'intentions'. Once the trial lawyer has proved the 'handing over,' together with the canonical verbal utterances, the proof process can stop. The lawyer sits down. The gift has been proved. Contrary evidence of the true 'intention' of the parties may not even be admissible.

Ritual invokes multifaceted symbolic belief structures, but the ritual itself can work whether or not a specific propositional content is attached to the ritual's symbolism. The search for a 'purpose' underlying legal ritual assumes that there is some 'truth' underlying the practice. But the operative language of ritual does not constitute a type of expression which has conventional truth value. While the sentence 'the cat is on the mat' is meaningful if there are in the world such entities as cats and mats which stand in certain relationship to each other, the ceremony of a marriage has no specific meaning outside of the ritual context itself. The consequences of ritual action are quite determinate, but ritual itself lacks determinate truth value.

Because ritual lacks truth value, it can allow determinate social action to take place in the face of contrary and contradictory beliefs. This aspect of ritual makes it absolutely essential to the operation of any society. No society has a uniform set of moral ideals or consistent ideology. The fact that ritual permits determinate social action in the face of actual disagreements, disputes and conflicts is why ritual is such a crucial component of any legal system charged with resolving social conflict and discord.

Instead of thinking of legal rituals as expressing some independently existing purpose or end, one should think of them as providing the framework or context in which analysis of regulative rules takes place. An issue involving the interpretation of a regulative rule and its application to the facts will be presented to a court and debated in the context of pleadings, motions and, if a trial is required, the presentation of testimony -- that is, in an interrelated system of constitutive rules. The filing of a motion is first understood by reference to other instruments and ceremonies: the complaint, the answer, the affidavits which must accompany the motion, and to the ceremonies of oral argument before the court. Once on a motion for summary judgment, I watched a young lawyer make a winning legal argument to a judge, but the lawyer had failed to file a proper affidavit with the clerk's office. The facts were not seriously controverted by the parties, the motion itself contained all the factual allegations which would have been in the affidavit, and the law was settled. Nevertheless, the lawyer lost. His impeccable legal analysis was not presented in the proper ceremonial form, and so the court ignored it. There was nothing before the court on which the court could rule.

At a deeper level, the facts to which regulative rules apply are often themselves institutional facts, understandable only within a wider set of constitutive rules. Accordingly, our basic understanding of legally significant behavior is often structured and controlled by the ritual forms of our legal experience. When this happens, legal ritual does not express an independent legal understanding; it is the very mode by which our legal understanding takes place. Gifts, wills, deeds, motions and trials cannot exist apart from the rituals attendant upon their creation. The rituals do more than mark, define and alter rights and obligations of people within a community -- they create the very institutional facts which make those obligations intelligible to us. Because of the constitutive nature of legal ritual, the social facts against the legitimacy of the ritual is judged are themselves constituted by the ritual. To paraphrase Clifford Geertz, through the legal ritual, the world as lived and the world as imagined are fused through the agency of a single set of symbolic forms.[15] In the words of Maurice Bloch, 'what is being said is the right thing because by acceptance of the formalization of language it has become the only thing.'[16]

II

Legal Ritual and the Speed Limit in Keokuk

Ritual theory not only has interesting theoretical implications, but has practical implications as well. To show this I conclude with a problem from negotiable instruments law. A negotiable instrument is a promissory note containing various formal attributes, and which reflects a debt that one person (the 'maker') owes another person (the 'payee'). For a promissory note to be a negotiable instrument, it must be (1) signed by the maker; (2) contain an unconditional promise to pay a sum certain in money and no other promise; (3) be payable on demand or at a definite time; and (4) be payable 'to order' (i.e., to the person named on the instrument) or 'to bearer' (i.e., to whomever possesses the instrument).[17]

If the required form is used on the promissory note, precise legal consequences follow. Unlike an ordinary promise to pay, the negotiable instrument can be transferred to a third person free of the underlying defenses that the maker might assert against the payee.[18] For example, A gives B a promissory note for $100 in the form of a negotiable instrument to pay for the value of some goods supplied by B. B endorses the note to C, and C gives B value for it. The defenses that A could assert against B (for instance, that the goods were non-conforming or defective) cannot be asserted against C. A must pay C and seek a separate legal remedy against B.[19] C is called a 'holder-in-due-course' and 'takes free of the maker's defenses' to the underlying transaction, even if the goods supplied were defective or worthless.

Negotiable instruments were a common payment mechanism used in the 18th and early part of the 19th century when no official system of paper money existed. By the middle of the 20th century the practice had ceased to have much if any commercial importance.[20] However, in the area of consumer transactions, a practice became common in which unscrupulous salesmen would sell a product, for instance, aluminum siding, in exchange for the promissory note of a homeowner. The promissory note might often be accompanied by a mortgage or deed of trust on the home. The siding was often prone to defects or worthless. The seller, however, could sell the note to a third party factor who would hold and enforce the note in the event of default, but remain free of the buyer's claims of breach of warranty against the seller. In the meantime, the seller might be insolvent or have skipped town.

Occasionally, in litigation between the payee and the holder, courts held that a holder or purchaser of consumer commercial paper was too 'closely connected' to the seller of the goods or services to enjoy holder-in-due-course status.[21] However, it was not always possible to show that purchasers of commercial papers were 'closely connected' in this way. Furthermore, because these transactions were often tied together with a home mortgage, especially in states with procedures for non-judicial foreclosure, if the seller wished to keep his home, he had the expensive burden of initiating a lawsuit, with the outcome of his suit by no means clear.

In response to the problem, 44 of 50 state legislatures passed statues which attempted to limit the holder-in-due-course doctrine in consumer transactions. The California version of the statute, used by several other states as well, provides:

> An assignee of the seller's rights [under a consumer contract] is subject to all equities and defenses of the buyer against the seller arising out of the sale, notwithstanding an agreement to the contrary . . . .

These statutes did not stop the problem. Sellers were able to draft around these statutory restrictions by inserting so called 'waiver of defenses' clauses in the underlying instruments. If the debtor had no defenses against the original payee, he had none against a subsequent holder either. The beneficiary of the 'waiver of defenses clause' ended up in the same place as a holder-in-due-course.

In 1975 the FTC ended the legislative and judicial impasse by promulgating a startling simple rule. The new FTC regulation made it an unfair and deceptive practice for a seller to take a note or the proceeds of a note (made to a finance company or bank) from a consumer unless the note contained the following language:

> ANY HOLDER OF THIS CONSUMER CREDIT CONTRACT IS SUBJECT TO ALL CLAIMS AND DEFENSES WHICH THE DEBTOR COULD ASSERT AGAINST THE SELLER OF GOODS OR SERVICES OBTAINED PURSUANT HERETO OR WITH THE PROCEEDS HEREOF. RECOVERY HEREUNDER BY THE DEBTOR SHALL NOT EXCEED AMOUNTS PAID BY THE DEBTOR HEREUNDER.[22]

This language, when placed on the standard promissory note form, renders the note non-negotiable and harmless. The note is still a functioning debt instrument, but no one who takes it can become a holder-in-due-course. Unlike previous judicial and legislative efforts, the FTC's language worked. The abuses associated with the 'aluminum siding' type scams have largedly disappeared.

Why did the FTC's rule succeed so effectively where so many courts and legislatures before it failed? Probably not because of fear of any sanctions for violating the rule. Although the FTC may bring a cease and desist action against someone who fails to include the language on their standard form,[23] and may file a civil action to seek relief for a consumer,[24] the FTC is a relatively small agency and lacks the resources to bring such actions against sellers in all 50 states.[25] Although some states have passed consumer protection statutes, no private cause of action exists under the FTC Act.[26] Nevertheless, after FTC promulgated the rule, the language of the rule eventually found its way into standard commercial forms and form books.[27] With the change in the form books, the abuses stopped. Nobody drafts from scratch, not even con artists.

Strangely, in their discussion of the FTC rule, White and Summers, probably the two most prominent commentators on commercial law in the United States, expressed nothing short of outrage. I quote at length from the second edition of their widely respected treatise on commercial law:

> One might properly ask who gave the FTC authority to help tear down one of the pillars of commercial law . . . . Generations of lawyers and law teachers are surely turning in their graves . . . . Here is not the place for extensive debate on the power of the FTC; White and Summers share the view that the FTC has, at the very least, far exceeded its appropriate reach. Indeed, one might ask what are the bounds of FTC rulemaking? If it can abolish the holder-in-due course doctrine, can the FTC effectively enact its own consumer credit code? Set the Speed limit in Keokuk? All this has occurred without a single Congressman or Senator putting a pen to paper or

> voting on so much as a word of this new quasi legislation. One should distinguish between the process by which the consequence was accomplished and the consequence itself. We are not advocates of the holder-in-due course doctrine in consumer transactions . . . . We believe that on balance the world is better off with abolition of the holder-in-due course doctrine in consumer transactions. Moreover, one's distaste for the process should not obscure his judgment about the cleverness of the rascals at the FTC. They did not mount a frontal assault on the holder-in-due course doctrine; they did not purport to have the power to render any state law invalid; they did not submit their proposal to the winds in the halls of Congress (a place where they may have lost). Rather they simply required that a legend be placed on most consumer paper. Having studied the Uniform Commercial Code carefully, they correctly concluded that paper which included such a legend would not under state law be negotiable. So make no mistake, the kids at the FTC are often wrong, seemingly devious, but far from stupid.[28]

The vehemence of this prose from commentators normally as reserved as White and Summers is remarkable. But their appeal to the doctrine of state's rights is misplaced, given the number of states that have passed statutes to limit the holder-in-due-course doctrine in consumer transactions. Likewise, their attack on the FTC's rulemaking authority seems misplaced, since, as they themselves concede, the D.C. Court of Appeals concluded that the FTC was in fact delegated such legislative power by Congress.[29]

What White and Summers clearly object to are the unorthodox tactics of the FTC. As they note, the FTC did not adopt a legislative, or regulative, rule at all. The FTC simply required certain canonical ritual language to be used on consumer credit paper. No regulative rule was changed at all.[30] The FTC changed the constitutive rules of using consumer promissory notes, and thereby effectively, cheaply, and painlessly subdued the monster of consumer negotiable paper.

Under the conventional model, consumer promissory notes are identified as contracts, perhaps contracts of adhesion, but contracts none the less. Contract law is conceived of as a system in which parties are free to arrange their economic affairs against the background of a fixed system of rules. The rules can be changed. For instance, some terms can be declared unenforceable, but the parties are free to order their affairs as they see fit. However, parties do not negotiate the terms of commercially packaged and printed forms. Actual agreement is irrelevant to their enforceability. Promissory notes are simply mechanical debt instruments. The FTC attacked not the background law but the instrumental form itself. Faced with a ritual problem, the FTC found a ritual answer.

However, the failure of the conventional model was more than a simple miscategorization of promissory notes as contractual agreements. Within the traditional model, the FTC solution could not exist -- could not even be conceived of. Its very success cast a cloud upon the metaphysical foundations of traditional jurisprudence. Steeped in that tradition, White and Summers could only react with dismissive anger. The FTC 'rascals' had to have used some slight-of-hand, some devious, unethical trick. This criticism is just silly, and White and Summers do not argue that the FTC's action was unlawful. The judicial and legislative failure to stop abuses associated with the holder-in-due course doctrine in consumer transactions was not a failure of will. It was a failure of metaphysics.

In spite of the success of the FTC solution, legal scholars continue to analyze legal ritual on the model of regulative rules. Much has been written, for instance, about the recognized problems of adhesion contracts. In the insurance industry, rental car industries, and in many other industries, standard form legal instruments continue to abuse consumers. Legislative and judicial solutions fail because these are not problems easily solved by regulative rules. Ritual problems sometimes require ritual solutions. Ritual solutions involve not changes in the background law but control of the ritual forms themselves.

* A closely related article, "Legal Ritual", was the basis for presentation at the Fifth Round Table. That paper is to be included in the Volume, *Law and Aesthetics*, R. Kevelson, 1992, ed.

ENDNOTES

1. Peter A. Winn is Assistant District Attorney in Austin, Texas.

2. J.L. Austin, 1965, *How to Do Things with Words*, Ed. J.O. Urmson, Oxford University Press: New York.

3. *Id.*, 5.

4. John R. Searle, 1969, *Speech Acts: An Essay in the Philosophy of Language*, 33-42, Cambridge: Cambridge University Press.

5. *Id.*, 33.

6. *Id.*, 50-53.

7. *Id.*, 51.

8. *Id.*, 52.

9. Lon Fuller, 1945, *Consideration and Form*, 45 Col. L. Rev. 799, 801.

10. S.F.C. Milsom, 1981, *Historical Foundations of the Common Law*, 250 2nd ed.

11. *Id.*

12. *Id.*

13. See e.g., *Danby v. Tucker*, 1883, 31 W.R. 578.

14. This was recognized by Lord Esher in *Cochrane v. Moore*, 25 Q.B.D. 57., 1890.

15. Clifford Geertz, 1973, "Religion As a Cultural System," in *The Interpretation of Cultures*, 22 New York: Basic Books.

16. Maurice Bloch, 1975, "Introduction," in *Political Language and Oratory in Traditional Society*, ed. Maurice Bloch, 30-31 London: Academic.

17. Uniform Commercial Code, sec. 3:104, and secs. 3:105-112.

18. Edward L. Rubin and Robert Cooter, 1989, *The Payment System: Cases, Materials and Issues*, 1989, West Publishing Co., St. Paul, Minn., 3-4.

19. *Id.*, 3-4.

20. Grant Gilmore, 1954, "The Commercial Doctrine of Good Faith Purchase," 63 *Yale L.J.* 1057; Albert J. Rosenthal, 1971, "Negotiability--Who Needs It?, 71 *Columbia L.Rev.* 375.

21. *Unico v. Owens*, 1967, 50 N.J. 101, 232 A.2d 405; *American Plan Corp. v. Woods*, 16 Ohio App.2d 1, 240 N.E.2d 886.

22. 16 C.F.R. 433.1-433.3 1991 effective date May 14, 1976.

23. 15 U.S.C. sec. 45m, Supp. IV 1974.

24. 15 U.S.C. sec. 57b, Supp. V. 1975.

25. For discussion, Jim L. Banks, 1983, "The FTC Holder In Due Course Rule: A Rule Without A Remedy," 44 *Montana L.Rev.* 113.

26. *Holloway v. Bristol Myers Corp.*, 1973, 485 F.2d 986, D.C. Cir.

27. Since the rule was promulgated, I have found only one case in which the Seller used a form which lacked the FTC language and the subsequent holder's claim against the buyer was enforced, *Capital Bank & Trust Co. v. Lacey*, 1980, 393 So. 668, La., and in this case, it does not appear that the underlying transaction was in any way questionable.

28. White and Summers, 1980, *Handbook of the Law Under the Uniform Commercial Code,* sec. 14-8, 571-572, West Publishing, St. Paul, Minn. 2nd ed.

29. *Id.*, n. 60, citing *National Petroleum Refiners Ass'n v. FTC*, 1973/1974, 157 U.S.App.D.C. 83, 482 F.2d 672, cert. den., 415 U.S. 951, 94 S.Ct. 1475, 39 L.E.2d 567.

30. White and Summers, *Uniform Commercial Code,* 1988, 3rd ed., West, St. Paul, Minn., 639, 'Moreover the FTC radicals could argue that they had not changed even one word of the sacred state law on holders in due course'.

Chapter 25

Is There An Anthropological Semiotics of Law?

Irene Portis Winner[1]

I

The following general assumptions underlie what I would construe as a semiotic anthropological approach to law which, I consider, pertains to the nature, meaning and functioning of law in a comparative and universal context: 1. Every functioning society has a legal system communicated by 'culture texts', verbal and nonverbal, generated from various systems of signs, given that the use of the term legal here is understood broadly as applicable in varied ways to any and all aspects of a culture that have the capacity to exert *social control,* that is to contribute to the enforcement of, and regulate deviations from, prescribed social norms. 2. Law is contextual, that is it reflects in various ways cultural world views, values, basic cultural categories such as perceptions of space and time, and beliefs and values, all of which act to organize social structure, norms, customs, habits, and traditions which may pertain to the domain of social control and to its various institutions. Nor is this a one-way process since legal traditions can alter other aspects of the culture.

Asking whether anthropologists have so viewed law requires a rehearsal of early and later approaches to the domain, anthropology of law, starting with Edward Tylor's definition of culture in 1871 as, in its wide ethnographic sense 'that complex whole that includes knowledge, belief, art, morals, law, custom and any other capabilities and habits acquired by man as a member of society.' And culture as it exists everywhere is a subject apt for the study of laws of human thought and action. Thus Tylor dismisses the earlier view that primitive man lives in an essentially precultural state where anarchy and brute force prevails.

While Tylor's holism supports the universality of law, there has been little agreement among students of culture about the nature of law in simple as opposed to complex societies. The root issues are what kind of relationship pertains between law and custom; what are the specific criteria that are essential to law and to any body of customs subsumed as part of law; and how do we study these issues in a preliterate society.

Thus questions include: in primitive society do all customs have as at least one of their functions that of social control and is all custom law, or are there societies ruled by custom and not by law? What is the relation of primitive law to ritual, to change and to deviant behavior? Does law require an authority and must there be specialized institutions to enforce a law? Must a legal system be ultimately sanctioned by legitimate use of coercion and if so must it be physical? Must law be based on secular sanctions only? Finally, if the semiotic dimension is introduced, an important question concerns the implications of the opposition literacy /nonl-iteracy for underlying cognitive styles and thus for the development, meaning and functioning of law?

The last issue is taken up by the British social anthropologist, Jack Goody, who advances it as underlying all the apparent dichotomies we just mentioned. For Goody this contrast, literacy/non-literacy is best not looked upon as a dichotomy either. There are degrees of literacy, and their related cognitive styles interpenetrate. Indeed, Goody asks whether the posing of a dichotomy law and custom and the insistence on an absolute distinction between, or identification of, custom and law in all cultures, do not arise from misguided conceptualizations.

Finally, the above theoretical questions cannot be separated from the issue of methodology. How in fact do we study law in primitive or nonliterate societies?

This discussion can only note the high points of a dialogue about these theoretical and methodological issues that arise in an anthropological approach to law, most importantly from Maine to Malinowski to Radcliffe Brown to Hoebel to Goody. And here we confront the issues of intertextuality and the rereadings and reinterpretations of texts that become polysemic, invoking the overriding preoccupations dominating the present discourse of the species "semiotic".

Let us set the discussion by quoting from A. Hoebel's standard outline of the parameters of law in the anthropological sense (Herskovits, 1965 quoting Hoebel, 1946:839).

> A social norm is legal if its neglect or infraction is met by the application, in threat or in fact, of the absolute coercive force by a social unit possessing the socially recognized privilege of so acting.

Thus the essential element is authority. A custom becomes legal when, if it is disregarded, someone can *do* something about it. Thus 'while a custom that prevails need not be legal, it becomes so if it comes to appertain to what (is termed) 'part of the going order' of the group' (Herskovits, 1965:208 quoting Llewellyn and Hoebel, 1941:283). For Hoebel the sanction of physical coercion by some kind of leader is a prerequisite for law, but Hoebel cannot find any society that does not meet these criteria, so he sees law as universal.

II

Clearly the problem Hoebel attacks arises from the fact that in complex societies, specialized legal institutions and authority figures and written codes allow for the relatively unambiguous demarcation of the domain of law, thus distinguishing it from what it is not, while in simpler societies, and particularly in preliterate societies, such specialized institutions are limited or nonexistent making authority figures hard to detect and sanctions diffuse based on reciprocity, public opinion, morality, supernatural beliefs, etc. Can one always locate specific leaders who can exercise enforcement by coercion? These points lead to the question of how, in such a diffuse situation typical of simpler societies, can one study law?

As Melville Herkovits notes in his standard work on cultural anthropology (1965), 'No precision in the study of unwritten law could be attained until the case method was applied. Otherwise, only a kind of ethnographic statement of ideal or normative procedures could be arrived at' (209). The early anthropological studies of law in the first decades of the twentieth century were valuable in laying out general patterns. They have informed us of the many ways in which justice can be administered including the use of religious sanctions, such as the ordeal or the oath, or of secular ones such as citing proverbs or weighing testimony about the fact' (209). However, the problem of methodology needed to be faced and weighed heavily in the first truly anthropological study of comparative by Maine.

A. Sir Henry Summer Maine

In Maine's famous studies of comparative jurisprudence, notably *Ancient Law,* 1861, and *Village Communities in the East and West,* 1871, he inferred past legal structures by comparing present forms in which he discerned traces of ancient structures and practices in order to make inferences about ancient law. His study was path-breaking since he showed how ancient law was intertwined with custom and religion, and he found remarkable similarities in the law of ancient societies untouched by Roman law, from Ireland to India. Such legal traditions reflected fundamentally similar kinship structures, inheritance rules, and property ownership.

However, his most fundamental errors were first the results of a suspect methodology but the best available in his day, and secondly a suspect theoretical position that accepted certain evolutionary principles of culture and their associated dichotomies. Thus he saw the contrast as absolute between status-based societies where social positions are ascribed and contract-based societies where social positions are achieved. Furthermore, he believed that in early society ruled by kinship all property was communal, and in later contract-based societies political rule and territoriality, not kinship ties, bound people together and common property disappeared. And for Maine, in late tribal society after a despotic period, there arose regularized codified, ritualized customary law. Some problems are that evidence from present day primitive societies and from archeological remains of early primitive cultures do not justify the view that primitive societies were without contracts in some form or without some private property, or that primitive societies were originally ruled by willful despots, or that customary law and social control appeared only in the late tribal period. In general, while Maine showed the importance of kinship ties in primitive societies, he underestimated the territorial principle as a means of binding a group together. A fundamental problem setting one of the dialogical subjects was put clearly by Hoebel (1954:283):

> If ever Sir Henry Maine fixed an erroneous notion on modern legal historians, it was the idea that primitive law, once formulated, is stiff and ritualistic (and by implication weak in juristic method.)

And referring to his own studies of the Plains Indians and his reading of ethnographic studies of others, ranging from the simplest society known, the Eskimo, to one of the most complex preliterate societies, the Ashanti, he asserts that the data

> has surely shown a large amount of flexible action in haggling (viewed dimly) and argument (viewed generously) over substance and

> penalty. In most primitive trouble cases the situation is surprisingly fluid, but flowing within channels that are built on the preexisting law and moving to a reasonably predictable settlement (283).

Jack Goody's (1975:137) later statement that the introduction of writing may make erasure more difficult than in oral societies also whittles away the ritualist world Maine described.

B. Malinowski and Radcliffe-Brown and the question of the universality of law

The problem of methodology was greatly advanced by the fieldwork method which, in its early phases, did not however achieve the case method approach of the last decades. Thus following Maine, we consider two early fieldworkers both of whose studies appeared at about the same time: the functionalist, Bronislaw Malinowski, and the structure-functionalist, Radcliffe-Brown, both trained in Britain as social anthropologists but who were in many ways almost diametrically different.

Malinowski's dynamic outlook was shaped by his early Polish and German training in physics and mathematics before he came to England to study anthropology to which he was particularly attracted by the imaginative works of Frazier. His *Crime and Custom in Savage Society* appearing in 1926 was based on extensive fieldwork in Melanesia (*Argonauts of Western Pacific*, 1922), founding the participant observation method and laying down the modern approach to study of primitive society.

Malinowski saw, as did Maine, that law was intertwined with custom. In fact, for Malinowski, in primitive society all but the most neutral custom was law which could not be separated from supernatural sanctions and which did not require physical coercion for enforcement. On the other hand, Malinowski reacted strongly to the type of mistakes Maine made. The most fundamental difference is the field method.

For Malinowski, in distinction to Maine, nothing was inferred and all was based on empirical evidence of real behavior. Therefore he totally rejected pseudo-evolutionary history as well as the view that customary law is stiff and rule bound and that private property is completely absent in primitive society. As Malinowski wrote, the problem was 'not to study how human life submits to rules -- it simply does not; the real problem is how rules become adapted to life' (Hoebel, 1954:34 quoting Malinowski, 1926:127).

Malinowski wrote that law is 'a body of binding obligations regarded as right by one party and acknowledged as the duty by the other, kept in force by the specific mechanism of reciprocity and publicity inherent in the structure of . . . society' (Bohannon, 1967:48 quoting Malinowski, 1926:127). Thus, apparently, reciprocity was as binding as law. However, while Bohannan criticized Malinowski for reducing law to reciprocity, Hoebel's comments were more temperate. Noting that Malinowski's interest was in deviation, and that his approach was descriptive and thus not the case approach, Hoebel discerns only six cases in *Crime and Custom* and they are presented in quasi-narrative form. Yet Hoebel, as opposed to Bohannan, defends Malinowski's law as really law in Hoebel's sense, since he interprets Malinowski's reports as describing law enforced by coercion of authority that is exercized by leaders. Thus Hoebel believes Malinowski reported instances where force supplemented reciprocity although, writes Hoebel, Malinowski never clearly stated what he thought was punishable crime in primitive society. Hoebel's examples of crime from Malinowski's text were incest, murder, excessive sorcery, theft and physical and violent conflict (Hoebel, 1954:183).

Hoebel finds that Malinowski was wrong to conclude that 'the whole of Trobriand culture with its mutual obligations and exchanges rests upon economic sanction, personal vanity and public opinion' (206). While it is true that the concept of public crime as opposed to private delicts was not well developed among the Trobriands as compared with Hoebel's own Cheyenne materials, crime and coercion did exist. Thus Hoebel believes that while Malinowski shed much light on social control at large, in his major works he fused law with its social matrix, failing to separate out the more strictly legal phases of a culture, (although in his later life Malinowski paid more attention to the role of power in society over and above reciprocity) (Hoebel, 209).

Radcliffe-Brown's *Andaman Islanders* appeared in 1922 and his noted article on primitive law in 1926. While both Malinowski and Radcliffe-Brown saw custom as focal, for Radcliffe-Brown, somewhat in the tradition of Maine and clearly in Durkheimian fashion, rules were prior to behavior having the function of maintaining social solidarity. Thus we have an early anthropological version of the Saussurean priority of *langue* over *parole*. Never the modern fieldworker using participant observation techniques like Malinowski, Radcliffe-Brown relied instead on formal questionnaires and emphasized stability and equilibrium far more than deviation and change. He attempted to define social control and custom in such a way that it could be distinguished thoroughly from law which, he held, required the sanction of physical force in a politically organized society, while custom depended on other types of sanctions primarily moral and ritual. Thus Radcliffe-Brown leaves us with simple societies ruled by custom but without law, and less simple societies having private but not public law. The Andaman Islanders had no law at all, society's running depending on the diffuse sanctions of public opinion (Redfield, 1964:6).

Hoebel who, in the main, accepts Radcliffe-Brown's criterion of law as requiring punishment by an authority, finds formal authority reported in both Malinowski's and Radcliffe-Brown's texts where these thinkers did not. But for Malinowski the lack of formal authority did not mean the lack of law. Hoebel reinterprets Radcliffe-Brown's text describing the lawless Andaman Islanders, holding that Radcliffe-Brown hardly emphasized dispute behavior even though he reported it since formal structure and not actions of people were his primary interest.

These dialogues between Maine, Malinowski and Radcliffe-Brown, and Hoebel's attempt to resolve them, are inconclusive partly because of their entanglement in dichotomies reflecting the arguments of their day, and partly because of their sometimes awkward translations of, as well as reactions against, Western legal concepts. The search for underlying principles resulted in simplifications, notably Radcliffe-Brown's social solidarity, but also Malinowski's reciprocity. Even Hoebel's attempt to isolate his deeper logical postulates underlying law and order in primitive society resulted in lists of not well related and overly rational precepts.

The attempt to resolve the conflicts posed by Maine, Malinowski, Radcliffe-Brown and Hoebel has lead another scholar, Pospisil, to abandon the search for a unifying criteria for law. Law in primitive society is a kind of diverse, heterogeneous universal as is legal authority and it need not be physical, as Hoebel held. 'There is no social group . . . that does not possess leadership and regulatory devices for the conduct of it members (Pospisil, 1963:54). For Pospisil (Bohannon, 1967:26), law's authority can be psychological such as ostracism or ridicule and there is no such thing as a 'lawless functioning group.' For he states 'not one attribute but rather a whole pattern of them which coexist in time form the core of the social phenomena which we call law' (Pospisil, 27-8). Yet his attributes remain a list that do not attempt to reach to deeper organizing and relational levels which Hoebel at least attempted.

C. Law and Communication

Jack Goody's treatment of law reconsiders, in a contemporary and semiotic outlook, the variable of writing in the search for an underlying principle that has complex effects on other partially dependent variables including, importantly, law and social control. In a vein similar to the semiotics of culture history devised by Jurij Lotman, the Soviet semiotician, Goody looks to what Lotman would call the most abstract culture texts such as world view that organize cultural practices, while at the same time not suggesting that such deep principles are themselves unchanging, harmonious and unaffected by context.

Goody, in his *The Domestication of the Savage Mind,* 1977, calls for a reconsideration of the Grand Dichotomy as it bears upon the study of cognitive developments in human culture, a dichotomy that has the most varied forms which go back to the opposition primitive/complex societies, the transformations of which include:

1. *bricoleur*/engineer, hot/cold
2. nonlogical and nonrational / logical and rational
3. magic, rite, myth, symbol (in its traditional non-Peircean sense) / history, science, concepts, abstract thinking
4. open/closed [and similar pairs of opposition - *Editor's note*]

For Goody the shift to writing must be far more fully explored since it is of critical importance in both formalizing and increasing the flow of information' (Goody, 1977:148). For example, consider the relation of the spoken and written word in reference to magic. If magic is looked upon as 'a set of procedures to change the world' and if 'spells and other attempts to control the course of events are dependent on the magic of the spoken word, to this extent they tend to give way to the worship of the book' (149-50). But these are not equal and competing systems. There is a critical difference since

> The magic of the spell is dependent, at least in part, upon the virtual identity of the speaker and spoken. How can one separate a man and his words? . . . Writing puts a distance between a man and his verbal acts (150).

In contrast is the Ashanti witness whose word is accepted as true, and proof of his actually having witnessed an event is irrelevant.

Goody argues that since writing accounts for a 'cumulative growth of systematic knowledge' that involves 'elaborate learning procedures,' it contributes to a secularization process which, while having many discontinuities cannot 'be reasonably described either in dichotomous terms or in relativistic ones' (150), for it must be understood 'in terms of basic changes in the nature of human communication' (150). 'In this way we can avoid not only the Grand Dichotomy but also the diffuse relativism that refuses to recognize long-term differences, and regards each 'culture' as a thing on its own, a law unto itself' (151)

Goody emphasizes that the relative autonomy writing brings to thinking is based on a changing kind of self-reflection. Thus thinking increasingly frees itself from the all important social context, achieving a decontextualization. This is indeed a version of Peircean concepts.

For Peirce's ideal sign achieves a relative but never complete freedom from context, that is from iconicity and indexicality, since the ideal sign is dependent upon self-reflection or internal dialogue, essential for abstraction, itself a condition of human semiosis (cf., Portis-Winner, 1989 for a discussion of Peirce's human sign).

Similarly for Goody all speech is monitored by the inner ear, and only a small proportion of what we reflect upon 'turns up as an interpersonal communicative act' (159), while writing changes this relationship substantially. As he writes 'I want particularly to stress the relevance of this internal aspect since the role of the inner ear and the contribution of writing in clarifying one's own thoughts are rarely given much recognition by those who see the elements in communication as a matter of external relations between human beings (or social persons), (160). However, Goody reminds us, the internalization of the social setting is part of an internal dialogue and a prerequisite for such cognitive processes (161).

Such is the theoretical substructure for Goody's treatment of law, comparatively studied, which is recapitulated here.

> *First*: All law is concerned with right and wrong. Goody finds that a cluster of concepts referring to unwritten custom, written rules or law, and justice and rights overlap and together they refer 'to very central processes in any form of human interaction' (128).
>
> *Secondly*: When considering the influence of writing on the law we are examining the new modality that involves the creation of a separate organization (the court of law becomes to some extent separated from the court of kings and thus becomes partially autonomous) (129), but this is not a binary distinction. There are intermediate institutions. Similarly, for Goody a monopoly of force by certain officials is not the issue. It is rather the application and distribution of force that is important and it differs in for example tribal acephalous systems as opposed to states.
>
> *Thirdly*: A related problem is the partial autonomy of the text 'by creating a text 'out there'; a material object detached from man . . . the written word can become the subject of a new kind of critical attention.' The text which cannot answer back must be interpreted

> and translated and universalized by eliminating particulars and reordering and reclassifying leading to further commentary. Thus it extends, and is not opposed to oral modes of thought (129).

Goody reminds us that the traditional European distinction between law and customs means what was written and what was not, and codifying custom means 'to set it down in writing before proclaiming it as law' (129). Thus, says Goody, this distinction cannot apply to jural systems of societies without writing. And Goody believes that anthropologists have quite naturally tried to reassess European concepts, and search for more appropriate criteria for distinguishing or uniting custom and law, but they have met with only varying successes (130).

Summarizing the dialogue, Goody notes that the usual idea that customary law means unwritten law not yet part of a superordinate system is avoided by those who simply call law what some think of as customary law, as Pospisil did for New Guinea (Pospisil, 1958) and Barton for Ifugao (Luzon) law (Barton, 1919). And,

> earlier Malinowski extended law outside its usual sphere of societies having codes, courts and constables, wanting to make the point that the sanctions on human behavior could be considered as a total set, and hence applying the wòrd law to any norm that was not merely neutral custom, just as later Llewellyn and Hoebel (1961) inspired by American legal realism, saw law as a rule whose breach invokes active response, a breach that somebody does something about (132).

In another attempt at a solution, Goody recalls that Gluckman, found in his study of legal action among the Lozi of Zambia, that the best translation of the central concept, *mulao*, is rules of right doing, covering both law and custom (Gluckman, 1955).

For Goody it is not the dichotomy law/custom, but developing relations between them and their associated changing cognitive styles that is important. For when jurisdictions pertaining to a written code are promulgated, inevitably some conflict between national law and local custom and also religious law develops. Furthermore law and custom in this situation differ hierarchically. However, the sense that customary law is folk law in the process of being received into a code may be too simple and too optimistic (131).

In any case, Goody would like to leave behind treatments of law as 'a fuzzy set that covers all or most forms of social control.' And he also rejects an ahistorical approach and notion that law is just a form of discourse. For we need to focus on the far reaching consequences which are hardly described by 'changing one set of cultural clothes for another,' following from the 'encapsulation of oral practices as written rules' (133).

III

In conclusion, it appears that Goody's semiotic approach to law as a special form of contextual communication where the relations between custom and law are constantly being negotiated, has few echoes in a recent collection on anthropology of law (Starr and Collier, eds., 1989) that thematizes law as process, the study of which shall illuminate how it reflects and effects asymmetrical power relations, although the semiotic implications are there for others to draw out.

As the introduction tells us (Starr and Collier, 1989:1-28), earlier interests from Malinowski's investigation of social control exercized by interconnected institutions, to Radcliffe-Brown's studies of disputes to discover rules enforced by three parties and preoccupation with the troubling issues of how to conceptualize law for peoples who lack 'law' (Llewelyn and Hoebel, 1941, Bohannan, 1957, Pospisil, 1985), all were followed, in the sixties and seventies, by the shift to the issue of dispute processes rather than rules (Nader, 1965 1969, Collier, 1973). The focus became 'processes rather than laws, interests rather than rules, litigants rather than judges, and power rather than order'(4). Notions of structuralism and symbolism, according to the authors, had little impact on the anthropology of law (5).

But, the authors tell us, the emphasis on process alone was not enough; thus the call for a return to the consideration of rules and a broader approach, asking such questions as how disputes effect relations among kins and incorporate power relations, historical context and change. I conclude, however, that in spite of the call for broadening of horizons, the position advanced in the Introduction that legal orders should be integrated as ''codes', discourses, and languages in which people pursue their varying and often antagonistic interests' (9), is not yet sufficiently explored in an anthropology of law, although the metadiscourse traced here indirectly substantiates the semiotic dimensions of the issues at hand.

ENDNOTES

1. Irene Portis Winner is Professor of Anthropology at the Massachusetts College of Art.

REFERENCES

Barton, R.F. 1919, *Ifugao Law*, Berkeley, Los Angeles: University of California Studies in Anthropology and Ethnology, No. 15.

Bohannan, Paul, ed. 1967, *Law and Warfare. Studies in the Anthropology of Conflict*, Garden City, New York: The Natural History Press.

Collier, Jane F., 1973, *Law and Social Change in Zinacantan*, Stanford, California: Stanford University Press.

Gluckman, Max, 1954, *The Judicial Process Among the Barotse of Northern Rhodesia*, Manchester.

Goody, Jack, 1977, *Domestication of the Savage Mind*, Cambridge, New York: Cambridge University Press.

Herskovits, Melville, 1965, *Cultural Anthropology*, New York: Knopf.

Hoebel, E.A., 1946, 'Law and Anthropology,' *Virginia Law Review*, XXXII:835-54.

_____, 1954, *The Law of Primitive Man*, Cambridge, Massachusetts: Harvard University Press.

Llewellyn, K.N. and E.A Hoebel, 1941, *The Cheyenne Way*, Norman: University of Oklahoma Press.

Maine, Sir Henry S., 1871, *Village Communities in the East and West*, London.

_____, 1875, *Early History of Institutions*, New York.

_____, 1977, (1861), *Ancient Law*, London.

Malinowski, Bronislaw, 1922, *Argonauts of the Western Pacific*, London: Routledge.

_____, 1926, *Crime and Custom in Savage Society*, London: Routledge and Kegan Paul.

Nader, Laura and Harry Todd, eds. 1978, *The Disputing Process in Ten Societies*, New York.

Portis Winner, Irene, 1989, 'The Human Sign As An Integrative Concept in the Semiotics of Culture', *The Nature of Culture*, Walter A. Koch, ed., *Proceedings of the International and Interdisciplinary Symposium*, October 7-11, 1986 in Bochum. Bochum: Studienverlag Brockmeyer (=BPX 12).

Pospisil, L., 1958, *Kapauku Papuans and their Law*, New Haven: Publications in Anthropology 54.

Radcliffe-Brown, A.R., 1964, (1922), *The Andaman Islanders*, New York: Free Press Paperback.

_____, 1933, 'Primitive Law,' *Encyclopedia of the Social Sciences*, New York, 9:202-206.

Redfield, Robert, 1964, Primitive Law, *University of Cincinnati Law Review*, Vol 33, No. 1:1-22.

Starr, June and Jane F. Collier, 1989, *History and Power in the Study of Law, New Directions in Legal Anthropology*, Ithaca-London: Cornell University Press.

Tylor, Edward B., 1871, *Primitive Culture*, London: J. Murray.

Chapter 26

Prague Linguistic Circle and the Humanities

Thomas G. Winner[1]

I

Introduction

The hallmark of the Prague Linguistic Circle is its integrative, relational and dynamic approach, interconnecting all the verbal arts and even the visual and musical ones with linguistic studies, with philosophy and even the sciences. Eschewed are the Russian Formalists who saw the text as immanent and concerned themselves only with the linear ordering of devices, and the Saussureans who separated *langue* from *parole*, and were little concerned with the relation of sign to referent. Although many of their insights were incorporated into the broader outlook of the Prague Linguistic Circle which resuscitated history and context never forgotten by Bakhtin, and mapped a whole new way of looking at reality which no longer separates structure from function, where functions are always multiple and changing, and where meaning is always multiform. Although interrelationships and searches for underlying principles were the guiding ideas, never was this group tempted by the simple solutions of any kind of reductions. This is its richness, this is why it speaks to all disciplines. The interest is eminently contemporary; that is in communication in all its functions, in all its meanings, in full socio-cultural context. Thus in the late 20s the Prague Circle addressed itself to the communication revolution that has become the most overwhelming task that we must understand today.

Taking off from the Prague Linguistic Circle's explorations, contemporary semiotics, especially the semiotics of culture developed in the sixties and seventies by the Moscow-Tartu school of semiotics, has demonstrated both in theory and in practice that such an enterprise is remarkably heuristic, avoiding the relativism and obscurantism of the postmodernists and deconstructionists who in a sense evaporate the text, reducing it to rhetoric and discourse and interpretation divorced from context.

What are then, within this interrelational outlook, the specifics of a work of art as opposed to other types of verbal texts, a scientific work, a news report, a legal document? Given that these are all narrations of a sort, if we do not insist that narratives must be linearly organized, how do these aesthetic narrations distinguish themselves from other types of narration? The first key issue we need to think of here is what I would call the ambiguous relationship of the artistic text to the world outside which it represents, where all types of tropes pull our attention back to the structure and meaning of the text and then return us, to lesser or greater extents, to new ways of looking at the world outside. Exactly the opposite for nonaesthetic texts where the rules of ordering information are aimed at the most unambiguous relationship to the referent and where the text itself is primarily a crutch to help us look at what is being referred to. Insofar as it distorts reality, it is devalued, while an aesthetic text must distort reality and must even question the reality of earlier aesthetic rules and devices. But this dichotomy is too simple. The opposition aesthetic/nonaesthetic is one of changing hierarchies, point of view and interpretation as well as inner qualities within the text. Which is better: a legal argument which passes all scientific criteria for describing a legal occurrence but which is cast in the driest and unimaginative of styles, or a text describing the same situation but exploiting the aesthetic devices, although the aim of those devices is not to call attention to the text primarily but to force us to think more sharply about what is being described? The answer is, I think, not what is better, because it depends upon the values of the interpreter and the goals of the sender, but that, as Jakobson has told us so often, there is no absolute separation between the aesthetic and nonaesthetic spheres, and yet they must be distinguished.

Perhaps it is not so surprising in a world which demands simplification in the face of all the complexities of human culture that the insights and demanding goals of a group such as the Prague Circle should be misunderstood as is so frequently the fate of the works of revolutionary thinkers such as for example Freud, Marx, Peirce to name a few. There are many interpretations of the theories of the Prague Circle today that are incorrect, such as: that their findings are formalistic, that the structures they discerned are abstract and out of context, that they did not take into consideration the pragmatic dimension, that they outlined a kind of semiotics which is imperialistic reducing all other disciplines to itself. And in fact, while every criticism always has a germ of some kind of truth, all of these are wrong. That is why I am today going to give you a brief history and synopsis of this important movement, relevant to scholars of all disciplines, since the Prague Circle's views open us to what I would call contemporary and heuristic ways of understanding how humans think and create. Not that their findings are the last word. In fact that is their strength; they lead us to new kinds of syntheses with other thinkers of whom at first they were unaware, like for example Peirce, and with contemporary explorations in all the disciplines. For example, Jakobson had fruitful discussions with physicists such as Einstein, with psychologists such as Lacan, with philosophers such as Cassirer, with anthropologists such as Boas and Levi-Strauss, not to speak of his earlier inspirations resulting from contacts with the revolutionary Russian avantgarde in the 1910s and 20s before the Stalinist repressions set in.

I shall begin by a brief historical overview and then discuss the main propositions of the Prague Linguistic Circle.

II
Historical Background

A. Buhlerian and early Prague functionalism

The first major step beyond the traditional concentration on the solitary sign from the Greeks through Peirce and Saussure came with the teleological communication model of the German psychologist Karl Buhler who in revitalizing Plato's view of verbal communication, depicted a speech event as a triangular scheme, linking a *sender*, a *receiver* and a *referent* (i.e. the things 'talked about in the communication') (Buhler, 1934:24). Buhler described three functions of discourse, function being defined later as an orientation towards a goal intended by the communication. Buhler's three functions were the following: the expressive function (*Ausdrucksfunktion*), by which the speaker characterizes himself, the representative function (*Darstellungsfunktion*) which describes extralinguistic reality, and the conative function (*Appellfunktion*) which acts upon the receiver of the linguistic message, all of which implied larger-than-the-word communications and went beyond the sign's structuration.

Buhler's three functions became the basis of the Prague school's functional approach to linguistics, semiotics and aesthetics. Soon to be added was a fourth function, the poetic function, a concept later expanded into the aesthetic function, characterized by the orientation of the message onto its own structuration.

An early fundamental document emerging from the Prague Linguistic Circle was its *Theses* (*Theses*, 1929), a collective work presented to the First International Slavic Congress held in Prague in 1929, which stressed the relation of diachrony and synchrony, the functional approach to language, and the aesthetic function, the necessary condition for a work of art which is activated by the orientation of a message onto its own structuration. The tenets of this document laid the groundwork for much of the later development of Prague aesthetic semiotics, but we cannot discuss them here for lack of time.

B. Broadening of the Buhlerian Model of Communication: Roman Jakobson

In 1960, in his renowned paper, 'Linguistics and Poetics,' Jakobson extended the Buhlerian and early Prague models of communication, outlining his well-known six-factor six-function model which added two more functions, the phatic and metalinguistic, to the earlier Prague model, and developed the notion of language *factors* the orientation on which determined the *function* of an utterance. A dominant interest of Jakobson became that of the relations of grammar and poetry. Elaborating on his earlier insight, Jakobson noted that while grammar in a referential text has the function of organizing the experience of the participants in the speech act, in an utterance dominated by the aesthetic function, grammar becomes itself part of the experience as it turns back on itself. For the referential level of language grammatically untranslatable cognitive data are not admissible. But when language is shaped towards an aesthetic function, it may approach untranslatability, as it inflates ambiguous meanings. Thus in poetry, grammar lends itself to meanings beyond the coded logical cognitive realm (Cf. Jakobson, 1959:237-38; also 1930; 1931; 1952). Thus Chomsky's famous 'Green dreams sleep furiously' which he called an ungrammatical sentence, and thus a meaningless one, may have semantic value in the aesthetic realm, even though not in the strictly cognitive one. This is well expressed in Jackobson's later metaphor

'The poetry of grammar and the grammar of poetry' which underlies his structural principle that 'the poetic function projects the principle of equivalence from the axis of selection onto the axis of combination' (1960:358).[2]

. . .

Jackobson's model goes beyond the Russian Formalists' 'device' where parallelism and other techniques 'make things strange'; for Jakobson the formal and the semantic are polar equals, while in the Formalist's view, the semantic is seen as subsidiary. Jakobson primarily chose texts from lyric poetry as examples. If we think of narrative poetry we must search for other aesthetic principles. As Jakobson was well aware, prose and poetry can intermingle in the most radical manner. Jakobson even went so far as to claim that the relationship between lyric poetry and the diary does not merely parallel the relationship between *Dichtung* and *Wahrheit*, but that both aspects are equally valid.

. . .

III

The Arts as Communicative Systems

A. The functional model

It is important to realize that the six-factor six-function entity is seen as always there, or potentially mobilizable. But this structure does not place a limit on the many further contextual factors and functions, or discoverable universal components not detected as yet. Nor need we assume that this or any model will not receive new revisions or find itself dissolved into new paradigms, etc. Yet the pithy insights of the Jakobson model are yet to be fully realized. We shall briefly outline Jakobson's position. 1) The *emotive* function arising when the orientation is on the addressor, may exploit the signifier by modifying the phonemic system, introducing extra-systemic sounds (e.g. vowel lengthening as in [bi:g]), special interjections containing peculiar sound sequences (shhh, ts-ts, whistling sounds, ouch, etc.). Normal syntax is also altered. Thus such emotive utterances may be substitutes of sentences (e.g. 'shhh' can be understood as a substitute of the sentence 'be quite!', 'ouch'= 'it hurts!'). In this way attention is focussed on attitudes of the *addressor*. 2) The *conative* function, focussing on the receiver, may utilize marginal grammatical forms, such as the imperative and the vocative which frequently deviates phonemically, syntactically or morphologically from other nominal and verbal categories and which cannot be challenged by the question 'is it true or false' and cannot be converted into negative statements. The goal of the conative is the evocation of a certain attitude or action in the addressee. 3) The *referential* function is present when an utterance is oriented on the *referent* and it is an accessory, even if only in highly attenuated forms, in most other functional utterances. 4) The *metasemiotic* function which dominates in statements that are concerned with the *code* has clearly become an almost obsessive preoccupation of contemporary art, for example, in postmodernism. 5) *Phatic* utterances 'check on the channel', their purpose being to ensure that *contact* is established; they are also a source of experimentation in present-day art forms. 6) Finally, contemporary art inquiries suggest that the *poetic* or *aesthetic* function, characterized by an *orientation upon the message* itself, is striking intertwining with the metasemiotic function, although Jakobson saw these as opposed; and the *aesthetic function* performs also in texts in which it is not dominant (rhythmic scything, wood chopping, the desire to have a job done well and beautifully, etc.).

B. The nature of 'literary language'

The functional approach overcame the view that poetic (literary) and prosaic (nonliterary) languages are two distinct linguistic dialects. Rather, Jakobson saw every work of literature as having a dual system, that of the *natural language* from which it is constructed and that of the *literary* code (i.e., the norms and strictures) of its time and genre. The grammar of a literary text is in part that of the language employed, English, French, Russian, etc. and in part that of specific literary codes, such as the code of the English Renaissance, the code of neoclassicism, the code of an individual author, etc. We cannot empirically define a *qualitative difference* between language when it expresses an *aesthetic function* and language dominated by *other functions*; they use the same linguistic arsenal on all levels of expression. We know the language of advertising and political slogans and speeches also exploits aesthetic devices such as rhyme, alliteration, anaphora, etc., but here these devices serve a different function. This does not mean that Jakobson denied aesthetic specificity. Rather, it remained for the semantic and pragmatic spheres to complete a syntactical aesthetic level.

C. Norm and norm violation

The notions of *code, norm* and the important one of *value* were investigated mainly by the chief aesthetician of the Circle, Jan Mukarovsky (Mukarovsky 1932, 1936, 1940). The dominance of the *aesthetic function* makes of the object an *aesthetic fact.* But functions are not fixed entities; they are dynamic and changeable. Thus an aesthetic object can be decoded by a receiver in such a manner that other functions are propelled into dominance. Thus Tolstoy's *War and Peace* and Stendhal's *The Red and the Black* can be read as an historical text. *Value* is the measure of success of a work in fulfilling its dominant function. It is thus a teleological concept. A communication is evaluated in certain ways because the author and/or receiver(s) imbue it with a certain hierarchy of functions and see one function as governing its structure. The *aesthetic norm*, always in dynamic relations with the aesthetic function, is the force regulating man's aesthetic attitudes towards things. The norms underlie the constraints or rules of the *code* that inform a structure. In creating a text, an artist can choose between normativity and anti-normativity or norm-breaking. And there are historical periods which tend toward maximum normativity (e.g. neoclassicism), and periods which tend toward anti-normativity (Romanticism, the interwar avantgarde). In the most extreme cases we can envisage on the one hand a completely normative text which becomes redundant from the aesthetic viewpoint (the rhythm is too perfect, the meaning is banal, there are no surprises), and on the other a totally anti-normative text, a text in which all rules are subverted (e.g. a text in an invented language), and such a text cannot be understood. However, from the point of view of the Prague school, aesthetic value always requires a certain amount of norm violation since such violations impart a necessary tension by defying expectation, introducing novelty, and thus increase the text's artistic information. This is a more exact way of saying imagination and originality must be there. Mukarovsky compares the aesthetic norms in an artistic text to grammatical rules in non-aesthetic language texts, the difference being that grammatical norms are relatively binding whereas aesthetic norms are not.

IV

The Author, The Reader and the Text

A. The author

A semiotic approach must include the pragmatic dimension of the author, but not in a reductive way. For in some shape or form, most obviously as the 'omniscient author,' the author is an agent in the text's structuration and unification. But then he is no longer the *biographical author* but an entity frequently labelled the *implied author*, a concept corresponding to Mukarovsky's *semantic gesture* (*semanticke gesto*), namely that entity 'by which the author fuses the work into a unified semantic whole' (1939:113). Such an implied author or semantic gesture is not given outside the work of art but is a function of its structure. Since this implied author must be seen as an abstraction, he is, in part at least, a result of the projection of the psychic state of the reader. Since the hypostacized implied author exists in the reader's mind on the basis of the presumptions of the work alone, he cannot be identified with the psychophysical personality of the author himself, the 'real' author whose full personality may not necessarily be reflected in the work.

For Mukarovsky, the primary interest for artistic analysis is not the psychobiological personality of the author but the relationship between this personality and that of the implied author (Mukarovsky calls these two entities the 'artist's personality' (*umelcova osobnost*) and 'author's personality' (*autorova osobnost*) (Mukarovsky, 1943-45:228). However, we cannot, in practice, ignore the living author or his spokesmen (family, friends). If they offer interpretations which become part of the 'universe of discourse,' such information can and does change the context and affect the reader's interpretation. Thus the boundary drawn between real author and the implied author remain to some degree problematic.

The relation between the psychobiological author and the reader of the text is also a polar one and makes problematic the boundary between the two. Mukarovsky observed (1943:91, 1946-47:61) that the creator of a work of art may, during the act of creation, assume the role of the perceiver: the painter as he steps back from his easel and critically contemplates what he has done, the composer as he plays a few bars on the piano, and the writer as he reads over what he has written, aloud or silently, in order to revise it, all become the receiver.

B. Text and code

The Soviet semiotician Jurij Lotman (1964) redefined the concept of text as it bears upon poetic structures, and defined the poetic (literary) text as a graphically fixed artistic whole (or its fragment) which does not exist alone by itself, but is inescapably part of a context with which it is in relations of opposition. Like the Prague scholars, Lotman also made explicit the fundamental distinction between texts in which the aesthetic function is dominant and those in which it is not. In the latter, the signifier itself is not uniquely important, it can be replaced by another. Indeed, such a text can be readily translated from one language or medium to another, and it can be paraphrased without irreparable loss of meaning. Not so in an aesthetic text, or rather in Prague parlance, a text in which the aesthetic function dominates. Such a text does not admit substitutions on the plane of expression without loss of some elements of meaning (Lotman, 1964:155-57).

In art, the concept of intertextuality has replaced the interest in tracing direct influences. This means that an artistic text, having multiform context, obtains its full meaning only in relation to other texts, both those cast in the same code and those representing different semiotic systems. Thus not only would we examine the internal structure of Günter Grass's *Blechtrommel,* but would also pay attention to its relation to the code of the novel of the mid-twentieth century, as opposed to the so-called realistic novel; to surrealism and German expressionism, and on a broader scale we would also weigh its connection to the entire cultural system which would include the questions of the peculiar cultural-political situation of Danzig before World War II, the relations in Danzig of Germans and Poles, the relations of Poles to Kashubians, the East German dialects used by Grass, the general epistemological revolution of the twentieth century as well as the specific German post-war cultural and emotional crisis.

If the text is perceived as dominated by the aesthetic function, this implies that the art object must engage some degree of norm violation, if it is to call attention to itself, and therein lies aesthetic value. Since such encroachments on the norm increase the tension between what is expected and what actually happens in the text, they increase the aesthetic information of the text. Norms, Mukarovsky held, do not have the force of legal rules, but are changeable. But aesthetic norms are charged with a peculiar dynamism since they must be challenged. To change them in a limited way is not necessarily a marked behavior in aesthetic texts, while the opposite is true when the grammatical rules of language when it does not adhere to the aesthetic function are challenged (Mukarovsky, 1936:28). We can question whether this position is sufficient to explain aesthetic value in highly stereotyped art, as for example Egyptian art or some primitive art. But such a position would hold that the dynamism is there, though to a far less conscious degree in art where norm change is slower and less detectable.

C. The reader

Today the reader is no longer unnoticed or dissolved into an effect of the text as in Aristotle's catharsis and later interpretations. The scholars at the University of Konstanz have formulated the concept of the implied, abstract reader. Others go farther and account for the effect on the text of reading by concrete individuals. In 1943 Mukarovsky emphasized (1943:106) that the reader projects upon the text his own intentional energy, thereby making his 'decoding' a dynamic act. In this spirit, Barthes (1970) pointed out that the reader is not merely a consumer but also a co-producer of the text. Thus the reader-text segment is reversible as Mukarovsky has already shown in the thirties. The deconstructionists have taken this to an extreme. In a sense it is their view that all we have is the reader and one reading is as valid as another. The text thus loses any independent ontological status.

. . .

In concluding our reflections about the reader, we cannot deal here with reader criticism or even censorship which may change the text. This carries us into the academic, political and ideological world, beyond the parameter of this discussion; but it is a relevant area of investigation. We can minimally agree here that how a twentieth century reader decodes and reconstructs a Shakespeare sonnet and how he reconstructs it, involves his knowledge of the literary tradition of Shakespeare's time, but involves also knowledge not available in Shakespeare's time (e.g. poetic developments since then) and probably his inadequate knowledge of the standard English spoken in Shakespeare's time. Thus this individual cannot perceive the same text as did a reader in Shakespeare's time. We need to see the whole process of reconstruction as involving decoding, recoding, encoding, interpreting, reconstruction and recreating, all of which is clearer in the performing arts, but nevertheless such processes are part of decoding which we need to rescue from passivity.

D. Translation

If semiotics is anything it is translation, its basic assumption being that all discourse can be open to such processes. Levels of translation include 1) intralingual translation (the transposition of a text into another text type within the same language system, e.g. the paraphrase of a novel), 2) interlingual translation, the translation of a text from one language to another, (e.g. the translation of an English text into German), and 3) intersemiotic translation (the translation of a text from one semiotic system into another one, e.g. a film from a novel, a ballet made from a novel, etc.). The area of translation then is an important semiotic domain.

The Czech literary scholar Jiri Levy has concerned himself in important ways with the peculiar problem of translation in art. For Levy, the search for the equivalence of aesthetic means is the goal of the translator rather than the traditional aim of achieving an agreement of stylistic devices (e.g. masculine rhymes for masculine rhymes, similar meters, rhythm, etc.) For Levy the translator needs first and foremost to bear in mind the relation of verse type to the structure of language (Levy, 1961). Let us give an example here, discussed by Mukarovsky (1940) and Jakobson (1926:52-53). It concerns the correct translation into Czech of Pushkin's line '*Burja mgloju nebo kroet*' as '*Boure mlhou nebe kryje*'. The Czech line follows the Russian in the trochaic tetrameter, in the word sequence, in the meaning of each word, in the rhythm and word boundaries, and even -- to a certain extent -- in the sound pattern. Yet the translation from Russian into Czech, relatively closely related to Russian, although it carries all grammatical, and apparently poetic forms, is flawed. As Mukarovsky pointed out, the translation has not taken into account the fundamental difference in the stress pattern of the two languages and also in the nature of syllable length. In Russian, word stress is free and phonemic, thus it distinguishes meaning, whereas stress is always on the first syllable in Czech and thus always coincides with the word boundary. While the coincidence of word stress and word boundaries in the Pushkin line is extremely rare in Russian and thus strongly marked, and is thus felt by a Russian to be a violation of norms, making the line sound new and fresh, in Czech, which mandates the stress on the first syllable, this coincidence is mandatory and not phonemic and thus not marked, its appearance in this line adds nothing new, and thus the line sounds hackneyed in Czech translation. Furthermore, the two languages differ in their attitude to vowel quantity which is a component of stress in Russian, but is phonemic in Czech.

How a translation of a work of art can compensate for such differences in the linguistic and other cultural systems, is the important issue here.

ENDNOTES

1. Thomas G. Winner is Professor Emeritus of Slavic Languages and Literature of Brown University; he directs the Program for Semiotic Studies at Boston University.

2. It was my initial editorial judgment to include, as Professor Winner suggested, only excerpts for this paper; but I included more than I originally intended because of value to Legal Semiotics. I regret omitting valuable passages of Professor Winner's poetic/semiotic/linguistic analysis also given in this paper, for reasons of space and the particular interests of this readership. *The editor.*

Chapter 27

The Body of Criminality: The Politics of Ordinariness

Alison Young[1]

I

A Working Paper[2]

This paper performs a fragmentary reading of a case in criminal law, *R v Clarke*[3]. In this case, a woman, named as 'May Clarke', was appealing against her conviction for theft. The trial had taken place before a judge, the Recorder, and a jury. The woman had originally pleaded not guilty to theft but had changed her plea during the trial to guilty and had received a conditional discharge by means of sentence. The text under consideration inscribes the Court of Appeal's examination of her case against the conviction.

Three judges heard the woman's appeal: Lord Widgery CJ, Sachs LJ and Ackner J. The judgment of the court was ready by Ackner J. The woman's appeal was allowed. Ackner J said: 'Since in the view of this court the assistant recorder mis-stated the law this court has jurisdiction to quash the conviction ... The conviction is duly quashed.'[4] The entire event of the appeal and judgment had required only two days to take place in the Court of Appeal and only two and a half pages to be set down in the annals of the *All England Law Reports* (that catalogue of law reports which, through its naming, achieves a connotation of both comprehensiveness and a suitable patriotism). These two and a half pages, the lexias of this text named '*R v Clarke*,' constitute the object of my interest.

The report is placed at page 219 of a volume that stretches to 1248 pages. The report occurs after a case which describes its interest as the substitution of a second party as plaintiff in a judgement previously made by the court. The report is followed by a case dealing with the construction of a will. There appears to be no connection between the cases -- other than that they are all *case reports*. We are presented with 'a chronological accumulation of cases reported in the form of a reference book under the names of the litigants and providing a formulaic account of what happened in court, nothing more or less, nothing to the side nor before nor after.'[5] The text is not free-floating; it is fixed spatially and temporally, by stating at the outset 'Court of Appeal, Criminal Division' and 23rd November, 7th December 1971'. This commemorates the event, gives it an historical and institutional credence.

The text then drops its hitherto realist tone; relating a list of words and phrases connected by dashes and printed in italics: '*Criminal law -- Insanity -- Defect of reason from disease of the mind -- Necessity of proving the accused was deprived of reasoning.*' Such an index of legal bons mots purpots to fix the event doctrinally, to list the issues with which the court has been dealing. The case can therefore be slotted into the body of criminal law created by English legal doctrine which demands that the law be constructed as a corpus of cases. Although allocated only two and a half pages in the *All England Law Reports*, the list of keywords is a reminder that *R v Clarke* makes its own significant contribution to the gradual and inexorable development of English criminal legal doctrine.

That doctrine is then elucidated in a brief paragraph, which states that the rules relevant to the defence of insanity 'do not apply to those who retain the power of reasoning but who in moments of confusion or absent-mindedness fail to use their powers to the full.'[6] In addition to elaborating the titillating crumbs of keywords already offered to us, the paragraph implies that the purpose of the appeal was to determine this point of doctrine. Nothing is said about the status of the person who is apparently so important that her name constitutes the title of the text. Title in land imports ownership and, thereby, power. The title in a case report imports no such power to the legal subject, who is reduced to a functional actor in the doctrinal narrative.[7]

The eponymous Clarke does not feature in the text until almost the bottom of the first page. Before reaching her textual debut, the report has still to point out various questions of authority. The curious reader is referred by a Note to 'Halsbury's Laws', for 'the defence of insanity in criminal cases'[8]. Criminal law is therefore both doctrinal and traditionally 'text-built'. Of the many texts on criminal law, only one will suffice, only one will merit citation: Halsbury's. Thus, implicitly and immediately, the hierarchy of texts that is English criminal law confronts the reader. As is to be predicted, a list of cases follows the citation of a learned text. Six cases are named; these are separated into 'cases referred to in judgment' and 'cases also cited'. There is thus a hierarchy of reference which impacts upon the text of the report and upon the future evaluation of the cases mentioned: to be 'referred to in judgment' awards a case a certification of merit; to be 'also cited' notes merely its relevance.

At this point in the text, the protagonist makes her appearance. The place was Leicester; the arena the Court of Quarter Sessions; the other main player the Assistant Recorder, E.F. Jowitt Esq QC. The titular heroine, May Clarke had at trial pleaded guilty to theft and was now appealing against her conviction. The court quashed her conviction. To state: 'the court quashed her conviction' indeed conveys the result of the appeal and performs a short if poignant narrative. Guilt had been attributed; guilt was later washed away. Innocence was restored.

II

Between the two textual points which mark May Clarke's appearance and the court's announcement that the conviction was quashed lies a longer narrative. Within that narrative there is created a body of criminality which has two characteristics: one is that it is a gendered body; the other is that it is a textual body. The rest of this paper will examine the ways in which the judgement of the court, as stated by Ackner J, inscribes those characteristics.

According to the judgment, Clarke was 'a lady of 58 years' and had been tried 'for what is commonly known as shoplifting.'[9] A case report will normally state the sex of the accused; what is striking here is that Ackner J is stating the accused's *gender*. It should also be noted that, whereas Clarke's crime was described doctrinally as 'theft,' in Ackner J's story it is described as 'shoplifting.' The theft of goods from a shop or store is a crime which is traditionally associated with women; shoplifting and prostitution are the two crimes which are viewed as quintessentially feminine by criminology. Morris[10] demonstrates how explanations for shoplifting differ according to the sex of the offender. Women are thought to shoplift as a result of subconscious motivations (sometimes leading to kleptomania), depression (often resulting from pre-menstrual tension or the menopause) or poverty (for example in order to fulfill their sex-role for providing food for children). Accounts for men, however, more frequently describe the causes of shoplifting as peer-group pressure and the search for excitement or risk-taking.

Criminology has also been reluctant to accept statistical studies which seek to show that the association of women with shoplifting is over-determined. Buckle and Farrington[11] found that men were twice as likely to shoplift as women. Campbell[12] found that over twice as many boys as girls had shoplifted. The polarization of explanations across the masculine/feminine dichotomy in criminological accounts and critical questioning of the criminal statistics demand an immediate questioning of the unproblematic association of women with shoplifting that appears in Ackner J's statement. His translation of the legal term 'theft' into 'what is commonly known as shoplifting' represents an underwriting of the cultural eagerness to see shoplifting as an appropriately feminine crime. It may be feminine for various reasons: in support of sex-role assumptions (woman takes goods as part of nurturing instinct) in agreement with psychosexual concepts about the feminine mind (woman as prone to disorders such like kleptomania); or as part of a medical-sexual model of feminine disorder (woman as susceptible to disorders produced by her menstrual cycle). The story about femininity that Ackner J begins in his opening sentence is elaborated and clarified in the remainder of the judgment.

Clarke's story and defence are described by Ackner J as 'nothing out of the ordinary.'[13] I will return to the notion of ordinariness later. For the moment, let us examine, as Ackner J does, the details of her story. Details function to elicit either sympathy and compassion (as here, where we *recognize* the ordinariness of Clarke's actions) or revulsion and censure (as in accounts of violent crimes). Clarke went shopping in a supermarket in Leicester. She chose various items from the shelves of the supermarket and put them in the wire basket provided by the store. Before going to the checkout, she transferred some of those items into her own bag: these items consisted of a pound of butter, a jar of coffee and a jar of mincemeat. She did not pay for these three items. She was stopped and charged with theft.[14]

Clarke's explanation, and defense, was that she had no intention to steal. She claimed that this was evidenced by her not feeling well on the day in question. She had not been feeling well for some time and had been forgetful on several occasions. She claimed that her act of putting the three items from the supermarket into her bag without paying for them had been one more act of forgetfulness, rather than an act of theft. Plato has written that a crime *is* an act of forgetting: the forgetting of the rational and calculating self. Ackner J comments that any jury, upon hearing such a tale, would have felt bound to acquit her. For Ackner J her forgetfulness is acceptable: this is astonishing given that a forgetfulness of the law earns many individuals long periods in prison. His faith in the jury's reactions to her tale also tells us that he sees its ordinariness as universally familiar. We have thus two issues here: Clarke's legitimized forgetfulness and the court's belief in her recognizability as an icon of feminine late middle age. The court therefore (and, Ackner J felt sure, the jury) does not doubt a story of illness and forgetfulness from 'a lady of 58 years.'[14] Her vagaries and ill-health are acceptable and predictable; this makes her story believable and natural, inspiring no doubts or questions. Unfortunately, Clarke had adduced the evidence of 'medical experts' to substantiate her story, not anticipating that the court would find her ill-health so believable.

The medical experts, 'these two gentlemen' as Ackner J calls them, [16] were her general practitioner and a consultant psychiatrist. They agreed with Clarke that she had been feeling depressed. One went so far as to call this a minor mental illness. According to the general practitioner, as paraphrased by Ackner J: 'The patient feels a lack of energy -- *he* finds it difficult to concentrate -- *he* may be short tempered or absent-minded.' [17] [my emphasis] According to the psychiatrist: '[depression] can produce states of absent-mindedness in which the patient would do things *he* would not normally do.'[18] [my emphasis] Note this instantiation of this patristic economy, in which male experts seem to notice no dissonance when describing a woman by means of the male pronoun.

As Ackner J tells us, the effect of this expert evidence was indeed to convince the Recorder that Clarke was not guilty of theft; however, he also became convinced that she was not guilty 'by reason of insanity.' At this point, Clarke changed her plea to guilty. Ackner J expresses juristic outrage at Clarke's conviction. Clarke was not guilty of theft, nor was she insane. Clarke was no doubt delighted to have her conviction quashed; however, it is my contention that Ackner J's discussion of her case results in an intensification of the legal representation of femininity as irrational, labile and inherently diseased. The illness as evidence of an abnormality, therefore implying that the norm of memory and reason and health was available (to women as well as men). His conclusion that Clarke was legally insane is lamentable and incorrect; unable to respond to such an error without normalizing, universalizing and legitimating the equation of femininity and insanity.

Let me demonstrate how this is achieved. Ackner J goes into much detail in describing Clarke's ill-health. This may have been in order to establish the familiar and recognizable nature of Clarke's actions; however, the effect is to constitute the appellant as an object to be studied: *R v Clarke* is therefore as much a case history as a case report. He states: 'She suffers from sugar diabetes. In the previous year she had gone down with diabetes. In the previous year she had gone down with 'flu and . . . her husband had broken his collar-bone. He had to look after her and was, in fact, because of his own condition, off work for several months. What with one thing and another she had become very depressed . . . On the morning in question she woke up with a very bad head which persisted despite her taking her pills.'[19] Diabetes and flu can both be serious illnesses; however, most people who are diabetic can stabilize this condition with medical help, while most people recover from 'flu in a matter of weeks at the latest. It certainly does seem odd to mention a 'flu which was suffered a year previous to the alleged crime. The oddity is not the point, however, which is rather that Ackner J is willing to delve back into the past to come up with illnesses that substantiate his claims of Clarke's ill-health. It is also worth noting Ackner J's use of the expression 'her pills.' This presumably refers to medication that had been prescribed by a doctor. There exists a dynamic between women and the medical profession through which women tend to be prescribed pills more frequently than men suffering from similar ailments.[20] Once pills are prescribed, they are seen as part of the woman's identity; she possess them in the same way that she possesses brown hair or dark skin or an ability with mathematics. Woman is constructed through her medical condition.

Clarke's alleged forgetfulness is also discussed by Ackner J. He states: 'On a number of occasions she had been very forgetful; for example, she had put sugar in the refrigerator instead of in the cupboard and the sweeping brush in the dustbin and then put the dirt where the brush should have been put.'[21] For Ackner J, for the criminal law, everything has a proper place. Such *appropriateness* gives order its topography. Theft, with its *dishonest appropriation* of goods belonging to another, literalizes a fear of disruption in our ordering of property. Disruption of that propriety, that order, invites comment; indeed, demands restoration and repression. Although, for Ackner J, this disruption of order does not connote insanity, he constructs it as an abnormality, a moment of difference. By doing so, he inaugurates the process of repression that will restore the order of propriety. The Platonic forgetfulness that underlies our taxonomy of crimes represents a failure to concur with the mnemonics of order. Clarke's failure to remember caused her to take goods from a shop without paying for them: Ackner J's problem is now to show why this is due neither to her insanity nor to her criminality, but rather to her femininity.

It is this moment of difference which is awarded judicial investigation. Ackner J has inspected the protagonist, 'a lady of 58 years,' situated in a marriage: her husband features, not as a minor player in a drama starring May Clarke, but in a celebrity role. His illness is documented as faithfully as that of the wife; their relationship of reciprocal care is recounted for the court. The organization of their domestic life is examined: 'Her husband rang up at about 11:00 a.m. to say that he would be home for lunch late. She put their meal in the oven on a low flame and went out to fetch the groceries.'[22] Their dietary regime performs a crucial role in the consideration of her guilt or innocence: the previously mentioned jar of mincemeat that she had put into her own shopping bag without paying for it was not an item of food that they were accustomed to eating. The Clarkes' usual menu thus implicitly becomes an index of guilt or innocence, reason or insanity. Menus represent order: items of good take their allotted places within the regime of eating, representing rationality as well as desire.[23]

Ackner J tells us: 'as for the jar of mincemeat neither she nor her husband ever ate this.'[24] It seems that the other two items (butter and coffee) did feature on the Clarkes' menu, but the shunning of mincemeat by both was given heuristic impetus in making out the argument that Clarke had picked it up *without thinking*. It is the 'out-of-placeness' of the mincemeat that gives weight to Ackner J's normative argument that Clarke must have been confused, forgetful (of their order of food as well as the order of private property). There is a certain sharpness in the consideration of both wife and husband's dietary likes and dislikes; the sharpness resides in the judicial acceptance of May Clarke's role as nurturer. Woman gleans the food, for herself and, as importantly, for her husband. This husband is allowed to feature in the investigation of May Clarke's mind *as if* he were physically fused to her own self.

At the outset of the judgment, Ackner J states that the case is an ordinary one. This 'ordinariness' appears to consist in the structures with which May Clarke had organized her life. She was married, she was shopping at the time of the alleged crime, she was engaged in an activity designed to nurture another person. But the ordinariness that Ackner J finds so striking exists in other, unremarked, aspects of the story. May Clarke was 58 years old and had come through the menopause. She was under medical treatment and was taking medication. She seemed to feel unwell frequently. These facets of her life are produced by a medical discourse which analyzes Woman as a combination of pathologies: psychiatric instability (suffering from depression, 'a minor mental illness'); physical weakness (diabetic, taking medication); irrational (confused, failing to exercise the powers of reason available to her).[25] May Clarke was also living with her husband in a relationship involving mutual care. She undertook some domestic tasks such as shopping, cleaning, cooking. The fact that her husband appears also to have taken part in some domestic tasks ('he had to look after her')[26] is played down in the text. These facets of her life fix her in a matrix of domesticity which evaluates her as traditionally feminine: nurturing and caring.

Whereas the Recorder felt that the evidence presented a picture of abnormality which could only be construed within the criminal law as insanity, the Court of Appeal felt that the disruptions of order presented by Clarke's story were, on the contrary, part of normality. Allen shows that defenses in criminal law divide into those which set up the accused as normal and those which establish the accused as abnormal. Insanity is of the latter type.[27] The moral insanity of diminished responsibility (into which the court's discussion of Clarke seems to shift her) belongs to the former type. Ackner J states that Clarke was 'a woman who retained her ordinary powers of reason but who was absent-minded or confused and acted as she did by failing to concentrate properly on what she was doing and by failing adequately to use her mental powers.'[28] The discourses of domesticity and medicine combined to construct femininity in their interstices; a legal femininity that is indeed a disruption of order, but a disruption that is exactly to be predicted. The proprieties of behavior and place and duty were overturned by Clarke, who put three items in her bag without paying for them. But in doing so, Clarke was merely acting out her role as a 'lady of 58 years': absent-minded, unhealthy, engaged in gathering food.

III

At the beginning of the case report were listed the legal keywords which summarize, in telegrammatic form, the subject of the case. My aim has been to show how the case is important, not for its examination of the defence of insanity (which is how it is assessed in criminal law textbooks)[29], but rather for its contribution to the creation of a body of criminality. The criminal actor is usually identified by its acting with a particular state of mind, usually intention, recklessness or negligence. None of these states is said to be the result of a lack of reason: when some 'defect of reason' does lead to the commission of a crime, the actor is then acquitted as not guilty by reason of insanity. The criminal individual acts on a place of rationality in the same way that the law-abiding actor does. It is my contention that criminal law produces the category of the criminal as gendered; produces the feminine shoplifter as an epistemological category of the ordinary, the everyday. Behavior and mental state are assessed, not merely by reference to a standard of reason, but also according to a dichotomy of reasonable gender *difference*. Within that moment of difference, Woman functions as topic and trope, locating the criminal discursively and culturally. The body of criminality, the body of criminal law, is a masculine body and the intrusion of femininity into that economy is indeed a disruption. It is a disruption not of right and wrong (as criminal legal doctrine asserts) but of the hierarchy of difference through which all our bodies are written.

ENDNOTES

1. Alison Young is Instructor in Law at University of Lancaster, England.

2. This paper contains work in progress from a large project on the textual bodies of criminal law and criminology. I am grateful to Peter Rush for his comments on this paper. A more developed version will appear in *Law and Aesthetics*, R. Kevelson, 1992 - *Ed. note.*

3. [1972] 1 All ER 219.

4. *Id.*, 221.

5. Goodrich, P., 1990, *Languages of Law*, London: Weidenfeld & Nicholson, 233.

6. *Id.*, 219.

7. It should also be noted that the exemption of the confused or absent-minded from insanity as legally defined -- see *McNaghten's Case* (1843) 10 Cl & Fin 200 -- does not clarify whether we can include them within the 'moral insanity' that was the precursor to the concept of the diminished responsibility; see Johnstone, G., 1988, 'The Psychiatric Approach to Crime' *Economy and Society*, 17, 3, 317. The discourse of 'moral insanity' is operating in *R v Clarke*, although, doctrinally, diminished responsibility is not available as a formal defence to the charge of theft.

8. *Id.*, 219.

9. *Id.*

10. Morris, A., 1987, *Women, Crime and Criminal Justice*, Oxford: Blackwell, 65.

11. Buckle, A. & Farrington, D., 1984, 'An Observational Study of Shoplifting,' *British Journal of Criminology*, 24, 63.

12. Campbell, A., 1981, *Delinquent Girls*, Oxford: Blackwell.

13. *Id.*, 219.

14. The judgement does not state whether she was stopped by the police, the supermarket staff or another shopper. The act of policing can be performed by all of us.

15. *Id.*, 219.

16. *Id.*, 220.

17. *Id.*, 220.

18. *Id.*

19. *Id.*

20. Eirenreich, B. & English, D., 1978, *For Her Own Good*, New York: Simon & Schuster.

21. *Id.*, 220.

22. *Id.*

23. Barthes, R., 1983, *The Empire of Signs*, London: Jonathan Cape; Mennell, S., 1991, 'On the civilizing of appetite' in M. Featherstone et al., eds., *The Body*, London: Sage.

24. *Id.*, 220.

25. See further on this Foucault, M., 1978, *History of Sexuality, vol. 1*, London: Penguin; Turner, B., 1984, *The Body and Society*, Oxford: Blackwell.

26. *Id.*, 220.

27. Allen, H., 1987, *Justice Unbalanced*, Milton Keynes: Open University Press.

28. *Id.*, 221.

29. See, for example, Smith, J. & Hogan, B., 1988, *Criminal Law*, London: Butterworths, 192.